24-gun frigate *Rose* (1757/1970)

MILLAR

12-gun sloop *Providence* (1768/1976)

ABOUT THE AUTHOR

JOHN FITZHUGH MILLAR received his A.B. from Harvard in 1966 and his M.A. in History from the College of William & Mary in 1981. He has taught history at three colleges and spent a decade as a museum director in Rhode Island. He has devoted years to the study of various aspects of life in the seventeenth and eighteenth centuries, such as architecture, decorative arts, classical & folk music, dance, ships and military history, and has lectured extensively on these subjects (anyone interested in hiring Mr. Millar to give lectures is invited to write to him in care of Thirteen Colonies Press). He has gained practical experience with eighteenth-century ships (including under sail) by arranging for the construction and operation of full-sized copies of the 24-gun frigate *Rose* (1757/1970) and the 12-gun sloop *Providence* (1768/1976). He served for many years on the Rhode Island Bicentennial Commission and in 1970 he founded the Bicentennial Council of the Thirteen Original States, an organization that successfully raised millions of dollars to assist Bicentennial projects in the Thirteen States. He lives with his wife Cathy in Williamsburg, Virginia.

His major published works include:

THE ARCHITECTS OF THE AMERICAN COLONIES, Barre Publishers, 1968 (out of print).

COLONIAL & REVOLUTIONARY WAR SEA SONGS & CHANTEYS, Folkways Records, FH 5275, 1975.

RHODE ISLAND: FORGOTTEN LEADER OF THE REVOLUTIONARY ERA, Providence Journal Books, 1975.

SHIPS OF THE AMERICAN REVOLUTION, Bellerophon Books, 1976.

AMERICAN SHIPS OF THE COLONIAL & REVOLUTIONARY PERIODS, Norton, 1978, (out of print).

ELIZABETHAN COUNTRY DANCES, Thirteen Colonies Press, 1986.

A COMPLETE LIFE OF CHRIST, Thirteen Colonies Press, 1986.

Forthcoming:

CLASSICAL ARCHITECTURE IN RENAISSANCE EUROPE 1419-1585, Thirteen Colonies Press, 1986.

EARLY AMERICAN CLASSICAL MUSIC, Thirteen Colonies Press, 1987.

COLONIAL ARCHITECTURE, I: BRITISH, DANISH, DUTCH, FRENCH, GERMAN & RUSSIAN HIGH-STYLE IN AMERICA 1100-1790, Thirteen Colonies Press, 1987.

COLONIAL ARCHITECTURE, II: EUROPEAN HIGH-STYLE IN AFRICA, ASIA & AUSTRALIA 1450-1790, Thirteen Colonies Press, 1988.

EARLY AMERICAN SHIPS

EARLY AMERICAN SHIPS

By *JOHN FITZHUGH MILLAR*

Thirteen Colonies Press

Williamsburg, Virginia

1986

Thirteen
Colonies Press
710 SOUTH HENRY STREET
WILLIAMSBURG, VIRGINIA 23185

© Thirteen Colonies Press, 1986
710 South Henry Street,
Williamsburg, Virginia, 23185

ISBN 0-934943-02-8 paperback
0-934943-05-2 hardcover

This book is set primarily in Baskerville type. John Baskerville (1706-1775) devised this beautiful type in the 1750s in
England and it remains unexcelled today. Benjamin
Franklin was most enthusiastic about Baskerville's type
designs, but they were not used in the U.S.A. until the end
of the eighteenth century.

Books of *Historical* interest, covering primarily from the Renaissance to 1800.

DEDICATION

This book is dedicated to my wife, *Catherine Louise Millar*. We first met aboard the frigate *Rose* at Long Wharf, Boston. All the frustrations and hardships incurred on behalf of *Rose* were thus well worth facing.

October 1775	Winds		Bearings &c at Noon	Remarks &c on board his Majesty's Ship Rose
Tuesday 17	NbE	The Ship Steady'd with the Stream Anch.r in Rhode Island Harbour, the Flagg Staff at the Fort bearing NWbW.		Little Winds and Cloudy, AM dry'd Sails. Punnish'd Jn.o Millar Seaman with 12 lashes for Disobedience to his Officers.

ERRATA

The artist inadvertently added two extra
stars to flag number 51, which should
have only 13 stars.

FOREWORD

In 1978, W. W. Norton & Company published American Ships of the Colonial & Revolutionary Periods, *which had taken me a decade to write. The book has been out of print since 1984, and even if Norton had been interested in reprinting it I was not satisfied with it. I thought it needed considerable rewriting and re-illustrating, which in turn has earned the rewritten book a new title.*

In adherence to the theory, "Where it ain't broke don't fix it," I have left much of the text and many of the illustrations untouched from the earlier book, but any reader familiar with the earlier book will quickly see substantial improvements. In some cases, no more than a word has been changed, while in others nearly everything about a particular ship has been written from a fresh perspective in the light of new information. A few ships have been dropped altogether, while others—including two important finds by archaeologists in South Carolina and New York—have been added in order to round out the picture of early American ships. A great many copies of period portraits of specific American ships have been added; indeed few existing such portraits from before 1790 have been omitted. The introduction has been enlarged with much useful information, including a comprehensive series of full-color reproductions of flags of the period.

In 1968 I sensed, perhaps before most people, the approach of the Bicentennial of American Independence, and realized what an exciting experience the occasion could be for Americans and others. For the most part the promises for that experience have fallen through, but in 1968 there was no indication that this would be so.

For Americans who wished to explore the tangible relics of their history during the Bicentennial period, at least one important side of that history was scarcely represented: the maritime side. Apart from the display at the Smithsonian Institution in Washington, D.C., of the relatively small gondola Philadelphia, *there were no ships from the Revolutionary period for people to see, and seeing such ships could fill a real gap in the experience of their history for curious Americans. The problem was all the more serious because most Americans automatically assumed that the two frigates* Constitution *and* Constellation, *on display in Boston and Baltimore respectively, were ships from the Revolution (they were not built until 1795–97); even worse, these two ships do not represent the configurations they had at their launching, nor even the configurations they had in their finest hours (the period before 1815), but they are instead a hodgepodge of periods with a heavy accent on the mid-Victorian era. Ships of the Revolution and the Colonial period bore no more resemblance to* Constitution *and* Constellation *(as they appear today) than a World War I destroyer bore to a modern guided-missile frigate.*

I decided to try to correct that imbalance by building full-sized reconstructions of Revolutionary period warships. The ships might possibly visit other ports, but they would be based in Newport, Rhode Island; Newport was my home, and that was reason enough, but Newport also had more pre-Revolutionary buildings still standing than any other community in the country. Further, it was because of Newport's economic ruin by a British blockade that the Rhode Island General Assembly initiated the bill in the Continental Congress that created the Continental Navy on 13 October 1775, and the first vessel authorized for that navy was "a swift sailing vessel, to carry ten carriage guns, and a proportionate number of swivels, with eighty men," which Silas Deane tells us was the Rhode Island sloop Katy, *later known as* Providence. *And it was in Newport on 9 July 1764 that the heavy guns of Fort George were fired on the British Customs schooner* St. John *by order of the governor and the General Assembly, an event that those who know about it call the "first shots of the American Revolution," twelve years before independence.*

At least one of the ships that I would build should be a ship whose plans survive, that would be big enough to persuade the curious to get out of their car to look at it, that would be small enough that I could borrow that much money to build it, and that had been in Newport at some point during the Revolution. Of all the ships that had been in Newport in the Revolution, there were no American ships whose plans were then known to have survived. Of the French ships, a few plans survived, but the ships were all bigger than my borrowing power could afford to build. Of the many British ships whose plans survived at the National Maritime Museum at Greenwich, just outside London, I chose one called the Rose, *mainly because her name appeared on almost every page of the collections of documents about the beginning of the Revolution. I knew very little about her history and significance at the time that I chose her, so my choice later proved to be a gratifying stroke of luck, for I found out that the* Rose *was the ship whose blockade of Newport caused the General Assembly to instruct its delegates in Congress to introduce the bill that created the Continental Navy. It could therefore be said that* Rose *was the direct cause of the founding of the American navy. I could not believe my good fortune.*

Rose *was variously described as a 20-gun or 24-gun frigate. She was built in 1756 in Yorkshire, and she was a little smaller than the Continental frigates* Boston, Montgomery, *and* Delaware, *and a bit larger than the corvettes* General Gates, General Washington, Ranger, *and* Saratoga. *She was scuttled by her own captain in 1779 to prevent the French fleet from entering the harbor of Savannah, Georgia, and assisting an American* army in besieging the British garrison at Savannah, but over the years various pieces of her have been salvaged. I was able to obtain some of these pieces, and they were incorporated into the construction of the new ship at Lunenburg, Nova Scotia. The yard of Smith & Rhuland at Lunenburg had been chosen primarily because it was the only one of the several yards in the United States, Canada, Britain, and the Far East, asked to bid on the construction job whose price I could afford to pay.

Rose was launched in March 1970 and sailed to Boston, and then to Newport in late May and early June of that year. With modern synthetic sails (and no engine) she sailed far better than anyone expected, a fact that has made many people wish that U.S. Coast Guard regulations and various insurance requirements were more relaxed so that the ship could sail more often than she has done. For many years, she was on more-or-less permanent display on Newport's historic waterfront, and went out sailing on average about once a year, usually for the purpose of making a film. I sold her in 1976, but never received payment. She had to be repossessed and sold no fewer than four times before she found a permanent home at Bridgeport, Connecticut in 1984, by which time rot was so far advanced in her that she has had to undergo a major rebuilding aimed at making her presentable under sail at Operation Sail 1986 in New York.

The other ship that I had planned to have built, the sloop Providence, had to wait a few years until money could be found to pay for her. This was accomplished by the founding of a nonprofit corporation called Seaport '76, and the sloop was launched in the autumn of 1976.

I founded Seaport '76 for the dual purpose of building Providence and taking over Rose. Unfortunately, in a parallel to the passage in Exodus, "And there arose a pharoah which knew not Joseph," there arose a board of directors which knew not the original purpose of the organization, and once Providence was built they severed all connection with Rose, the ship whose very existence had given their project enough credibility that money was able to be raised to pay for Providence. Alas, Rose and Providence, which together have such a great story to tell, will apparently never be exhibited together, but at least they both exist and they can both sail well.

Because the Rose was for many years the only visible part of my plan, I was heavily criticized for not reconstructing an American ship instead of an "enemy" ship. It did little good explaining that an American ship, the sloop Providence, was to be built as soon as money could be found for her. Nor did it make any difference when I protested that no plans existed for American ships of the Rose's size. A few of the critics announced that nothing short of changing the Rose's name would satisfy them. I can see now that it was really none of their business, but it set me to wondering whether I could have come up with plans for an American ship of the Rose's size and period if I had spent more time on research beforehand. Naturally, the point was entirely academic for the Rose was already built, and if I had waited even one more year before proceeding with the construction of such a ship, a year's inflation would have put the cost well out of reach of my meager borrowing power, even supposing that the few skilled but aged craftsmen would still have been available.

I therefore began a period of several years' research into the appearances of American ships (American-built, -designed, or -owned) in the Colonial and Revolutionary periods, and when I found much that had never been published and that was not available to the casual researcher, I decided that my findings should be made into a book.

My decision to write such a book was reinforced by one of my findings, which began to grow into an obsession. I found that there were many representations, including pictures, plans, and models, of American ships that were obviously giving an inaccurate portrayal of these vessels' true appearance. These ranged in date from about 1800, when the pictures in the Bailey collection at the Mariners Museum at Newport News, Virginia, were painted, to the present day, when Nowland Van Powell's numerous and interesting pictures were painted. These portraits generally contained serious errors in such details as rigs, flags, color schemes, and stern windows, to mention but a few, and, since most model builders and other artists generally had neither the time nor the resources to go beyond the information provided by such popular and widespread representations as the Bailey and Van Powell pictures, other pictures and models of Revolutionary period ships were bound to be produced having Victorian sterns, dolphin strikers, spanker booms on the wrong ships, ensigns at the gaffs, split gunport lids, and black-and-white color schemes, among other popular anachronisms. This book is an attempt to assist model builders and painters to go beyond those easy anachronisms, and may in the long run result in the public's being better informed about the ships that played such an important part in their past—a part that has been unfairly overshadowed in recent years by clipper ships, whaling ships, and other nineteenth-century craft, and of course by all the models and paintings of the nineteenth-century configuration of the frigate Constitution, as well as the ship herself.

My years of research have turned up actual lines plans of American ships of the period 1607 to 1789 that have never been published before, as well as period pictures and models. I have drawn or redrawn these plans at a scale of 1:48 (one inch equals four feet), which was the standard scale used by British shipwrights in that period, although they are much reduced to fit in the book. In some cases I have admittedly had to invent what a few of these ships looked like, based on slim evidence, such as recorded dimensions or a crude scratching on a powderhorn, and these inventions are clearly marked as such in the accompanying text; usually, but not always, these reconstructions are limited to profiles of the hull above the waterline. These reconstructions, I feel, are useful to the reader to the extent that they are my opinion (based on research and sober reflection) of the appearances of some of the more important ships of our history, some of the ships that model builders and painters would normally be more tempted to represent in spite of a lack of evidence about them.

For the sake of clarity in the drawings, and because such information was generally not available about most of the ships, I have totally omitted any information about deck plans; no doubt many model builders will resent this, but they can easily recreate deck plans by referring to some of the great standard works on ships of the period, such as the books by the late Howard Chapelle.

If I had known in 1968 what I now know about American ships, would I have found an American ship to build instead of the Rose? If I could have permitted myself the latitude of building a ship whose plans do not survive, but for which two rather vague portraits exist, I think I would have built the corvette General Washington. She was a bit smaller than Rose, but she was about the only Rhode Island ship of that period approaching Rose's size. Moreover, her history was as exciting and as long as that of any American ship in the Revolution, and she deserves to have a whole book written about her.

Very little is known about most of the ships in this book. A few previously unpublished facts—and a number of conclusions—are published herein, but nearly every one of these ships needs far more research than I have the capability or time to devote, and I fervently hope that many of these ships will eventually be the subjects of scholarly monographs by experts. Such monographs would add a great deal to what I have been able to offer in this book, and I expect that they would even refute a few of the imperfect pieces of information I have been able to present. Perhaps corrections and amendments can be made to some future edition of this book, based on research during the intervening years.

I apologize for not being a draftsman; I am self-taught, and the drawings show it, but I believe that my shortcomings in that field will not seriously hinder the reader from studying the designs.

Just as monographs on individual ships would be welcome contributions to scholarship, I would like to challenge at least one American museum to make plans to commission the construction of a collection of accurate models of a large number of early American ships. No such collection presently exists anywhere, although many capable model-builders would no doubt welcome such commissions.

Finally, I would like to thank my wife, Cathy, for being so patient with this lengthy project and for working as a registered nurse to support me financially; just because I actually owned and sold a full-sized frigate unfortunately does not mean that I have had at any time during this period an independent income! I also thank the late Barclay H. Warburton III, the loudest of Rose's critics, for goading me into the research on early American ship designs. I am most grateful to Mr. Merritt A. Edson, Jr., who read the original manuscript and made some valuable suggestions.

Subsequent to publication of the first book, I have received important information from many readers, including Jean Boudriot, John Harbron, John Sayen, Jr., Warren Riess, David Brewer, Robert Gardiner, Colan Ratliffe and D. J. Lyon, to name but a few. I hope they will not be disappointed in the result.

J.F.M.

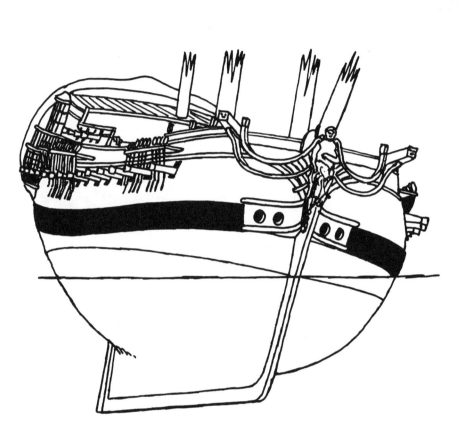

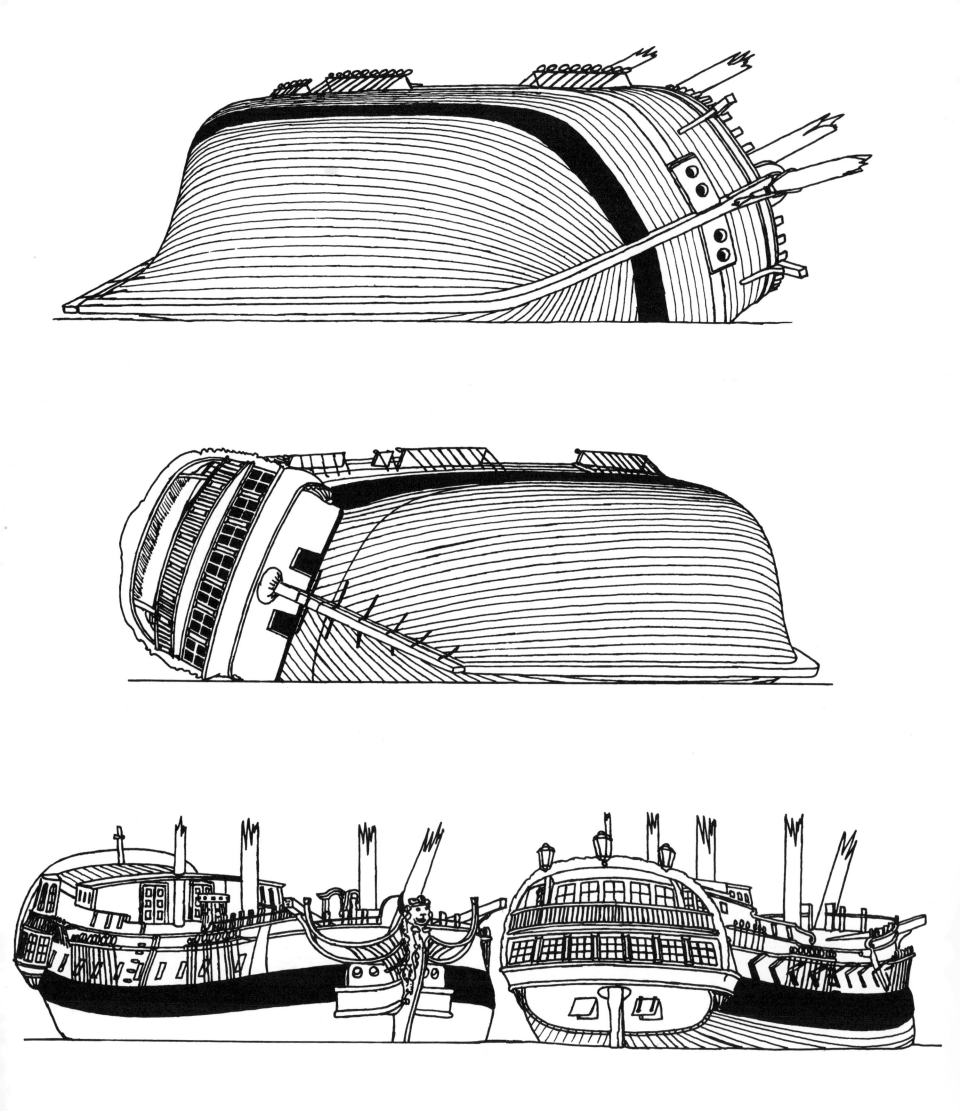

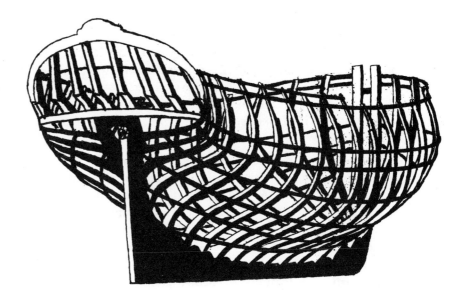

Part I

INTRODUCTION and BACKGROUND

THIS BOOK is about American ships of the Colonial and Revolutionary periods, 1607 to 1789, from the arrival of the first settlers at Jamestown, Virginia, and Sagadahoc, Maine, to the ratification of the constitution of a new nation. We have taken "American" to mean any ship designed, built, or owned by a resident or government of North America.

In most cases, this limitation will be seen to be more than a mere chauvinistic distinction. Most American ships were as different from European ships as the ships of the individual European countries were from each other. Putting aside the political, social, and military implications of being an American in the eighteenth century, one can easily discern a refining process at work in the American spirit that reveals itself in nearly everything the American produced. For example, American architecture of the period would generally not be mistaken for European architecture, although the parentage would be obvious; not only that, but it is usually possible to pinpoint within a few miles where a particular style of American architecture was developed. The steep, hipped roofs of Quebec, the shady galéries of Louisiana, and the heavy plantation houses of Martinique are all obviously of French parentage, but all obviously different from French designs in France and from each other, adapted to the environment and needs of their respective localities. Similarly, the step-gabled town houses and wide-gambrelled country houses of New York, the pastel, curvilinear gables of Curaçao and

the elegant houses of Paramaribo are all clearly Dutch, and yet different. The neat Colonial houses of New England are as different from each other as they are from houses in England, and there are some experts who can even tell a Rhode Island house from a Massachusetts or Connecticut house.

American furniture, too, can easily be distinguished from its European equivalents, and collectors can usually tell at a glance whether a fine piece was made in Boston, Newport, New York, or Philadelphia, and whether a country piece came from Pennsylvania or Connecticut.

The reasons for the American refinement of European styles are not hard to find. By the middle of the eighteenth century the European societies had reached a plateau which could be called the highest achievement of individual man, before the advent of mass man; being so highly civilized was somewhat a bore to the European upper classes, and they sought relief from boredom by ostentatious competition with each other. With plenty of money and other resources at hand, the man who wanted a more impressive house built a larger and more massive house, and the man who wanted more impressive furniture made it more massive and ordered that it be dripping with carvings and gilded decoration. There was little refinement of design.

Such competition was not confined to Europe by any means, but it took a different form in the New World. Instead of building a more massive house, the American made his house more impressive by hiring an architect to make it look more perfect in proportion and detail. Similarly, American furniture, with its delicate but robust grace, is generally more perfectly proportioned than its European counterparts. The Townsends, Goddards, Saverys, and others were not only the best cabinetmakers in America, they were probably the best in the world.

This refinement of design in American furniture and architecture was partly the result of the lack of resources available in the New World to build something bigger at that early date, but it was also a result of the American spirit, a spirit that was shaped by the first hundred years of European life in North America, where one had to make do with what one could get, and where one seldom had more than one needed.

In the seventeenth and eighteenth centuries Americans were forced into an overwhelming dependence on the sea. It was by sea that they had arrived from Europe and by sea that they would have to leave if they found life too rough for them. Many of the necessities of life—and nearly all the luxuries—had to be imported by sea from Europe, just as southerners had to ship tobacco and other crops to Europe to pay for their imports, and northerners had to earn credits in Europe by fishing on the Grand Banks and by carrying anyone's cargo anywhere in the world. If an enemy were to attack, he probably would come by water (either across the ocean or a lake), and the Royal Navy was regarded as the only sure defense against an enemy attack. In addition, roads were so bad that the only sensible communications between the various American Colonies were by sea.

With the Americans depending to such an extent on the sea, we might expect to find that there emerged various recognizable features in American vessels, in the same way that we saw them in American architecture and furniture, and we would be right, at least in part.

Americans did not actually invent the schooner rig; the rig is believed to have originated in Holland. However, Americans developed the rig to a high degree of perfection and used it widely while it was virtually unknown in Europe. The schooner rig was ideal for handling coastal traders of under 130 tons with three or four men; its simplicity made it almost essential for coasters and fishermen who would be out in all kinds of weather, while its weatherliness made it helpful in furthering one of America's leading industries—smuggling.

Another rig that prospered in America more than in Europe is that of the sloop. The sloop, however, could carry a great deal more sail than a cutter, and so could be built with fuller lines for longer voyages, or with fine lines for smuggling. American sloops frequently ventured into the Indian Ocean and the Pacific, even though they were usually no longer than 60 feet on the deck. Rhode Island and West Indian shipowners are known to have relied heavily on sloops, and Rhode Islanders and West Indians were more heavily engaged in smuggling than other Americans.

Americans did not limit their development to rigs, but experimented with hull shapes as well. The fishing pink was well suited to riding the sea on the choppy waters around the Grand Banks, while the sharp Marblehead "heeltapper" sped the catch back to New England ports before the fish could spoil. Further south, a sloop, and sometimes a schooner, with a high cabin in the stern came initially from Jamaica and then spread to Bermuda and the Chesapeake, and was recognized the world over as a Bermuda sloop. In Virginia, a pilot boat was developed with very fine lines, and was used for smuggling and escaping from British patrols during the Revolutionary War. Because of their fine lines and light construction these vessels could not profitably carry much cargo, but armed with a few light cannon they made ideal privateers, for they had the speed to escape from pursuers and catch up with potential victims, while with even only a few guns they were usually more heavily armed than most merchant vessels; in addition, they were nimble enough to place themselves in advantageous positions so as to rake their opponent but prevent him from returning fire.

Sloops, schooners, fishing boats, and pilot boats are all relatively small, and it was in such small craft that the majority of American commerce was carried. However, larger vessels were built in America, and after a while they developed their own special characteristics, too. The first large vessel known to have been built in North America was the 44-gun *Falkland,* built for the Royal Navy under contract in Portsmouth, New Hampshire, in 1690. She was followed seven years later by the 34-gun *Bedford Galley,* and there were others.

The navies of all the European powers were proud to the point of chauvinism of their native oak as a shipbuilding wood, but were quite worried about the growing scarcity of the wood; it took several acres of 200-year-old forest to build the hull of the largest battleships of the day (100 guns and over), and so the chauvinism was tempered with a desire to find a substitute for home-grown wood. At first it was thought that New England oak was the answer to Britain's need, but when the first ships built in New Hampshire for the Royal Navy showed a high rate of deterioration it was thought that American wood was inferior, and so very little attention was given to building more vessels of any size in America.

It seems likely that the problems encountered with American oak by the Royal Navy were chiefly a result of poor preparation and seasoning of the wood, as many American-built ships of later years lasted as long as their British counterparts. The British, however, had lost interest in American hardwoods, but increased instead a trade in American softwoods for spar timber. The standard British mast timber used to come from Scandinavia, where pitch pine was abundant. However, the firs and spruces of New England were a cheap and satisfactory substitute, and many pines of New Hampshire and Maine were marked with the king's "Broad Arrow," which meant that no one but the king's men was allowed to chop down the tree in question. The Americans themselves also used softwoods in construction of hulls. Southern builders in particular found that long-leaf yellow pine was an excellent and long-lasting wood, but it had its drawbacks in battle; yellow pine was found to splinter badly when hit by a cannonball, and more Americans were killed and injured by pine splinters than by cannonballs in the celebrated battle between the *Chesapeake* and *Shannon* during the War of 1812.

The Spanish had the exact opposite luck of the British in finding shipbuilding wood in their American colonies. A massive and dense species of mahogany grew in Cuba and Santo Domingo which they used so extensively for shipbuilding and other purposes that the wood is to all intents and purposes extinct today, although a few isolated trees may still be found in Haiti. This heavy mahogany is perhaps the most beautiful furniture wood ever found, and its shipbuilding properties were equally impressive. It seemed to be vastly superior to native Spanish oak in strength, longevity, and ability to resist dry rot and teredo worms, and some vessels built in Havana lasted over a hundred years without major rebuilding. The West Indies, however, contained no wood suitable for use as spars, and so all mast timber had to be imported from Spain or smuggled in from New England.

Strangely enough, there are no records to indicate that the French ever made use of that same mahogany that grew in their share of Santo Domingo (Haiti), nor that the British built anything other than small sloops out of that same mahogany that they found growing in Jamaica. For that matter, it also seems that the British and Dutch settlers in the Demerara area (now Guyana and Surinam) made no shipbuilding use at all of the abundant stocks of greenheart that still grow there. Greenheart, which is virtually impervious to rot and shipworm, is said to be over twice as strong as oak, and it is one of the heaviest woods grown anywhere; it has the disadvantage, however, that it can not easily be bent, and it tends to split under certain conditions.

It may come as quite a surprise to many readers that while hundreds of wooden houses from the seventeenth century survive today and quite a few wooden yachts are over a century old, typical wooden ships of the seventeenth and eighteenth centuries were lucky if they survived even ten years before requiring a major rebuilding due to damage by rot. Poor construction plus unseasoned or unsuitable timber could doom a ship to a mere year or two. Excellent construction plus excellent timber and good perpetual maintenance could give a ship up to 25 years, but such life-spans were rare unless island mahogany had been used. Rot is caused by a fungus that requires the right

combination of moisture, air and temperature. Since ships float in water, moisture is always present in the form of water vapor. More water is added from rain, which entered early ships in the upward-sloping seams of the tumble-home of the topsides and through the naturally-occurring checks and cracks that can be found in large pieces of wood as they expand and contract in reaction to changes in temperature and humidity. Most rot is confined to areas above the waterline, since salt in the water below the waterline inhibits the rot fungus. Some ships have even added to their life-span by filling the gaps between their frames with salt. Short life-span was normally not regarded as a serious drawback for a mechant ship, since the cost of construction could usually be recovered in about two trading voyages. Warships were often rebuilt from the waterline up about every ten years if they survived possible severe damage in battle, but most were scrapped after about two "great repairs," since their designs had become obsolete by then.

Before the American Revolution, larger merchant ships could usually be divided into two categories, both ship-rigged. The East Indiaman, with its two-decked stern, generally measured between 600 and 1,000 tons, and carried enough guns to be roughly equivalent to a frigate; there were almost none of these built in America before the end of the Revolution, probably because their size and shape were better suited to the longer voyages of the Pacific Ocean and Indian Ocean than the shorter ones of the Atlantic, and trading in the Pacific area was limited to certain large monopolies which had their own shipbuilding facilities in Europe.

The smaller West Indiaman, however, was in common use in the transatlantic trade, and measured from 200 to 600 tons. These ships, of which a good number were built in America, carried as many as 20 guns, although some carried no guns at all. For the most part these ships were simple workhorses, with little elaboration. Some, resembling North Sea colliers like Cook's *Endeavour,* were extremely blunt at each end, and had neither head nor quarter gallery. Although there was little to distinguish them from their European equivalents, by the time of the American Revolution certain regional characteristics had emerged, such as the disposition of the decks of a Philadelphia merchant ship.

At the outbreak of the American Revolution, it is estimated that between a quarter and a third of all vessels under British registry were American built; this includes both those ships owned and operated by Americans, and those sold to British owners as American exports. These American-built ships ranged typically from 60-foot sloops and schooners through 80-foot brigs to 100-foot ships.

During the two wars against the French and Spanish (the War of Austrian Succession or War of Jenkins' Ear, 1739–48, and the Seven Years' War, 1756–63), Americans were quick to outfit privateers and took a heavy toll of enemy merchant shipping. It is perhaps surprising to note that, with few exceptions, these privateers

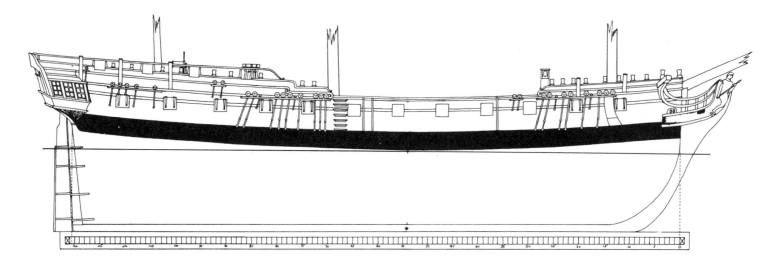

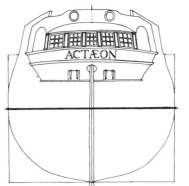

A Draft of His Majesty's 32-Gun Frigate *Actaeon,* built at Woolwich in 1775

Length on the Lower Deck	120′ 6″
Length of Keel for Tonnage	99′ 6″
Breadth	33′ 6″
Depth in Hold	11′ 0″
Tonnage	594

An English East Indiaman, ca. 1770.

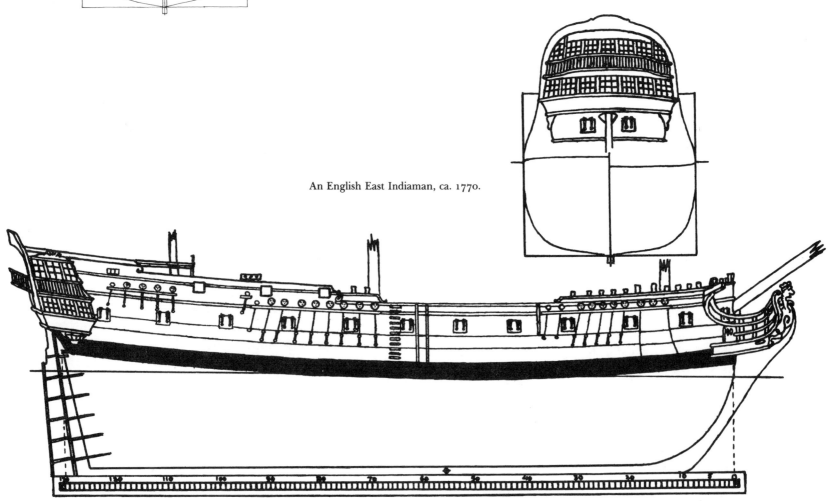

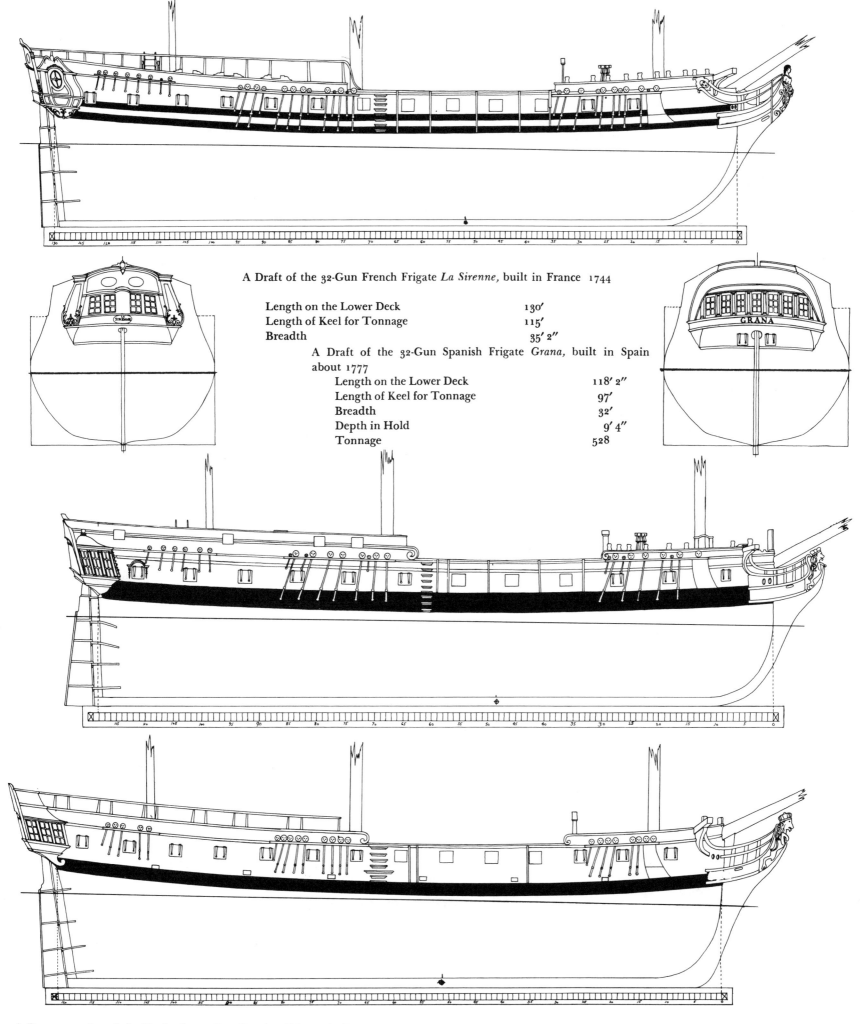

A Draft of the 32-Gun French Frigate *La Sirenne*, built in France 1744

Length on the Lower Deck	130'
Length of Keel for Tonnage	115'
Breadth	35' 2"

A Draft of the 32-Gun Spanish Frigate *Grana*, built in Spain about 1777

Length on the Lower Deck	118' 2"
Length of Keel for Tonnage	97'
Breadth	32'
Depth in Hold	9' 4"
Tonnage	528

A Reconstruction of the Draft of a 32-Gun Russian Frigate, built about 1780

Length Between Perpendiculars	121'

5

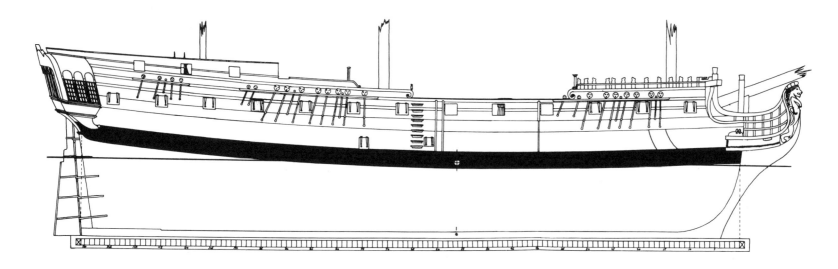

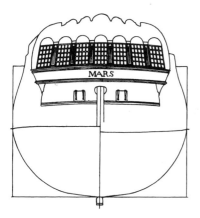

A Draft of the 32-Gun Dutch Frigate *Mars,* captured in 1780

Length on the Lower Deck	130' 9"
Length of Keel for Tonnage	108' 10"
Breadth	34' 10"
Depth in Hold	11' 10"
Tonnage	703

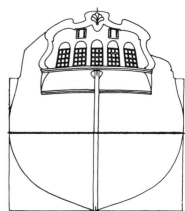

A Draft of the 32-Gun Swedish Frigate *Jaramas,* built at Stockholm before 1768

Length Between Perpendiculars	121' 4"
Breadth	32'

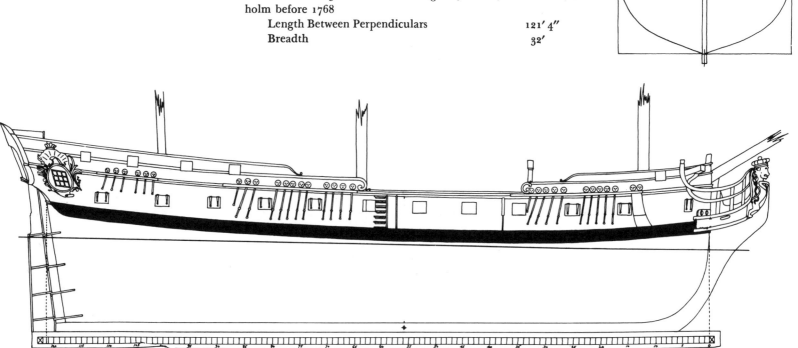

were tiny sloops and schooners armed with perhaps six small guns. Some of these same privateers, especially those from Rhode Island, were rightly accused by the British of trading with the enemy French West Indies (during the Seven Years' War) at the same time as they were attacking French shipping, and the truth of this accusation was one of the main reasons that the British placed severe restrictions on American trade and smuggling immediately after the Seven Years' War.

Privateers, incidentally, were privately-owned warships, whose owners posted substantial financial bonds with their government in order to be granted a license to attack enemy ships in time of war. Captains and crews without such a license or commission were liable to be hanged as pirates if caught on the high seas by the enemy. The reason for the posting of the bond was to enable restitution to be made if a court eventually determined that a particular ship had been a friendly or neutral vessel that had been captured or damaged by mistake. Similar to a privateer was a Letter of Marque and Reprisal (often shortened to Letter of Marque). This was a regular merchant ship engaged in commerce, but heavily armed so that she could under license attack and capture enemy vessels she might encounter. Both categories of privateering have been outlawed in modern warfare by international agreement.

Although the Continental Navy unfortunately amounted to very little during the Revolution when stacked up against the might of the Royal Navy, yet as a shipbuilding feat it was nothing short of spectacular. With only a handful of exceptions, no vessels of any size had hitherto been constructed in the Thirteen Colonies. In the space of a few years, during which they were dragged down by the considerations of waging an exhausting war, the colonists were able to produce one 74-gun battleship (with the frames cut for several more 74s), more than twenty frigates of 24 to 36 guns, and hundreds of lesser ships and privateers.

Some of the smaller vessels revealed innovation in design, while others were merely continuations of what had been produced earlier. But it was in the frigates and 74s that American initiative is most impressive. For the most part, these vessels were marginally larger than European ships of the same rate, which showed an understanding of the long-term evolution of warship design. As for their shapes, the American ships were related more to British precedent than to the ships of any other nation, but they were by no means copies of anything in the Royal Navy. Some of the American builders had doubtless served apprenticeships in British shipyards, and were thus attracted to the British concept of the shape of the midsection, the stem, and the rudder post. Pictures of 32-gun frigates from the 1760s and 1770s from Britain, France, Holland, Spain, Sweden, and Russia have been included in this book for the sake of comparison, and it will be seen that the American designs are more closely related to the British designs than to any others, in the same way as American domestic architecture was related to British domestic architecture during this period, but it is also obviously different from the British precedent.

While the British scorned the Yankee officers and men, they sometimes praised the products of Yankee shipyards when they were able to capture them, and many were taken into the Royal Navy after their capture and their lines taken off in British dockyards so that experts could attempt to analyze why they were so fast and so stable. The British described one captured American frigate as "the most beautiful and fastest frigate that ever swam."

Since American ship designs owed a good deal to their British parentage, a quick look at British ship design would be helpful in understanding the progression of designs through the years. While the British claim that their interest in sea power goes back to King Alfred in the ninth century, they did not make much of an impression on their neighbors until the sixteenth century, when Henry VIII traveled to France on a huge ship named after him. Under his daughter Elizabeth, British warships became smaller, faster, and more seaworthy. The exploits of the Elizabethan "seadogs" in defeating the superior forces of the Spanish Armada and in voyaging to the far corners of the globe are legendary, and the success of these intrepid mariners was partly due to the shape and size of their ships. While they had high, narrow sterns (supposedly so that they would lie head-to-wind in fierce gales), they were not top-heavy like the Spanish ships that were in effect floating castles. Serious thought had gone into their underwater lines, the theory being that they should bear some resemblance to the shape of a fish; the maximum breadth was well forward of amidships, a shape sometimes described as "cod's head and mackerel tail." They usually had three masts, of which the fore and main were square-rigged, and the mizzen had only a lateen sail on it. Merchant ships of the period looked much like the warships, and examples can be seen in the replicas of *Susan Constant* at Jamestown, Virginia, and *Mayflower* at Plymouth, Massachusetts. There is also a copy of Drake's *Golden Hinde*, based for a time at San Francisco, but she is not quite so representative, since the designer appears inadvertently to have given her a beam about four feet too small. This defect was subsequently overcome by the expediency of adding "blisters" to each side of the hull below the waterline to give the ship more stability.

Ship design continued in this fashion for about a century, with the most powerful classes of warship becoming progressively larger, but otherwise with no new ideas. Charles I took an interest in his navy, but neither seems to have benefited from that interest. His son, Charles II, on the other hand, spent a great deal of time in his dockyards, and his reign happens to coincide with both improvements in design and construction and the amending of Charles I's classification systems. At the same time, a number of wars against the Dutch and French contributed to the evolution of fleet tactics, which in turn began to influence design and classification.

As E. H. H. Archibald so well explained in his book *The Wooden Fighting Ship in the Royal Navy*, the Admiralty classified its warships in six rates. A First Rate, the largest size, carried 100 or more guns; a Second Rate mounted 90 or more, and the other rates spread downward in unequal amounts until the Sixth Rate, which carried 20 or more guns. Below Sixth Rate were any number of dispatch vessels. The battle tactics of the day called for opposing fleets to form columns, known as the "Line of Battle," and blast away at each other until one side had inflicted enough damage on the other to force it to withdraw from the conflict. Naturally, only the larger rates would be of any use in the direct line of battle.

The Admiralty would periodically issue "Establishments" for each rate. In other words, the Admiralty would decide what the minimum dimensions for each rate would be, and how large each rate's guns would be. Almost invariably, each Establishment was for a longer and wider ship for a given rate than the previous Establishment, until by the time of the American Revolution the tonnage of a given rate had more or less doubled in roughly a century of development.

The Admiralty owned its own dockyards, including those at Portsmouth, Plymouth, Chatham, Deptford, and Woolwich, but it frequently purchased ships from private shipyards. These private contractors knew the latest Establishment, and were permitted to draw their own designs around the Establishments, often drawing them a few feet larger than the Establishment for good measure. In order to be awarded the contract to build the ship, the builder frequently had a model built of the hull, leaving off most of the deck planking and all the planking below the wale, thus exposing the deck beams and ribs. The Admiralty could inspect the model far more thoroughly than they could inspect a set of drawings, and then either approve the design, correct it, or disapprove it. This type of model is therefore known as an Admiralty model, Admiralty board model, or Admiralty dockyard model. Strictly speaking, Admiralty models were not rigged, because the rigging would get in the way of a close inspection, because the rig would make the model even more expensive, and because it would take up far too much room to transport or store. The rigs of the ships varied little, and in any case were usually the prerogative of the ship's first captain. Nevertheless, one finds a large proportion of beautifully rigged Admiralty models on display today, but it must be remembered that the rig was usually not part of the model's original purpose, and was thus added much later as a rule.

Admiralty models from the seventeenth and eighteenth centuries are among the finest examples of the woodcarver's art, and if they are available at all these days they sell for $50,000 apiece and more. Fine collections of them can be seen at the National Maritime Museum at Greenwich, just outside London; the Science Museum, Kensington, London; the Nederlands Scheepvart Museum in Amsterdam; the Musée de la Marine at the Trocadéro in Paris; the Museo Naval in Madrid; and the United States Naval Academy Museum at Annapolis, Maryland. There is also a splendid collection of recently built Admiralty-type models, every bit as well made as the real ones, at the Smithsonian Institution in Washington, D.C. Admiralty models were generally, although not always, built to a scale of one inch equals four feet (1 : 48), the same scale as the plans were drawn.

The arrangement inside these ships followed a definite and repeated scheme. In the bottom, near the keel, was an area running the length of the ship known as the hold. In this large space was stored all the food, drink, ammunition, and spare parts of ship and rigging that was likely to be needed on a voyage of several months' duration. Above that, on larger ships, was the orlop deck, where the boatswain and carpenter had their stores, where some cables and gunpowder were stored, and where some of the crew slung their hammocks. The headroom on the orlop, as also on all the other decks, was sometimes less than five feet, reflecting a desire on the part of the Admiralty to keep the ship's center of gravity low, the fact that the average height of a seaman was over a foot less than the average height today, and the fact that seamen were regarded as being among the lowest forms of human life in those days, so no one much cared about their headroom.

Above the orlop, and on smaller rates above the hold, was the gun deck, sometimes called the lower gun deck. This carried the heaviest battery of guns, again to keep the center of gravity low, and was so close to the waterline that its guns often could not be used in rough

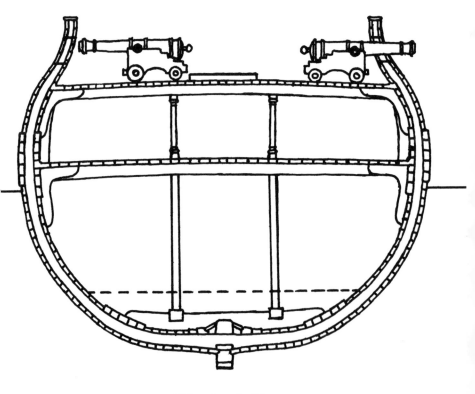

Mid-section of a frigate.

weather, thus effectively reducing the ship's fighting strength by almost one-half. More than a few fine ships have sunk because they left their lower gun deck ports open too long, allowing the sea to rush in over the sills. When the ship was not cleared for action, the gun deck would have hammocks for about half the crew slung over the cannons. At the forward end were the hawse holes, through which led the anchor cables, and a clear space was left aft of the riding bitts all the way to the capstan (a large hand-powered winch, usually located on more than one deck between the main mast and the mizzen mast). In the stern were two or four gunports facing aft, known as stern-chasers, in between which ran the huge tiller. On earlier ships the tiller was connected to a vertical staff on a pivot, known as a whipstaff, and thus the ship could be steered by men standing one or two decks above the tiller, but by the end of the seventeenth century the tiller was connected by means of ropes to a wheel on the upper gun deck or even higher.

The upper gun deck was covered only at the forward end and aft of the mainmast. The open section forward of the mainmast was called the waist, and was usually crowded in with the ship's boats and spare spars. The section of deck over the forward end was called the forecastle or fo'c'sle, while the section over the after end was the quarterdeck, so called because it originally stretched only a quarter of the length of the ship. On the larger rates, the quarterdeck was covered at its after end by another deck, known as the poop (please, not poop deck), and there were even a few First Rates that had a tiny deck above the poop, known as the poop royal.

Under the quarterdeck was the captain's sleeping cabin and great cabin (office and dining room), although on the largest rates the great cabin would be on the middle gun deck (in any case, this is where the modern word "quarters" comes from, describing a place to live). All these large cabins in the stern were well lit with banks of windows, which made them attractive places to live but which also made them extremely vulnerable to damage from enemy shot. These cabins were well suited for carrying admirals, their aides, distinguished passengers, and others, in addition to the captain.

In sharp contrast to the spartan living accommodations for the crew, the great cabins in the stern were frequently decorated in lavish style. For example, John Drew, a prominent house carpenter and joiner who was responsible for the excellent woodwork in many of Portsmouth, New Hampshire's finest homes, was requested by a certain Captain Warren in 1722 to do work on the great cabin of his newest ship, including "Sashes and Lockers," "a hansom beaufait" (obviously a buffet or sideboard), "& raised Arched pannels" similar to those he had recently installed in the east parlor of the MacPhaedris House. The cabin was also to have "Mouldings" and "Collums" (probably pilasters rather than columns), a canopied bed, a table, and a chest. Captain Warren's cabin was painted in contrasting colors: "the Mouldings done with vermillion the sides or mergents with green & the Collums with blew."

First and Second Rates had three complete gun decks and an armed quarterdeck, but the difference between them was more in the weight than the number of the guns. The First Rate's lower gun deck carried 42-pounder cannon compared to the Second Rate's 32-pounders, and the First Rate's middle gun deck carried 24-pounders compared to the Second Rate's 18-pounders. Both carried 12-pounders on the upper gun deck and 9-pounders on the quarterdeck. Some French and Spanish ships even had light guns on the poop and on the gangways that led from the forecastle to the quarterdeck.

Among Third Rates were six distinct classes of ships. The three-decker, 80-gun ships were top-heavy and clumsy, and could not open their lower deck ports in any kind of wind. The two-decker, 80-gun ships, on the other hand, were too long for their height, which meant that they strained and hogged until stronger construction techniques were devised after the American Revolution. The two-decker, 70-gun ships were considered a little smaller than they needed to be, but the 74-gun ships proved to be such a happy medium that they became the workhorses of the battle fleet. The 60-gun ships, also Third Rates, were designed for the line of battle, but seem to have been better employed as independent cruisers. They were in any case largely replaced at the time of the American Revolution by the stronger and larger 64s, which, however, were still relatively much smaller and weaker than the 74s.

In practice, the First Rates usually stayed in home waters for coastal defense, while the Second Rates were the flagships of cruising fleets. Every fleet had a large number of 74s and a sprinkling of 64s, although these were phased out by the end of the eighteenth century because they were too small to stand the kind of punishment that could be dealt out by the larger ships. One practical reason for leaving the First Rates in home waters and sending the Second Rates to sea was the number of seamen required to man them. The First Rates needed over 850 men, while the Second Rates needed only 750; but since sometimes even that was regarded as extravagant, many admirals were sent off to sea with only a 74 for a flagship.

The Fourth Rates were all of 50 guns. They were originally designed for the line of battle, but as the eighteenth century progressed they were obviously too small for the task. They were, however, very useful as independent cruisers, and as flagships in peacetime on foreign stations where they were not likely to run up against any superior enemy. They carried only eighteen-pounders on their lower deck, nine-pounders on the upper deck, and six-pounders on the quarterdeck. With their smaller size, requiring only about 350 men in peacetime, they were reasonably inexpensive to maintain.

Only a little smaller was the Fifth Rate, theoretically the smallest size of two-deckers. Just as the smallest three-deckers were considered failures (80 guns), so were the smallest two-deckers, although they were still useful as independent cruisers, a number of them having been thus employed in North American waters during the Revolution. These carried 40 or 44 guns. Their death knell was sounded by the invention of the large frigate (about which more later). The Fifth Rates could not sail as well as the frigates, and in rough weather they could not even fire as many guns as the frigates. In the late seventeenth century, there were also some smaller Fifth Rates that mounted about 30 guns, but these were phased out early in the eighteenth century. When the British began to build frigates in the second half of the eighteenth century, the larger ones were called Fifth Rates out of a stubborn sense of tradition, but they bore no resemblance at all to genuine Fifth Rates.

Sixth Rates generally used their lower gun decks for oars, which helped them get in and out of harbors. They always had one loading port on each side of the lower gun deck, and sometimes had as many as four guns to a side. The main battery, however, consisted of six-pounders or nine-pounders on the upper gun deck, with occasionally a few extra guns on the quarterdeck. The stern generally had only one level of windows across it. This type of vessel was unsatisfactory in a number of ways. It was slightly top-heavy because of the height it required to keep the lower deck ports well clear of the water, and in practice its lower deck gunports and oarports leaked considerably. The concept of a Sixth Rate, with its 20 to 30 guns, was rescued by the French, with their invention of the frigate.

The word frigate, from the French *frégate,* had been around for years. Its actual meaning in earlier years was simply a small armed ship that had relatively great speed and that could be used to carry messages for the admirals. Many writers give early dates for the first frigate, but they are mistaken since the French invented the frigate (as we know it) in the 1740s. It is not entirely clear how the French arrived at their breakthrough, for while the British interpreted the new concept as being related to their Sixth Rates the French saw it as being related to the East Indiaman, a large class of armed merchant ship.

For the British, to make a frigate meant to take a Sixth Rate design and alter it. They lowered the lower gun deck until the deck itself was almost as low as the waterline. They removed all guns from that deck, except the stern-chasers, and removed all gunports, loading ports, and oarports, although they left the hawse holes, riding bitts, capstan, and tiller. The main battery was then exclusively on the upper gun deck. This caused a paradox in nomenclature, for the tradition-bound British called the lower deck the gun deck, while it had in fact no guns on it at all (other than temporary stern-chasers). Modern writers have tended to ignore this and call it a berth deck, which is what in fact it was.

Oars, if retained at all, were usually placed between the gunports on the upper deck.

As a class the frigate cut across the boundaries of the rates, for frigates could have anywhere from 20 to 50 guns merely by making them longer, but still with the same deck arrangements. The smaller frigates were usually armed with nine-pounders, although a few appeared with only six-pounders, and the French preferred eight-pounders. Those of 28 to 40 guns usually carried 12-pounders for their main armament, although two American frigates built in Rhode Island in 1776 caused a stir by mounting 18-pounders, and the French-designed, Dutch-built, 40-gun frigate *South Carolina,* built in 1777, carried 36-pounders; in this, she was a forerunner of the large American frigates of the War of 1812, for they were the first to mount guns as large as 24-pounders on a regular basis, but *South Carolina* was also identical to East Indiamen being built in France at that time, so here the distinction between frigate and East Indiaman was blurred.

Frigates were fast, maneuverable, and good fighters in bad weather. Moreover, they were economical on crews. A 20-gun frigate could be manned with 70 men in peacetime, and could carry as many as 200 in wartime. The extra men were useful in manning any prizes they might capture. While frigates were extremely useful to the battle fleets for running up and down with messages in a battle or for scouting ahead for the enemy, they were also at their best as independent cruisers and as convoy guards. The British built frigates in classes of 20, 24, 28, 32, 36, and 38 guns. The French built them in classes of 26, 32, 36, 38, 40, and over.

Here it should be said that a ship that was "rated" at 20 guns may actually have carried 24 or more. Her owners would still describe her as a 20-gun ship, while anyone who captured her would gloat over having captured a 28-gun ship. This system seems to have been a widely-accepted form of jingoism at the time, but it has caused endless confusion for historians. Similarly, the number of gunports in a hull did not necessarily conform to either the rate or the number of cannons actually mounted.

The standard way to describe the size of a gun was to rate it by the weight of the cannonball it fired. However, not all measurements were the same. A ball that weighed nine pounds in England weighed only eight French pounds. This means that a French 36-pounder ball weighed over four pounds more than an English 36-pounder—a considerable difference when multiplied by the whole lower-deck broadside of a battleship. The British disadvantage in throw-weight, however, was counterbalanced by the fact that when the British captured a French ship they could use British balls wrapped in wadding in the French-built guns, but the French could never use their balls in captured British cannons. Cannons generally measured in length from 15 to 21 times the diameter of the ball they fired, although carronades were much shorter than regular cannons.

Weights were not the only area of metrical divergence. Thirty-five English feet equalled 36 Swedish feet, and 16 English feet equalled 15 French *pieds*; this last has caused

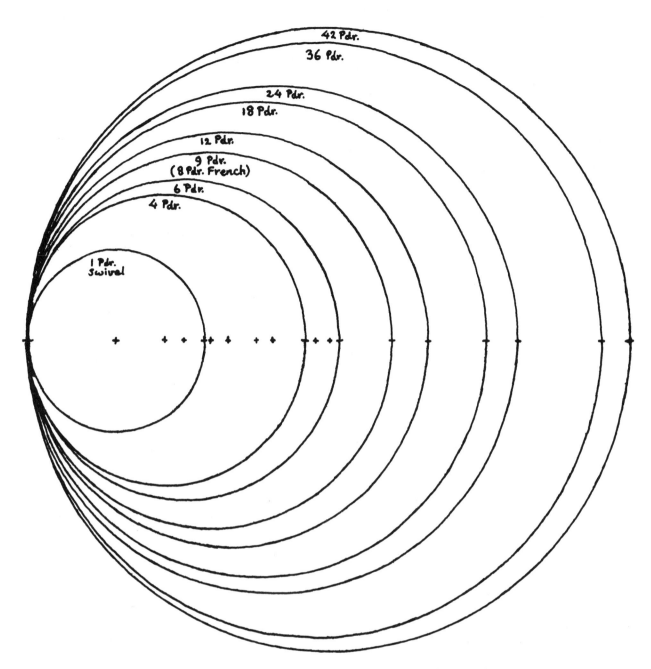

Relative sizes of British and American cannonballs.

considerable confusion, for more than one writer has mistakenly translated *pieds* into metres as if the *pieds* were the same as feet, as in the case of Admiral Paris' account of the frigate *South Carolina*. *South Carolina* now turns out to have been an even larger ship than had previously been recognized.

Smaller than the smallest frigates were a variety of craft. The largest of these were known as sloops-of-war, a term that had nothing at all to do with the sloop rig. For that reason, to avoid confusion we will refer to them by their French name in this book, *corvette*. The ship-rigged corvette was not especially common in the British navy, but a number appeared in the Continental Navy, where they generally gave a good accounting of themselves. Their speed and their shallow draft enabled them to escape from larger ships, except in rough weather, when they could not carry enough sail to escape from, say, a 74. The larger sort of American privateer was usually this type of vessel, mounting any-

where from 14 to 20 six-pounders. Their deck arrangement was generally the same as a frigate's, although with even less headroom, but some dispensed with the raised quarterdeck and forecastle, preferring instead to cover the whole gun deck with a flush spar deck from stem to stern. This was an innovation that was echoed a few years later in the designs of some of the large American frigates that fought in the War of 1812.

Smaller corvettes were rigged as brigs, both in Britain and America. While a few followed the deck pattern of a frigate, the majority had only a raised quarterdeck and no forecastle. These vessels generally mounted anywhere from 10 to 18 guns, mostly six-pounders or smaller. They were particularly useful as commerce raiders. The Americans used them as privateers, and the British used them to catch American privateers, as well as for more mundane duties.

Smaller still were the various schooners, sloops, cutters, and luggers, mounting anywhere from 6 to 14 guns,

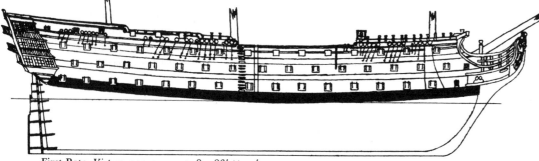

First Rate, *Victory*, 104 guns, 1758, 186' × 52', 2142 tons.

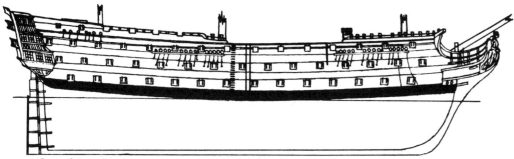

Second Rate, *London*, 90 guns, 1759, 178' × 49', 1840 tons.

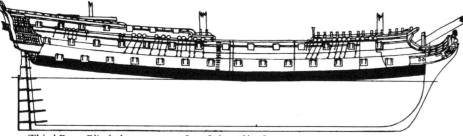

Third Rate, *Elizabeth*, 74 guns, 1765, 169' × 46', 1612 tons.

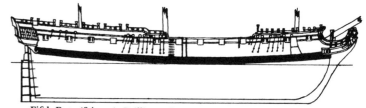

Fifth Rate (frigate), *Brilliant*, 36 guns, 1757, 128' × 39', 718 tons.

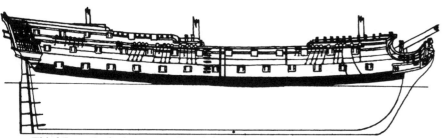

Third Rate, *Eagle*, 64 guns, 1765, 160' × 44', 1374 tons.

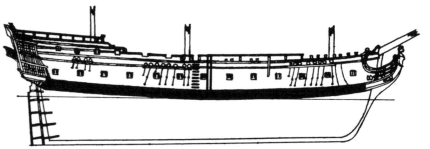

East Indiaman, *Princess Royal*, 32 guns, 1769, 142' × 38', 878 tons.

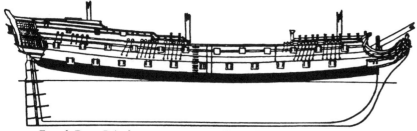

Fourth Rate, *Bristol*, 50 guns, 1771, 146' × 41', 1043 tons.

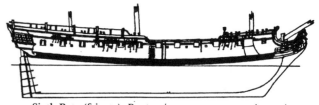

Sixth Rate (frigate), *Rose*, 20/24 guns, 1757, 110' × 30', 444 tons.

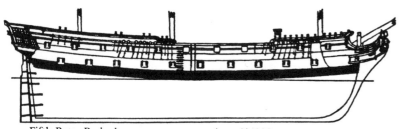

Fifth Rate, *Roebuck*, 44 guns, 1771, 140' × 38', 886 tons.

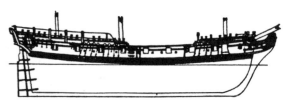

Ship-sloop (corvette), *Falcon*, 14 guns, 1768, 96' × 27', 302 tons.

Relative sizes of different rates of English ships.

mostly six-pounders or smaller. These, however, were not called corvettes or sloops-of-war. The sloops and schooners usually had either a raised quarterdeck or at least a small "cuddy" or roofed cabin in the stern, while the cutters and luggers had completely open gun decks, with cramped and ill-ventilated quarters in the hold along with the supplies. Schooners and sloops were far more common in America than luggers and cutters, which, however, were more common in European navies.

In the middle of the American Revolution, a new type of gun was invented by the Carron Foundry in Scotland, and it was therefore called a carronade. This was a short-barreled gun that could only be used at close range, but for a given size of ball the weight of a carronade was only a tiny fraction of the weight of a regular cannon. This meant that a tiny sloop or schooner could carry large-bore guns, but the practical implications were not realized until the French revolutionary wars later in the century. Only a few carronades were actually used in the American Revolution.

Just as the shape of a hull or rig was often a clue to a ship's country of origin, some countries had differing practices in launching ships. For example, the Dutch generally launched their ships bow-first (and thus built them with bow facing the water and the forward end of the keel downhill), while everyone else launched their ships stern-first. Although the stern-first launch had the potential for damaging the rudder, it made sense from the point of view of the builders; most ships were designed to float with the aft end of the keel deeper than the forward end (which theoretically caused less damage should the ship run aground), and constructing the ship with the waterline more or less horizontal meant that many items in the construction could be exactly vertical or exactly horizontal. Most builders who followed English practice tried to complete construction of a hull, including the carving, before launching it, because it is always easier to work from platforms built solidly over the ground rather than over a float. However, French builders, and presumably Quebec builders as well, launched their ships before they were fully

planked or decked and before any carving had been applied. The theory behind this was possibly that launching-beds were in short supply and the sooner a ship could be turned out, the sooner a new ship could be started on the same bed.

In the period under discussion in this book, the principal motive power of larger vessels was provided by square sails. Each of these sails was rigged in essentially the same way, so that even if a ship had a great many of these sails anyone who knew how to handle one square sail could theoretically handle all of them. For this reason, it was a relatively simple matter to train the "green" crews that usually were found for naval vessels in time of war.

Sails were set on masts above the ship. The largest ships had three masts, and rarely a fourth, as well as the bowsprit that was present on nearly every sailing vessel, large or small. The three-masted vessel was described as ship-rigged, and her masts were the fore, the main, the mizzen. Two-masted vessels could have a variety of rigs. The ketch had a main and a mizzen, but the others —brig, snow, bilander, and schooner—had a fore and a main, while the lugger was the equivalent of a three-masted schooner. Single-masted vessels were almost invariably sloops or cutters.

Since trees did not grow tall or strong enough for the required sail area to be set from one piece of wood, the mast was usually made from more than one tree, portions overlapping each other for a few feet. At the doublings or joints between the masts were a pair of trestletrees on which the second mast could stand, with a band around both masts a few feet higher up. This system enabled the crew to remove the upper masts without difficulty in case of storm or to make repairs.

As a rule, each mast had one square sail that could be set from it, although for the highest section this rule was not always observed in light weather. The lowest sail, set on the lower mast, was called the course, and this corresponded to the mainsail of medieval and earlier ships. The sail above that in late medieval times

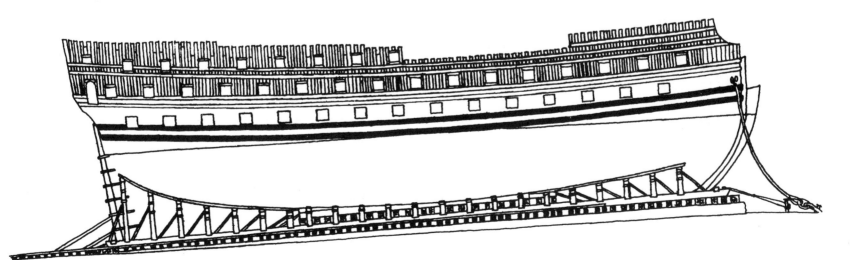

A French battleship ready for launch.

was thought to be as high as it was possible to rig a sail, so that was known as the topsail, set on the topmast. When someone eventually rigged a mast and sail still higher, it was thought that only the most gallant (meaning brave) seamen would go up that high, so it was called the topgallant sail or t'gans'l, set on the topgallant mast. Above that was flown the royal standard of the king when he was present, so when someone dared to set a sail in fair weather on the flag staff, that was called the royal (not the royal sail).

Even the bowsprit was often in more than one piece, known as the bowsprit and the jibboom, and each of them could have a square sail set under it, known as a spritsail. In the seventeenth and early eighteenth centuries, the bowsprit had a small mast stepped vertically on the end in place of the jibboom, known as the spritsail topmast, upon which was set the spritsail topsail, but this was often more trouble than it was worth.

Each square sail was suspended from a horizontal wooden spar known as a yard. All the yards were hoisted up when the sail was set by means of a rope attached to its center, known appropriately enough as a halyard. When the sails were not set, but furled on their yards, the yards were lowered to the level of the top of the mast below them, although the course yards remained where they were. One yard, however, the mizzen course yard, also known as the crossjack or cro'j'k, did not have any sail set below it; it was used simply to spread the bottom of the mizzen topsail.

In light weather, additional square sails could be set by means of extensions lashed onto the ends of the regular yards. The sails set on these extensions were called studding sails or stu'ns'ls. During the Revolution and the years immediately before it, American vessels had to be fast to escape from British patrols, and so Americans made full use of their light-weather sails, such as studding sails and royals. Sometimes they held onto these sails in fresher winds with disastrous consequences; either the masts would break or the ship would literally sail herself right under—and this happened more than once. American masts were often taller and their sails larger than those of their European counterparts; British captains complained that American ships they had captured were "overhatted." American masts were also frequently more raked than European masts, the foremast being vertical or inclined slightly aft, the mainmast being raked farther aft, and the mizzen being raked even farther aft.

On all three-masted ships, the space between the foremast and the mainmast was always much greater than the space between the mainmast and the mizzen. As the eighteenth century wore on, however, the foremast was placed farther and farther aft, the Americans being leaders in this trend. Another trend was in the steeve or slope of the bowsprit; except in cutters and luggers, whose bowsprits were horizontal or even sloping downward, bowsprits sloped upward at quite a steep angle, but as the American Revolution began bowsprits started to slope a little less.

Masts were held upright by guy ropes, called stays, from all sides. The side stays, known as shrouds, were the most numerous; there were sometimes more than a dozen on each side of a main lower mast. These shrouds were kept taut by means of a tackle running between two special blocks known as deadeyes. The lower deadeyes were pushed outward from the side of the ship by a chainwale (pronounced "channel," and sometimes spelled that way too); the deadeyes were connected to the ship by means of the chains or chainplates below the chainwales.[2]

The topmasts and topgallant masts were also supported by shrouds in a similar manner. The topmast shrouds were held out by the platform known as the fighting top, and the topgallant shrouds were held out by the crosstrees. Instead of chainplates they were secured to a point on the mast below by cables known as futtock shrouds.

The backstays from every level of mast went all the way down to the chainwales on the side of the hull; to all appearances, they were merely extra shrouds placed immediately aft of the regular shrouds. So that the seamen could climb into the rigging, light lines were lashed and tied horizontally across the shrouds on each side of the ship at intervals of about one foot all the way up. These were called ratlines, and where the shrouds grew too close together to insert one's foot between them the ratlines were extended onto one or more backstays.

The forestays ran quite differently from the backstays. For the lower masts, the forestays ran over the center line of the ship until they reached a point where the next mast entered the deck, or, in the case of the foremast, where they reached the end of the bowsprit. Lower forestays were frequently doubled for extra strength. The forestays for the upper masts led to the top of the next level of the mast next forward of them, except on the foremast whose forestays went to various positions on the bowsprit and jibboom. As for the bowsprit and jibboom, they had stays as well. A heavy stay led from the stem of the ship just above the waterline to a point near the end of the bowsprit; this was called the bobstay, and there were sometimes more than one of them. Sometime in the 1790s (outside the scope of this book) a strut pointing downward from the end of the bowsprit served as a spreader to give a more direct pull to the martingale stay that held down the end of the jibboom. This is generally known as a dolphin striker for obvious reasons, and it appears in many modern models and paintings of ships from the Colonial and Revolutionary periods, which is totally incorrect. Putting a dolphin striker on models or pictures of pre-

---

[2] Once while talking with some salty Nova Scotia riggers, I decided to play a joke on them by letting it be known that just as "chainwale" is pronounced "channel," so "chainplate" was actually pronounced "chimplet" (which it is not). A year or so later, I heard some other Nova Scotians from another part of the province talking knowledgeably about "chimplets."

A late-nineteenth-century painting of *Sukey*, a complete fabrication.

1790 ships is one of the most common mistakes found on such models, and there should be no excuse for it.

The British model of the captured American brig *Fair American* (now at the U. S. Naval Academy Museum), which was almost certainly made about 1783, has a dolphin-striker, but old photographs of the model have recently been discovered showing her before that spar was added early this century. Dominic Serres (who died in 1793) painted an English collier with a dolphin-striker, but the painting is undated and could easily have been done the year he died. The French painter Mesnier painted the Philadelphia ship *Pigou* in 1793 with a dolphin-striker (in the J. W. Henderson Collection, on loan to the Philadelphia Maritime Museum), and this ship, built in 1792, may well be the earliest datable user of such a spar. Both the Royal Navy establishments and Steel's book incorporated dolphin-strikers by the mid-1790s, but many ships went without such spars well into the nineteenth century. For further discussion, see the entries for the ship *America of Charleston* and the sloop *Providence*.

Although it took many years before the advantage of setting sails on the forestays was recognized, forestaysails, loosely known as jibs, began to appear on the various stays between the foremast and bowsprit/jibboom. These were small triangular sails that were at their most useful when the wind was coming from the side or slightly ahead of abeam. As the eighteenth century progressed, bold captains began to experiment with setting staysails between the other masts as well. The experiments were pronounced to be a success, and the staysails grew bigger and more numerous, many of them being quadrilateral. While the staysails did not have quite the driving power of the square sails, and while they were of practically no value at all when the wind was aft, there are cases on record (and I have pictures to prove it) of large square-riggers sailing to windward using nothing but staysails. It looked mighty peculiar, but on rare occasions when a ship had to claw off from a lee shore or beat into a crowded anchorage such a sail arrangement provided the right combination of speed and control to accomplish the task.

Finally, there was one more fore-and-aft sail on a ship. This was set on the lower mizzen mast. In the seventeenth and early eighteenth centuries, this was a lateen [3] or triangular sail set on a yard hung on the side of the mizzenmast, sloping in such a way as to be parallel to the mizzen forestay; about as much of the yard projected forward of the mast as aft of it, and it was thought to be a great nuisance. Its only real function was in balancing the ship to make her steer more easily. As the eighteenth century progressed, the forward end of the yard lost its part of the sail, so that a quadrilateral sail was set on the after end only. By the time of the Revolution, most, but not all, ships had replaced the lateen yard with a simple gaff, which was all the quadrilateral sail needed. The sail was known as a mizzen (loose-footed) or driver (extended by a boom); we usually call both kinds by the nineteenth-century name of spanker. In light weather, a form of studding sail known as a ringtail could be added to the spanker. This was not actually an extension of the sail, but a narrow square sail that was only used for sailing downwind. In the 1790s, this sail was modified to be an actual extension of the spanker, and it could then be used for sailing to windward in light weather.

---

[3] The word *lateen* has nothing to do with Latin, but is a corruption of *la trina*, which means "three-pointed."

Before 1790 the spanker was quite a small sail, and almost invariably did not have a boom on ship-rigged vessels until after that date. As soon as it was married with a boom, its foot increased greatly in length until the sail projected considerably beyond the stern of the ship. Essentially the same sail had been set for years on the mainmast of brigs, snows, and schooners, and here it almost invariably had a boom, although the sail was attached to the boom only at the tack and the clew.

On a few American frigates in the Revolution, a few extra square feet of sail area was gained by the use of a fourth mast, aft of the mizzen. This was actually the staff for the ensign on which a lateen sail was set from a yard, and an extension was provided on top from which the ensign flew. The purpose of this little sail was probably to aid the helmsman in balancing the ship while she was sailing to windward. Incidentally, in this period the ensign was always set on a staff mounted on the stern just forward of the tafferel, and it was never flown from the gaff of the spanker; this is another all-too-common mistake among modern painters and model builders when they are dealing with ships of this period. This custom of flying the ensign from a staff began to be abandoned in the 1790s when the length of the spanker booms made it impractical to change tacks while the ensign staff was in position.

Brigs, snows, and bilanders were the two-masted rigs closest in configuration to the ship rig. Each was a ship rig missing its mizzen mast, and there are accounts of vessels that spent parts of their lives rigged both ways. On the brig, the spanker was borrowed from the missing mizzen and placed on the main, and therefore the main course yard became the crossjack with no sail set on it. The snow was identical to the brig except in that one place; the snow set its spanker on a vertical spar mounted only about one foot aft of the mainmast, thus allowing its gaff jaws to travel up and down without interfering with the set of the main course. The bilander, a rare rig, had no main course, but it set a huge lateen or quadrilateral sail on a lateen yard in place of the spanker.

While the previous three rigs were like a ship rig minus its mizzen, the ketch was similar to the ship rig but minus its foremast. The mainmast was stepped in or close to its usual place, thus leaving an enormous gap between it and the bowsprit. The gap was often profitably used to house one or more giant mortars for lobbing explosive shells on enemy positions; with virtually no rigging in the way, the mortar shells could be fired with relative safety.

The schooner had two masts, although in the nineteenth century there were some schooners that had three or more masts. The essence of the schooner rig was its fore-and-aft sails. The mainsail, which resembled the spanker on a ship, was slightly bigger than the fore-sail, but otherwise the two sails were nearly identical. There were from one to three fore-staysails or jibs. For sailing downwind; many schooners could carry a square topsail on the foremast, and some even had one on the mainmast as well. There are occasional pictures of schooners setting   a fore course as well in fine weather, but this was the exception. The schooner rig never went higher than the topmasts, and sometimes not higher than the lower masts.

Just as steam propulsion and the submarine were invented in the eighteenth century but not perfected until many years later, a refinement in the schooner rig appeared on small schooners in eighteenth-century America (probably originating in Bermuda). This was the Bermudian or (later) Marconi sail, which was a triangular sail with no gaff that was set aft of the mast. In practice, the masts were placed forward and raked sharply aft, and there was usually no jib or forestaysail. The masts were often of about equal height, and the effect was rather like that of the popular cat-ketches that appeared in the 1970s. No record has yet been found of the Bermuda sail on larger schooners or on sloops or cutters; that development had to wait until the twentieth century.

The schooner is thought to have originated in Holland. A similar rig, which must have been developed over many centuries in the Mediterranean, is the lugger. This rig was used extensively by the French, both in the Mediterranean and in northern waters, but it was seldom seen on American vessels. The lugger had two masts positioned roughly as they would be on a schooner, and a third mast tacked on almost as an afterthought, just aft of the rudder post. Each of these masts carried a lugsail, which is a quadrilateral sail suspended from a tilted yard that ran fore and aft. The mainsail was slightly larger than the foresail, and the mizzen was much smaller. One jib was usually carried on the horizontal bowsprit, which carried no jibboom. In light weather, lug-topsails were set on spindly topmasts above the lugsails. Luggers were fast and light, and therefore made good smugglers and commerce raiders.

To catch the luggers, the British used the cutter. The cutter generally had an identical hull shape to the lugger, but had only one mast. On this was set a regular gaff-mainsail, similar to the spanker on a ship, but with a long boom. One or more jibs were set on the horizontal bowsprit, which, like the lugger's bowsprit, never carried a jibboom. Many cutters could set a square topsail and even a course in fine weather, and a few even had a square topgallant set above the topsail on the same mast pole. Cutters could carry tremendous sail area for their size, and they were very fast in the right conditions.

The cutter rig is thought to have been a variation on the Dutch sloop rig. Like the cutter, the sloop had only one mast, and could set essentially the same sails as the cutter. The only major difference in the rig was the bowsprit; in the sloop, the bowsprit was steeved up at an angle, and could carry a jibboom, thus allowing more jibs to be set. One might well wonder why enterprising mariners did not employ the sloop rig on a cutter hull, and vice versa, but there is no record of its ever having been done, and the two classes of vessels developed independently; Americans preferred the sloop and the

British preferred the cutter, although, of course, the British built a number of sloops and the Americans built a few cutters.

Rigs were not the only distinguishing features between ships of different nationalities. In many cases, the hull shapes were very characteristic of their countries of origin. Most of these characteristics were based on the common practice in either Britain or France, and it was not uncommon to find, say, a Spanish ship that combined obvious French features with obvious British features. This is largely because the other countries tended to hire French and British shipwrights to rebuild their navies between wars.

With warships, one of the most obvious differences between the French and British practices was that the French ships were generally much larger than the British ships of the same number of guns. Theoretically, this made the French ships faster and more weatherly than the British, but the French frequently threw away their advantage through poor seamanship and lack of experience. Nevertheless, the British kept enlarging their ships throughout the eighteenth century in an effort to keep up with the French.

The midship section of French ships was frequently different from that of British ships. The French section had a nearly flat floor, followed by a pronounced knuckle, followed by a fairly flat slope up to the waterline to another knuckle. The supposed advantage of this shape is that the ballast could be kept lower, contributing to stability, but the more simply rounded British bottoms apparently did not suffer greatly from lack of stability.

It was in the frigate classes that British ships differed the most from their French counterparts, as Robert Gardiner has so clearly pointed out in his excellent series of articles in *Warship* magazine, vol. III (Conway Maritime Press, 1979). French frigates were longer, narrower, shallower and much more lightly constructed than their English counterparts of the same rate. This caused them to sail faster in light weather, especially off the wind, but their performance to windward and in heavy weather was greatly inferior. Their ammunition, food, water and other supplies comprised a much greater proportion of their displacement than on British frigates, which meant that their trim was likely to change drastically on a long cruise. French frigates when roughly used needed more frequent major rebuildings than British. All this reflects the different purposes for which they were built. British frigates were built essentially for constant patrol to control the seas, while French frigates were intended for short cruises and commerce-raiding. The French viewed naval strength as something with which to assist the army, while the British viewed sea power as a goal in itself.

Other national characteristics will appear from time to time in the commentary on individual ships later in the book. Among those to look for and compare are the shape of the tafferels, the head rails, the quarter galleries, the rake of the stem and sternposts, the degree of sheer, the fineness of the entry, and the number and placement of fenders and wales along the topsides. While the French seem to have been largely the innovators—and indeed they explored the science of ship design and construction far more thoroughly than did the British—the British did invent one important advance in design which nearly everyone copied. This was the round tuck stern. Previous to the middle of the seventeenth century all ships had square sterns, which caused a great deal of drag in the water. The British invented a means of fairing the underwater part of the stern upward to a horizontal transom beam, which made for rounded underwater lines in the stern, hence the name "round tuck stern." By the early nineteenth century, nearly every major ship built anywhere in Europe or America had the round tuck stern.

Other national characteristics had to do with the proportions of the length and breadth of the vessel to each other. The Dutch, because of their shallow, muddy coastline, came up with a midsection that was shallower than others, and therefore wider in order to support the same cargo and the same rig; Dutch vessels also had much flatter bottoms than others in case they should have to sit on the mud to await the next high tide. Many smaller American craft also had great beam, particularly at the time of the Revolution, but in this case the goal was speed coupled with stability. Many late eighteenth-century American bottoms, therefore, were far from flat, but had great deadrise, almost like a *V*, and also had sharp entries to match. The American design might have caught on faster in Europe if it had not usually been accompanied by extremely light construction scantlings in an effort to obtain still more speed. Light construction did not stand up well in the foul weather frequently found in European waters. Europeans were also impatient with the fact that American vessels were only fast when not overloaded, which, with their sharp deadrise, it was far too easy to do.

While the shape and appearance of ships varied somewhat from country to country, the actual construction varied little. The keel, a massive timber or timbers of oak or elm, was laid with the stern toward the water (although the Dutch launched their ships bow first). On it were mounted the stem and the sternpost. Frames were added in a sequence, usually starting from the stern.

Frames were of oak, and were sawn to the desired shape. The natural shapes and crooks of trees were a help, but only to a certain extent. Frames had to be built up out of a series of short, curved pieces, and they were usually but not always built in pairs, so that the butts or joints in one frame were overlapped by the wood of the other. Each of these short lengths of curved wood was called a futtock. The two frames were held together sometimes by iron bolts, sometimes by iron spikes, and sometimes by wooden tree nails (pronounced "trunnels"), usually of locust wood. The port pair of frames was joined to the starboard pair by a floor timber at the bottom, and by a number of tem-

17th-Century Ship

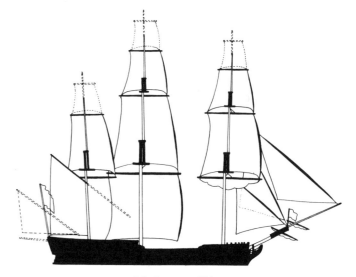

18th-Century Ship

Brig

Snow

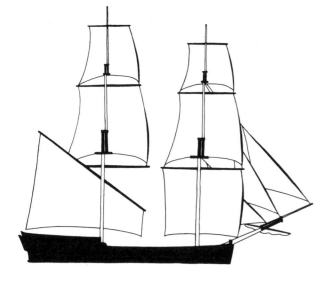

Bilander

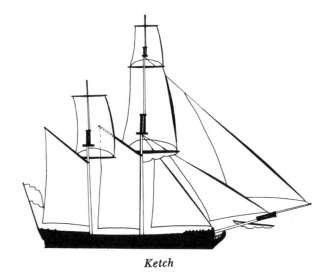

Ketch

Row Galley

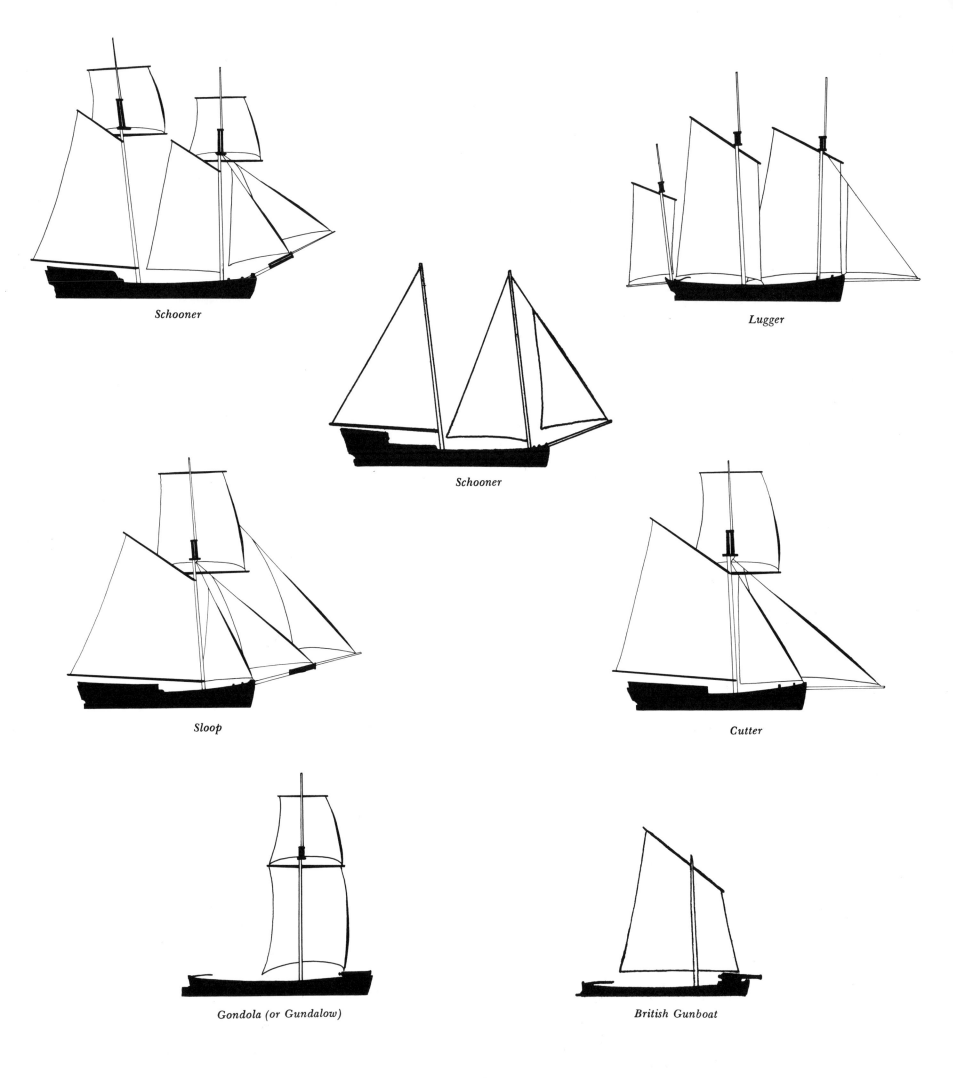

Schooner

Lugger

Schooner

Sloop

Cutter

Gondola (or Gundalow)

British Gunboat

Detail of anonymous 18th-century painting of a Maryland ship-yard, from a wooden overmantel panel originally at Spencer Hall, Maryland; Maryland Historical Society.

porary braces nearer the top.

When all the frames had been erected on top of the keel, another heavy longitudinal member, known as the keelson, was fastened on top of the floors. At this stage, it would be seen that there were large gaps between the forward frames and the stem, and the after frames and the sternpost. Into these gaps, where the planks would have very pronounced curves, were placed special frames and parts of frames, set at right angles to the curve of the planks. These were called cant frames, and they were usually more solidly spaced than the regular frames. Many ships, however, were built with regular frames in the place of cant frames, their edges drastically bevelled to follow the bend of the planks. The reproduction of *Rose* was built this way in Nova Scotia in 1969, and archaeologists have found an American ship of the early eighteenth century with frames similarly marching up the stempost at right-angles to the centerline.

As soon as all the frames were set up, they were joined longitudinally by temporary braces or ribbands. The first planks to be fastened to the ship were usually those of the main wale, which we have drawn as a thick dark line curving along the topsides in all our drawings. The wale planks were at least an inch thicker than the regular planks, both to provide extra longitudinal strength and also to serve as rubbing strakes when the ship was bumping against another ship or against a dock. The wale was usually situated at the widest point of the ship.

Above the wale the frames sloped inward, so that the ship was quite a bit narrower at the top than at the waterline. This is called tumblehome, and its purpose has been explained in a variety of different ways. Some say that it was to make it more difficult for an enemy to capture the ship by boarding, while others claim that it came from a misunderstanding of the principles of

the center of gravity. Regardless of its origin, it was a typical feature of nearly all ships in the period under discussion in this book, and tumblehome only began to disappear in the nineteenth century. Tumblehome contributed to the rigidity of the hull, but it was also the place where rainwater could most easily get behind the planks to cause rot.

The planks above the main wale were interspersed occasionally with more wales, usually only one plank wide, and usually molded into an interesting decorative shape. These naturally provided additional strength and longitudinal rigidity to the ship, but it is hard to imagine that some of them were more than decorative, for they were often intersected every so many feet by a gunport.

In the nineteenth and twentieth centuries, when a plank had to be bent around a tightly curved part of a ship it was placed in a steam box and impregnated with steam. When it came out of the steam box it could be bent to the desired shape, and it would hold that shape after it had dried. Earlier shipwrights had a more difficult time. Sometimes they would cut the planks from a naturally curved tree, and sometimes they tried charring the plank on one side. Some used green lumber, which is more likely to bend than seasoned wood, but which is almost certain to rot in a very short time. Others soaked the wood for months in brine. Some form of steam preparation may have been available by the time of the Revolution, especially since one American frigate is said to have been launched only sixty days after her keel was laid, and yet she had not rotted appreciably by the end of the war; the shipwrights would not have had time to search for naturally crooked trees for the planking in her bow and stern and then allow it to season, so they must have used whatever wood they had on hand.

When the outside planking was complete, a similar amount of work remained to be done on the inside of the ship. Along the underside of where the deck beams would go a timber was placed along the back of the frames. This was called the clamp or shelf, and part of its duty was to provide still more longitudinal bracing. Decks were nearly flat from end to end of the ship, and did not follow the sheer line. Deck beams were frequently not long enough to stretch all the way across the ship, so they were pieced together. They were supported near the middle of the ship by two carlines, which were timbers running the length of the ship; the carlines themselves were supported at intervals by vertical posts, some of which ran down as far as the floor timbers and up as high as the upper decks, where they could be used as bitts or supports for bitts.

After the decks had been planked, the inside surface of the frames was covered over by planking as thick as the outside planking, although often of an inferior wood. These inner planks were known as the ceiling (what we normally think of as the ceiling in a house was called the deckhead or the overhead), and they served as further longitudinal stiffening. In some ships there were gaps in the ceiling to allow air to circulate

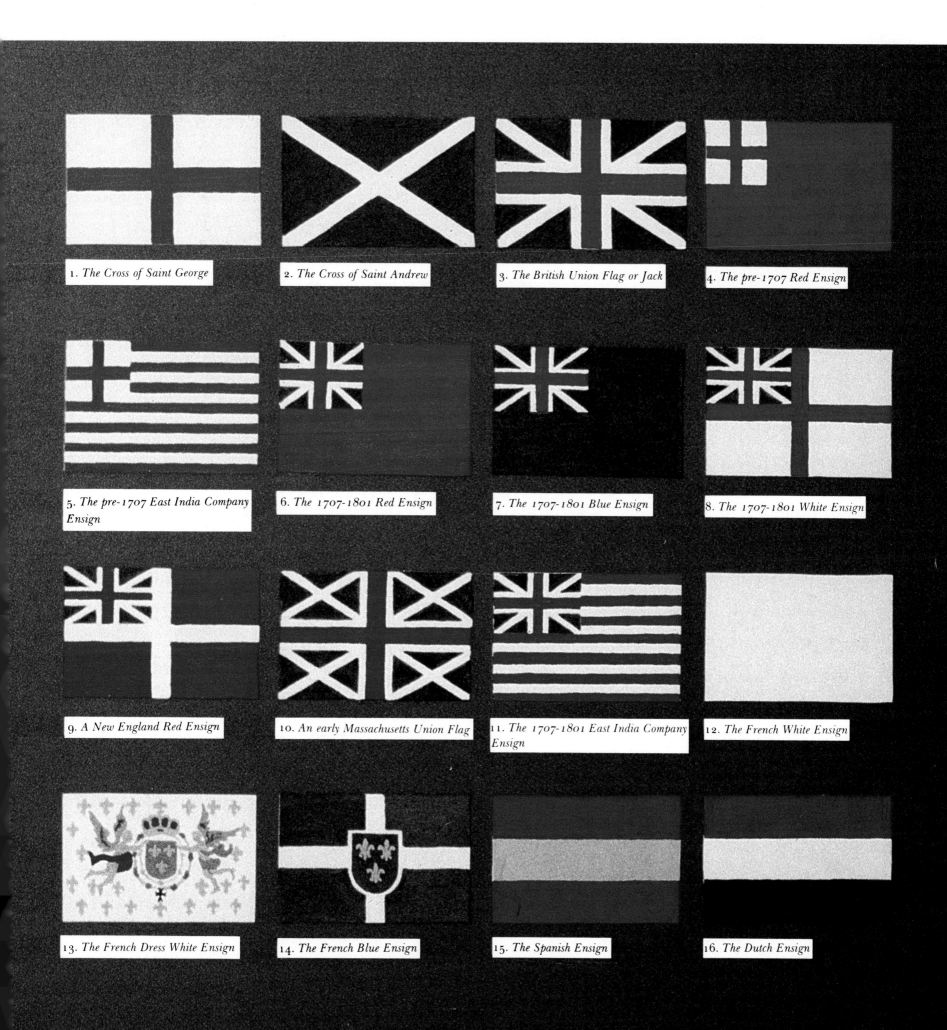

1. *The Cross of Saint George*

2. *The Cross of Saint Andrew*

3. *The British Union Flag or Jack*

4. *The pre-1707 Red Ensign*

5. *The pre-1707 East India Company Ensign*

6. *The 1707-1801 Red Ensign*

7. *The 1707-1801 Blue Ensign*

8. *The 1707-1801 White Ensign*

9. *A New England Red Ensign*

10. *An early Massachusetts Union Flag*

11. *The 1707-1801 East India Company Ensign*

12. *The French White Ensign*

13. *The French Dress White Ensign*

14. *The French Blue Ensign*

15. *The Spanish Ensign*

16. *The Dutch Ensign*

17. *The Danish Dannebrog*

18. *The Russian-American Company Ensign in Alaska*

19. *The Massachusetts Pine Tree Flag*

20. *An Appeal to Heaven*

25. *The Pine Tree & Stripes Ensign*

26. *The Grand Union Ensign, version I*

27. *The Grand Union Ensign, version II*

28. *The Grand Union Ensign, version III*

33. *The Grand Union Ensign, version VIII*

34. *The Grand Union Ensign, version IX*

35. *The Grand Union Ensign, version X*

36. *The Grand Union Ensign, version XI*

41. *The Merchant Ensign, version I*

42. *The Merchant Ensign, version II*

43. *The Merchant Ensign, version III*

44. *The Stars & Stripes, version I*

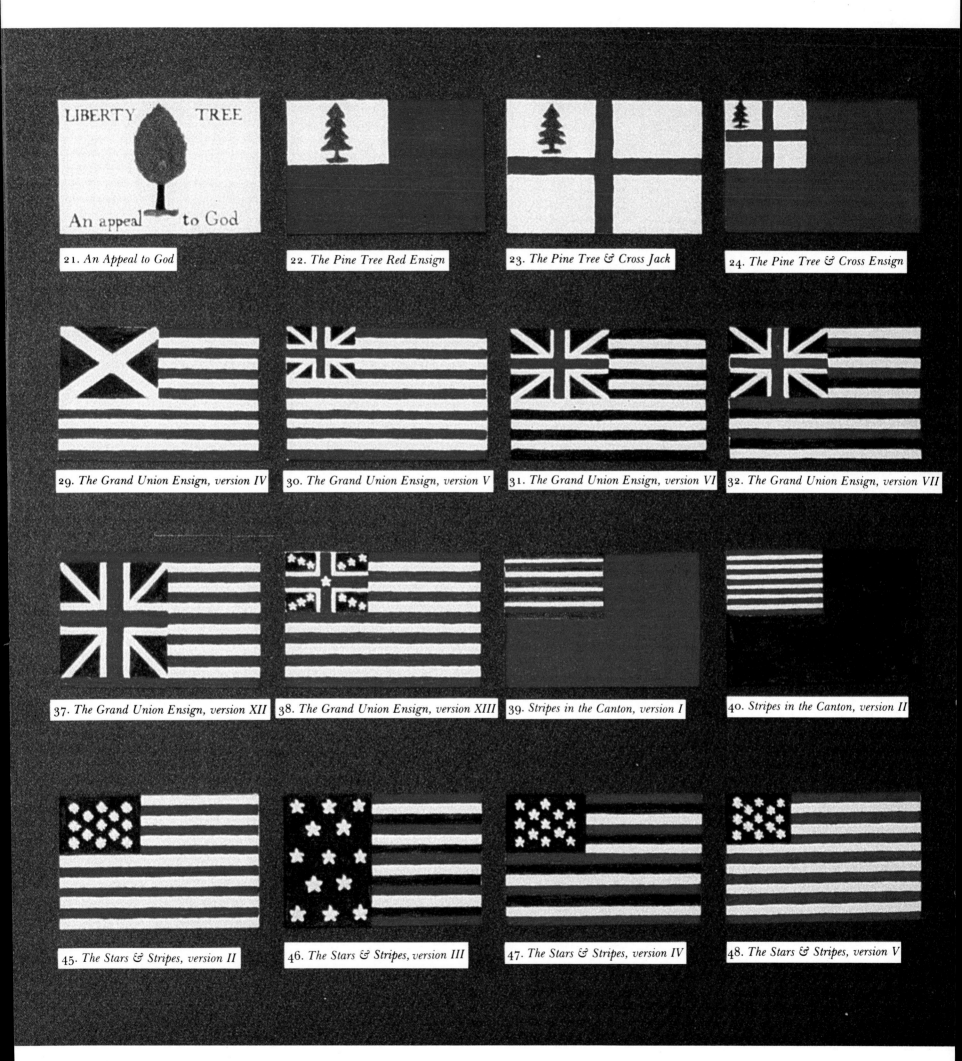

21. *An Appeal to God*

22. *The Pine Tree Red Ensign*

23. *The Pine Tree & Cross Jack*

24. *The Pine Tree & Cross Ensign*

29. *The Grand Union Ensign, version IV*

30. *The Grand Union Ensign, version V*

31. *The Grand Union Ensign, version VI*

32. *The Grand Union Ensign, version VII*

37. *The Grand Union Ensign, version XII*

38. *The Grand Union Ensign, version XIII*

39. *Stripes in the Canton, version I*

40. *Stripes in the Canton, version II*

45. *The Stars & Stripes, version II*

46. *The Stars & Stripes, version III*

47. *The Stars & Stripes, version IV*

48. *The Stars & Stripes, version V*

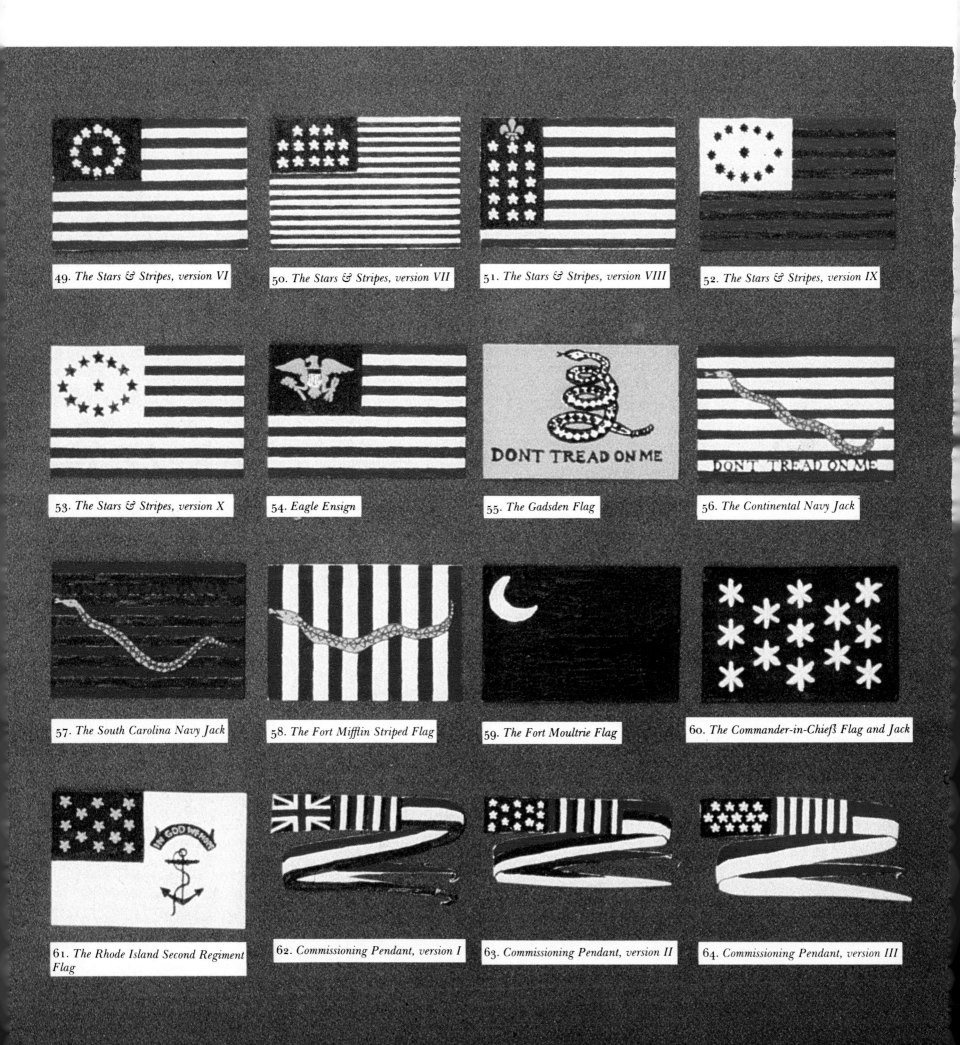

49. *The Stars & Stripes, version VI*

50. *The Stars & Stripes, version VII*

51. *The Stars & Stripes, version VIII*

52. *The Stars & Stripes, version IX*

53. *The Stars & Stripes, version X*

54. *Eagle Ensign*

55. *The Gadsden Flag*

56. *The Continental Navy Jack*

57. *The South Carolina Navy Jack*

58. *The Fort Mifflin Striped Flag*

59. *The Fort Moultrie Flag*

60. *The Commander-in-Chiefs Flag and Jack*

61. *The Rhode Island Second Regiment Flag*

62. *Commissioning Pendant, version I*

63. *Commissioning Pendant, version II*

64. *Commissioning Pendant, version III*

between the frames, but others were completely sealed up and some were even caulked for extra rigidity. In these latter cases, salt was sometimes placed in large quantities between the inner and outer planking; this pickling was intended to preserve the wood from the rot that usually attacked it when it was denied full circulation of air.

For some ships no further construction was done, but for others knees had to be fitted. These were right-angled trusses cut from a natural crook in a tree or, more frequently, from tree roots. In America the hackmatack tree was traditionally used for this purpose. Some knees were placed under the deck beams so as to bind them to the sides of the ship; these were called hanging knees. Other knees, placed horizontally between the deck beams themselves to keep them straight, were called lodging knees.

For many of those ships that had a head, planking in the bows did not bend around to the stem for about the upper six feet of the topsides, but stopped instead at a bulkhead that was set a few feet aft of the stem. This was called the beakhead bulkhead, and it provided a small platform from which it was easier both to reach the head itself and to manage sails on the bowsprit. However, the beakhead bulkhead was a particularly weak point on ships that had it, for it was prone to leak in bad weather and it was very vulnerable to being pierced by shot from an enemy ship in a maneuver known as raking. The beakhead bulkhead began to disappear for this reason soon after 1750, and by the time of the Revolution the majority of warships smaller than the First and Second Rates were built with round bows.

The sterns, too, with their flimsy construction and wide expanse of window area, were vulnerable to raking fire from enemy ships, but the traditional sterns did not give way to solid round construction until about the 1820s.

Among the most common misconceptions about ships of the period of this book are the notions about their color schemes. Many people think that because the 44-gun frigate *Constitution,* now on display in Boston, is painted black with white trim all ships of the period were so painted. This is doubly misleading. To begin with, the *Constitution* was not painted this way until well into the nineteenth century, so in terms of color (as well as countless other details, both major and minor) she is not representative of the late eighteenth century. When she was first built, she was painted ochre with a black wale strake; the two uppermost panels of planks on the topsides were vibrant colors, probably blue and red; much of her head and tafferel were gilded or painted yellow, while her rails were black and her deck furniture was largely red. At least two period paintings show her this way, in addition to two of her sistership *United States,* and they merely confirm that she was painted more or less the same as other ships of her day. Over $4 million were spent on *Constitution* to put her in good condition for the 1976 Bicentennial, and it is to be deplored that she has not been restored to either the shape or the colors of her original appearance, or at least

of the way she looked in the War of 1812, her finest years.

How did these colors become so standardized, and whence did they come? In the seventeenth century, the topsides of ships were usually oiled with linseed oil or coated in a linseed-based varnish. Linseed oil was available in large quantities because it came from the same flax plant as linen fibers, which were in great demand for clothing and sails. It was noticed, however, that the older a ship grew and the more it had to be oiled or varnished for protection, the darker it became. Thus, it would be easy for a potential adversary to tell roughly how old (and weak) a ship was by its color, and hence the enemy would be able to include that information in making its decision as to whether or not the ship could be easily captured. Therefore, while some ships continued to be oiled, most were no longer oiled but were painted to resemble the color of newly-oiled oak. Nearly all the ships in the period covered by this book were ochre in color, varying from almost yellow to light brown, some being almost orange. There were exceptions, of course. Some hulls were all black, and some Spanish ships are said to have been painted in red stripes (but the MGM version of the merchant ship *Bounty* for the film *Mutiny on the Bounty* is definitely wrong in blue).

After the ochre, the next most obvious element of color on the topsides was the main wale. The main wale was a band of planks (thicker than the rest) that followed the sheer of the hull. The wale essentially provided longitudinal rigidity for the hull, but it also served a useful function as a rubbing strake; since it was located at the widest part of each section of the ship, it was the piece that would grind against a dock or against another ship when the ship lay alongside. Consequently, since before Elizabethan times the wale had been coated with pitch or pine tar to give it maximum wearing durability. Thus, the wale was almost always black.

Towards the end of the eighteenth century, the areas of black gradually were expanded and the ochre diminished, leading to the nineteenth-century scheme of a narrow ochre (later white) stripe marking the row of gunports.

The bottoms of ships were given the benefit of much experience and research, for without a healthy bottom the ship would surely sink. The greatest enemy of the ship's bottom was the teredo worm, a borer worm (related to the clam) that lives in salt water from the arctic to the equator. It does not actually eat wood, but riddles all kinds of wood with tunnels that are invisible from the outside, and feeds on microscopic organisms that float past the hull. Without protection a wooden hull would be useless in only a few years.

Since worms would not cross the layer of tar between two planks, one solution frequently used called for the bottom to be sheathed in an additional layer of planks that could be replaced every few years when the worms had destroyed enough of it. Another solution called for the coating of the bottom with an evil-smelling and poisonous substance that would discourage worms from making the ship their home. This substance was usually included in tallow, so the ships' bottoms were usually a dirty-white or off-white color. For longer bottom life, the tallow compound could be applied on top of wooden sheathing, the whole operation being done with the ship still in the water, by "careening" or pulling the ship over onto her side and doing one side of the bottom at a time. The tallow compound was also reasonably effective in discouraging the growth of seaweed, barnacles, mussels, and other marine life on the bottom that can reduce the ship's speed by as much as one-half, but the tallow compound had to be applied at least once a year.

The tallow compound was obviously far from perfect, so frequent attempts were made to find substitutes. Lead sheathing was tried, but it was both expensive and heavy, and besides it seemed ineffective against marine growth. In the 1760s, experiments were made with copper sheathing, which would quickly turn a light green in color. The copper plates were effective against borers and marine growth, but they caused all iron parts of the ship under water, such as plank fastenings and rudder hinges, to disintegrate under electrolytic or galvanic action. A few years later, all iron fastenings below the water were replaced by bronze or copper fastenings if copper plates were to be fitted. The Royal Navy made immediate and extensive use of the discovery, but few American or French ships had copper sheathing before 1790. One of history's little ironies is that during the wars of the French Revolution and Napoleonic expansion the French continued to sell the British tons of copper (and brandy) which the British were quite openly using to make their ships go faster and last longer, which inevitably resulted in defeat for the French.

One area of the ship's hull that varied in color was the area between the main wale and the waterline in the bow and the stern. Most ships continued the ochre color down into these areas, but some continued the tallow up to the wale all the way around, thus making the areas off-white, and others continued the black of the wale down to the waterline.

Most ships were arranged in such a way as to have a panel running along the topsides immediately below the gunwale. This was often painted a bold color, such as blue or green, although sometimes it was left ochre, and sometimes it was even black, especially in later ships. Another similar panel immediately above this one in the way of the quarterdeck and forecastle was often painted a contrasting bold color, such as red, although these were also occasionally black in later ships. These bold panels were frequently decorated with leafy scrolls or classical frieze-type designs picked out in gold leaf or even carved in light relief.

Ships in the late seventeenth century were dripping with carving, but the amount of carving was cut back sharply in the eighteenth century as a cost-cutting measure. Particularly notable among the carvings on the earlier ships were the circular wreaths that surrounded the gunports on the upper decks, and the statues that filled every conceivable niche on the stern. Most of the carved parts, at least of the earlier ships, were covered in gold leaf. Later ships restricted the carving generally to the figurehead and possibly a little on the stern and quarter galleries.

Figureheads varied from ship to ship and country to country. The most common design by far was that of a crowned lion. The lion was stylized rather than sculpted from life, and resembled a heraldic lion, although at various times when national taste turned to things Oriental the lions acquired a distinctly Chinese flavor. Lookouts on a British ship could usually tell from the shape of the lion's crown if another ship were British or from a continental nation.

Lions began to give way to other designs by the middle of the eighteenth century. Gods and goddesses or other figures from classical mythology were the most popular, although an individual ship could have a figurehead that reflected her name: the frigate *Unicorn*, for example, would have a unicorn, while a ship named after a general would most likely have a statue of that general. Captain Cook's *Resolution* had a horse, as did a number of other ships. First Rates and Second Rates rarely had lions at any period; instead, they often had a collection of allegorical or mythological figures, or a member of the royal family seated on a horse.

In our practical age, we might well wonder what was the point of wasting time and money to stick a long cut-water and figurehead onto the bow of a ship some 200 years ago. While the carving itself was decorative and had no functional purpose other than as a morale builder, the space between the figurehead and the bow was extremely practical. This was called the head, and it was the lavatory facility for all the enlisted men on the ship (officers had pots in their cabins), which one might imagine could be quite uncomfortable in a cold winter storm. It was thought that having these facilities in the bow would ensure that they were kept clean by frequent large waves and hence there would be less risk of disease, but cleaning the head was a daily chore that was usually not helped much by waves. American ships, incidentally, are said to have been infamous the world over for their poorly kept heads.

On larger ships, the head was equipped with two enclosed privies for use in bad weather, but on smaller ships everything was out in the weather. The most obvious features of the head that could be seen from afar were three curved (and sometimes carved) rails leading from the bow out to the figurehead. The lowest rail was well placed for the seaman's feet, while the middle one was for sitting and the upper served as a backrest. Head rails were gilded on some ships, and painted black or yellow, or both, on others. This whole triangular contraption was temporarily covered by a grating where men could stand to assist in weighing anchor. The grating and the headrails were supported by ribs as if the structure were to be planked (which it actually was in the Victorian era). When the ships were in port, they often disguised their heads with brightly painted canvases.

Deck furniture and the inside of bulwarks on warships were almost invariably red. Red was also used on bulwarks below decks, and on the deck itself for the deck below the lowest gun deck. It is said that the reason for this was that it was believed that seamen who were used to the color red all about them would be less likely to panic in the crucial moments of battle when they might find blood around them. As a practical matter, however, historians believe that the abundance of red paint did little that had not already been done by discipline and training. On merchant ships, the insides were usually painted a light color so that the crew could see what they were doing.

The spars, too, were painted according to an almost invariable rule. All the yards and gaffs and booms were black, probably from being coated with pitch. All the doublings, crosstrees, and fighting tops were also black. All other spars were either oiled or painted ochre; none was ever painted white until well into the nineteenth century.

This book contains drawings of over 200 ships that were designed, built or owned by Americans in the period 1607-1790. These drawings can be divided into three basic categories, the complete lines, the hull profiles and the waterline drawings. In most cases, but not all, the complete lines reflect the fact that the original plans or a model of the ship still exist, while the profile and waterline drawings are more conjectural, based on paintings, written evidence or other rather scanty data.

In a few cases, complete drawings have been included of ships for which only enough evidence exists to warrant a waterline drawing, but these are mostly ships of greater interest to model builders and artists, and the fact that the plans are conjectural is clearly stated.

The complete plans consist of three parts: the outboard profile, the plan, and the sections. The outboard profile (or "sheer" or side elevation) is simply a view of the side of the ship from stem to stern and from keel to rail cap. Many draftsmen like to include a few interior details on their outboard profiles, such as the deck levels, but it was thought that such details would needlessly complicate our drawings. For the same reason, much carving has been omitted, although figureheads have nearly always been included, contrary to the practice of the period. To emphasize the prominence of the main wale, this has been shaded dark, the way it would look on the real ship, although as a rule this was not usually done by eighteenth-century draftsmen.

Quarterdeck rails in this period were nearly always open, and in this book they have been drawn that way, in spite of the fact that surviving plans and paintings show that the rails on some ships had been lightly planked or covered in canvas so as to give the appearance of being a solid bulwark. Such planking was often done some time after the ship was built. On the other hand, many paintings and plans of the period omit certain details on the topsides, such as the boarding stairs, the barrel fenders, the chestrees, and the anchor fenders, but such details have usually been included in this book regardless.

The plan drawings, otherwise known as the half-breadth, show a view of one side of the bottom of the ship, and are located immediately underneath the outboard profile. Many draftsmen like to include details of the deck plan superimposed on this, but we have not done so for two reasons: (1) it would clutter up the drawings more, and (2) there is precious little information about the deck plans of most individual ships, although they generally did not vary much from one ship to another within a type and period.

The section or body plan shows the shape of the ship looking from the bow and the stern, so that the shapes of certain selected frames (and, by extension, all the frames) can be shown. The left half shows all the stations from the stern to the point of maximum breadth (usually more than half the distance to the bow), while the right half shows the stations between the point of maximum breadth and the bow. These stations are sometimes brought up to the top of the quarterdeck rail, but sometimes only to the top of the sheer.

Many modern draftsmen include diagonal lines on their drawings, used for making sure the planking would be "fair" and have no bumps or indentations in it. We have not included such diagonals so as not to clutter up the drawings.

The general practice was to draw these lines to the inside of the planking, but we have not been consistent with this practice in every case. The difference between lines drawn to the inside and those drawn to the outside of the planking would be negligible at the scale these plans are reproduced in this book.

The originals for these plans were drawn, following British and American practice, to a scale of 1:48, or one inch equals four feet, but they have been printed much smaller than that in this book. Because of the great difference in size between, say, a battleship and a small schooner, the plans have been reproduced at varying scales in such a way as would best allow them to fit on their particular page. However, the scale is drawn on every plan.

We have noted a number of different dimensions of these ships, which should aid in comparison. Length overall is a measurement not generally used 200 years ago, but we find it useful. It extends from the nose of the figurehead to the after part of the quarterdeck rail, and does not include any spars.

Length between perpendiculars, or length on the deck, is a measurement that varied somewhat with the whim of the measurer, and we have not been consistent. Within a few inches, it was the length of the ship from where the planking underneath the wale met the stem to a similar point on the sternpost, in which case it was called the "length between perpendiculars." In most cases, a deck would be laid inside, corresponding roughly with the level of the ends of the lower part of the wale, and the measurement was then known as "length on the lower deck," or "length on the range of the deck." The deck, of course, was far more nearly

Construction of a frigate at Philadelphia, William Birch, ca. 1799.

level than the wale, which curved in imitation of the sheer.

Length of keel for tonnage was a measurement made for tax purposes, and should be of little or no interest to most readers.

Breadth was the width of the ship at her widest point, usually a point just above the waterline a short distance forward of the midpoint of her length. This measurement varied somewhat depending on whether it was made to the inside or outside of the planking. On a small boat this could mean only about three inches, but on a battleship this variation could be over a foot.

Depth in hold is another measurement that should hold little interest for most readers, since it was used primarily to calculate taxes. It varied somewhat from measurer to measurer and could be the distance from the keelson to the underside of the berth deck or even to the gun deck.

Draft, on the other hand, might be of more use to the reader, but it varied considerably, depending on how heavily laden the vessel was. We have taken the draft as the measurement from the bottom of the keel

at the sternpost to the waterline, and we have drawn the waterline so as to be consistent with good trim and sailing practice; the waterline we show is not always the same as that shown on original plans of the ships, since these only reflect the trim as it was on the day the plans were made. In most cases the keel had a slight drag, which means that the draft was greater at the sternpost than further forward.

Tonnage is another figure intended for tax purposes. This was a measurement, not a weight, and it was obtained by a mathematical formula that showed theoretically how many "tuns" or large casks of wine could be stowed in the available space on the ship. The actual weight or displacement tonnage was usually a much larger figure, sometimes half again as much. In 1694, British tonnage was computed by the formula: Length of Keel × the square of the Breadth divided by 188. By 1703, it was Length of Keel × Breadth × Depth divided by 95. The French used a totally different system, arriving at a much lower figure. From an early date, Americans were often accused of conniving at under-valuing their tonnage figures by anywhere from a quarter to a third in an effort to avoid paying a portion of taxes and light-house fees. For this reason, among others, tonnage is not always a useful guide for the comparison of different ships. Even in Royal Navy service, tonnage calculations varied by as much as five percent on the same ship over a period of years (depending on the measurer) and similar variations are found between identical sisterships built over a period of years.

No account of ships of this period would be complete without a description of the clothes worn by the crew and officers, and the flags flown by the ships. Before the middle of the eighteenth century, the Royal Navy had no uniforms for any of its officers or men, other than the red coats with white facings for the Marines. An individual captain could and occasionally did specify that the oarsmen of his personal gig wear a uniform of his own invention. When Commodore George Anson arrived in Canton on his victorious flagship *Centurion* in 1744, he found that the Chinese authorities treated him with more courtesy if he made a great show with uniformed personnel around him. When he was promoted to a position of real authority in the Royal Navy in 1748, he instituted a system of dress and daily uniforms for all officers and some warrant officers. This, in turn, encouraged some captains to try to dress their seamen in uniforms, but the majority of seamen wore what they pleased.

Over the years, fashions changed and Anson's uniforms were thought to be too elaborate as well as out of style, so they were gradually replaced. During the American Revolution, a Royal Navy captain wore white stockings, breeches and single-breasted waistcoat. His double-breasted dress coat was blue with white facings edged with a single stripe of gold lace, while his daily coat was all blue; in the double-breasted daily coat, the buttonholes, edged in gold lace, were arranged in four groups of threes on each facing. Lieutenants wore a coat similar to the captain's dress coat but without the gold lace. The master, the senior warrant officer, wore a coat similar to the lieutenant's but with blue facings, and pursers, gunners, carpenters, boatswains and surgeons were theoretically supposed to wear the same coat as the master, but the rules were not always observed. The typical seaman wore a frock coat cut slightly shorter than usual and generally blue or brown. His waistcoat might be any color, but it was often striped or red, as were his trousers or breeches. Often, a seaman wore a white canvas skirt over his breeches to protect them from tar, paint or moisture. On their heads, seamen wore tricorns or flat straw hats (in summer) or flat tarred hats or knitted stocking-caps. Midshipmen, many of whom were but thirteen years old, wore white small-clothes with a blue, single-breasted coat trimmed with white tabs on the collar and white cuffs; the buttons on the cuffs are said to have been placed in such a way as to inhibit the youngsters from the habit of wiping their noses on their sleeves (hence midshipmen are sometimes known as "snotties").

In the French Navy, the rank of captain was divided into three grades, *capitaine de vaisseau* (battleship), *de frégate* (frigate), and *de brûlot* (fireship); this was a mark of seniority and had little to do with the types of ships they actually commanded. The level of captain was marked by the amount and placement of gold lace on the coat. The French captain wore red stockings, red breeches, a red waistcoat trimmed with gold lace and a blue coat trimmed in red and gold; his dress coat was single-breasted, and his daily coat was double-breasted with red facings trimmed in gold, including gold buttonholes. He also had a "fatigue" uniform that omitted the gold. His rank on all three coats was denoted by a pair of gold epaulettes, while British captains never wore epaulettes in this period (British admirals did). French lieutenants, like their captains, were divided into three grades. Their uniforms, and those of the midshipmen, resembled the captains' uniforms with correspondingly less gold lace. Each different type of French warrant officer had a slightly different uniform (no doubt the nobles at Versaille had spent weeks working out the system to their satisfaction and to the exasperation of those who served in the Navy), but they all shared red small-clothes with gold trim. French marines were actually from army regiments drawn from coastal towns, so their uniforms differed from town to town, but most had white small-clothes and blue double-breasted coats with red facings. For a more complete description of French Navy uniforms of the period, the reader is directed to the excellent color plates in volume IV of Jean Boudriot's *Le Vaisseau de 74 Canons*.

Uniforms in the Spanish and Dutch services differed only slightly from the French uniforms.

Uniforms of the Continental Navy in its first two years steered a different course. Captains wore white stockings, blue breeches, red waistcoats trimmed in gold lace and blue double-breasted coats with red facings. These facings were either plain or trimmed with gold lace, depending on which tailor made the coat. Lieutenants wore a similar uniform but without any gold lace. There was no difference between dress and daily uniforms. Although Congress never sanctioned it, starting in 1777 many of the Continental Navy officers adopted a new uniform, replacing all the red with white and switching to white breeches. They also added epaulettes. The reason for this was that all possibility of surprising a British ship was lost if officers could be plainly seen wearing red. From 1777 on, American midshipmen wore the same as their British counterparts but without the white trim on the coat. American warrant officers in practice wore what they pleased. American marines began the war with white small-clothes and green double-breasted coats with white facings trimmed in green piping, but because the coats were difficult to keep clean they were replaced in 1779 by green coats with red facings.

To outsiders, people in the United States may seem to be overly attached to flags (usually the national flag and the Confederate flag from the Civil War), and yet Americans are surprisingly ignorant about the rich variety of flags that contribute to the American heritage of the seventeenth and eighteenth centuries. For the purposes of this book, a selection has been made of some of the most interesting and important flags associated with early America. The selection is weighted towards those flags that are known to have been flown on ships, as well as those that may yet appear to have been flown on ships (one of the difficulties involved in finding and identifying early American ships is that researchers may not be aware of the diversity of American flags that such ships may be flying), and a few "missing links" in the development of American flag design.

The text describing each of 64 such flags is keyed to a series of four color plates on which each flag is numbered. The pictures begin with flags of the major European powers that colonized North America and hence of the colonists themselves, but the majority of the pictures are devoted to American flags used during and just after the struggle for independence. The variety is astonishing, particularly since a large portion of these flags were used or even designed after Congress apparently made the design of the official United States flag quite clear in June 1777.

1. The Cross of Saint George

The simple red cross on a white field has been the national flag of England for many centuries. It is still appropriately displayed today, even though England has been united with Scotland, Wales and Northern Ireland for many years.

2. The Cross of Saint Andrew

The diagonal white cross on a blue ground, recalling the unusual crucifixion of Saint Andrew, has been the national flag of Scotland for centuries.

3. The British Union Flag or Jack

This combination of the crosses of Saint George and Saint Andrew represents the union of the kingdoms of England and Scotland that occurred in 1603. It was first proclaimed in 1606, but in 1634 it was reserved exclusively for royal or naval vessels (merchant ships were expected to revert to the single cross of their respective country); it was abolished in 1649 under the Commonwealth but revived again in 1660 by Charles II for royal and naval vessels, and merchants flying it were subject to arrest. It became more widely used after 1707 when the parliaments of England and Scotland were united, and gradually the government stopped prosecuting merchant ships for flying it. The red diagonal cross of Saint Patrick found in the modern British Union flag was not added until 1801 when the Irish parliament was united with the British parliament, and so is completely wrong if shown on a model or portrait of any ship in this book.

4. The pre-1707 Red Ensign

On ships, the Union flag came to be flown from the forward part of a ship, where it was known as a Jack, or from a masthead. The ensign staff at the stern was reserved by at least 1625 for the Red Ensign, which consisted of a red flag with the Cross of Saint George in the upper-left canton. Later, in order to distinguish the commands of different admirals, the Blue Ensign and the White Ensign were introduced, in which the red fly was replaced by a blue or plain white fly. Merchant ships flew only the Red Ensign.

5. The pre-1707 East India Company Ensign

The East India Company was chartered in 1600 and felt that it was unfairly handicapped by not being permitted to fly the Union flag. At least as early as 1656 it developed a distinctive version of the Red Ensign by dividing the red fly

into a number of stripes by the addition of several white stripes. The number of stripes varied from as few as seven to as many as 19, with 13 being common. The British government permitted the Company to fly the striped flag anywhere south and east of the island of Saint Helena off the west coast of South Africa, but Company ships are known to have flown this flag in North America and even in London.

6. The 1707-1801 Red Ensign

In 1707 the Act of Union united the parliaments of England and Scotland, and accordingly the Red Ensign received the addition of the Cross of Saint Andrew in the canton in union with the cross of Saint George. This was the standard ensign flown by British and Anglo-American merchant ships as well as most naval ships.

7. The 1707-1801 Blue Ensign

For ships acting under the orders of an "admiral of the blue" the Blue Ensign was usually flown; it resembled the Red Ensign but with the red fly replaced by a blue fly. It was not for merchant ships.

8. The 1707-1801 White Ensign

For ships acting under the orders of an "admiral of the white" the White Ensign was usually flown. It did not resemble an up-dated version of the pre-1707 White Ensign because its canton was not set into the corner of a plain white fly, but rather in the corner of a large Cross of Saint George. It is believed that this design first appeared as regimental colors of British Marines, whose coats were red with white facings. It was not used by merchant ships. While the modern White Ensign has come to be almost the only ensign flown by the Royal Navy, it was relatively rare in the eighteenth century, when the Royal Navy generally used the Red Ensign.

9. A New England Red Ensign

Sailor-artist Ashley Bowen of Marblehead, Massachusetts recorded a version of the Red Ensign flown by a New England merchant ship on at least two occasions. Its fly was the reverse of the White Ensign, for it consisted of a large white cross on a red ground. No doubt this design did not become popular for fear of confusing it with the Danish flag.

10. An early Massachusetts Union Flag

American merchants, like their British counterparts, chafed under the regulations that prohibited them from flying the Union Flag, and this example clearly shows how inventive they could become in getting around the regulation. This flag, flown at Boston, was a Cross of Saint George with four Crosses of Saint Andrew, one in each corner. It does not appear to have been widely used.

11. The 1707-1801 East India Company Ensign

When the Red, Blue and White Ensigns were brought up to date by placing the British Union in the canton, the East India Company made a similar alteration to its Ensign. The number of stripes still varied considerably. An engraving by Heap shows a Company ship visiting Philadelphia in

1754 with nine stripes in the flag, but 13 stripes was also a common configuration, foreshadowing the American Grand Union Flag.

12. *The French White Ensign*
The ensign most commonly flown by French ships was a plain white flag with no decoration whatsoever. Surprisingly, the French government, which went into excruciatingly detail in promulgating regulations for differentiating naval uniforms, never really developed a cast-iron policy about flags, and consequently a variety of other flags were used.

13. *The French Dress White Ensign*
For use on important occasions, such as the launching of a ship or a salute to some notable personage, the French used an elaborate ensign. In the center was the Bourbon blue shield with three gold fleurs-de-lys, surrounded by a wreath and chain and surmounted by the Bourbon crown, which was usually (but not always) supported by a pair of cherubs. In the white fly were from 24 to 42 or even more gold fleurs-de-lys. Flag charts of the period show that versions of this flag also existed with a red fly and a blue fly. The sheer expense of making such complicated flags probably explains why they were seldom flown, for elaborate flags wear out just as fast as simple ones.

14. *The French Blue Ensign*
In 1661, Louis XIV decreed that French merchant ships should fly an ensign consisting of a white cross on a blue ground with a blue shield in the middle holding three gold fleurs-de-lys. He later extended the decree to cover warships, but it seems that the plain white flag was more commonly used.

15. *The Spanish Ensign*
For most of the eighteenth century, the Spanish Ensign (for government vessels) was a plain Bourbon-white flag with the royal arms in the center. However, in the last quarter of the century, this was replaced by a flag consisting of two horizontal red stripes enclosing a yellow or gold stripe, sometimes (but not always) with the royal arms superimposed over the stripes.

16. *The Dutch Ensign*
The Dutch Ensign is three horizontal stripes, from top to bottom, red, white and blue. Certain chartered companies, such as the Dutch East India Company and the West India Company were permitted to emblazon a device made out of their initials in the middle of the white stripe.

17. *The Danish Dannebrog*
The basic Danish Ensign was a simple white cross over a red field, but, unlike all the other flags shown here, it was generally not rectangular; the fly ended in two or three pointed tails. This flag was used throughout the Danish Virgin Islands.

18. *The Russian-American Company Ensign in Alaska*
The Russian-American Company was encouraged to fly a special flag in Alaska rather than the regular Russian flag. This ensign had a wide horizontal white stripe at the top,

and under it were a narrower blue stripe and red stripe. On the left half of the white stripe was a two-headed black eagle with other devices and a legend in Russian.

19. *The Massachusetts Pine Tree Flag*
In its simplest form, this flag was a green and black pine tree on a white ground. Its theme referred back to the Massachusetts coin of the seventeenth century, the pine tree shilling. This flag was flown on ships of rebellious Americans at the beginning of the War of Independence. It can be clearly seen at the mainmast head in the powderhorn engraving of the 74-gun ship *America*, or "AMARACA" as the carver spelled it.

20. *An Appeal to Heaven*
When George Washington commissioned ships to attack British shipping in September 1775, his secretary, Colonel Joseph Reed, wrote a letter proposing that their ensign be "a White Ground, a Tree in the Middle—the Motto (Appeal to Heaven)—This is the Flag of our floating Batteries." Most modern artists have interpreted the letter to mean a pine tree with the motto above it, but a close inspection of a contemporary sketch of one of the floating batteries in question shows an oak tree with the motto at the bottom.

21. *An Appeal to God*
Obviously related to number 20 is a flag shown in the background of a portrait of Commodore Esek Hopkins in a naval engagement. This is a white ground with a deciduous tree (with leaves on) and the words "Liberty Tree" at the top, and "An appeal to God" at the bottom. It was probably not used as an ensign but rather as a battle flag or signal flag of sorts.

22. *The Pine Tree Red Ensign*
The Pine Tree Flag of number 19 could be used anywhere on the ship, including as a Jack in the bow. The ensign corresponding to such a Jack was a simple red ground with the Pine Tree Flag placed in the upper left canton. Such a flag appears in a picture of the Battle of Bunker Hill.

23. *The Pine Tree & Cross Jack*
A powderhorn now in the Massachusetts Historical Society was presented by the Assembly to Major-General Richard Gridley in February 1776 as a token of thanks for his services as an artillery officer at the siege of Louisbourg in 1745, at Fort William Henry and Fort Edward in 1775-6, Louisbourg again in 1758, Quebec in 1759 and at Charlestown Heights in 1775. One of the three flags flying over the scene is a Cross of Saint George with a pine tree in the upper left quadrant.

24. *The Pine Tree & Cross Ensign*
If number 23 were used as a Jack, the corresponding ensign might be a red fly with the Jack placed in the upper left corner. In fact, various representations of such an ensign have been found, but so far always with land forces. One even uses a blue ground instead of red.

25. *The Pine Tree & Stripes Ensign*

When John Paul Jones had his coat of arms drawn, he incorporated a number of flags, including this one. It had a pine tree on a white field for its canton and thirteen horizontal stripes, red, white and blue in order down from the top. The canton was five stripes deep. There is no indication as to how Jones used this flag, but it is likely that it was used as the ensign of a privateer ship that Jones may have owned in part.

26. *The Grand Union Ensign, version I*

Once the Continental Navy had been created in October 1775, it was quite clear that the fighting was going to continue to grow and that the flags with pine and oak trees in use in New England would be insufficient to represent the aspirations of the thirteen United Colonies. A new flag was developed, apparently without any prompting from Congress, and versions of it were instantly adopted the length of the seaboard. The Grand Union Ensign combined the British Union flag in its canton with thirteen horizontal stripes in the fly, and it was first hoisted by Lieutenant John Paul Jones aboard Esek Hopkins' flagship *Alfred* in the Delaware River on 3 December 1775. Which version Jones hoisted is unknown, but the most likely are numbers 26 and 34. The version shown here has seven red stripes and six white stripes, and its canton is seven stripes deep. This is the version that appears in Holman's four oil paintings of the frigates *Hancock*, *Boston* and *Fox*, and may have been the most pervasive version. It also appears on North Carolina currency.

27. *The Grand Union Ensign, version II*

A watercolor painting of the American fleet on Lake Champlain (now in the Public Archives of Canada) shows the schooner *Royal Savage* flying an ensign with seven red stripes and six white; the canton is six stripes deep. Congress apparently never passed any resolution to this effect, but it seems that the Grand Union Ensign in all its forms was supposed to be reserved for vessels in the Continental service, meaning that vessels in the various state navies, privateers and merchant ships had to use some other flag (usually a simple flag of thirteen stripes with no canton). Occasional exceptions appear in the records, but the rule seems on the whole to have been obeyed.

28. *The Grand Union Ensign, version III*

A second contemporary portrait of the schooner *Royal Savage* is in the Schuyler Papers at the New York Public Library, and the principal difference in the flag is that its canton extends for only four stripes.

29. *The Grand Union Ensign, version IV*

An interesting variation is found on at least two powderhorns depicting the flag flying over Fort Schuyler, NY in 1777. The canton is seven stripes deep, but it has dropped the Cross of Saint George and contains only the Cross of Saint Andrew. Some writers have suggested that the carver lacked the room to engrave both crosses, but that theory must be discarded in the face of two separate horns showing the same variation. The same variation appears on a portrait of a brigantine called *Sukey*, but because the hull of the ship and its rig (including a dolphin-striker) are patently of nineteenth-century design the picture is obviously a forgery.

30. *The Grand Union Ensign, version V*

A number of powderhorn engravings show a flag identical to number 26, but with the canton extending for five stripes.

31. *The Grand Union Ensign, version VI*

An unusual version painted on the spot by the British artist/engineer John Montressor flew over Fort Mercer in the autumn of 1777. It had seven blue stripes and six white, and its canton was seven stripes deep.

32. *The Grand Union Ensign, version VII*

The Holman portrait of a sloop that this writer has identified as *Providence* in 1777, shows a flag whose canton extends seven stripes deep, but the stripes are white, red and blue in order from the top. Curiously, many other flags had white stripes at the outside, which was detrimental to good visibility.

33. *The Grand Union Ensign, version VIII*

When the brig *Lexington* was captured in 1777, both an oil painting and a watercolor were painted of different stages in the battle. Both clearly show the stripes in order from the top as red, white and blue and the canton extending five stripes deep.

34. *The Grand Union Ensign, version IX*

John Paul Jones included a number of flags in his drawing of his coat of arms, and one was a version of the Grand Union. Its stripes were red, blue and white in order from the top down, and the canton extended down only four stripes. It is possible that this is the flag that Jones personally hoisted as the first official ensign of the Continental Navy on *Alfred* on 3 December 1775. Jones was especially proud of this achievement, which is why he may have made a point of including this version of the flag in his arms.

35. *The Grand Union Ensign, version X*

As part of the decoration for a map of the region of Charleston, South Carolina in the period 1776-1777 is an attractive local variant of the Grand Union. The top half of the flag had the Union canton on the left and a green palmetto tree (symbolic of the repulse of British naval cannonballs by the springy palmetto logs that comprised the walls of Fort Moultrie in 1776) on a white ground. The bottom half of the flag was seven thin red horizontal stripes, and six white stripes. Each of the other States could easily have adapted this flag by putting their own emblems in the upper right quadrant, but there is no evidence that any ever did.

36. *The Grand Union Ensign, version XI*

At the Essex Institute at Salem, Massachusetts is the 1777 bookplate of Continental Navy officer Stephen Cleveland, showing a handsome corvette (see under *Hero*) flying the Grand Union Ensign, but this version has thirteen *pairs* of stripes or 26 stripes in all. It seems to have been general practice that flags of 26 stripes had a white stripe at the top and a red stripe at the bottom.

37. *The Grand Union Ensign, version XII*
The powderhorn engraving of the 74-gun ship *America* (spelled AMARACA) mentioned in number 19 shows a version of the Grand Union flying from the ensign staff in which the Union is centrally located along the pole. It extends down for 11 stripes with one stripe above it and another below it. This could be attributed to careless engraving, but matches some versions of the Stars & Stripes that appeared over the next few years.

38. *The Grand Union Ensign, version XIII*
Congress voted on 14 June 1777 that the official flag of the United States would thenceforth be "13 stripes alternate red and white, that the union be 13 stars, white in a blue field representing a new constellation." It would appear that this resolution allowed only a limited number of variations, but variations proliferated, some of them within the congressional guidelines and others outside. Doubtless many people who had fought and bled under the Grand Union remained partial to it, and the version shown here is probably an attempt to reconcile the Grand Union with the addition of stars. It had seven red and six white stripes, and the canton extended down for six stripes. In the canton, replacing the Cross of Saint Andrew were three white stars on each diagonal, with a thirteenth star in the middle of the Cross of Saint George. This version is known to posterity only through its having been included in the Italian Scotti flag sheet of 1796, now at the John Carter Brown Library, Providence, Rhode Island, but Scotti was undoubtedly referring to a picture or description from about 1777 and now lost.

39. *Stripes in the Canton, version I*
Many regimental flags placed their thirteen stripes, either horizontally or vertically, in the canton, leaving the fly either plain (in any color) or decorated with a regimental emblem. A primitive watercolor in the collection of the Abby Aldrich Rockefeller Folk Art Museum at Williamsburg, Virginia shows the Pennsylvania privateer frigate, *Manda*, in 1779. Her ensign has a plain red fly and the canton consists of red, white and blue horizontal stripes. Unfortunately, the artist was unable to squeeze more than eleven stripes into the canton, so it is not clear in which order they were intended to be. A good guess would be blue at top and bottom, in the order blue, white and red.

40. *Stripes in the Canton, version II*
An English engraving of a battle on Lake Champlain shows some of the American vessels flying a flag similar to that in number 39. However, a contemporary colorist has colored one copy of the engraving, and he used blue for the fly. The stripes could be either red, white and blue or red and white. The latter arrangement forms the base for what may be a surviving flag of the period, the so-called Easton Flag from Easton, Pennsylvania, which also contains an arrangement of thirteen white stars in the fly.

41. *The Merchant Ensign, version I*
While the Grand Union Ensign was supposedly reserved exclusively for the use of vessels in Continental service, ships in state navies, privateers and merchant ships were left to pick something else. What they picked often enough that it became widely known as the Merchant Ensign was one or other arrangement of horizontal stripes, of which three versions are shown here. The striped flag remained in at least limited use until about 1800. The simplest version had seven red stripes and six white stripes, but sometimes it appeared with seven white and six red stripes. Occasionally it consisted of blue and white stripes, or red and blue stripes.

42. *The Merchant Ensign, version II*
The Merchant Ensign was also found in arrangements of red, white and blue stripes in any of the six mathematically possible orders.

43. *The Merchant Ensign, version III*
Sometimes the stripes were arranged in thirteen pairs of red and white stripes with white uppermost. This version appears in a Dutch engraving of Conyngham's lugger *Surprise* capturing a British packet, and also in the background of a portrait of Conyngham.

44. *The Stars & Stripes, version I*
When John Paul Jones set sail from France in 1779, he arranged that each ship in his little fleet should fly a different version of the American flag in order to facilitate recognition. After Jones had returned victorious to the Texel, a Dutch artist recorded the appearance of the flags flown by the remaining two ships. The flag flown on the captured *Serapis* (and presumably on his previous flagship, *Bonhomme Richard*, before she sank) had a canton that was five stripes deep containing its stars in three horizontal rows of four, five and four. The unusual order of its stripes from top to bottom was: blue, red, white, red, white, blue, red, white, red, blue, white, blue and red. It is possible that this order resulted from the fact that the flag was constructed out of available pieces of old Dutch flags.

45. *The Stars & Stripes, version II*
The Dutch artist at the Texel painted the ensign flown by the frigate *Alliance* as having seven white stripes and six red stripes. The stars were arranged in five rows of three-two-three-two-three, the most typical of all arrangements of stars in early flags, and the canton extended over six stripes. While the Grand Union Ensign had been reserved for United States ships the Stars & Stripes was intended for use by anyone and everyone American.

46. *The Stars & Stripes, version III*
An oil painting of *Alliance* in European waters in the 1790s (in a private collection) shows her to be flying an ensign whose stripes ran red, white and blue in order from the top, but whose canton extended down the whole depth of the flag.

47. *The Stars & Stripes, version IV*

During the first few years of independence, perhaps the most frequently used—and most handsome—American ensign had its stripes arranged in order from the top, red, blue and white. The canton, which extended down six stripes, contained its five-pointed stars in the 3-2-3-2-3 pattern. This flag appears on many European flag sheets, and can be seen flying from Fort Mifflin in the background of the well-known painting of the explosion of the British ship *Augusta* in the Delaware.

48. *The Stars & Stripes, version V*

In a 1783 European flag book is a version with seven red stripes and six white stripes. The canton, containing its six-pointed stars in the 3-2-3-2-3 pattern, extended down five stripes. This may be the same version that Copley painted on a ship in the background of his portrait of Elkanah Watson in London in December 1782. Less than two months later, the American ship *Bedford* arrived on 3 February in London to trade, the first American ship to do so, before all the peace-treaty documents had been signed, but which version of the Stars & Stripes she flew is not recorded.

49. *The Stars & Stripes, version VI*

British marine artist Dominic Serres died in 1793, but in 1806 his son arranged for the publication of a book containing engravings of many of the father's paintings. On one of the subsidiary title-pages is a flag entitled "America" with seven red stripes and six white stripes. The canton, which extends down six stripes, contains a circle of twelve five-pointed stars with a thirteenth in the middle. This arrangement is recorded in a number of non-maritime flags of the period.

50. *The Stars & Stripes, version VII*

David Rittenhouse of Pennsylvania, using the pseudonym Abraham Weatherwise, published *Weatherwise's Town & Country Almanack* in 1782, containing an illustration of a flag with 26 presumably red and white stripes. The canton contains its five-pointed stars in horizontal rows of three, five and five. The star patterns offered almost limitless opportunity for variety. A circle of thirteen was also known (although probably with no connection to the legendary Betsy Ross), and horizontal rows of four-five-four were used as well.

51. *The Stars & Stripes, version VIII*

The 1782 Lotter flag sheet at the J. Carter Brown Library in Providence, Rhode Island records a version of the Stars & Stripes designed specially to pay tribute to the Franco-American alliance. It had seven red stripes and six white stripes. The canton extended down through eleven stripes. Its six-pointed stars were arranged in three vertical rows of 4-5-4 and above the middle row was a gold fleur-de-lys. A variation of this theme appeared on the 1781 Mondhare flag sheet, but it contained only twelve five-pointed stars plus the fleur-de-lys.

52. *The Stars & Stripes, version IX*

In a primitive picture of the large frigate *South Carolina*, now at the Peabody Museum, Salem, Massachusetts, former crewmember J. Phippen painted an ensign with unusual colors. The stripes were red (top and bottom) and blue. The canton, seven stripes deep, was white with blue eight-pointed stars arranged in a circle with one star in the middle. Similar flags are known: Lieutenant-Colonel John Simcoe painted one in his view of the Battle of Yorktown, 1781, in which the canton was blue and extended over ten stripes, and had its six-pointed stars arranged in the 3-2-3-2-3 pattern. The so-called Guilford Flag survives at Raleigh, North Carolina in a tattered condition. It now has twelve blue and red stripes (blue at the top) and a wide white canton eight stripes deep containing thirteen eight-pointed stars. Some experts feel that this is a later 15-star/15-stripe flag that has been cut, but such an interpretation is not necessary.

53. *The Stars & Stripes, version X*

When E. H. Derby's ship *Astrea* sailed to Canton for the first time in 1789, her captain, James Magee, brought back a number of porcelain punchbowls and pitchers each showing a detailed picture of *Astrea* under sail. Most of these items have disappeared, but the Boston Marine Society still displays its bowl and pitcher. Her ensign appears to have seven white stripes and six red stripes and a white canton containing a circle of twelve five-pointed stars with the thirteenth one in the middle. The canton is six stripes deep.

54. *Eagle Ensign*

A late-eighteenth-century primitive oil painting of the Cannon House and Wharf (Dietrich Brothers Americana Collection) shows two ships and one fort each flying an ensign with seven red stripes and six white stripes (actually, the artist added a few more stripes for good measure) and a blue canton seven stripes deep emblazoned with a gold eagle. Variations of this flag are known from as early as about 1780, and the United States Army continued to use it well into the nineteenth century.

55. *The Gadsden Flag*

Christopher Gadsden of South Carolina, a member of the Naval Committee in Congress, designed a flag for Commodore Esek Hopkins to use as his personal standard. It was a yellow flag with a coiled rattlesnake and the legend underneath, "Dont tread on me," and it was sent to Hopkins on 13 January 1776. About four weeks later, Gadsden presented a copy of it to the South Carolina Provincial Congress. It is not known whether Hopkins ever used his.

56. *The Continental Navy Jack*

While all the Grand Union and Stars & Stripes flags were regarded as ensigns, to be flown from a staff in the stern or from a masthead, Continental Navy ships also needed a Jack to fly in the bow, the equivalent of the Royal Navy's Union Jack. The flag that filled this need had seven red stripes and six white stripes; a golden rattlesnake stretched uncoiled across the flag, and in the lowest white stripe were the words "Dont tread on me." This flag appears in a portrait of Esek Hopkins, which suggest that it was in use in 1776, and it was also flown on the bowsprit of the frigate *Alliance* at the capture of *Serapis* in 1779. It should be noted that while many modern ships remove their Jacks while they are under way ships in the eighteenth century did not, so it is quite correct to paint a picture of an eighteenth-century ship under way with her Jack flying.

57. *The South Carolina Navy Jack*
Somewhat similar to the Continental Navy Jack, the South Carolina Navy Jack had seven red and six blue stripes. Its rattlesnake was slightly smaller, and the motto, "Dont tread on me," appeared on the second red stripe from the top. No original information about this flag survives, but it is believed that the author of an 1880 flag book, Admiral G. H. Preble, had access to original information about it that no longer can be found.

58. *The Fort Mifflin Striped Flag*
A scurrilous British cartoon, published 1778, entitled "The Taking of Miss Mud Island," referred to the capture by the British of Fort Mifflin in the Delaware. A flag flying above the island consists of seven vertical red stripes and six white stripes with an uncoiled golden rattlesnake stretched across the flag. This flag could be the result of the imagination of the cartoonist, but it is likely that such a flag existed, perhaps on American privateers operating near the coast of England.

59. *The Fort Moultrie Flag*
In June 1776 the various batteries around Charleston, South Carolina are reported to have flown a blue flag with a white or silver crescent in the top left corner, and at least one of them also had the word "Liberty" in white across the bottom. The flag had been designed by Colonel William Moultrie some months earlier to conform to the uniforms of the militia at the forts, since they wore blue uniforms and silver crescents on their hats. This same flag is documented to have been used by vessels of the South Carolina Navy. In 1780, a British officer reported seeing a similar flag at Charleston, but with the crescent replaced by thirteen stars.

60. *The Commander-in-Chiefs Flag and Jack*
The Valley Forge Historical Society has a silk flag that textile experts confirm is from the late eighteenth century. It is blue with thirteen six-pointed stars arranged in the 3-2-3-2-3 pattern. Because it has been cut on all four sides to fit into its present frame experts speculate that it may once have been the canton of a Stars & Stripes flag, but this is not necessarily correct. Washington is known to have had such a flag, and a shield emblazoned with the same device appears in a handkerchief picture at Winterthur of the stern of the frigate *General Washington*. The flag would also have been very appropriate for use as a Navy Jack after the earlier Jack with its rattlesnake had outlived its usefulness; in fact, it appears as the Jack on the bowsprit of the frigate *Alliance* in a 1781 primitive painting by Matthew Parke, who was a captain in her Marines.

61. *The Rhode Island Second Regiment Flag*
Rhode Island remained an independent nation until 29 May 1790, a considerable time after the other twelve States had ratified the Constitution, and even then she joined the Union only after Washington had threatened to lead an army to conquer Rhode Island and divide the spoils between Massachusetts and Connecticut! She had valid reasons for wanting to remain outside, but they need not concern us here. What kind of flags might Rhode Island ships have flown in that period? Two period flags survive, those of the First and Second Regiments, but estimates as to their dates vary between 1776 and 1783. The Second Regiment flag would have been the most appropriate. It had a white fly on which was a blue fouled anchor and above that a blue banner with the words "In God we hope." In the upper left canton was a blue ground against which were gold stars (points facing down) in the 3-2-3-2-3 pattern. Some say that it was from a Rhode Island flag such as this that the Stars & Stripes received its stars, but it could easily have been the other way around.

62. *Commissioning Pendant, version I*
All Royal Navy ships, except when a commodore or admiral was aboard, flew a long streamer with two tails from the mainmast head. Before 1707 this took the form of an elongated Cross of Saint George with a long red forked tail, and afterwards the British Union replaced the Cross of Saint George. Occasionally the tail was blue for ships that flew the Blue Ensign, or red, white and blue for ships flying the White Ensign. The Royal Navy tried in vain to prevent civilian ships from flying similar pendants, and eventually settled for forcing merchant ships to remove their pendants only when in close proximity to a Royal Navy ship. The American Congress, normally interested in promoting freedom, agreed with the Royal Navy, for on 29 October 1776 it resolved:

> That no private Ships or Vessels of War, Merchant Ships and other Vessels belonging to the Subjects of these States, be permitted to wear pendants when in Company with Continental Ships or Vessels of War, without leave of the Commanding Officer thereof.

> That if any Merchant Ship or Vessel shall wear pendants in Company with Continental Ships or Vessels of War without leave first obtained from the Commander thereof, such Commander be authorised to take away the Pendants from the Offenders.

> That if private Ships or Vessels of War, refuse to pay the Respect due to the Continental Ships or Vessels of War, the Captain or Commander so refusing shall lose his Commission.

It should be noted that such pendants should not be described as "homeward-bound pennants," which is a modern term and usage. Quite a variety of American pendants were known, the simplest being a forked streamer whose top half was red and bottom half white. The Continental brig *Lexington* in 1777 flew one that had the British Union next to the mast, followed by thirteen vertical stripes in order blue, red, white, etc., and a tail that was red in the upper fork, blue in the lower and white in the space between. The Pennsylvania privateer *Manda* in 1779 flew a similar pendant, but minus the British Union and having the vertical stripes in order red, white, blue, etc.

63. *Commissioning Pendant, version II*
A German flag sheet at the end of the War of Independence showed a pendant whose Union consisted of thirteen white, five-pointed stars on a blue ground in an elongated 3-2-3-2-3 pattern, followed by thirteen vertical stripes in order red, blue, white, etc., and a red tail on top with a white tail at the bottom and a blue space in between. This is likely to have been the most common American pendant of its day.

64. *Commissioning Pendant, version III*
The French Mondhare flag sheet (1781) shows a pendant with a blue Union and thirteen five-pointed stars arranged horizontally in a 4-5-4 pattern (actually, Mondhare replaced one of the stars with a fleur-de-lys, but that can be regarded as unusual) followed by seven vertical red stripes and six white stripes; the upper tail was red and the lower tail white.

For further information about early American flags, the reader may wish to consult Edward W. Richardson, *Standards and Colors of the American Revolution*, The University of Pennsylvania Press, 1982, or W. R. Furlong & B. McCandless, *So Proudly We Hail*, Smithsonian Institution Press, 1981.

Sources for the drawings in this book are almost as varied as they are numerous. However, the majority of drawings that were done from existing plans came from the National Maritime Museum in Greenwich, just outside London. Historical researchers know that the Latin countries have kept the most thorough records of their colonial activities; such absurd figures—such as the number of nails required to build a privy for an obscure fur trader in Quebec—are carefully preserved in vast archives. However, when it comes to ship design we find that Great Britain has more plans and models than all the rest of the world put together. This is partly because most of the French and Dutch drawings were destroyed in the fighting of two world wars, and partly because the British were so keenly interested in ship design that they kept most of their own plans, and even made plans of many of the ships they captured from the French, the Dutch, the Spanish, and the Americans. The majority of these plans repose at Greenwich, and nearly all of them are available for reproduction.

A few plans were included in books over the years that do not appear in the archives at Greenwich. Most notable among them are the Swedish shipwright Fredrik Henrik af Chapman's *Architectura Navalis Mercatoria*, and *Souvenirs de la Marine* by the nineteenth-century French admiral Paris. The collection of plans in this book would probably not have been possible without the pioneering research work conducted over nearly a whole lifetime by Howard I. Chapelle, and reflected in many of his books (see our Bibliography) as well as in the superb exhibits of ship models at the Smithsonian Institution, where he was a curator.

We have tried to indicate the sources for our plans in the text that accompanies each drawing. Some of these sources are admittedly quite tenuous, for which we make no excuse, but, in explanation, shedding even this bit of light is one of the primary purposes of the book. Over the years, beginning at least as early as the first two decades of the nineteenth century when a collection of watercolor paintings of Revolutionary War ships was produced (now at the Mariners Museum, Newport News, Virginia), artists and model builders have attempted to show their contemporaries and future generations what they thought Colonial and Revolutionary period ships looked like. Unfortunately, in most cases they have been highly inaccurate and misleading. Sometimes this was only the addition of a dolphin striker or spanker boom where none existed, flying the ensign in the wrong place, flying the wrong ensign, or use of the wrong color scheme, but frequently it was more than that.

The Bicentennial of American Independence has produced a new spate of models and paintings of ships of the Colonial and Revolutionary periods. While this book is admittedly far from perfect, there should be no excuse for any model builder or artist who has access to this book to make such egregious mistakes as most (but not all, I am happy to say) have made in the past. Let us indeed joyfully celebrate the glorious—and not so glorious—deeds of men like Silas Talbot, John Rathbun, John Barry, Abraham Whipple, and John Paul Jones, but let us at least represent their ships as accurately as possible.

Part II

The SHIPS

L'ABENAKISE/AURORA, 38

DATES	LENGTH HULL	LENGTH DECK	LENGTH KEEL	BEAM	DEPTH	DRAFT	TONNAGE B. M.
1756-1763	168	146	134	37	15	18	946

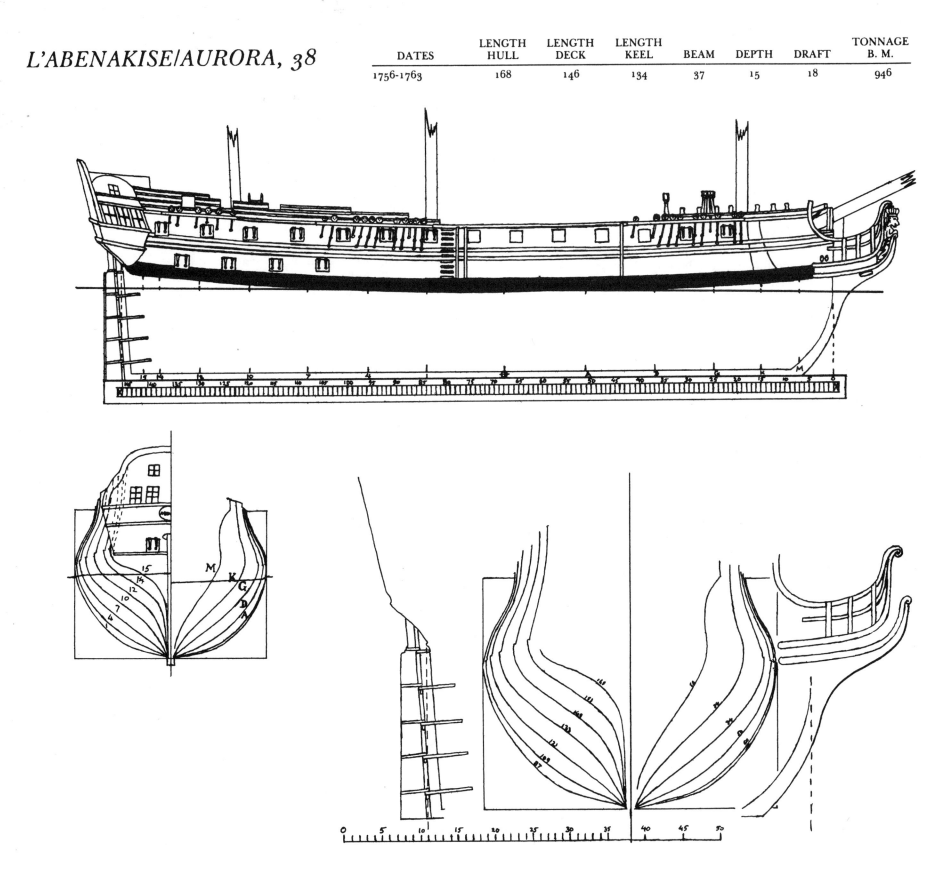

Tracing of surviving plan of *L'Abenakise*, National Maritime Museum, Greenwich.

33

L'ABENAKISE/AURORA, 38

THE 38-gun ship *L'Abenakise* (sometimes spelled *Bon Acquis* and even *A Bien Acquis* in the British records) was apparently built along the St. Lawrence River in Quebec Province about 1756. She was designed as a frigate for the French navy. She had the classic shape of an East Indiaman of the period, and was quite similar in size and shape to the French East Indiaman *Le Duc de Duras* which later became the more famous *Bonhomme Richard*. We suspect that her name was intended to have been *L'Abenakise* (which is French for "girl of the Abenaki tribe"; the Abenakis were one of the tribes of the Algonquin group), and that illiterate crewmembers called her *A Bien Acquis* (which is French for "cheap") in much the same way as British sailors on the ship *Bellerophon* sometimes called their ship *Billy Ruffian*.

She was captured on 23 January 1757 at the beginning of the Seven Years War by the much smaller British frigate *Unicorn*. Being a powerful vessel herself, she was renamed *Aurora* and taken into the Royal Navy as a Fifth Rate of 36 guns. Her builders had apparently used inferior wood, for she was ordered broken up at the end of the war in April 1763. If she had been sound she could have been sold to private owners and used as an East Indiaman.

If the ship herself did not last long, her influence was felt for years. She apparently sailed so well that the British Admiralty requested that other ships be built to her design. While certain characteristics were incorporated into British ship design, the chief British surveyors reported to the Admiralty that her design was not suited to enlarging or reducing to other rates without adverse consequences. As a result, one class of frigates only, the *Lowestoffe* class, was actually based on her design, and even that class was smaller and somewhat different.

Aurora's success depended in part on the fact that her upper gundeck was unusually high above the water, and this was not due to any theory of placing guns that high, but rather to the fact that, unlike frigates, she had eight 18-pounders on the lower deck in the manner of some early East Indiamen. She also carried twenty-eight 12-pounders on the upper deck and two 6-pounders on the forecastle. Naturally, the *Lowestoffe* class had no guns on the lower deck at all.

Her plans were drawn in abbreviated form and still exist in the British Admiralty records. All that was drawn was the profile of the bow, the profile of the stern, and the body plan, all rendered on graph paper. The midship section shows the characteristic French form with the pronounced double knuckle.

Quite a number of ships were built in Quebec for the French, but no plans have been found for any others yet; they included the 500-ton corvette *Le Canada* in 1742; the 700-ton, 22-gun ship *Le Caribou* in 1744; the 22-gun ship *Le Castor* in 1745; the *Le Martre* in 1747; the 60-gun ship *Le Saint-Laurent* in 1748; the 70-gun ship *L'Original* in 1750; the corvette *L'Algonquin* in 1753; and the frigate *Le Québec* in 1757.

Although we have shown a standard French crowned lion for a figurehead, she may well have had an Indian maiden instead.

ADVENTURE, 6

DATES		LENGTH HULL	LENGTH DECK	LENGTH KEEL	BEAM	DEPTH	DRAFT	TONNAGE B. M.
1790 ff	ESTIMATED	59	50	44	17	8	7	40

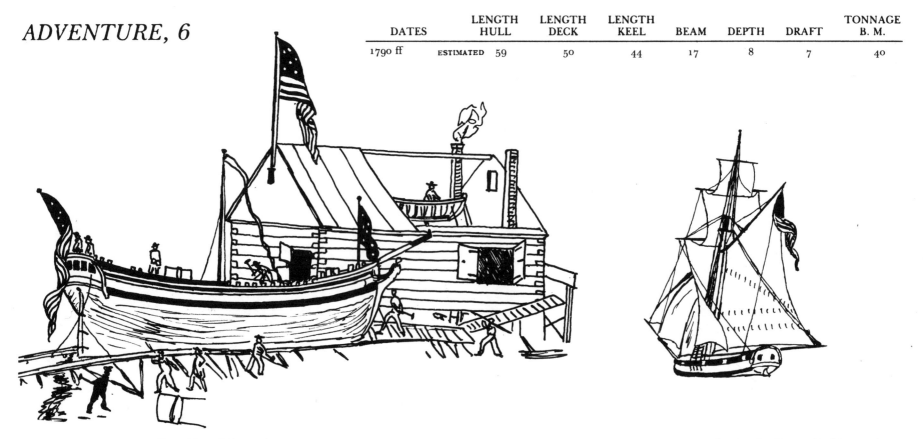

Launching of sloop *Adventure*, 1792, drawing by George Davidson, private collection.

Sloop *Adventure*, 1792 drawing by George Davidson, private collection.

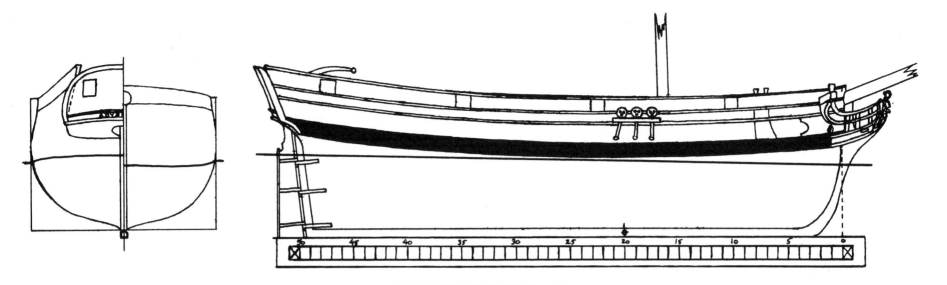

ADVENTURE, 6

WHEN Captain Robert Gray left New England in 1790 on his second voyage to the northwest coast of North America, he carried in the hold of his ship *Columbia Rediviva* the sloop *Adventure*. She had been built in Boston and then carefully dismantled so she could be stored in the hold for re-assembly in the northwest. Samuel Yendell, Columbia's ship-carpenter, served as shipwright. The keel was laid on 3 October, 1791 at Fort Defiance, Clayoquot Sound, Vancouver Island, in what is now British Columbia. She stuck on the launching ways on 12 April, 1792. A detailed painting shows her shortly before launching but before her bulwarks were added. Although she carried one 3-pounder and four swivels, she eventually had ports cut for eight carriage guns, according to another painting of her under full sail. The latter painting shows that she set not only a square topsail but also a course and topgallant.

Her captain was Robert Haswell, aged 24, former chief mate on *Columbia*. He took her on two cruises that combined coastal exploration with trading for skins of sea lions and sea otters. At the close of the season, she was sold for 75 prime otter skins to the Spanish governor, Don Juan Francisco de la Bodega y Cuadra (or Quadra, as spelled in American notes), who sent her to San Blas, Mexico. It should be noted that British adventurers and explorers on that coast had been harshly treated by the previous Spanish administration, and Gray had been spared largely because the Spanish officials had thought that *Columbia* was a naval vessel (and Gray did nothing to undeceive them), so the sale of the sloop served in part as a token of gratitude to Cuadra.

Adventure was the first United States-built vessel on the west coast, but the British explorer Meares had built the lugger *Northwest America* in 1788, only to have her seized by the Spanish. A second vessel was brought by Meares knocked down for assembly in the northwest, but the Spanish seized it and assembled it themselves. The Russians hired an English shipwright, James Shields, to build them the small (length 73 feet) full-rigged ship *Feniks* (*Phoenix*) in 1794 at Resurrection Harbour, Blying Sound, the Kenai Peninsula, Alaska; Shields was killed when the ship was wrecked on the Alaskan coast four years later, returning from a voyage to Siberia. British explorer Captain George Vancouver built a small sloop for the king of Hawaii in 1792, and British and American castaways built a second one for him in 1795, so he could more easily invade and conquer neighboring islands.

ALEXANDER, 28

IN 1780, the merchants of Portsmouth, New Hampshire, were sorry to learn that the British had captured the 18-gun Continental Navy corvette *Ranger* at Charleston, South Carolina. The *Ranger* had been built at Portsmouth three years earlier, and many of her crew came from the Portsmouth area. In a fit of patriotism, they commissioned a larger ship to be built at Portsmouth and presented to the Continental Navy. She was to mount 28 guns, and was to be named *Alexander*, presumably after the Macedonian conqueror. Unfortunately, when she was finished they changed their minds and decided to outfit her as a privateer, to be owned by the merchants who had put up the money. Under the circumstances, they cannot be blamed for their change of heart, since the Continental Navy was in such terrible shape as to inspire practically no confidence in the future of such a fine ship if she were to be donated to the navy. As a privateer, she would have had little trouble recruiting a sufficient crew, in contrast to ships in the navy; in fact, virtually the whole crew of the *Ranger* signed on aboard *Alexander* once they were released from British custody. Her captain was Thomas Simpson of Portsmouth, and she was bonded on 5 January 1781.

The privateer *Alexander* had few initial successes, and she was captured by the 44-gun British ship *Mediator;* in fact, *Mediator* captured *Alexander,* the privateer brig *Amiable,* the French ship *La Ménagère,* and two others—all in the same action on 12 December 1782.

It is at least conceivable that if the Allied ships had stayed together instead of allowing *Mediator* to pick them off one by one they might have beaten off their assailant, if not even captured her, but the naval history of the Revolution affords few examples of close cooperation between American ships under adversity. The battle was painted by Samuel Atkins, Robert Dodd and Dominic Serres, and prints made from the paintings are at the New-York Historical Society. The Henry Francis DuPont Winterthur Museum in Delaware has a pitcher with the image of a ship very much like *Alexander*. Since the peace treaty was all but signed by the time that the captured *Alexander* reached Britain, the Royal Navy had no use for this fine frigate, so she was sold to private owners,

who no doubt used her as a merchant ship in some long-distance trade. Her dimensions are not recorded.

Our source for this drawing of *Alexander* is a mixture of looking at the above-mentioned paintings (the artists had without doubt seen *Alexander* when she arrived in England), the lines of the frigate *Raleigh,* which had been launched from the same yard, and a print of the bow of *Alliance* (also built by the same builder), which, being rather finer and more extended than *Raleigh*'s, shows some development from the original model over the years. Our assumption here is that *Alexander*'s design was related to *Raleigh*'s in the same way that *Virginia*'s was related to *Randolph*'s, or any 28-gun frigate to any 32-gun frigate by the same designer.

ALEXANDER, 28

DATES	LENGTH HULL	LENGTH DECK	LENGTH KEEL	BEAM	DEPTH	DRAFT	TONNAGE B. M.
1780-ca. 1790 ESTIMATED	140	118	100	32	15	16	550

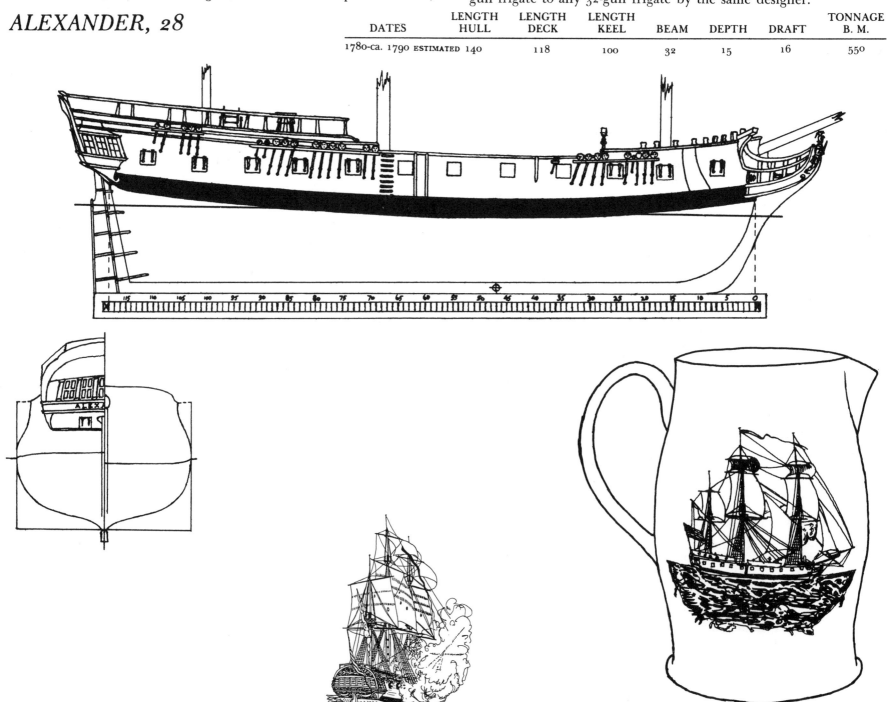

Frigate *Alexander*
From an engraving after Dominic Serres, 1782
New-York Historical Society

(?) Privateer *Alexander*, porcelain pitcher, Henry Francis DuPont Winterthur Museum, Delaware.

ONE of the most easily recognizable shapes among American ships of the Colonial period is that of the Philadelphia merchant ship. Such ships were generally about 90 feet long on the deck, had blunt bows (with or without a head), usually had no quarter galleries, and were completely decked over, the quarterdeck being raised about two feet above the deck over the waist.

When the Continental Navy was established in the fall of 1775, it had ready access to smaller craft such as sloops, schooners, and brigs, all of which were suitable for certain kinds of work. The navy eventually had a number of larger warships built to its specifications, but for the first few months it had to make do with converting some Philadelphia merchant ships by adding gunports and generally strengthening their hulls. Such a ship was *Black Prince* (named after the dashing son of King Edward III), built about 1774 for a syndicate headed by Robert Morris and John Nixon, and commanded by the famous John Barry. She had a figurehead of the Black Prince in full armor.

Purchase of *Black Prince* for the navy was authorized by Congress on 30 October 1775, and fitting out began a few days later under command of Dudley Saltonstall. Commodore Hopkins came aboard early in December, and she left Philadelphia on 4 January 1776 as flagship of the first American fleet. Her name had been changed to *Alfred,* in honor of the ninth-century British king who is said to have founded the Royal Navy.

Her first navy assignment was to carry home powder and cannons acquired in a raid on Nassau, which had been captured in March 1776. While thus heavily laden the fleet encountered the 24-gun British frigate *Glasgow* off Newport, Rhode Island, in the middle of the night. *Alfred* herself had about 24 guns (some accounts say 20, others 24, and still others 28), so she should have been able to inflict punishment on the frigate, and with the rest of the fleet in the action there should have been no chance of escape for *Glasgow*. As it happened, the fleet bungled the job; they allowed *Glasgow* to damage them considerably, and then, being slow because of their heavy cargos, they watched helplessly as she escaped into Newport. Commodore Esek Hopkins was eventually eased out of his job because of this incident.

Although Congress appointed Elisha Hinman as her new captain in October, word did not reach New England in time and *Alfred* set sail under command of John Paul Jones in company with the sloop *Providence*. She had a successful cruise of about five weeks, in which she captured a number of enemy ships, burned part of the town of Canso, Nova Scotia, and escaped from the frigate *Milford*. After her return, she lay more or less idle for the next nine months, needing repairs and being short of crew.

In mid-August 1777 she departed for France under Hinman in company with the frigate *Raleigh*. As a merchant ship in 1775, she had logged almost 240 nautical miles in one 24-hour period, but the way she was loaded in 1777 made her a slow sailer and she was unable to keep up with *Raleigh*. Although they took a few small prizes early in the voyage, *Alfred*'s slow speed proved a handicap when they attacked a lightly-guarded convoy and were beaten off. They arrived at Lorient on 7 October and departed for home once more late in December, choosing a route that took them close to Africa.

East of the Windward Islands they encountered two lightly armed British ships, *Ariadne,* 20 guns, and *Canso,* 16 guns. *Raleigh* clapped on all sail and ran while *Alfred* surrendered without much of a fight. For this disgraceful conduct Captain Thompson of *Raleigh* was dismissed, and Hinman was absolved of all blame, so that he could turn up as an ineffectual captain of the frigate *Trumbull* later on. *Alfred* was used as an armed transport by the Royal Navy until 1782 when she was sold.

The Continental Navy was not the only navy to use Philadelphia merchant ships as warships. The Royal Navy did, too. One of these was an exact sistership of *Alfred,* so we are told, and it is possible, though not certain, that her original name was *Resolution*. She too had a figurehead of the Black Prince. When she was purchased by the Royal Navy in 1777 she was given the name of *Drake* (after the famous Elizabethan admiral) and fitted out with anywhere from 14 to 20 guns (the accounts differ). She was captured by John Paul Jones on the 18-gun corvette *Ranger* off Belfast, Northern Ireland, on 24 April 1778. He sent her to France with a prize crew under the insubordinate Lieutenant Simpson, but partway there Jones replaced Simpson with Lieutenant Hall. *Drake* was then sold.

One of the chief disadvantages of placing a heavy armament on a Philadelphia merchant ship was that the guns had to be below the main deck, both for the sake of the stability of the ship and to protect the gunners. This meant that the gunports were perilously close to the waterline, thus making it difficult for the ship to fight in heavy weather. One can well imagine that *Alfred*'s men were reluctant to engage the *Glasgow* with her gunports even closer to the waterline than usual because of the great weight of captured cannons in the hold.

The plans we show here are derived from the Admiralty plans of another Philadelphia merchant ship, *Lord Camden,* whose dimensions were very close to those of the *Drake* and the *Alfred*. A confusion exists as to the dimensions of the *Alfred;* the British records say she was 440 tons, but this is a measurement to the underside of her main deck. If they had used the more common measurement to the bottom of her gun deck they would have come up with 275 tons.

Four contemporary pictures purport to represent *Alfred*. One, a seaman's sketch in ink and watercolors, is obviously inaccurate since it shows quarter galleries and an odd deck layout; another, a pen-and-ink sketch in the Roosevelt collection is supposed to show *Alfred* capturing the supply ship *Mellish*, but *Alfred* actually appears as no more than a speck on the horizon, for the sloop *Providence* made the actual capture. The third is a crude engraving on a powderhorn in the U. S. Marine Corps Museum. The fourth is a distant view of her through the stern windows of

the brig *Andrew Doria* in the background of Charles Peale's 1787 portrait of Lieutenant James Josiah as he was in 1776. No contemporary portraits of *Drake* are known to exist.

I am indebted to Mr. John J. McCusker, Jr., for his careful research into the facts and myths about *Alfred*'s appearance.

ALFRED (ex-BLACK PRINCE) & DRAKE, 20 ESTIMATED

DATES	LENGTH HULL	LENGTH DECK	LENGTH KEEL	BEAM	DEPTH	DRAFT	TONNAGE B. M.
ca. 1774-ca. 1782	110	91	76	26	12	14	275

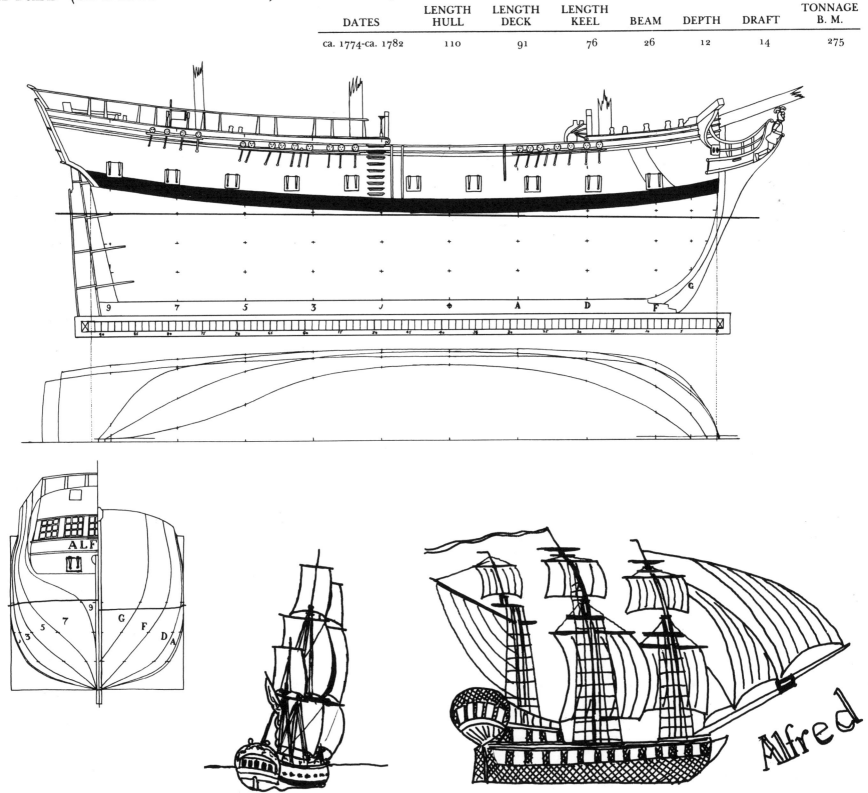

Ship *Alfred*, detail of portrait in oils of Lieutenant James Josiah by C. W. Peale, 1776/1787, recently sold.

Ship *Alfred*
From a powderhorn engraving by H. Mack, 1776
U.S. Marine Corps Museum, Quantico, Virginia

Ship *Alfred*, detail of anonymous grisaille of capture of *Mellish*, Roosevelt Collection, Hyde Park, NY.

Commodore Esek Hopkins.

ALLIANCE (ex-JOHN HANCOCK), 36

AFTER the initial thirteen frigates were constructed for the Continental Navy, Congress ordered several more in 18-gun and 36-gun sizes. Of the latter, only three were actually built, one of them being *Alliance*.

Alliance was built in 1777 on the Merrimack River at Salisbury, Massachusetts, by the Hackett family of builders, who came down from nearby Portsmouth, New Hampshire, to do the job. She was somewhat smaller than the other two ships of this class, but she was apparently well built, a fast sailer, and a popular ship. She was launched on 28 April 1778 and originally named *John Hancock*, since the earlier frigate *Hancock* had already been captured, but a few days later she was renamed *Alliance* after the Franco-American alliance that was ratified by Congress on 4 May.

No plans of her have survived, but there are more contemporary and near-contemporary portraits of her than of any other American ship of the period. Of these portraits, some are valuable to the historian and others are useless or even misleading. The best is a view from ahead from an engraving of the battle between *Bonhomme Richard* and *Serapis* that apparently survives only at the Musée de la Marine in Paris. Another engraving and an oil painting of the same subject are not as good. Also useful are a pair of paintings dated 1789 showing the ship from astern as she approached Boston

Light in 1781; one is by Captain Matthew Parke, who had been a marine in her crew, and the other, an overmantel from Waltham, Massachusetts, is by Jonathan Edes, and both are quite primitive. A watercolor at the U.S. Naval Academy Museum, showing her with all sails set, including royals and studding sails, seems to date from the 1790s and is reasonably accurate, but a "copy" of that same painting in oils at the Peabody Museum, Salem, Massachusetts, shows essentially a nineteenth-century ship. A Dutch oil painting in a private collection in Massachusetts shows a broadside view, but includes a dolphin striker, which had not yet been invented. One other contemporary picture is a small sketch of her in battle off Cuba in early 1783, but it has little detail. Our plan is based on the two most accurate pictures, plus a record of her principal dimensions, and the existing plan of the frigate *Raleigh*, which had been designed and built the previous year by the Hackett family.

Her first captain, the mad Frenchman Pierre Landais, who had been made an honorary citizen of Massachusetts, took her to France with Lafayette as a passenger. In August 1779, *Alliance* put to sea as part of John Paul Jones's squadron, but Landais refused to obey Jones's signals. During the battle off Flamborough Head, Yorkshire, on 23 September, Landais deliberately fired into *Bonhomme Richard* so as to sink her and then presumably gain the glory of having defeated *Serapis*. The plan did not work and Jones had Landais removed from command when they arrived at Texel, Holland. Jones himself took command of *Alliance* and on 27 December very boldly sailed right through a powerful British squadron that was waiting to catch him.

While Jones dallied with a mistress on shore, Landais seized back control of the ship, and, after being briefly detained by an irate Jones and the French authorities, set sail for Philadelphia with Arthur Lee as a passenger on 8 July 1780. On the voyage, Landais had to be replaced by Lieutenant James Degge, who brought her into Boston. At Boston, Landais was dismissed from the service for his conduct, and Degge was also dismissed because Landais had accused him of mutiny.

John Barry was made *Alliance*'s new captain, but he had difficulty finding enough crew to man her. On 11 February 1781 Barry was forced to take her to sea, grossly undermanned, to bring Thomas Paine and Colonel John Laurens to France. Many of the crew were former British prisoners and they plotted mutiny, but the ship reached France before they could do much. After they had left Lorient at the end of March, Barry found out about the mutiny and had all the plotters whipped. During the rest of the long voyage back to Boston, *Alliance* captured two brigs and the two corvettes *Atalanta* and *Trepassey*. She was then forced to remain idle in Boston for lack of crew.

March 1783 found her in Havana, Cuba, with a load of 100,000 Spanish dollars to take back to the Continental Congress. She left Cuba in company with the smaller ship *Le Duc de Lauzun* and was immediately chased by three British frigates. The appearance of a large French ship on the horizon caused the British to give up the chase, whereupon Barry turned on one of them, the 28-gun *Sybil*, and completely disabled her. This was the last sea battle of the Revolution, for when *Alliance* arrived at Newport, Rhode Island, on 20 March Barry learned that the war had ended.

The new nation felt no need to maintain a navy during peacetime, so the few remaining ships were sold, *Alliance* being the last. She was auctioned off for $26,000 at the Merchants' Coffee House in Philadelphia on 1 August 1785, even though some members of Congress had wished to maintain just one ship "for the honor of the flag" and for protection against pirates. She was bought by Robert Morris, who found her well suited to be an East Indiaman. Her first voyage to Canton in 1787, under the command of Thomas Read, was remarkable in that she avoided the seasonal headwinds in the East Indies by following the fierce westerlies to the south of Australia and she surprised watchers in Canton by arriving there out of season two days before Christmas. Her dimensions were close to those of a typical East Indiaman, except that, like the larger *Confederacy* class, she was unusually narrow for her length. She was eventually wrecked at the mouth of the Delaware River in 1800, probably the last warship of the Continental Navy still afloat.

ALLIANCE (ex-JOHN HANCOCK), 36

DATES	LENGTH HULL	LENGTH DECK	LENGTH KEEL	BEAM	DEPTH	DRAFT	TONNAGE B.M.
1777-1800	178	151	120	36	13	17	910

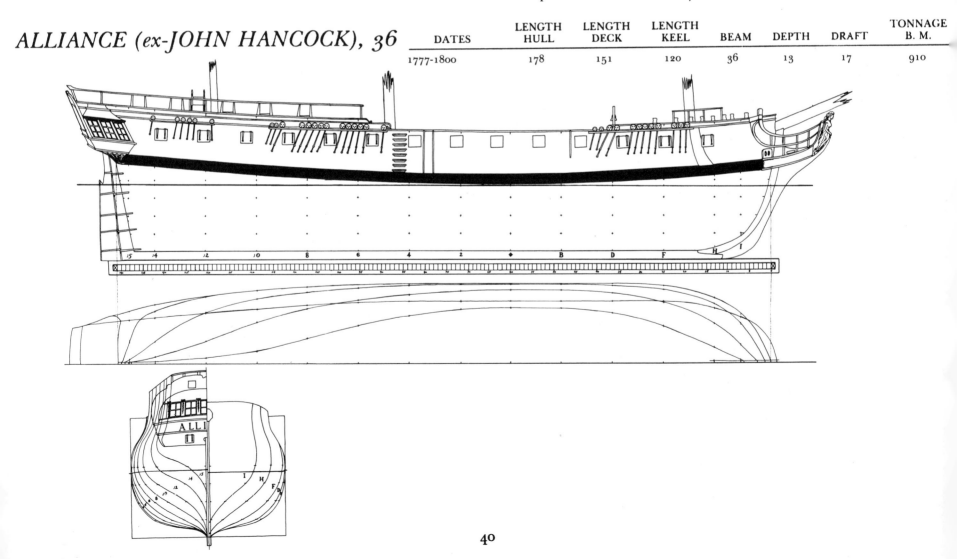

Frigate *Alliance*
From an anonymous engraving, ca. 1779
Le Musée de la Marine, Paris

Frigate *Alliance* in European waters late in her career, anonymous oil painting, private collection.

Frigate *Alliance*
From a primitive oil painting
by Captain Matthew Parke, U.S.M.C., 1781
Naval Historical Foundation, Washington, DC.

Frigate *Alliance* late in her career, anonymous painting, Peabody Museum, Salem.

Frigate *Alliance*, detail of view of Boston, grisaille by Pierre Ozanne, 1778, Library of Congress.

Captain Pierre Landais.

Captain Matthew Parke, U.S.M.C.

Captain John Barry.

Crew of *Alliance* in Canton, ca. 1790.

AMERICA/BOSTON, 44

ONE of the few ships built for the Royal Navy in what is now the United States was the 44-gun ship *America*. She was built at Portsmouth, New Hampshire, by Nathaniel Meserve in 1748–49. A 24-gun ship, *Boston,* was built in Boston at the same time, and when the latter proved unseaworthy because of extensive rot in 1756, *America* was renamed *Boston*. She herself, however, was also rotten, and she was sold out of the navy in September 1757; she must have been in terrible shape, for the navy practically never sold anything that could float while a war was in progress.

In appearance she was fairly typical of British warships of her class, except that she was several feet longer than the Establishment then in force for 44-gun ships; this seems to be an American trait—designing ships of a certain rate to be larger than others of that rate. Her appearance is known to us through the preservation of a beautifully built model, now kept at the Athenaeum at Portsmouth, New Hampshire. The model had been allowed to deteriorate over the years, but it was carefully restored by James A. Knowles. One record states that the model was lodged at the library at Harvard College in the 1750s (along with skeletons of various animals), and that it was at that time fully rigged. The model is not now rigged.

America's first captain, Henry Barnsby, sailed her to Spithead and then to Chatham. He reported that she sailed very well, being a sharp ship with a round buttock, and that she would need very few changes. Her guns were probably eighteen-pounders on the lower deck, nine-pounders on the upper deck, and six-pounders on the quarterdeck.

AMERICA/BOSTON, 44

DATES	LENGTH HULL	LENGTH DECK	LENGTH KEEL	BEAM	DEPTH	DRAFT	TONNAGE B. M.
1748-1757	159	139	118	38	15	17	863

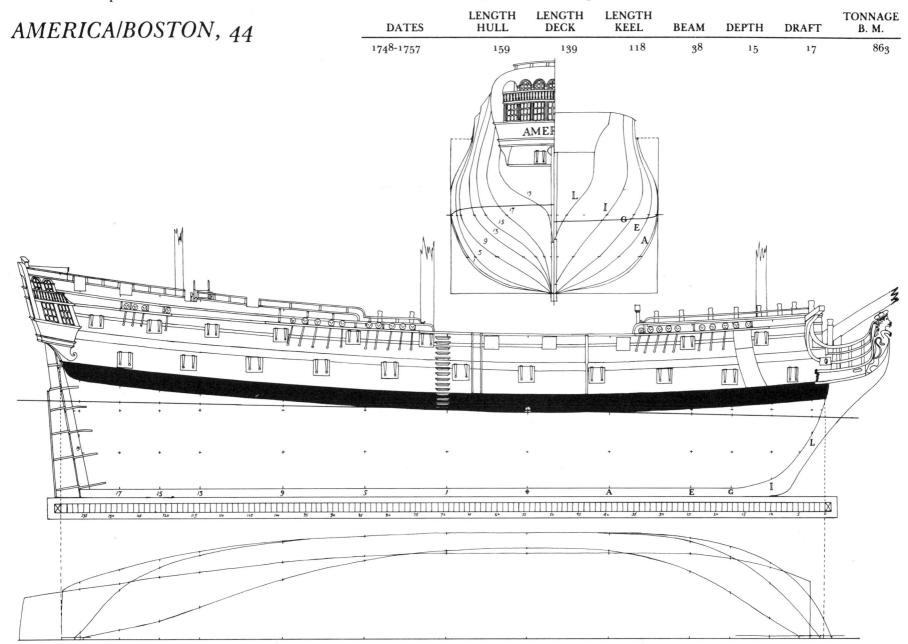

AMERICA, 74

At the time of the American Revolution, all the major navies of the world had battleships of 74 guns and more. The infant United States had nothing larger than a 32-gun frigate in 1776, so Congress set about rectifying the situation and on 9 November 1776 ordered three 74s built. Shortly thereafter, on 15 January 1777, the New York Committee of Safety also ordered that the timbers be cut to build a 74 far up the Hudson River. Shortages of funds forced the cancellation of the New York ship and of two of the national 74s, but the other was built at Portsmouth, New Hampshire, by the Hackett family of shipbuilders. She was laid down in May 1777.

The Hacketts were responsible for building many of the major ships used in the Revolution, including the frigates *Raleigh, Alliance,* and *Alexander,* and the corvettes *Ranger* and *Hampden.* As far as we can tell, they supplied the designs for all these ships themselves, not making use of the designs supplied by Congress. However, they did build their 74 to designs sent up from Philadelphia (which were modified as building progressed). An early form of the design is preserved in a half-model that can be seen at Independence National Historical Park in Philadelphia, and the official design, as approved by Congress, is preserved in the National Archives. Both the model and the design have been attributed to young Joshua Humphreys, and the design is certainly by the same hand as the design for the frigate *Randolph,* but what the connection with Humphreys was we will leave for others to debate.

Construction was delayed by lack of money, and there were even schemes to cut her down to a ship of 60 guns or smaller from time to time, but happily these came to nought. In 1781, John Paul Jones was appointed her commander and the resident inspector in the hope that construction would be speeded up. Jones found her to be well behind schedule but he had little luck in speeding up the construction. He also apparently ordered some changes made in the upper works, some of which are not reflected in our drawing, which is based on the official draft. Finally, *America* was launched on 5 November 1782. Jones had put all his efforts into completing the ship for so long because he looked forward to commanding such a fine ship, and also because he was sure that Congress would create the post of admiral just for him while he commanded *America.* Jones's dreams were not to be realized; already on 3 September, two months before her launching, Congress had presented her to the French navy out of gratitude for past favors and to replace *Le Magnifique,* a French 74 that had been wrecked in Boston Harbor. The chevalier de Martigne, former captain of *Le Magnifique,* was given command of her immediately after launching.

The French, probably noting that her sharp bow did not have enough buoyancy to support the forward cannons as it should, reported that she did not combine all the qualities that a vessel of her class should have. In 1786 she was surveyed and found to be totally rotten. Minister Castries ordered that she be broken up at Brest and another ship of 74 guns be built and given her name. Many historians have been misled into believing that the original *America* somehow survived in the French navy until being captured by the British in 1794, but an examination of the lines of this ship show her to be totally French in design; just to confuse matters further, the British also had a 64-gun ship called *America,* which was burned at Portsmouth, England, by accident.

There is a painting of *America* at Mystic Seaport in Connecticut. It was painted by John S. Blunt in 1834 and shows her under American colors, which she never flew under sail. The painting, while attractive, is merely fanciful; Blunt was not even born until 1798. A crude sketch on a powderhorn shows 38 guns arranged on two decks, but the artist had probably never seen the original plans. The powderhorn is dated 1776, but the ship was obviously added later—not too much later, for she is shown flying the Grand Union Ensign, which was superceded in June 1777.

America was not to be exceeded by any United States ship until the end of the War of 1812.

AMERICA, 74

DATES	LENGTH HULL	LENGTH DECK	LENGTH KEEL	BEAM	DEPTH	DRAFT	TONNAGE B. M.
1777-1786	221	180	147	49	19	24	1982

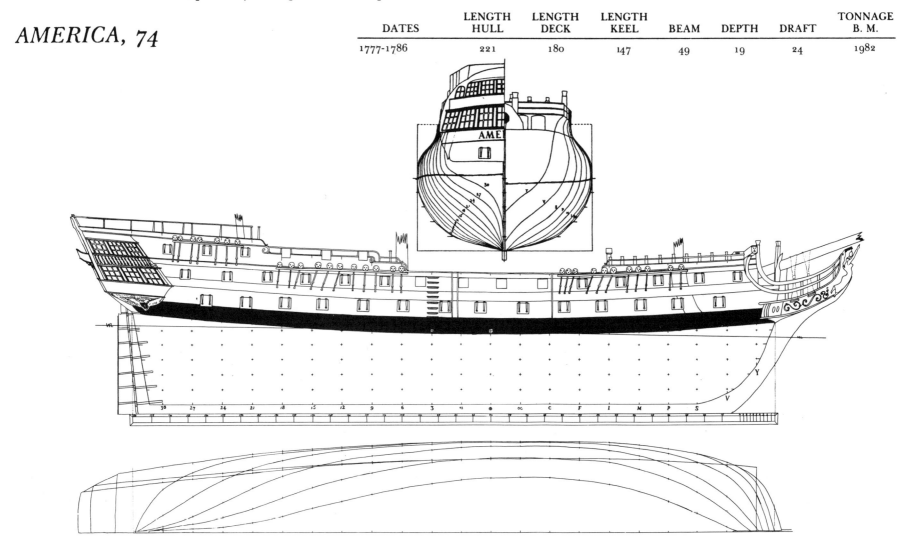

AMARACA

Powderhorn engraving of battleship *America*, 1777, Massachusetts Historical Society.

AMERICAN, 10

IN the fall of 1775, American forces launched a two-pronged invasion of Canada; one force under Benedict Arnold marched through Maine to Quebec, while another marched up to Montreal, using the Lake Champlain route. The American troops captured Montreal and Trois Rivières, but were badly defeated in front of Quebec. Arnold built a number of small warships on the St. Lawrence River to assist with the land operations, and probably all of these were gondolas or "gundalows."

Gondolas were easily, quickly, and cheaply built, for they had flat bottoms, nearly flat sides, and were double-ended. They were powered by oars, but could sail when the wind was fair. When Arnold had to evacuate the St. Lawrence area in the face of British reinforcements, at least one of his gondolas fell into British hands. Her name has been variously given as *American*, *American Convert*, and *Convert*. When the British found her, they called her *Loyal Convert*.

The British reassembled their gondola at St. John's on the Richelieu River at the northern end of Lake Champlain and used her against Arnold's naval forces on the lake. Presumably she was dismantled at the end of the war. The British kept the American rig of a square topsail and course with one jib, and they added a gaff mizzen. There are a few pictures of her sailing with the new rig, one in the Public Archives of Canada and the other in the Royal Collection at Windsor Castle in England. In addition, her plans survive at the National Maritime Museum at Greenwich, England. She mounted ten guns. In 1777, this large gondola capsized in a strong wind, and was only righted by cutting away all her spars and rigging.

Gondola *Loyal Convert* (*American*)
From a watercolor painting, 1776
The Royal Collection, Windsor Castle

AMERICAN, 10

DATES	LENGTH HULL	LENGTH DECK	LENGTH KEEL	BEAM	DEPTH	DRAFT	TONNAGE B. M.
1775-1777	70	63	59	20	4	4	109

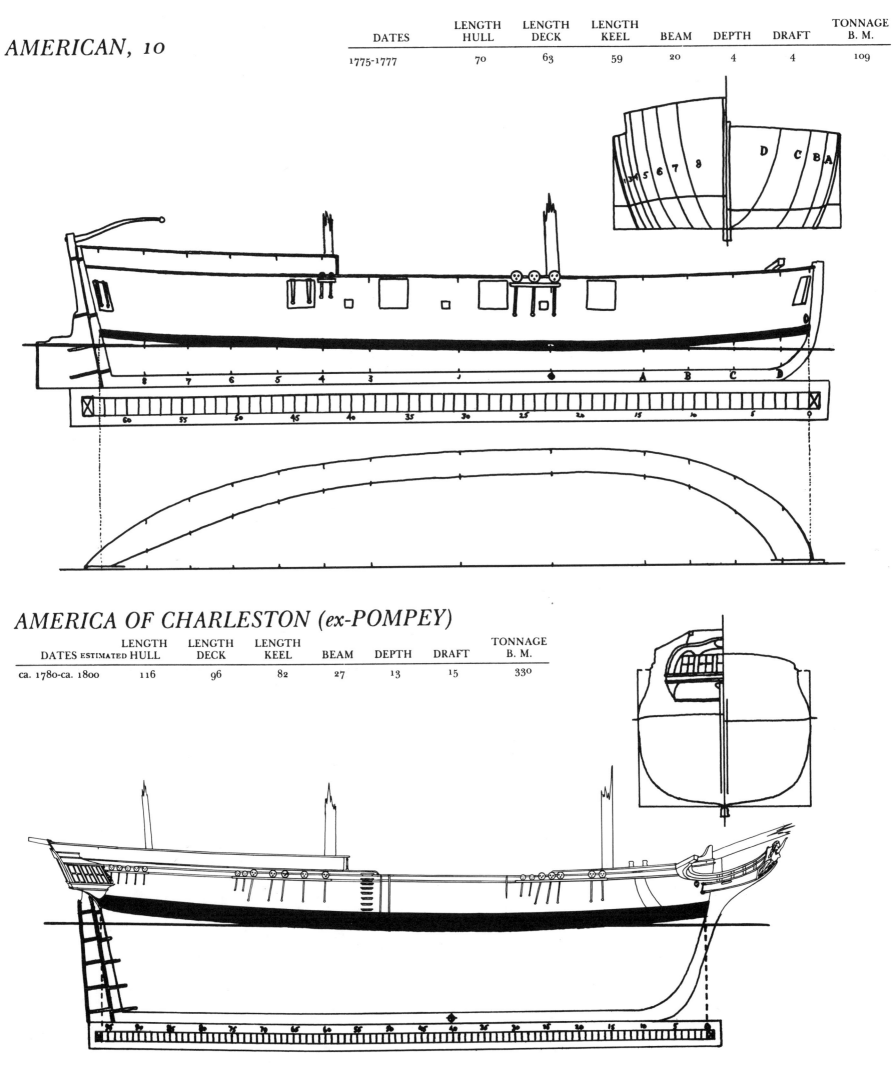

AMERICA OF CHARLESTON (ex-POMPEY)

DATES ESTIMATED	LENGTH HULL	LENGTH DECK	LENGTH KEEL	BEAM	DEPTH	DRAFT	TONNAGE B. M.
ca. 1780-ca. 1800	116	96	82	27	13	15	330

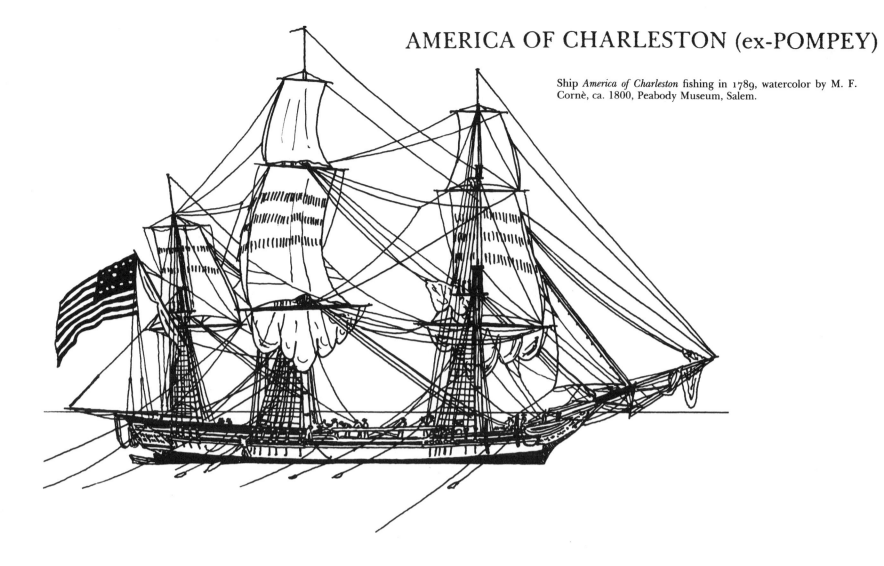

Ship *America of Charleston* fishing in 1789, watercolor by M. F. Cornè, ca. 1800, Peabody Museum, Salem.

America of Charleston, Upon Grand Bank May= 1789

in Salem- M. Cornè

THE Peabody Museum at Salem, Massachusetts has in its collection two pictures of an American merchant ship called *America of Charleston*. The pictures are dated 1789, which would suggest that they are the earliest pictures of a dolphin-striker in existence. However, since the artist, Michel Felice Cornè, did not come to America until 1799, it is certain that he was commissioned some time after his arrival to paint two incidents that had occurred a decade earlier, and thus he included a dolphin-striker by mistake.

The paintings, which are in the Mediterranean style made popular by Cammilieri and the Roux family, show the ship in two different weather conditions. The first shows her on the Grand Banks, more or less hove-to in a light breeze with all her fishing lines out; although she was hauling in cod as fast as the hooks could be baited, she was not in fact a fishing vessel. The second picture shows her with broken spars in a terrible storm, with the caption, "8 days from Grand Bank to the Channel of England," which is an exceptionally fast passage.

America of Charleston was formerly a British ship called *Pompey* that was captured by the Massachusetts privateer *Grand Turk* close to the end of the American Revolution. Her low freeboard, when combined with a long head and a raked sternpost, suggest great speed, but the low freeboard is probably more a reflection of overloading. She apparently had no provision for carrying cannons.

Ship *America of Charleston* in a bad storm, 1789, watercolor by M. F. Cornè, ca. 1800, Peabody Museum, Salem.

AMSTERDAM/OBSERVER, 12

THE appearance of the brig *Amsterdam* is known to us only through a painting by Robert Dodd. The painting shows her (after she was captured by the British frigate *Amphitrite* on 19 October 1780 and subsequently renamed *Observer*) doing battle with the Salem privateer *Jack* on 29 May 1782. Although *Jack* was the larger vessel, *Observer* captured her and took her into Halifax. Her commander during the battle was Lieutenant Crymes. She was sold on 21 October 1784.

Amsterdam was built in Massachusetts and named after one of the principal cities of Holland, which had become one of the allies of the United States toward the end of the war. Basically, she was a typical 14-gun brig that could be used as a privateer or a merchant ship, and could have passed for practically any nationality.

Brig *Amsterdam*
From an engraving after a painting by Robert Dodd, 1782

AMSTERDAM/OBSERVER, 12

DATES		LENGTH HULL	LENGTH DECK	LENGTH KEEL	BEAM	DEPTH	DRAFT	TONNAGE B. M.
1780-?	ESTIMATED	89	75	—	24	—	—	170

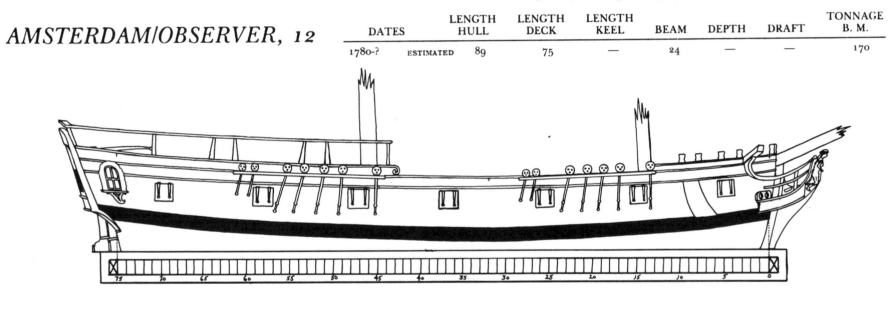

ANT, 8

SCHOONERS and sloops built in Bermuda had the reputation of being very fast, which is confirmed by a look at their sharp lines. *Ant* was an 8-gun schooner built in Bermuda in about 1788, and her lines appear to owe something to the developments in design that occurred not far away on the Chesapeake Bay at the end of the Revolution. She was taken into the Royal Navy, one source says by purchase and another says by capture from the French in 1797. In any case, she was put into drydock and her lines recorded in that year; the lines are on file at the National Maritime Museum. She was sold out of the navy in 1815. Since one of the most frequent complaints about Bermuda and other Ameri-

can fast schooners of the period was that they were so lightly built (for speed) that they fell apart after only a short period of use, it is surprising to see this schooner last perhaps thirty years.

The most noticeable features about her design are the sharp deadrise and the taper of the keel; the fact that the lines are drawn, as was the usual custom in those days, parallel with the top of the keel makes the drawing look a little strange to the modern eye.

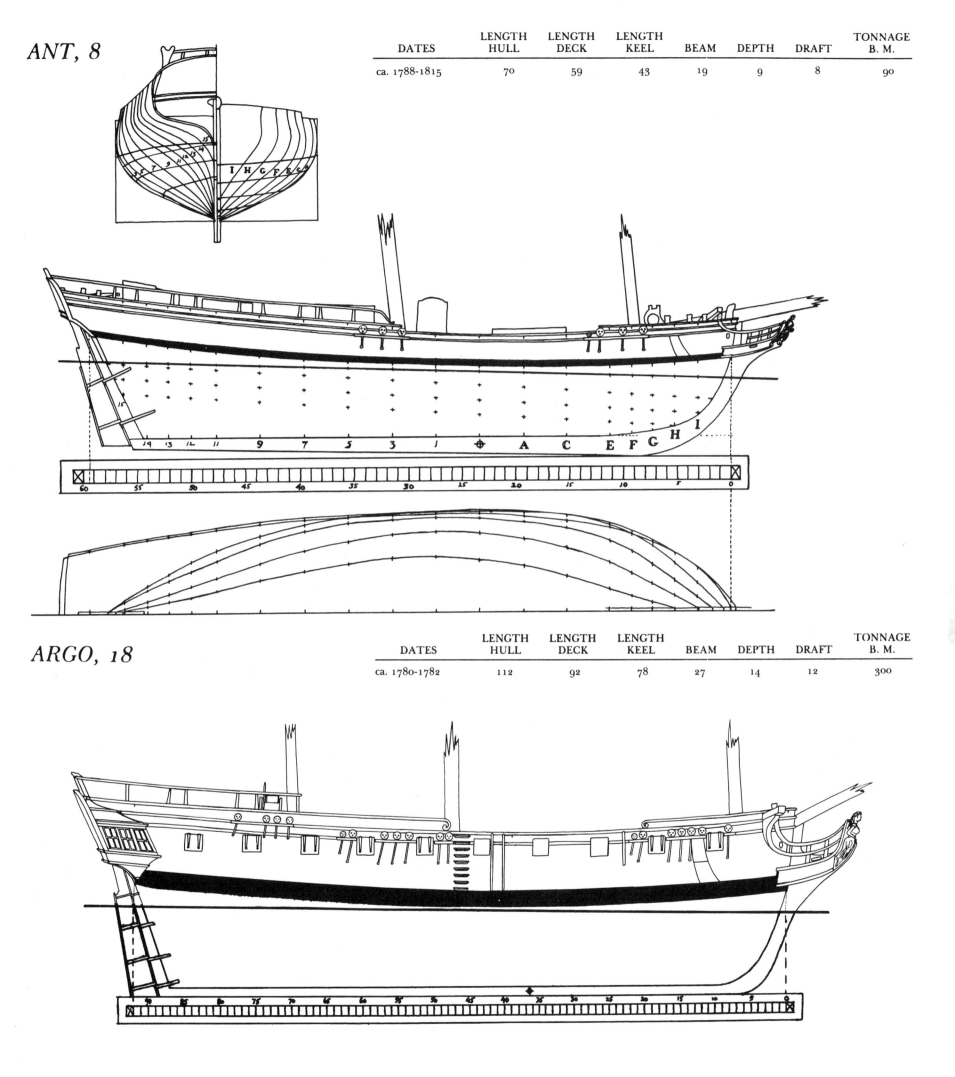

ANT, 8

DATES	LENGTH HULL	LENGTH DECK	LENGTH KEEL	BEAM	DEPTH	DRAFT	TONNAGE B. M.
ca. 1788-1815	70	59	43	19	9	8	90

ARGO, 18

DATES	LENGTH HULL	LENGTH DECK	LENGTH KEEL	BEAM	DEPTH	DRAFT	TONNAGE B. M.
ca. 1780-1782	112	92	78	27	14	12	300

ARGO, 18

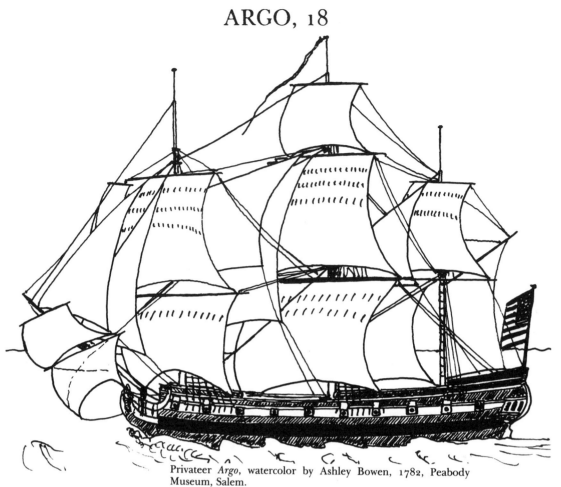

Privateer *Argo*, watercolor by Ashley Bowen, 1782, Peabody Museum, Salem.

ABOUT 1780 a syndicate of businessmen from Marblehead, Massachusetts, ordered the construction of
an 18-gun privateer to be called *Argo*. She was probably
built in Salem. From the two rather crude contemporary
paintings of her at the Peabody Museum in Salem (these
watercolors were by a seaman called Ashley Bowen, who
lived in Marblehead; one shows *Argo* under full sail returning from France in 1782, and the other shows her
scudding before a gale in a snowstorm with only three
reefed sails set) she looks equally suited to being a merchant ship or a privateer, for she has a full-bodied hull
and looks like a miniature frigate. Her career lasted no
more than two years, for she was wrecked near York,
Maine, in November 1782, shortly after the pictures
were painted. Her captain was Samuel Russell Trevett,
who fortunately escaped death in the wreck; interest-
ingly enough, her previous captain, John Williamson,
was also aboard at the time of the wreck.

Ship *Argo*
From a watercolor painting by Ashley Bowen, 1782
Peabody Museum, Salem, Massachusetts

ARIEL, 20

IN 1780, when John Paul Jones lost his command of
the frigate *Alliance* to mad Captain Pierre Landais,
he was presented with a much smaller frigate called
Ariel, which he found was quite inadequate to do the
job he had been asked to do: to ferry across to the
United States over 300 tons of military equipment, including 11,000 muskets, 10,000 uniforms, and 800 barrels of powder. *Ariel*'s French armament of 26 guns was
reduced to 16 to make more room, but it was not
enough. After many delays (some caused by Jones's hav-

ing affairs with ladies on shore) and a false start, *Ariel*
finally got to sea on 7 October, just in time to run into a
terrible storm. All the masts had to be cut away to avoid
going on the rocks. She returned to France for repairs
and finally sailed on 18 December. As he neared the
American shore Jones nearly captured the loyalist privateer *Triumph* (formerly the Massachusetts privateer
Tracy); this was his last battle under American colors.
Ariel arrived at Philadelphia on 18 February and was
handed back to the French, who sailed her back to

France in the summer.

Ariel was built at the Perry yard at Blackwall on the Thames (a private contractor rather than a Royal Navy yard) in 1777. She mounted 24 guns, and was captured in September 1779 by the French frigate *L'Amazone* (*L'Amazone* was at one point commanded by the great explorer de la Pérouse, but whether he was in command at this instant has not been determined). She was lost at sea in 1793. She formed a part of the French fleet under D'Estaing that attempted to capture Savannah.

Ariel's plans have been lost, but we have drawn here the lines of a typical British ship of her size, type, and date.

ARIEL, 20

DATES	LENGTH HULL	LENGTH DECK	LENGTH KEEL	BEAM	DEPTH	DRAFT	TONNAGE B. M.
1777-1793	130	110	89	30	9	14	429

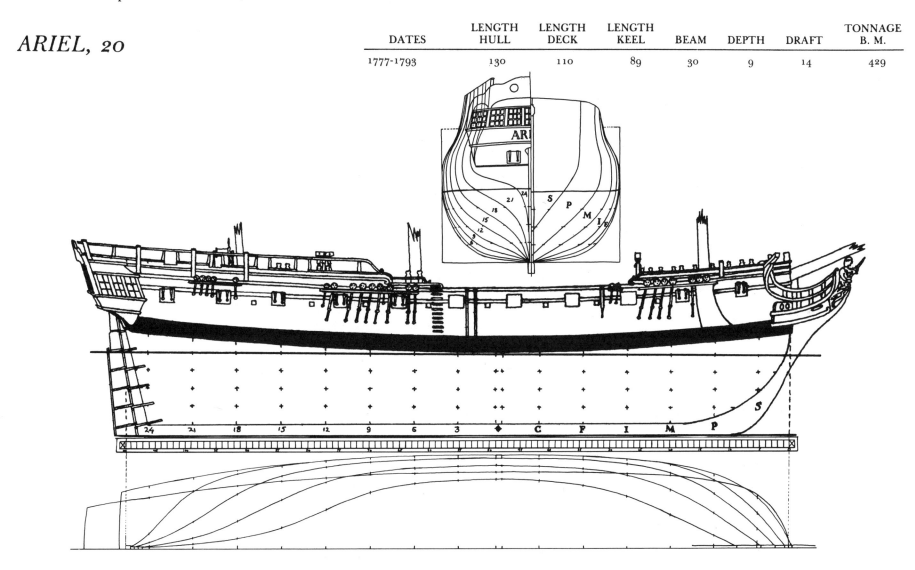

ASTON HALL

Although the Royal Navy was opposed to ordering construction of frigates or larger warships in America, it frequently purchased American-built ships for transports or fire-ships. Some of these were undoubtedly built in the Chesapeake Bay, such as *Maryland Planter,* later renamed *Proserpine*; she was purchased in 1757 as a 12-gun fireship, and sold at the end of the war in 1763. Although no plans have been found, her length between perpendiculars was 91 feet, beam 25½ feet and she measured 253 tons.

A similar, slightly larger ship from the Chesapeake Bay was *Aston Hall*. She was built in Maryland in 1773 for T. Curtis, and she was used in commerce between Halifax and London under the command of J. Parker. In 1778, the British government chartered her as a transport for the first time under the command of J. Austin, and the charter was continued for at least two years. In 1780, she sailed to Jamaica, and she disappeared from the register in 1782. A handsome portrait of her in oils was painted by Francis Holman, and now hangs at the Mariners Museum, Newport News, Virginia. John Sands kindly supplied information about this ship.

ASTON HALL

DATES		LENGTH HULL	LENGTH DECK	LENGTH KEEL	BEAM	DEPTH	DRAFT	TONNAGE B. M.
1773-1782	ESTIMATED	103	92	80	28	14	15	300

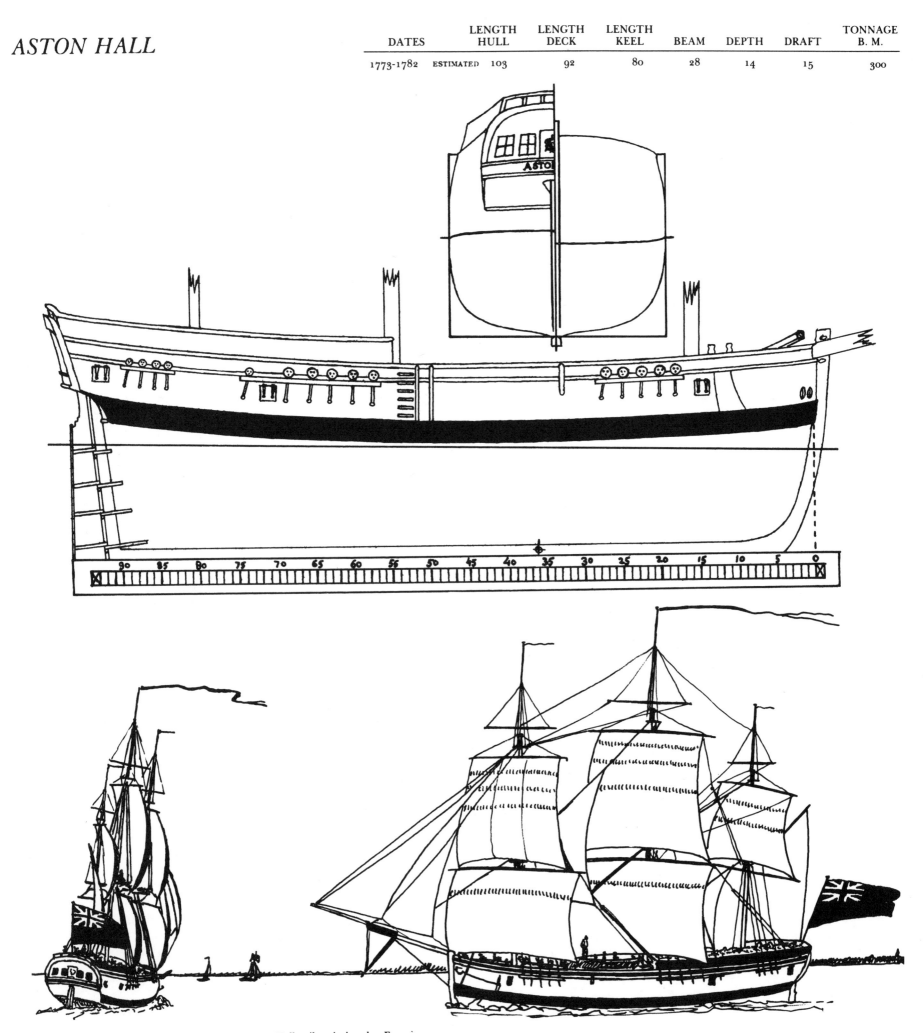

Maryland merchant ship *Aston Hall,* oil painting by Francis Holman, 1777, Mariners Museum, Newport News.

ASTREA & TARTAR, 20

DATES		LENGTH HULL	LENGTH DECK	LENGTH KEEL	BEAM	DEPTH	DRAFT	TONNAGE B. M.
1782-1792 1782-?	ESTIMATED	119	99	85	29	12	12	360

Detail of portrait of Elias H. Derby, possibly showing *Astrea* or *Grand Turk*, Peabody Museum, Salem.

Privateer *Astrea*, 1789, from Canton porcelain pitcher and bowl, Boston Marine Society.

ASTREA & TARTAR, 20

THE merchant-prince Elias Haskett Derby of Salem, Massachusetts commissioned the construction of the 20-gun privateer ship *Astrea* at Pembroke (several miles upriver in the Plymouth area) in 1782. She made her first long voyage to France in 1783 and returned with the first news of the official peace treaty. After the end of the war he employed her in the transatlantic trade, and she was particularly fast. She made many voyages to London and to Baltic ports, including Saint Petersburg, Russia. In 1788, Derby decided to enter her in trade to Batavia and Canton, but she did not actually depart until February 1789 under the command of James Magee; *Grand Turk*, a smaller ship owned by Derby, had already made a profitable voyage to Canton and back in 1787. She made various other voyages to the Orient until she called at Burma in August 1792. There she was seized by the Sultan of Pegu to carry supplies for his army in his war with Siam. At the end of this duty she was in such bad condition that she had to be sold at Calcutta for $7780, half her appraised value from a few months earlier. The sultan refused to pay any compensation.

On his first trip to Canton, Captain Magee commissioned several porcelain punchbowls and pitchers to commemorate his visit, each with clear portraits of *Astrea* on the side. The Boston Marine Society apparently owns the only surviving set. This picture has formed a basis for our reconstruction, which resembles an updated version of the frigate *Hancock* reduced to *Astrea*'s known tonnage size. Her bottom was surprisingly not coppered. Quantities of documents, such as manifests and logbooks, survive from *Astrea*, which was named after the Greek goddess of Justice.

Another Massachusetts vessel that may have resembled *Astrea* was the 20-gun ship *Tartar*; she was under construction for two years for the Massachusetts State Navy under the supervision of Captain John Hallet. She first went to sea in March 1782 under Captain John Cathcart, but since the war was clearly ending she was ordered sold in November. She was bought as a privateer, and, still under command of Cathcart, was captured by the British privateer *Bellisarius* (not to be confused with the American-built Royal Navy ship of that name).

ATLANTIC & PATTY

DATES	LENGTH HULL	LENGTH DECK	LENGTH KEEL	BEAM	DEPTH	DRAFT	TONNAGE B. M.
fl. 1763	ESTIMATED 102	80	—	24	—	—	185

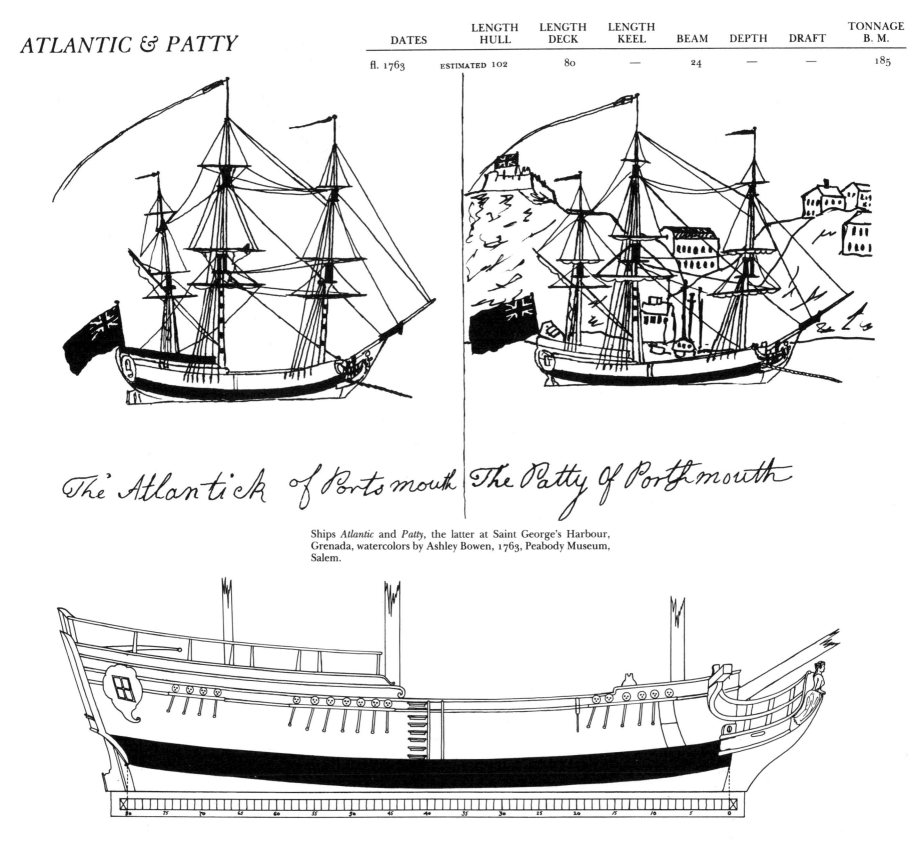

Ships *Atlantic* and *Patty*, the latter at Saint George's Harbour, Grenada, watercolors by Ashley Bowen, 1763, Peabody Museum, Salem.

ATLANTIC & PATTY

The Marblehead seaman Ashley Bowen, who left us a splendid record of his life and times in the form of several illustrated journals, painted crude watercolor sketches of many of the ships he either sailed on or encountered in his travels. Two of these were the merchant ships *Atlantic* and *Patty*. Both were Portsmouth, New Hampshire, ships, but although we have drawn them as identical, because of the apparent similarity between them evidenced by Bowen's drawings, they

may not have been sister ships. Bowen says he had charge of *Atlantic* for a brief while in 1763, loading her at the Isle of Shoals, although he also says that George Dimon was the "master Chief Mate" and William Temple the owner.

Bowen then shipped on *Patty* as chief mate under Captain Monsieur Bunbury to Grenada in the West Indies, expecting to continue with her to London, but she was sold at Grenada and he had to find his way home some other way.

BEDFORD GALLEY & BOSTON, 34

DATES	LENGTH HULL	LENGTH DECK	LENGTH KEEL	BEAM	DEPTH	DRAFT	TONNAGE B. M.
1697-ca. 1722 1692-?	121	103	85	29	11	14	372

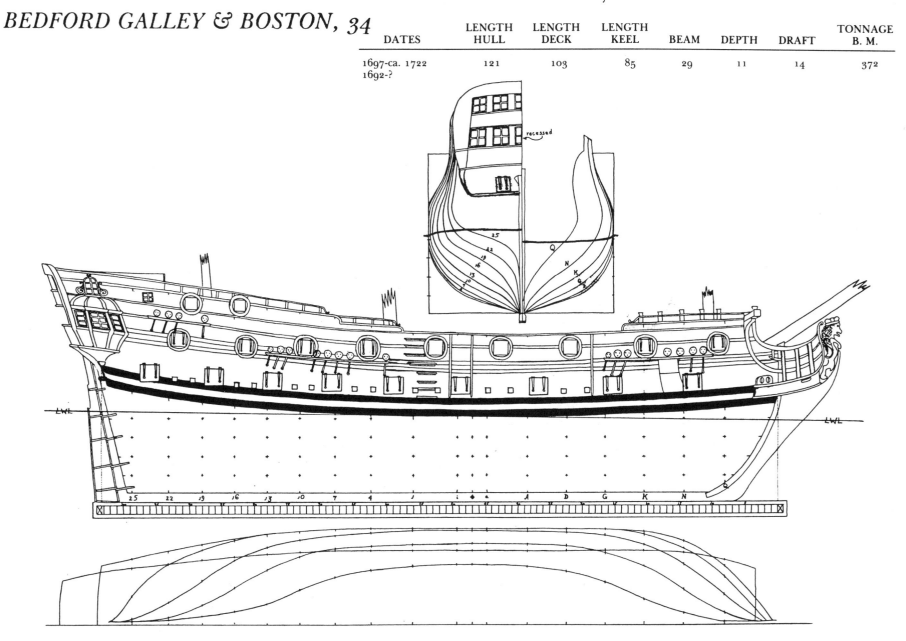

BEDFORD GALLEY & BOSTON, 34

In 1697, flushed with his recent success in having built the 44-gun ship *Falkland* and sold her to the Royal Navy, a shipbuilder by the name of Holland at Portsmouth, New Hampshire (actually New Castle, a neighboring village), built a second ship for the navy on

speculation. This was the 34-gun *Bedford Galley* (not to be confused with the 70-gun ship *Bedford* that was in the Royal Navy at the same time). The Royal Navy purchased her the same year.

Unfortunately, she quickly showed areas of rot that caused her to need rebuilding in 1709, and at the time she was enlarged slightly to 410 tons although we are not told what was done that would increase the tonnage measurement by only 38 tons. She fought in the Mediterranean early in the century, and was converted into a fireship in 1716. No occasion was found to use her as a fireship, so she was sunk in either 1722 or 1725 to be a foundation for a new building at the Sheerness dockyard.

No plans of her have survived, nor any portraits. However, we do know her length, breadth, and tonnage, and we know the typical appearance of ships of her day; we also have plans of the earlier *Falkland* that was built by the same builder. It is on that basis that we present this reconstruction of her plans. She was a two-decker, with nine ports per side on each deck. On the lower deck there were fourteen oarports per side, arranged in pairs between the guns, hence the word *Galley* as part of her name; the oars must have been helpful when she was fighting in the Mediterranean. She was overmasted at first, and her spars were later reduced.

Another ship that must have looked much the same as *Bedford Galley* was the 32-gun warship *Boston*, about which we unfortunately know very little. She was built in America in 1692, possibly by Holland at Portsmouth, and presented to the Royal Navy by the citizens of Boston in 1694. She did not remain long in the Royal Navy, for she was captured by the French in the Atlantic in January 1695. No trace of her has been found in French records.

BELISARIUS, 24

DATES	LENGTH HULL	LENGTH DECK	LENGTH KEEL	BEAM	DEPTH	DRAFT	TONNAGE B. M.
ca. 1780-?	132	111	94	31	9	13	514

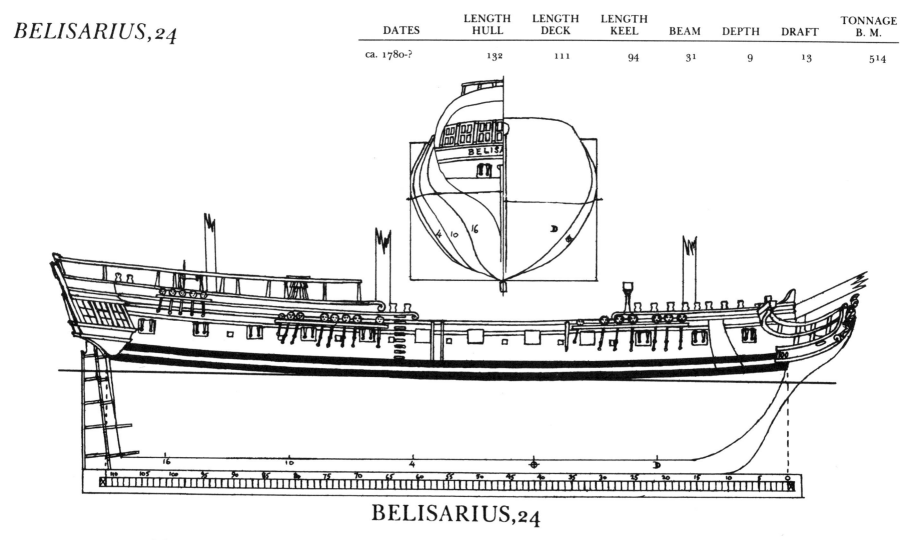

BELISARIUS, 24

ONE of the larger American privateers in the Revolution was an unusual ship called *Belisarius*. She was built at Paul's shipyard in Boston about 1780 to plans by a maverick designer named John Peck, who was apparently also responsible for the privateer *Rattlesnake* and the East Indiaman *Empress of China*. Very little is known about her. An advertisement appeared in the *Gazette* at Providence, Rhode Island, in April 1781 announcing that she was ready for sea at Boston and would cruise for five months as a privateer under the command of James Munro, who had previously commanded the *General Washington*. However, she never finished her five-month cruise, because she was captured in a flat calm in August 1781 by the British frigate *Medea* because someone had forgotten to bring along any sweeps. She was taken into the Royal Navy and sometimes described as a 20-gun ship and sometimes as a 24-gun ship. She was sold at the end of 1783.

Joshua Humphreys, the well-known builder from Philadelphia, visited Peck after she was built and he wrote down her measurements and the notation that she was "one of the fastest sailing ships that ever swam the seas." He also sketched a few of her frame designs and we have used this information to try to reconstruct her lines for this book. The British, however, were not as enthusiastic as Humphreys, for one admiral said that she "did not answer all that was expected," although he did not enumerate her faults. He described her as a good sailer and stiff in a moderate breeze. He also said that she had a sharp entrance but with no hollow in the waterlines, and that she had a great deal of deadwood and a large gripe or forefoot. Some of the British dimensions do not agree with Humphreys; the British measurements could have been taken at different stations or taken carelessly, but Peck, scatter-brained as he was, could have given Humphreys only approximate figures. We have used Humphreys's figures.

Various commentators have made much of the supposed French influence in Peck's designs, but it seems that Peck was influenced by no one and the fact that *Belisarius*'s midsection resembles the typical French midsection is probably mere coincidence. If Humphreys's drawing is correct, and there is no saying that it is, Peck continued the pronounced knuckle of the lower bilge all the way aft, which is a most peculiar and un-French design, slightly reminiscent of the after lines of the 12-meter yacht *Mariner* that was an unsuccessful candidate for the defense of the America's Cup in 1974. She was unusual for a vessel of her size in that she had a square stern. Peck is known to have designed a number of other vessels, including the privateer *Rattlesnake*, the Portsmouth ship *Leda*, the Continental packet schooner *Mercury*, and the merchantship (ex-privateer) *Empress of China*.

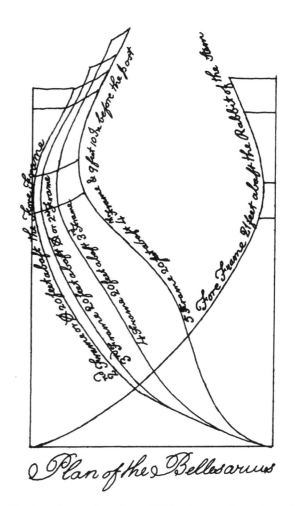

Plan of the Bellesarius

Tracing of surviving plans of *Belisarius* as redrawn by Joshua Humphreys, 1780.

BERBICE, 8

THE 8-gun schooner *Berbice* was built in America, probably in the Chesapeake Bay area, about 1780. She was captured in the West Indies, and was purchased for the Royal Navy under orders of Admiral Rodney. Rodney used her as a tender, and we may assume that this included carrying messages back and forth between the islands, since she was very fast for her size. She was, according to one record, condemned and sold out of the navy at Antigua in September 1788, but another record says that she was (again?) purchased in 1793 by the Royal Navy when war broke out against France, and that

she was wrecked on the island of Dominica in the West Indies at the end of 1796. If this is so, she lived a long life for such a lightly built boat. Her design should be compared to the schooner *Ant*.

Two copies of her lines survive, one at the National Maritime Museum at Greenwich and the other in private hands; however, they do not agree. Howard Chapelle synthesized the two designs, and we have followed his lead.

	DATES	LENGTH HULL	LENGTH DECK	LENGTH KEEL	BEAM	DEPTH	DRAFT	TONNAGE B. M.
	ca. 1780-1796	79	73	54	21	8	9	121

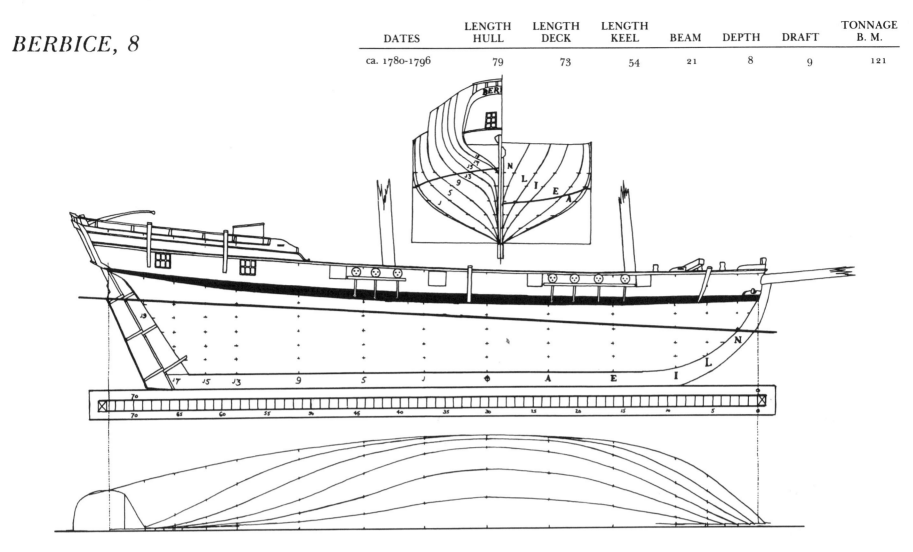

BETHEL, 16

A FINE contemporary oil painting exists of the Massachusetts privateer *Bethel*. The picture, true to a popular convention of the day, shows her under sail in two different poses as if there were actually two ships in the picture. It is said to be the earliest portrait of an identified American ship, and was painted in 1748. *Bethel* belonged to the Quincy family of Boston, and may have been built only a few years earlier by the well-known Boston builder Benjamin Hallowell.

In 1748, she captured the polacca (pole-masted ship) *Saint Joseph* in the Mediterranean. Later, off the Azores, she had the good fortune to capture the Spanish treasure ship *Jesus, Maria and Joseph* of 26 guns and 110 men in the middle of the night, after a "serenade of French horns and trumpets &c." *Bethel* herself, under the command of Captain Isaac Freeman, had only 38 men and 14 guns, her six other guns being wooden dummies. Such dummies were often known as "Quakers," to rhyme with the Elizabethan name for a certain class of cannons known as sakers. An unusual feature for such a small ship is the double-decked stern gallery, resembling the stern of an East Indiaman. Her later history has not yet been discovered.

No plans of her are known to exist. However, we have reconstructed lines for her, based on the portrait and on other ships of her period.

Privateer *Bethel*, detail of anonymous oil painting, 1748, Peabody Museum, Salem.

BETHEL, 16

DATES		LENGTH HULL	LENGTH DECK	LENGTH KEEL	BEAM	DEPTH	DRAFT	TONNAGE B. M.
ca. 1746-?	ESTIMATED	101	84	68	26	12	13	240

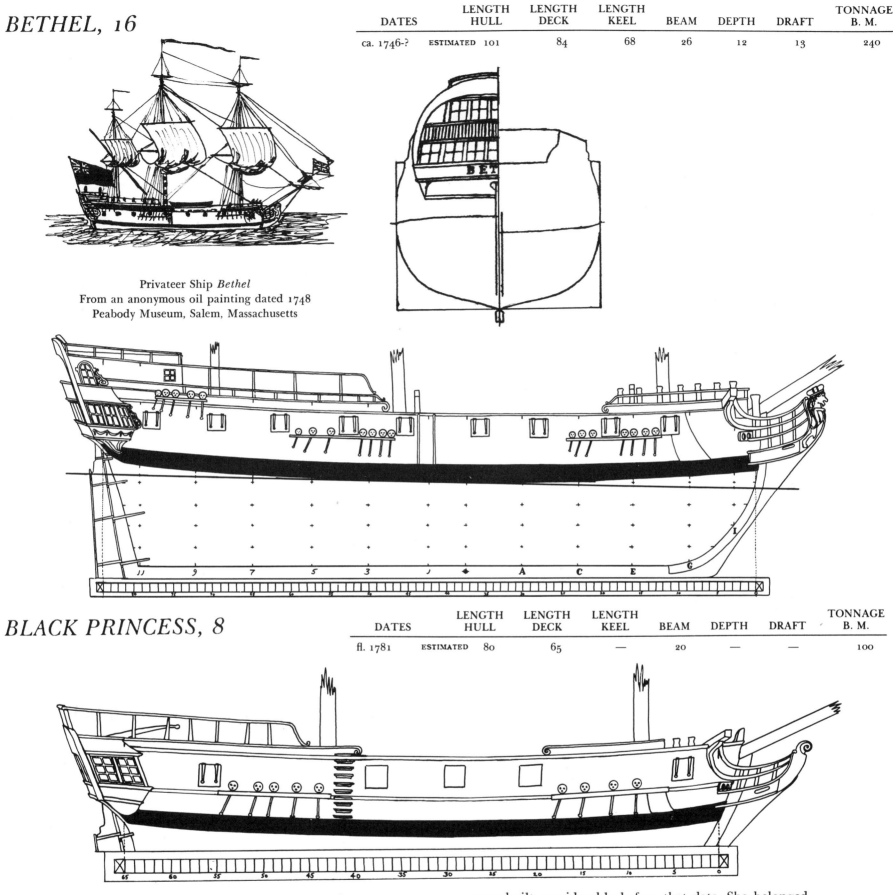

Privateer Ship *Bethel*
From an anonymous oil painting dated 1748
Peabody Museum, Salem, Massachusetts

BLACK PRINCESS, 8

DATES		LENGTH HULL	LENGTH DECK	LENGTH KEEL	BEAM	DEPTH	DRAFT	TONNAGE B. M.
fl. 1781	ESTIMATED	80	65	—	20	—	—	100

BLACK PRINCESS, 8

ONE of the many merchant ships that were fitted out with a few cannons and issued a letter of marque by a state governor in the Revolutionary War was the Connecticut brig or snow *Black Princess*. She mounted eight or ten guns, and sailed under the command of Humphrey Crary in 1781, although she looks as if she were built considerably before that date. She belonged to Dudley Woodbridge & Co., and cruised to St. Maarten in the West Indies with a crew of only twelve men. On her return voyage she was chased into Stonington, Connecticut, by a frigate. There is no record of any captures made by her.

A crude sketch of her exists at the Connecticut Historical Society and we have based our simple plan on that sketch.

Sketch of Connecticut brig *Black Princess*, Connecticut Historical
Society, Hartford.

BONHOMME RICHARD (ex-DUC DE DURAS), 42

DATES	LENGTH HULL	LENGTH DECK	LENGTH KEEL	BEAM	DEPTH	DRAFT	TONNAGE B. M.
1765-1779	188	155	135	39	16	19	1050

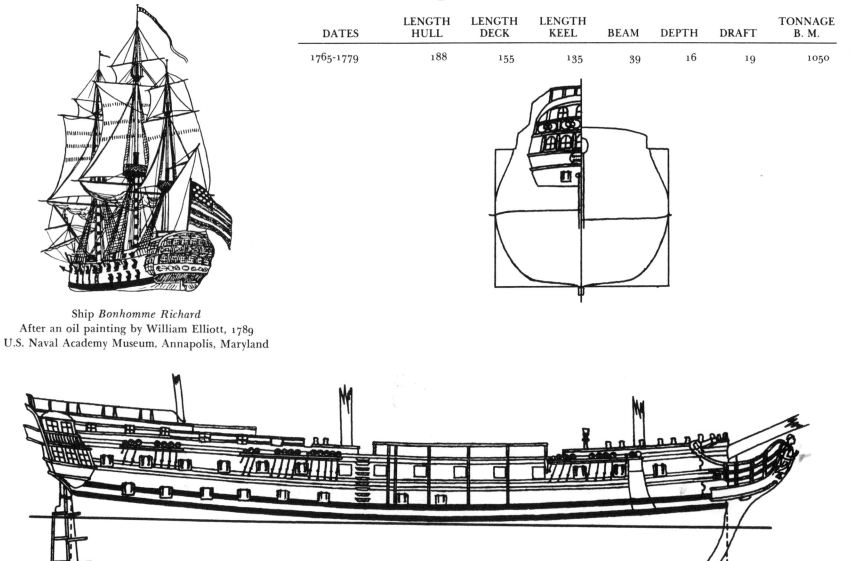

Ship *Bonhomme Richard*
After an oil painting by William Elliott, 1789
U.S. Naval Academy Museum, Annapolis, Maryland

BONHOMME RICHARD (ex-DUC DE DURAS), 42

JOHN PAUL JONES spent a good deal of time in France in the hope that the French might outfit him with a fleet of heavily armed ships to do battle with the British; he was convinced that he would never get such a fleet if he waited around Philadelphia for Congress to present it to him. When he got his fleet, it was not exactly what he had wanted in terms of the quantity and quality of men and ships under him, but he used it to good advantage so that the favorable publicity that he gained from the fleet's single major (but insignificant) engagement with the enemy far outstripped the reputation of more important naval combats.

Jones's flagship was a tired French East Indiaman by the name of *Le Duc de Duras,* equipped with 36 guns. Carpenters made a number of gunports on the lower deck, filling them with obsolete eighteen-pounders (that exploded in the battle), bringing her strength up to 42 guns. The little fleet left France in June 1779 to go clockwise around the British Isles. In all of Jones's efforts with the fleet, he was not supported at all by Pierre Landais in the *Alliance,* and hardly supported by any of the other captains. Time after time he was frustrated in his plans to raid a section of British coast and hold a town for ransom. Finally, off Flamborough Head, Yorkshire, he spotted a large convoy arriving from the Baltic, guarded by only a 44 and a 20. As good convoy guards should, the two British ships sheered off to do battle with Jones so that the convoy would have time to escape. One of Jones's 20s engaged and captured the 20-gun guardship, and Jones himself did battle with the larger ship, whose same was *Serapis.*

In deference to his patron, Benjamin Franklin, the author of *Poor Richard's Almanac,* Jones had named his ship *Bonhomme Richard* (i.e., *Poor Richard*). The contest was unequal, but Jones fought with such deter-

mination that he carried the day (or actually night), in spite of having to put down mutinies and in spite of the fact that his ship was not only leaking faster than the pumps could handle but was also on fire. It was in this battle that Jones is reported to have uttered his immortal words "I have only just begun to fight." After the victory, Jones put his own crew and the crew of *Serapis* to work at plugging the leaks, pumping her, and putting out the fires, but after a while he realized it was hopeless and gave the order to abandon her. This must be one of the strangest outcomes to a sea battle, for the winner was the ship that was sunk.

This battle so close to British shores struck terror into the British population, who fully expected a large invasion at any moment. Nevertheless, the *Serapis* had done her job, for the convoy arrived in Britain unscathed, and any ordinary captain would have surrendered *Bonhomme Richard* long before the actual end of the battle, so much damage had she sustained.

Many portraits of *Bonhomme Richard* in this battle exist, either from the bow or the stern, but none full on from the side. No plans of the ship survive, but some of her dimensions are known, and the designs of at least one other East Indiaman drawn by her designer, Antoine Groignard, can be studied. She made one voyage to China in 1766-1767, during which she had a crew of 160 men. An expedition in the 1970s searched the floor of the North Sea with sophisticated equipment, but was unable to find any trace of the ship.

Captain John Paul Jones.

DATES	LENGTH HULL	LENGTH DECK	LENGTH KEEL	BEAM	DEPTH	DRAFT	TONNAGE B. M.
1748-1752	142	118	98	33	7	15	555

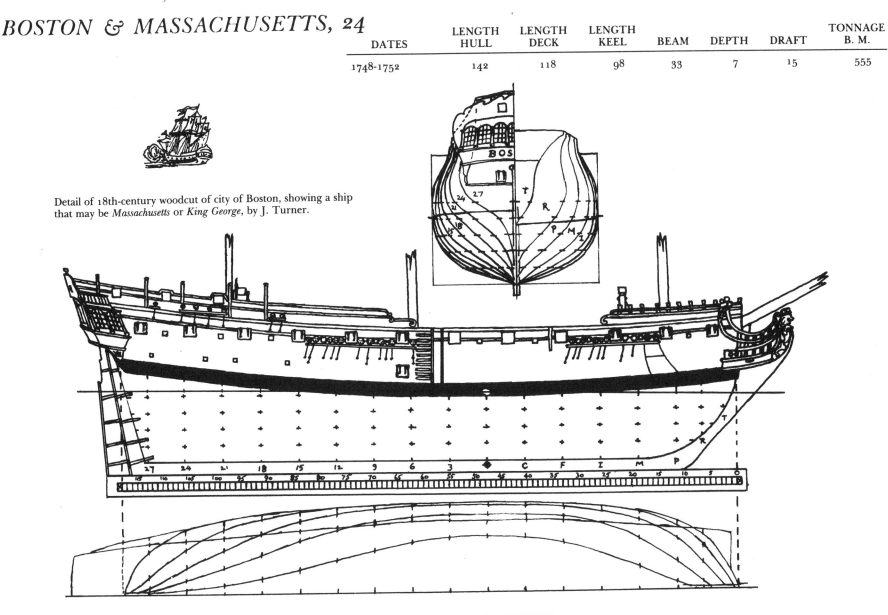

Detail of 18th-century woodcut of city of Boston, showing a ship that may be *Massachusetts* or *King George*, by J. Turner.

BOSTON & MASSACHUSETTS, 24

AFTER the New England troops and ships had played such a major part in the capture of the French fortress of Louisbourg in Nova Scotia in 1745, pressure was exerted on the Royal Navy to build some of its ships in America. The navy initially agreed rather reluctantly to build four, which they then scaled down to two. The 44-gun ship *America* was built at Portsmouth, New Hampshire, and the 24-gun ship *Boston* was built by Benjamin Hallowell in Boston. She was soon found to be rotten and in 1752 was ordered broken up after only four years. Although the British and Americans thought of her as a Sixth Rate, and although she had one port on the lower deck (probably used only as a loading port and not as a gunport), she approached very close to the concept of a frigate. As such, she may have been the first frigate-type ship built in America, as far as we know. She was very similar to other ships of her type built in England, except that she followed the American custom of making a ship of a given rate a few feet larger than other ships of her rate. Her plans survive at the National Maritime Museum, Greenwich.

The Province of Massachusetts commissioned a 24-gun frigate that was built by Captain Berry in February 1744/5, possibly to the same plans as *Boston*. Her name was *Massachusetts* and she was commanded by Edward Tyng, who served briefly as commodore of the motley New England fleet that attacked Louisbourg with such surprising success in 1745. She had a crew of 130 men, but may have carried as many as 200 at Louisbourg. She was later commanded by Moses Bennett. After the war, several Boston merchants attempted to use her to import Protestant servants from northern Ireland, but that plan failed. About 1753 she was sold for use as a West Indiaman. She may be the ship firing the salute in J. Turner's woodcut view of Boston.

BOSTON/CHARLESTON & PROTECTOR/HUSSAR, 24/26

O<small>F</small> the initial thirteen frigates ordered by Congress in 1775, *Boston*, one of the three 24-gun ships, was built at Newburyport, Massachusetts, by Green-leaf & Cross. She was an exceptionally pretty ship, judging from the set of contemporary oil paintings of her by Francis Holman. Her rig was unusual in that she set a lateen sail on the ensign staff, thus giving her a fourth mast. Her armament was nominally that for a 24-gun ship, but her builders made her a scaled-down copy of the 32-gun frigate *Hancock*, which they were building at the same time, so that she could actually carry 32 guns if necessary. When the British captured her, they rated her as a 28-gun ship. Due to shortages of nine-pounder cannons, some of her initial cannons were twelve-pounders. Her first captain was Isaac Cazneau, but he was replaced before she got to sea.

Under Captain Hector McNeill, she departed from Boston in May 1777 on her first cruise, in company with *Hancock*. The two of them had the good fortune to take a British frigate of 28 guns, the *Fox*. A good deal of chivalry was displayed in this battle as each side ceased fire to allow the other to put out fires caused by hot wadding lodged in awkward places. *Fox* was soon re-taken by *Flora*, 32 guns, and *Hancock* was taken by *Rainbow*, 44 guns, in a disgraceful episode in which *Boston* deserted her companions in flight. McNeill was dismissed as a result. There is no doubt that the three frigates together had the strength, if not the determination, to defeat the two British ships. After this, *Boston* lay in Boston, nominally under command of Samuel Tucker, but with no crew. He got her to sea on 15 February 1778 with John Adams as a passenger. Five days out, lightning broke the mainmast. Then she narrowly escaped from a 36-gun frigate, but captured the 16-gun brig *Martha* before arriving in the Garonne River at the end of March.

In May, she set out on a cruise in the Bay of Biscay with a troublesome crew of Frenchmen, but returned to St. Nazaire to get rid of her crew in August. In September she set sail for home in company with *Providence* and *Ranger*, arriving at Portsmouth, New Hampshire, in October 1778. She lay mostly idle until the following July, when she took eight prizes on a short cruise with the frigate *Deane*. In September 1779 she was ordered to Charleston, South Carolina.

She was still in Charleston the following May when the British captured the city. Under the terms of the city's capitulation the ships had to be surrendered intact, so *Boston* entered the Royal Navy but with a new name: *Charleston* or *Charlestown*. She was sold out of the navy in 1783.

The Massachusetts State Navy undertook an ambitious project in 1779: the frigate *Protector* was built in New-buryport, Massachusetts. Little is known about her appearance, for neither her lines nor her measurements nor even a portrait of her survive. We do know that she rated 26 guns and that her tonnage was 586, a bit more than *Boston*'s 514, but not enough more to mean that the two measurements were of a different design (tonnage measurements of the same ship varied widely, depending on who was the measurer). It is our suspicion that the two ships were built in the same ship-yard to essentially the same design, and that is how we have drawn them.

Protector did not get rigged until 1780, so she missed being a part of the disastrous Penobscot Bay expedition that had been organized by Massachusetts state forces. On her first cruise, under Captain John Foster Williams, she ran into heavy fighting. On 9 June 1780 she fought the 32-gun Liverpool privateer *Admiral Duff*. *Admiral Duff* was weak from old age and from the fact that she was once a merchant ship (an East Indiaman), but her crew fought like wildcats and her high sides must have seemed terrifying to those on *Protector*; one of the *Protector*'s crew wrote that she was "large as a 74." After a long period of furious fighting *Admiral Duff* sank, and there were only 55 survivors. *Protector* herself was badly cut up and so headed back to port. On the way she encountered the 32-gun British frigate *Thames*, and fortunately escaped from her after a long, running fight.

In May 1781 *Protector* encountered two British ships, the 44-gun *Roebuck* and the 28-gun *Medea*, and this time there was no escape. She was taken into the Royal Navy and given the name of *Hussar*. She participated in the capture of a number of American vessels in the twenty months of the war that remained, and was sold out of the navy in August 1783. Edward Preble, later a famous captain in the U.S. Navy, had been a midshipman on *Protector*, but was fortunately exchanged before he could get a taste of British prisons; this is mentioned here because Congress, not wishing the individual states to continue to maintain their own navies, normally refused to allow crewmen of state vessels to be figured into national prisoner exchanges. Captain Williams had to wait seven months to be exchanged, and he was lucky compared to his men.

Protector was apparently armed with cannons supplied by the French, and so they are likely to have been larger in calibre than typical British and American guns of the same nominal weight. An entertaining account of her career was published in 1838 in *The Revolutionary Adventures of Ebenezer Fox*.

Our drawing of *Boston* and *Protector* is based on paintings of *Boston* (at the Peabody Museum, Salem), on the recorded dimensions of *Boston*, and on the lines of *Hancock* that are preserved at Greenwich. No dimensions survive for *Protector*.

Captain Samuel Tucker.

Frigate *Boston*
From one of a set of four oil paintings by Francis Holman, 1779
Peabody Museum, Salem, Massachusetts

Captain Edward Preble.

BOSTON/CHARLESTON & PROTECTOR/HUSSAR, 24/26

DATES	LENGTH HULL	LENGTH DECK	LENGTH KEEL	BEAM	DEPTH	DRAFT	TONNAGE B. M.
1776-? 1779-?	139	114	93	32	10	14	514 586

& AMERICAN TARTAR/HINCHENBROKE, 28

(see also pp. 208 – 209)

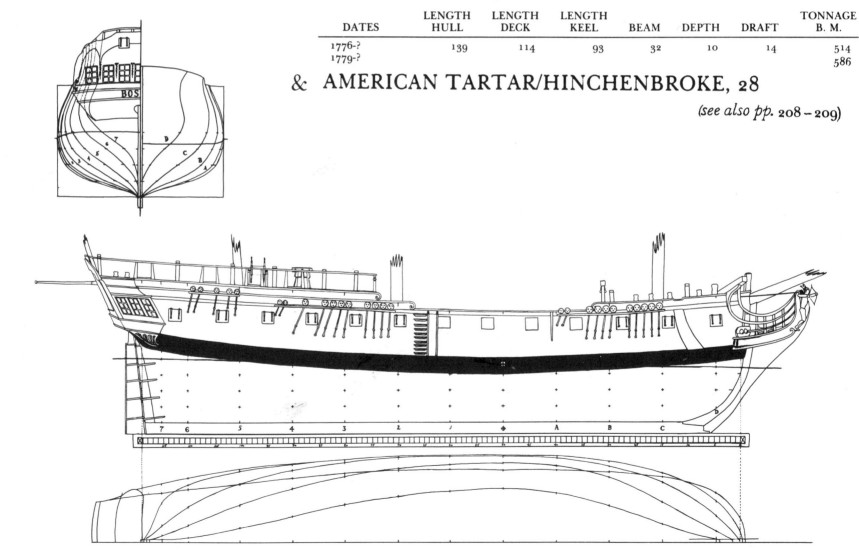

LA BRICOLE, 44

WHEN Admiral D'Estaing brought his French fleet to Savannah in 1779 in an unsuccessful effort to capture it from the British, he outfitted two of his transports with heavy cannons. These two ships, *La Bricole* and *La Truite* (meaning "odd-job" and "trout") were subsequently donated to the South Carolina Navy, which proceeded to arm them with even more guns. Transports built to the official French designs, as these were, were particularly narrow for their length, so it is obvious that D'Estaing never intended them to carry their armament outside the sheltered waters of the Savannah River. The South Carolina authorities agreed, reserving the ships for harbor service only in Charleston.

La Bricole, the larger of the two, was built at Le Havre in 1759 by Ginoux as a "flute" of 750 French tons. In 1764 she served as a troop transport in French Guiana and was armed with 20 to 28 guns. At Charleston, additional gunports were cut in her sides and she mounted 44 guns, although one report said she could have been fitted with 64. These were 18 and 24-pounders, some of which are said to have been given to Charleston years earlier when the Royal Navy removed the French cannons from the captured French 80-gun battleship *Le Foudroyant*. In the event, when the British took Charleston in 1780, *La Bricole* had been hurriedly stripped of her guns and sunk to block the harbor. Jean Boudriot has kindly supplied details of her design for incorporation into this book.

LA BRICOLE, 44

DATES	LENGTH HULL	LENGTH DECK	LENGTH KEEL	BEAM	DEPTH	DRAFT	TONNAGE B. M.
1759-1780	179	155	138	35	14	17	900

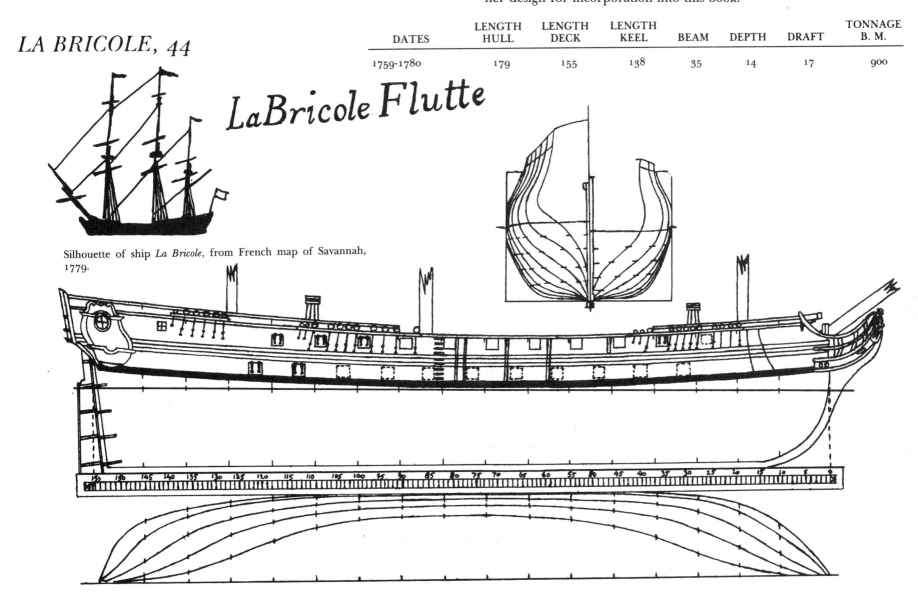

Silhouette of ship *La Bricole*, from French map of Savannah, 1779.

BRILLIANT/DRUID/BLAST, 16

WE know quite a bit about the larger ships that were built in New England and the Middle Colonies, but very little about those built in the South. The merchant ship *Brilliant* was built in Virginia about 1775. She mounted 14 guns, so she could defend herself. Although there is no sign of it on the Admiralty plans of the ship, one writer says that she was fitted with a timber port in the bow, presumably for loading cargos of long-leaf yellow pine, a southern wood. She was actually used principally for transporting tobacco. She was purchased for the Royal Navy in 1776 and renamed *Druid*. She was used as a convoy guard, and in that capacity in September 1777 she frightened off *Alfred* and *Raleigh*, although she suffered considerable damage herself.

In September 1779 she was fitted out as a fireship and renamed *Blast* (a suitable name), but was never used as a fireship so she was sold out of the navy in September 1783.

A large model of *Brilliant* is on display at the Smithsonian Institution, and a small booklet about her was published by the Tobacco Institute.

Her lines are on file at the National Maritime Museum at Greenwich:

BRILLIANT/DRUID/BLAST, 16

DATES	LENGTH HULL	LENGTH DECK	LENGTH KEEL	BEAM	DEPTH	DRAFT	TONNAGE B. M.
ca. 1775-1783	109	89	74	27	12	13	288

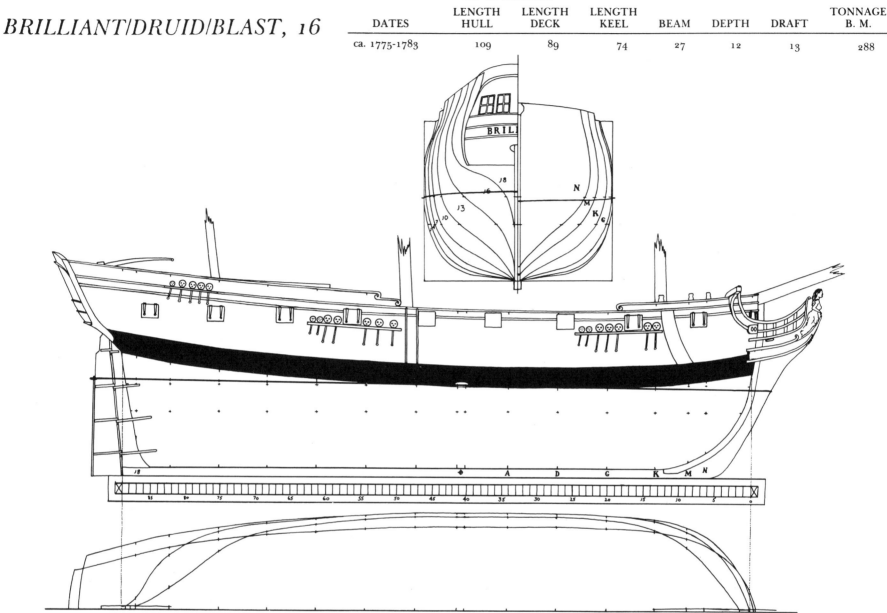

CABOT (ex-SALLY), 14

THE 14-gun brig *Cabot* was one of the first ships to be purchased by the Continental Navy in 1775, although she was not part of the 13 October bill that created the navy, as so many writers have claimed (according to Silas Deane, who seconded the bill, the first two vessels authorized were the sloop *Katy* and the brig *Minerva*). According to the Maryland Gazette of 19 December, 1775, her original name was *Sally* (the same name that the ship *Columbus* had before joining the Continental Navy). Congress renamed her *Cabot* in honor of the fifteenth-century explorer.

Commanded by John B. Hopkins, the son of the commodore, *Cabot* got to sea with the rest of the Continental fleet early in 1776, took part in the raid on Nassau,

and was the first to get into action against the frigate *Glasgow*; Hopkins was wounded in the latter battle, and four of his men were killed on the second broadside. A few months later her command passed to another Rhode Islander, Joseph Olney. Olney got to sea in the spring of 1777 with two Massachusetts Navy brigs, *Massachusetts* and *Tyrannicide*, and conceived a bold plan for the three brigs to capture the British frigate *Milford*, 28 guns. When they got close to their quarry, the two state brigs lost their nerves and abandoned *Cabot*. Olney was trapped and chose to run *Cabot* on the rocks at Chebogue, near Yarmouth, Nova Scotia. *Milford's* crew got her off the rocks and took her into the Royal Navy under the same name. She was the first vessel of the Continental Navy to be captured. She took part in the battle of Dogger Bank in the

North Sea against the Dutch in 1781 and was sold out of the Royal Navy in June 1783.

No plans exist of the original ship, but a complete set of her dimensions was recorded. A spy furnished other details of her appearance: she had a small white head, all her gunports had lids, and she mounted an additional 12 swivel guns. She carried sixteen 6-pounder cannons and 182 men, which must have made her rather crowded. A clear portrait of *Cabot* can be seen in a 1781 oil painting called "Action off the Coast of France;" the painting is the property of the Thomas Coram Foundation for Children, London, for whose benefit Handel played many concerts. She looked very different from the commercial model kit of her that is on the market. The British apparently re-armed her with fourteen 4-pounder guns.

CABOT (ex-SALLY), 14

DATES	LENGTH HULL	LENGTH DECK	LENGTH KEEL	BEAM	DEPTH	DRAFT	TONNAGE B. M.
ca. 1774-1783	88	75	64	25	11	10	189

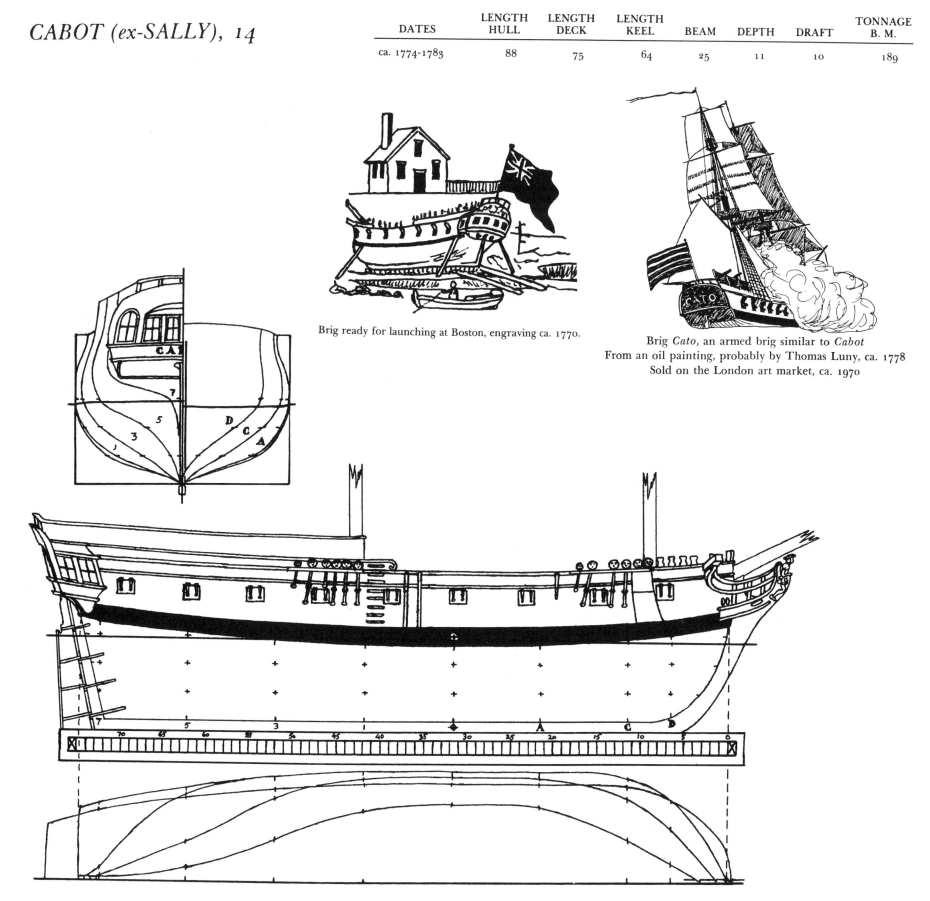

Brig ready for launching at Boston, engraving ca. 1770.

Brig *Cato*, an armed brig similar to *Cabot*
From an oil painting, probably by Thomas Luny, ca. 1778
Sold on the London art market, ca. 1970

Brig *Cabot*, detail of oil painting, possibly by Francis Swaine, 1781, Thomas Coram Foundation, London.

Lieutenant James Josiah, brig *Andrew Doria* (similar to *Cabot*)

CARLETON, 12

WHEN Sir Guy Carleton's Forces chased Benedict Arnold's troops out of Canada in 1776 the British decided to establish a fleet on Lake Champlain. One of these vessels was the little schooner *Carleton*. She mounted 12 guns and had the shallow draft necessary for navigating Lake Champlain. She was placed under the command of Lieutenant J. R. Dacres (we were unable to determine what relation he may have been to Captain Richard Dacres of the frigate *Guerrière* in the War of 1812). She seemed to sail rather better than the other British vessels on the lake, and that got her into trouble. She was the first British vessel to arrive at the American position behind Valcour Island, so she bore the full brunt of the American fire until she was disabled and most of her crew wounded or killed. Finally, to avoid further slaughter, Midshipman Edward Pellew (later Lord Exmouth, the celebrated British admiral), aged nineteen, bravely crawled out on the bowsprit to hold the jib aback in order to turn her away from the battle. She escaped with heavy damage.

No record of her later career has appeared to date; we can assume that she was repaired and used on the lake until the end of the war. There are a number of portraits of her, including several in the Public Archives of Canada and one in the Royal Collection at Windsor Castle. Her lines are on file at the National Maritime Museum, Greenwich.

Schooner *Carleton*, engraving published by Sayer & Bennett, 1776, National Maritime Museum, Greenwich.

DATES	LENGTH HULL	LENGTH DECK	LENGTH KEEL	BEAM	DEPTH	DRAFT	TONNAGE B. M.
1776-ca. 1783	66	59	47	20	7	7	99

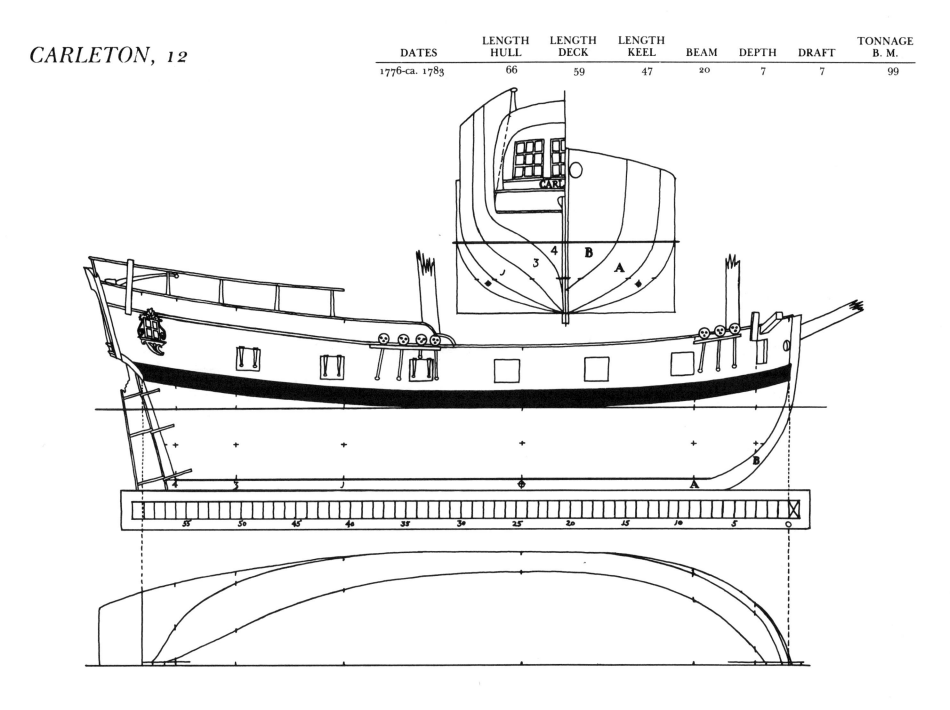

CHALEUR, 8

THE schooner *Chaleur* was built in the 1760s in either New England or Canada. She was purchased for the Royal Navy in 1764 and was thus one of its first schooners. Her purpose was to attempt to curb some of the smuggling that had for long been carried on with impunity by the New England Colonies, particularly Rhode Island. It was thought that a fast hull with a schooner rig would be more likely to catch the smugglers, which were themselves for the most part fast hulls with schooner or sloop rigs. There must have been something wrong with her, perhaps rotten timbers, for she was sold out of the navy at the end of 1768, when the navy had more need of schooners than ever before.

She is variously referred to as a 4-gun, 8-gun, or 12-gun schooner. Her lines show ports for a total of six carriage guns, but there was plenty of room for more ports to be cut later. One account says that she was captured from the French near the American coast by the corvette *Favourite,* but it is unsubstantiated. She was probably built as a merchantman, since she was so burdensome. Her lines are on file at the National Maritime Museum, Greenwich.

CHALEUR, 8

DATES	LENGTH HULL	LENGTH DECK	LENGTH KEEL	BEAM	DEPTH	DRAFT	TONNAGE B. M.
ca. 1762-ca. 1768	76	69	50	20	8	9	121

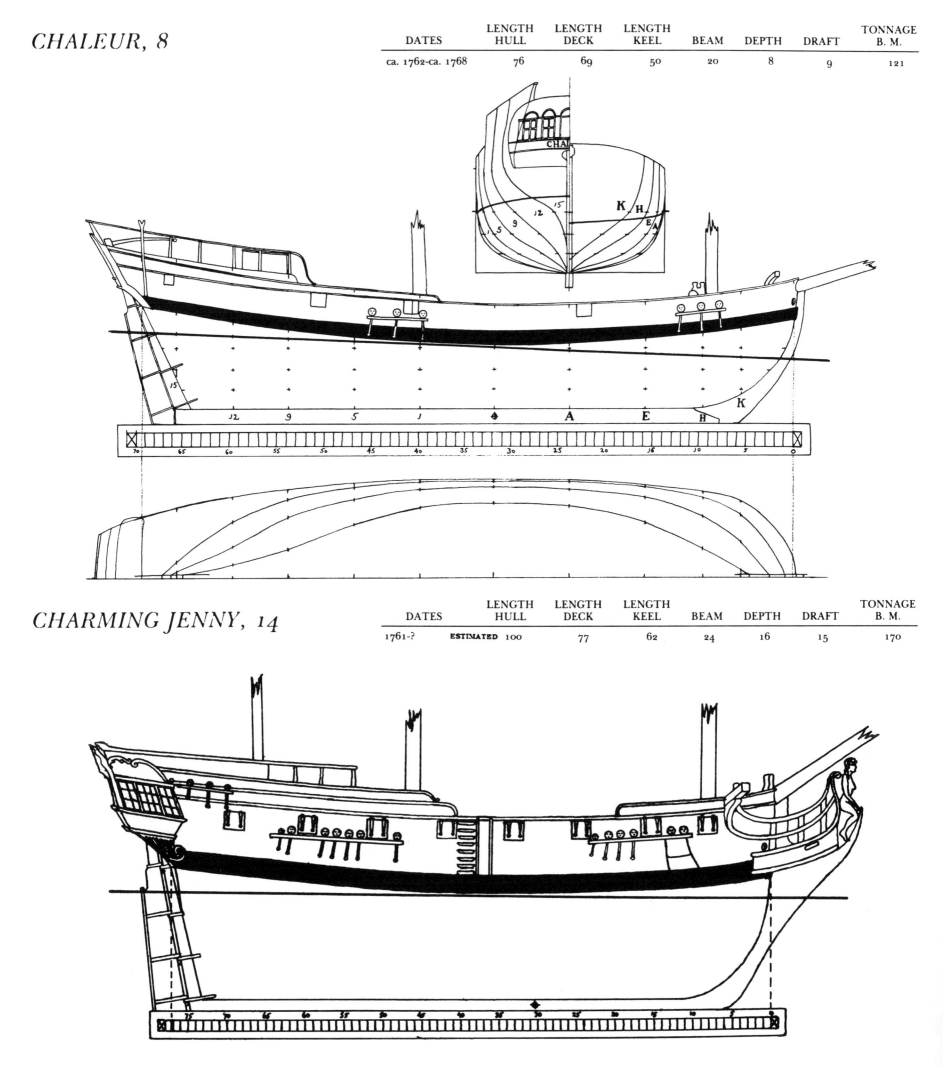

CHARMING JENNY, 14

DATES	LENGTH HULL	LENGTH DECK	LENGTH KEEL	BEAM	DEPTH	DRAFT	TONNAGE B. M.
1761-?	ESTIMATED 100	77	62	24	16	15	170

CHARMING JENNY, 14

IT is thought that something like a third of all the ships in the world flying the British flag in the 1770s were American built or owned. Such ships were commonly known as "plantation built." These ships were frequently built on speculation and sailed over to England (with a cargo, of course) and sold at auction. This kind of sale was often called "sale by the candle," because whoever's bid was on the floor at the time a particular candle went out was the winning bid.

A handbill advertising the "sale by the candle" of the 14-gun plantation-built, square-sterned ship *Charming Jenny* of 170 tons in London in August 1761 has recently been found in London. A fairly detailed portrait of the ship is engraved at the top of the paper, which is something of a rarity. We learn from the advertisement that she was regarded as suitable for trade with Virginia or the West Indies or in the North Sea,

and that her captain was Joseph Todd. Since Britain was at war with France and Spain in 1761 the 14 guns that she carried were a necessary part of her, although one suspects that the buyer would have to buy the guns separately, because they are not listed in the accompanying inventory of her gear.

For S A L E by the CANDLE
The good Ship *Charming Jenny*

CODRINGTON/CHEROKEE/DESPATCH, 6

A FINE merchant ship was built at Newburyport, Massachusetts, in 1773, possibly by Greenleaf or Cross. She was unarmed and was named *Codrington*, probably after the wealthy family of that name in Barbados. A large number of British-owned ships were built in North America, so it was not unusual for this ship to be purchased by the Royal Navy in September 1774. She was renamed *Cherokee* and fitted out with six three-pounder carriage guns, eight swivel guns, and 30 men for service in the southern part of North America doing survey work. After the Revolutionary War broke out in earnest, she was converted into a transport and renamed *Despatch* in April 1777. She was well suited to being a transport, having about as much carrying capacity as it is possible to build into a ship of her length, and she sailed well after the mainmast had been nudged forward a little. Nothing is known about her after this date. Her lines are on file at the National Maritime Museum, Greenwich.

Boston merchant ship on ceramic mug with legend, "Robt. H. Wilson 1784 Boston," formerly in Sussel Collection.

Boston merchant ship, woodcut on broadside about Boston Tea Party.

71

DATES	LENGTH HULL	LENGTH DECK	LENGTH KEEL	BEAM	DEPTH	DRAFT	TONNAGE B. M.
1773-?	88	77	60	24	17	14	178

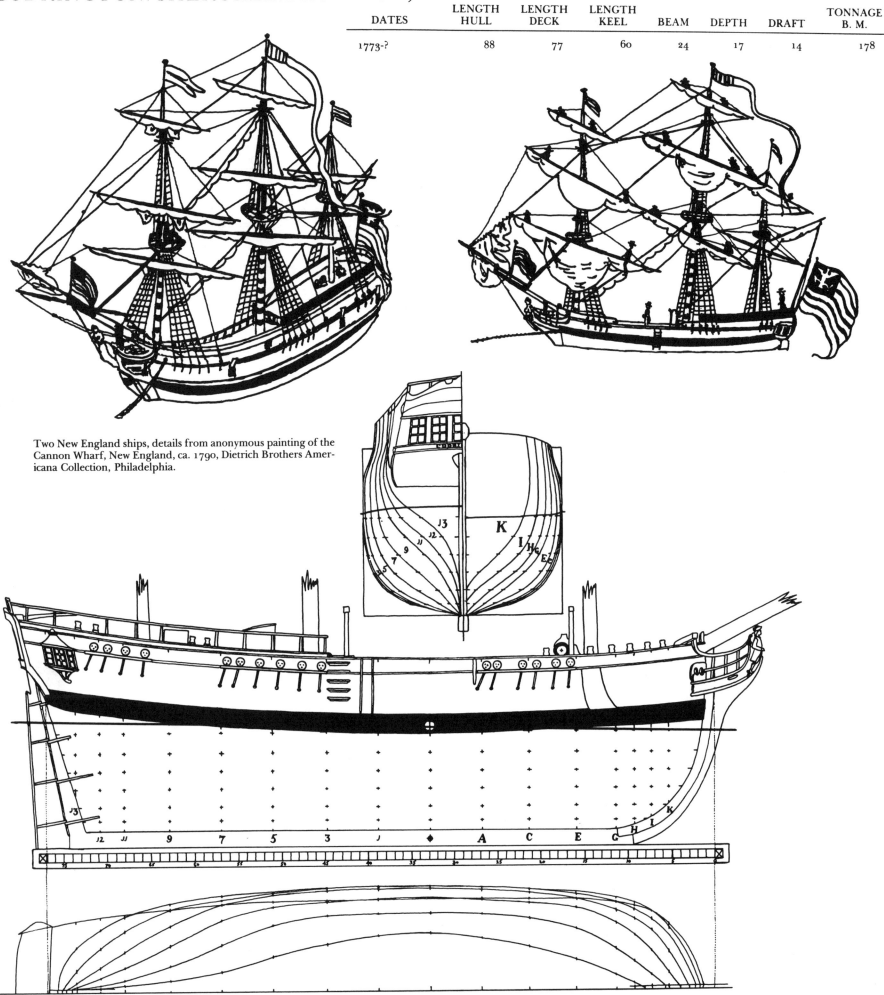

Two New England ships, details from anonymous painting of the Cannon Wharf, New England, ca. 1790, Dietrich Brothers Americana Collection, Philadelphia.

COLUMBIA REDIVIVA

The little merchant ship *Columbia* has been the subject of much disagreement among maritime historians. One side says that she was built in Scituate, Massachusetts in 1773 on the same slipway that had launched the Boston Tea Party brig *Beaver* the previous year. The other side says that she was built at Plymouth, Massachusetts in 1787 (and that the brig Beaver had been built in Rhode Island in 1770, according to *Lloyd's Register*). As the late William Baker has shown, the latter is at least partially correct. However, her full name was *Columbia Rediviva* (rediviva is Latin for "brought back to life"), and it is possible that she was so renamed, being an older ship that had required rebuilding in 1787. Under the command of John Kendrick of Wareham, Massachusetts, she left Boston in September 1787 to hunt seals and otters on the West Coast. Her consort, the sloop *Lady Washington*, arrived in Oregon a week before *Columbia* and was fiercely attacked by Indians. The two ships managed to trade with other Indians and then took the furs they had obtained to Canton, China. In China, Kendrick took command of *Lady Washington* and ordered Robert Gray of Tiverton, Rhode Island to give up his place as captain of the sloop to move up to command of *Columbia*. *Columbia* then sailed home after exchanging the furs for tea. She reached Boston in August 1790, the first ship to fly the American flag around the world.

She was received in Boston with great celebration, made the more exciting because she had brought back Attoo, a young chief from the Sandwich Islands (Hawaii) who marched in the welcoming parade in his full regalia. In spite of the fanfare, however, the voyage was a financial flop for her backers, who had put up the then-large sum of $50,000. But some of the backers were undaunted and they sent Gray and *Columbia* out again in the autumn of 1790. On this voyage Gray discovered the Columbia River (which he named after the ship), a fact that gave the United States a stronger claim to the land on the West Coast than Spain, Great Britain, or Russia, all of whom said that they had been there first. While there he met the British explorer George Vancouver. Gray returned in 1793 to learn that the second voyage had also been a financial failure and that the ship had to be sold at auction immediately. In 1792, Gray had built a small sloop in Oregon called *Adventure*. He had brought her frames out with him in *Columbia*'s hold. She was the first United States vessel to be built on the West Coast, although the British explorer Meares had built one there as early as 1788, and the Russians built their *Feniks* there in 1794. *Columbia* was broken up in 1801 after several years in the Havana trade.

No plans of *Columbia* have survived, but we do know some of her dimensions and there are a number of well-executed contemporary portraits of her; we have based our drawing on these. Disneyland in California has an operational, full-size copy of her on display, and it appears to be accurate, which is more than one can usually say for Hollywood's excursions into history. At the time of writing, a West Coast group is planning to build full-size, sailing copies of both *Columbia* and *Lady Washington* for the Bicentenary of their historic 1788 arrival in Oregon, Washington and British Columbia.

Ship *Columbia* in the Pacific Northwest, Robert Haswell, 1788, Massachusetts Historical Society.

Ship *Columbia* wintering in the Pacific Northwest, 1792, drawing by George Davidson, private collection.

Ship *Columbia Rediviva*, being attacked by Indian war canoes in the Pacific Northwest
From a painting by a sailor in her crew, dated 1792

Ship *Columbia* attacked at night by Indians at Chickleset, Vancouver Island, 1792, by George Davidson, Oregon Historical Society.

Ship *Columbia* with brig *Hancock* in the Pacific Northwest, Robert Haswell, 1791, Massachusetts Historial Society.

COLUMBIA REDIVIVA

DATES	LENGTH HULL	LENGTH DECK	LENGTH KEEL	BEAM	DEPTH	DRAFT	TONNAGE B. M.
1773/1787-1801	103	86	72	24	12	13	212

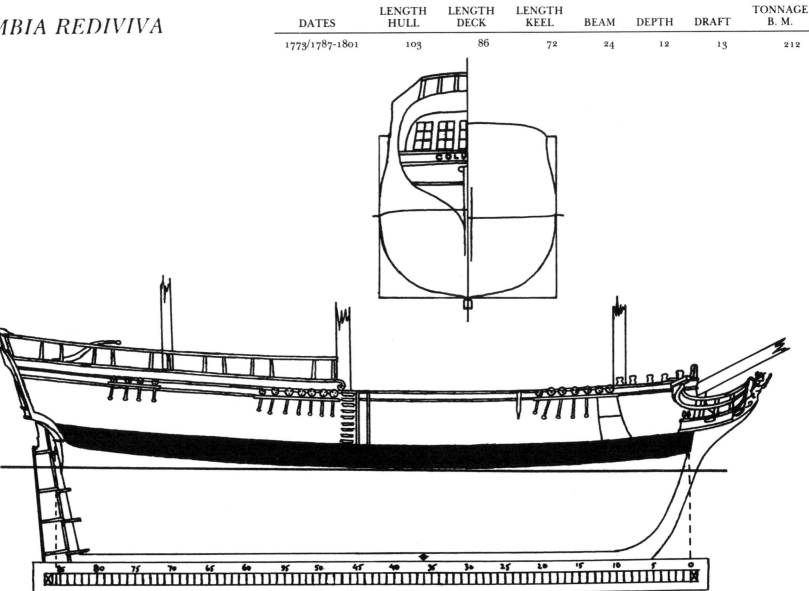

	DATES	LENGTH HULL	LENGTH DECK	LENGTH KEEL	BEAM	DEPTH	DRAFT	TONNAGE B. M.
	ca. 1773-1778 **ESTIMATED**	98	89	73	27	12	14	270

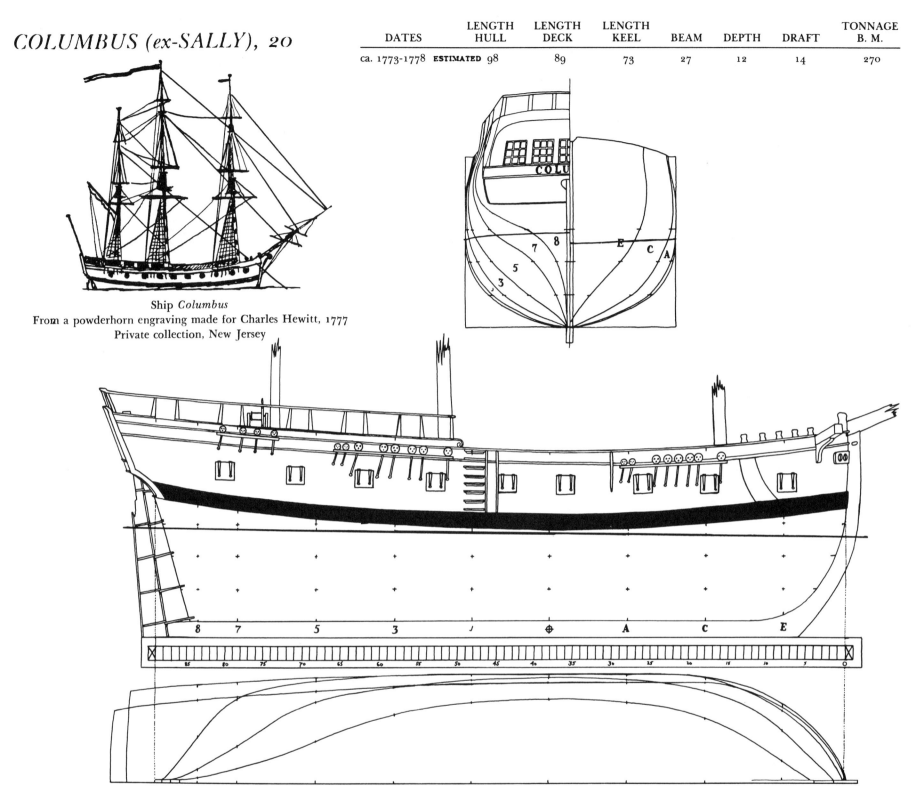

Ship *Columbus*
From a powderhorn engraving made for Charles Hewitt, 1777
Private collection, New Jersey

COLUMBUS (ex-SALLY), 20

ONE of the members of the first fleet of the Continental Navy in 1775 was the ship *Columbus*. She had formerly been the Philadelphia merchant ship *Sally,* and must have looked a lot like *Alfred* except for the fact that she had no head. According to the report of a British spy, she was painted all black. She mounted anywhere from 20 to 28 guns at various times, arranged with 18 on the gun deck and as many as required on the quarterdeck, and even on the waist. She had been built by Wharton & Humphreys.

Her first navy captain was Abraham Whipple, and she took part in the expedition to Nassau. She was blanketed by the other ships in the battle against the frigate *Glasgow,* and so did not actually take part in that action, apart from having one man hurt. After a brief stint at anchor in Providence, Rhode Island, Whipple took *Columbus* to sea on 16 June, only to run into the 28-gun British frigate *Cerberus,* which managed to pour three broadsides into *Columbus,* killing one man and cutting up her rigging rather badly; *Columbus* hit *Cerberus* with one answering broadside before escaping. She returned to Providence and found herself trapped there when a British fleet occupied Narragansett Bay in December 1776. She did not get to sea at all in 1777.

In the meantime Hoysted Hacker had been made her captain. He tried to get her to sea on a black night in March 1778; he had unloaded all her guns and stores first, so as to make her faster and so that the British would not get much if they captured her. The British

ships stumbled onto her by accident and forced Hacker to run her aground at Point Judith, where he stripped her of everything valuable. In the morning of 28 March the British burned her.

There are no surviving plans of *Columbus*, nor even dimensions, although there is a crude picture of her scratched on a powderhorn engraving of Providence in would not get much if they captured her. The British February 1777.

CONFEDERACY, BOURBON & [un-named], 36

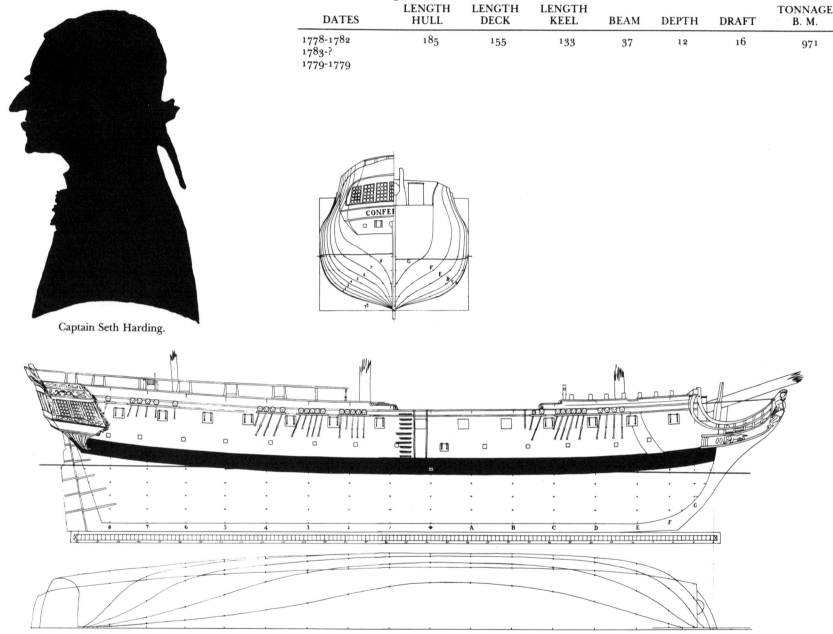

DATES	LENGTH HULL	LENGTH DECK	LENGTH KEEL	BEAM	DEPTH	DRAFT	TONNAGE B. M.
1778-1782 1783-? 1779-1779	185	155	133	37	12	16	971

Captain Seth Harding.

CONFE

CONFEDERACY, BOURBON & [un-named], 36

Among the ships authorized by Congress on 20 November 1776 were five frigates of 36 guns. Of these, *Alliance* was built in New Hampshire to local designs, an unnamed ship being built in Virginia was burned on the stocks by a British raiding party, and *Confederacy* and *Bourbon* were both built in Connecticut. Funds were lacking, which delayed construction of those that were built, and quite likely the fifth authorized frigate was never even begun for that reason.

Confederacy was launched in 1778, having been built on the Thames River at Norwich, Connecticut, by Jedediah Willets. The design was furnished by Congress, and is obviously related to the designs of the frigate *Randolph* and the 74-gun *America*. She was an unusually large ship for her rate and she was heavily ornamented with carving, which is surprising in view of the shortage of money. Although the hull form was quite sharp, making her potentially fast, she still retained the beakhead bulkhead which had been discarded by other frigate designers a long time previously. Her gun deck was pierced with fourteen ports per side, and it was high enough out of the water to allow for a complete deck of oarports, plus a loading port below the gun deck but above the wale. Her keel was slightly rockered forward, for no apparent reason.

In 1779, Captain Seth Harding was assigned to *Confederacy,* but he had so much trouble recruiting a crew that he impressed some French prisoners as they were released by the British on an exchange; this got him into trouble, so he was obliged to release the Frenchmen. On her first voyage *Confederacy* was ordered to take John Jay, U.S. ambassador to Spain, to his post, and Monsieur Gérard, French ambassador to the United States, back to France. To avoid the likelihood of contact with enemy ships, they took a circuitous route and on 7 November 1779 *Confederacy* was savaged by a hurricane, which neatly removed the bowsprit, all three masts, and the rudder. She put into Martinique for a few months of temporary repairs while the ambassadors continued to Europe on a French ship. Then she returned to Philadelphia for complete repairs in May 1780. She cruised in the Delaware River in company with the frigate *Boston.* In the spring of 1781 she went to the West Indies to escort home a large convoy, in company with the frigate *Deane* and the corvette *Saratoga,* and she herself was heavily laden with goods. She

was fallen upon by the 44-gun *Roebuck,* and the brand-new 32-gun frigate *Orpheus,* so Seth Harding surrendered without firing a shot. She was taken into the Royal Navy under the name of *Confederate,* but was broken up in March 1782. She was probably rotten.

As for *Bourbon,* she was not even laid down until early 1780 (at Middletown, Connecticut) and was launched in July 1783 into the Connecticut River. Still incomplete, she was sold in September 1783 by a Congress that had no further use for her. She would have been well-suited to service as an East Indiaman. She was bought unfinished and completed as a merchant ship by Daniel Parker of Philadelphia, who also owned the ship *Empress of China.* He sent her to Cadiz in 1784. It is not certain that she was built to the same design as *Confederacy;* it seems likely that she was, although perhaps a round bow was substituted for the vulnerable and out-of-date beakhead bulkhead.

The other frigate, built at Gosport, Virginia (near Portsmouth and Norfolk), was nowhere near finished when a British force occupied the area. The frigate, according to Sir George Collier, commander of the 44-gun *Rainbow,* was burned along with over 130 other ships in the area. It is likely that this frigate was identical to *Confederacy.*

No contemporary portraits survive of any of these three ships, but the British thoughtfully took off *Confederacy*'s lines, and these are the source for our plans.

CONGRESS, 32

AFTER only one of the initial four frigates built at Philadelphia managed to get to sea under American colors, Congress was understandably reluctant to order any more major warships built at Philadelphia. However, the shipyards were still there, and one of them turned out a fine frigate of 32 guns to be used as a privateer by Philadelphia merchants. She was named *Congress* and placed under the command of George Geddes as soon as she was finished in 1781. She took part in a bloody battle in September 1781 off Charleston against the 14-gun British corvette *Savage. Savage* was captured, but *Congress* suffered 8 killed and 30 wounded out of her crew of 215, and had to put into port for repairs. *Savage* was later retaken by the British frigate *Solebay* and sent into Charleston for repairs. *Congress* herself was captured not long after that, but she was not taken into the Royal Navy. (Chapelle errs when he says that the Philadelphia privateer *Congress* was captured and taken into the Royal Navy as *General Monk; General Monk* was formerly the Rhode Island privateer *General Washington.*)

Congress was renamed *Duchess of Cumberland* under British ownership and commanded by Samuel Marsh. In September 1781, she was sent to Saint John's, Newfoundland with a number of American prisoners aboard, to pick up more Americans and convey them to English prisons.

However, before she reached Newfoundland she was wrecked on a remote island on the night of the 19th, and twenty of her 170 people were lost.   There is a report that the famous Captain Thomas Truxtun served on her as a young lieutenant, but it could easily have been another ship called *Congress,* as there were naturally many of that name.

There are no surviving portraits of *Congress,* nor any plans. However, the British did record some of her dimensions, and these show, as might be expected, that she was nearly identical to the Philadelphia-built frigate *Randolph.* Accordingly, our plan shows a version of the *Randolph* plan, minus the outmoded beakhead bulkhead. One source says that *Congress* was built in the Eyre shipyard along with another frigate named *Franklin* of unspecified size.

Colonel Jehu Eyre of the Philadelphia firm of shipbuilders.

CONGRESS, *32*

DATES	LENGTH HULL	LENGTH DECK	LENGTH KEEL	BEAM	DEPTH	DRAFT	TONNAGE B. M.
ca. 1781-1781	154	131	108	33	17	16	685

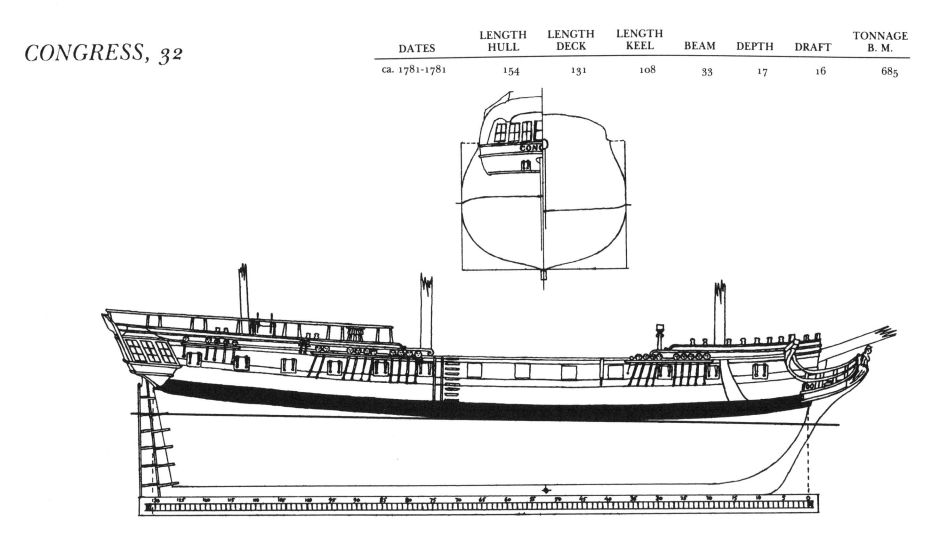

CONQUISTADOR (*ex-*JESUS, MARIA Y JOSÉ), *60*

DATES	LENGTH HULL	LENGTH DECK	LENGTH KEEL	BEAM	DEPTH	DRAFT	TONNAGE B. M.
1745-1782	189	156	137	44	20	22	1278

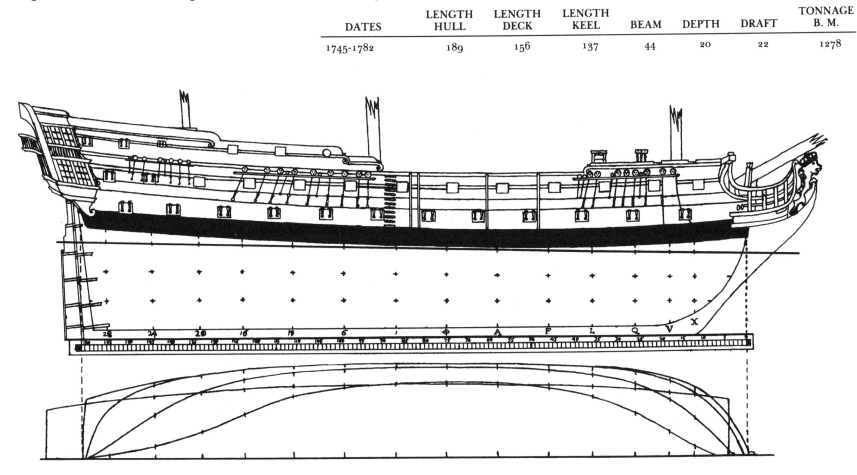

CONQUISTADOR (ex-JESUS, MARIA Y JOSÉ), 60

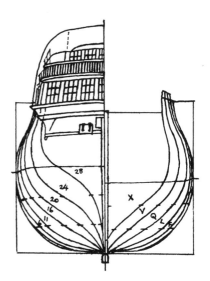

THE Spanish Navy was quick to take advantage of the excellent strength and durability of the special kind of mahogany that grew in Cuba (but which is now believed to be extinct), and built some of its finest ships in Cuba (see the entry under the ship *Santísima Trinidad* for a list of some of these ships). The Spanish usually hired master shipwrights from England and France to design and supervise construction, which explains why many of these ships looked more like British or French ships than the Spanish ships built on the west coast of South America. One such ship was *Conquistador* (spelled *Conquestator* in British records). This ship of 60 guns was built as the 70-gun ship *Jesus, Maria y José* in 1745 and later renamed. She stood particularly high out of the water. The British captured her in 1762 and found her to be still useful until 1782, when she was scrapped, although she had spent her last seven years limited to harbor service. Her plans, as taken off in a British dockyard, are preserved at the Science Museum, London.

LA COUREUSE

DATES	LENGTH HULL	LENGTH DECK	LENGTH KEEL	BEAM	DEPTH	DRAFT	TONNAGE B. M.
ca. 1785-ca. 1796	57	53	39	16	6	8	55

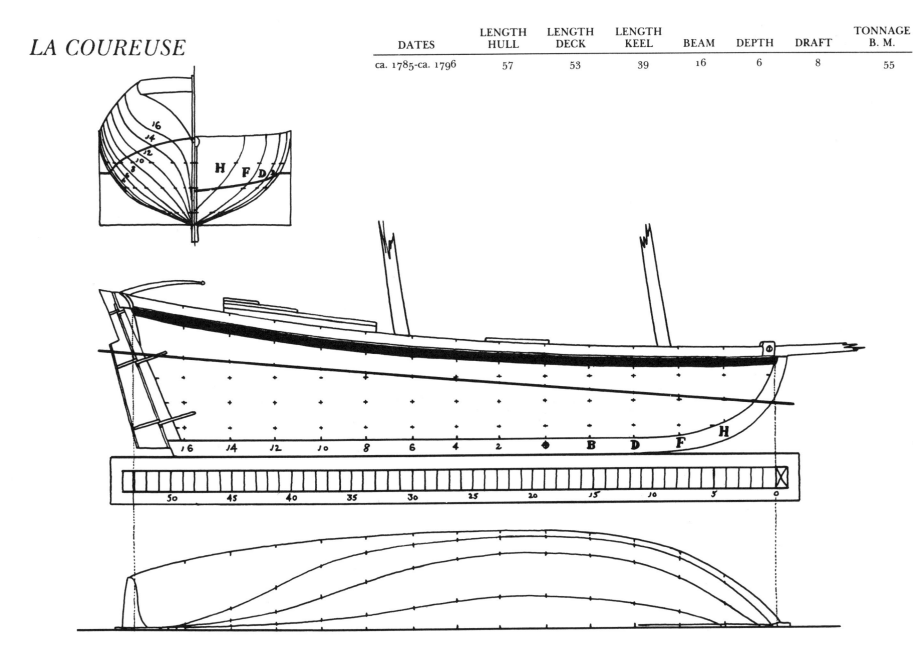

LA COUREUSE

WHEN the American Revolution was over and there was therefore no further need at the moment for fast privateer schooners, designers who knew the secrets of building fast schooners set their hands at building pilot schooners. With a fast schooner, a pilot could get aboard an incoming ship much sooner, and theoretically could thus pilot more ships in a given day and so derive a greater profit. One of these schooners was built at New York around 1785. When the French Revolution got under way she was purchased by some French Republicans, who renamed her *La Coureuse* and installed her in the French Republican Navy.

She was sighted by the British frigates *Pomone, Artois,* and *Galatea* off Isle Groix as she was guarding a convoy. The rest of the convoy was captured, but *La Coureuse* was not taken until the end of a nineteen-hour chase on 27 February 1795, which means that she was very fast if she could stay ahead of large and fast frigates. She carried eight two-pounder cannons, plus six swivels, but since these were added by the French we have omitted them from the drawing. Her crew numbered 23. Her lines were taken off at Plymouth Dockyard, and they are on file at the National Maritime Museum, Greenwich. After that, she was sent to the Mediterranean as a dispatch vessel for the Royal Navy, with a crew of 36. She was paid off in September 1796 and probably sold, but no record of her survives after this date.

This little schooner had a square-tuck stern, considerable drag to the keel, moderate deadrise, and slack bilges with quite a flair to the topsides. She had a trunk cabin aft, and her masts were apparently unstayed except for a forestay. She had a simple rig of only three sails. She would not be far out of place if used today as a yacht.

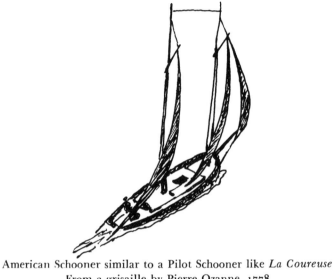

American Schooner similar to a Pilot Schooner like *La Coureuse*
From a grisaille by Pierre Ozanne, 1778
Le Musée de la Marine, Paris

CUPID, 14

DATES	LENGTH HULL	LENGTH DECK	LENGTH KEEL	BEAM	DEPTH	DRAFT	TONNAGE B. M.
ca. 1774-1778	111	93	75	27	12	16	290

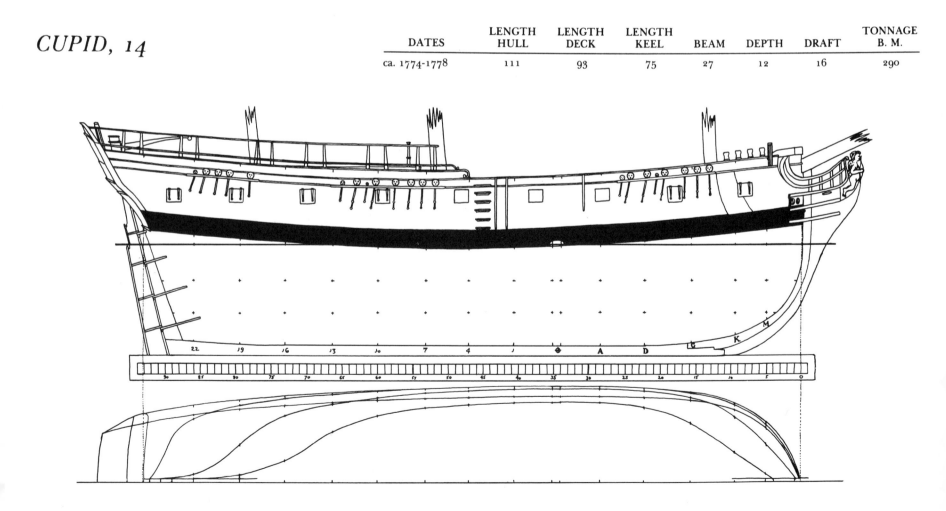

CUPID, 14

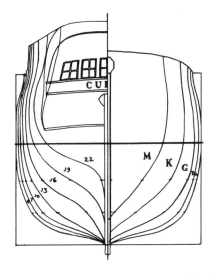

THE 14-gun armed merchant ship *Cupid* was purchased by the Royal Navy in 1777. She was presumably used as a convoy guard, but little is known of her. She foundered in a bad storm off the coast of Newfoundland on 28 December, 1778. She had an open waist that was not found on many American merchant ships of her size. It is reported that she had been built in Newfoundland about 1774. Her original name is unknown. Her plans are on file at the National Maritime Museum, Greenwich.

DEANE/HAGUE, 32

THE 32-gun frigate *Deane* was built at Nantes, France, in 1777 to the order of the American commissioners in Paris. She was a very small ship for her rate, partly so as not to attract the attention of British spies and partly because the commissioners had little money to spend. In fact, the French asked 58,000 Livres for the ship, but American agent John Williams, Jr. had to negotiate the price down to 55,500 at several months' credit. The ship was apparently going to be built regardless, for the shipyard had an alternate French buyer, who intended to name her *Le Lyon*. With Samuel Nicholson in command, *Deane* arrived in Boston in May 1778, where she had to stay for several months because of a shortage of crew and the severity of the British blockade.

On 14 January 1779 she left on a cruise on which she captured a 16-gun British ship called *Viper*, burned a London merchant ship, captured six prizes in the West Indies, and arrived at Philadelphia on 17 April. She left Philadelphia on 1 July, and by 27 July, so we are told, captured sixteen enemy vessels between the Delaware and the Chesapeake, and then captured two more while she was in company with *Boston*. She returned to New England where she was idled for want of a crew. In March 1781 she sailed with *Confederacy* and *Saratoga* to escort a rich convoy from the West Indies, returning to Boston where she was once more left without a crew.

She had been named *Deane* after Silas Deane, who had seconded the bill that had founded the navy in October 1775. However, in 1782 Silas Deane had publicly advocated reunion with Britain, so he was branded a traitor and forced into exile. In 1782 the frigate was renamed *Hague*, after the capital city of Holland, the latest ally of the United States. In September 1782 her original captain was replaced by John Manley who took her immediately to Martinique, making a number of captures on the way. After she left

Martinique once more, she captured a rich prize called *Baille* about 7 January 1783, the last significant prize of the war. On 9 January she was chased for thirty-six hours by five larger British warships until she ran aground on a reef off Guadeloupe. She remained aground for two days while the British kept up a long-range bombardment. Finally she got off and escaped to the protection of a French fort. She had completed repairs by 26 January and sailed for Boston, where she arrived in May 1783, some time after peace had been declared. As soon as *Hague* arrived, Captain Manley was arrested on trumped-up charges which appear later to have been dropped. *Hague* herself, one of the navy's last four ships, was left idle until she was sold at auction on 2 October 1783.

One account says that *Deane*'s plans were sent to Congress for approval before she was built, but the plans have never been found. We do know her dimensions, and we do know that she carried 24 twelve-pounder cannons, eight four-pounders on the quarterdeck, and two six-pounders on the forecastle; she therefore had the configuration of a standard French frigate, even if she was on the small size. Some writers have contended that she had two complete gun decks of 16 guns each, but this is clearly nonsense. We have taken the lines of a number of smaller French warships and combined features from them with what we already knew about *Deane* to produce the reconstruction of her lines shown here.   It will be seen that although she carried more and heavier guns she was approximately the same size as the 24-gun frigates *Boston* and *Delaware*.

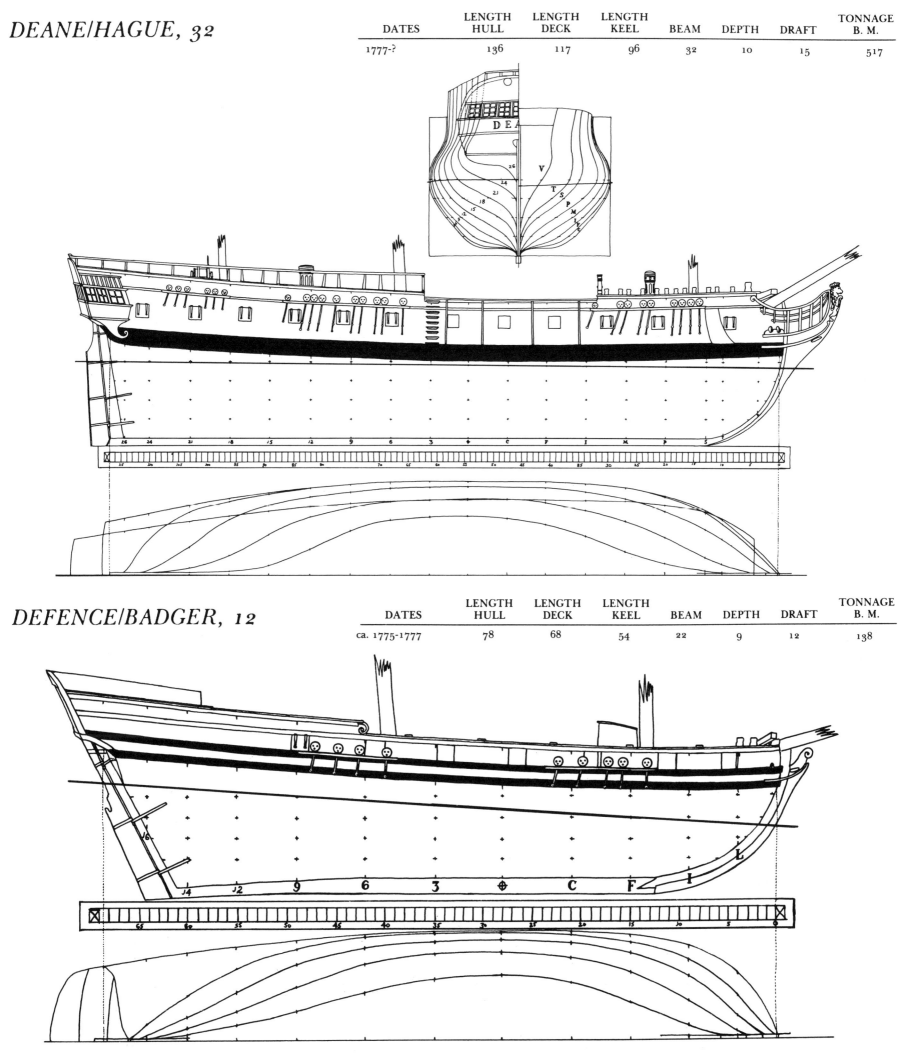

DEANE/HAGUE, 32

DATES	LENGTH HULL	LENGTH DECK	LENGTH KEEL	BEAM	DEPTH	DRAFT	TONNAGE B. M.
1777-?	136	117	96	32	10	15	517

DEFENCE/BADGER, 12

DATES	LENGTH HULL	LENGTH DECK	LENGTH KEEL	BEAM	DEPTH	DRAFT	TONNAGE B. M.
ca. 1775-1777	78	68	54	22	9	12	138

DEFENCE/BADGER, 12

Horatio Nelson

A FINE brig that had been built in the Chesapeake Bay area around 1775 found her way into the Royal Navy in 1776. Vice Admiral Clark Gayton named her *Badger* and rated her at 14 guns, although it seems she actually carried ten 4-pounders. Some records suggest that she had earlier had the name *Pitt*, but Chapelle believes she had been the privateer *Defence*. Gayton praised her performance highly, saying that she had captured 22 American ships in two cruises. He sent her to England in the summer of 1777, where she was put in the Portsmouth drydock for cleaning, repairs and drawing her lines. She returned to the West Indies in September 1777 with 90 crewmen, but she was in such poor condition that thought was given to replacing her. So many vessels in the Royal Navy were named *Badger* at this time that it is confusing to follow their careers. At least one remained on the Navy lists until 1783, and it may well have been this one. If so, she was commanded in 1778 and 1779 by young Horatio Nelson.

Typical of Chesapeake boats, she had a coach roof aft for her captain's cabin, but unlike others she had a small billet head on her stem. Her keel had plenty of drag and was built with an intentional hog in it, which makes taking off her lines rather difficult.

Her lines are preserved at the National Maritime Museum at Greenwich.

DELAWARE/DAUPHIN/UNITED STATES, MONTGOMERY & HERO, 24

TWO of the original thirteen frigates authorized by Congress in 1775 were *Montgomery* and *Delaware*, both of 24 guns and both apparently built from the plans approved by Congress. *Montgomery* was built in 1776 by Lancaster Burling at Poughkeepsie, New York, on the Hudson. Since the British occupied New York City and Lake Champlain, it was decided in October 1777 to burn and sink both the *Montgomery* and the 28-gun frigate *Congress,* which was built in the same town at the same time. Some historians think that the wrecks of these two frigates still lie undiscovered in the Hudson ten miles downriver from where they were built, just waiting for a concerted effort of underwater archaeology. *Montgomery*'s captain was to have been John Hodge of New York.

Delaware, on the other hand, was built at Philadelphia by Warwick Coates, and was completed in time to be employed on the Delaware River in operations against the British fleet that advanced up the Delaware in 1777. Her captain, Charles Alexander, was placed under the orders of Commodore John Hazelwood of the Pennsylvania State Navy. *Delaware,* in company with the Pennsylvania State Navy corvette *Montgomery,* came down the river on 27 September 1777 to attack British gun emplacements. Alexander anchored 500 yards away from the guns, but when the tide went out *Delaware* was hard aground. British gunners, having stepped up their shooting, soon had her on fire, and Alexander reluctantly had to surrender the most powerful ship then on the river.

The British got her off the mud and incorporated her into the Royal Navy. She remained for a time with the fleet that was proceeding up the river to Philadelphia.

A tiny sketch of her, marked "frégate," appears on a French map of the British operations on the Delaware that is in the possession of the Musée de la Marine in Paris. On 9 March 1779, she took part in the capture of the Connecticut State Navy ship *Oliver Cromwell* of about 20 guns.

Delaware was sold by the Royal Navy at the end of the war on 14 April 1783. She was acquired by Mary Hayley, an English widow living in Boston, Massachusetts. Mrs. Hayley amused herself by immediately renaming her *United States,* which she thought would annoy British authorities, and she used the ship for whaling, sealing, and trading. *United States* had to visit such out-of-the-way places as the Falkland Islands to do her mistress's bidding. The ship was then sold to French owners, who renamed her *Le Dauphin,* and there is a suggestion that they used her for whaling. In 1794 she was sold at auction in Charleston, South Carolina, and bought by a French privateer captain with the improbable name of Jean Bouteille. British consular officials were alarmed at this turn of events, and they combined with American officials to try to prevent Bouteille from doing anything with his new acquisition. Nevertheless, he fitted her out once more as a warship, and removed her quarter galleries and "upper deck," and painted her all black. The desired result was that she should look like an innocent merchant ship, so that she could blend in with British convoys unnoticed. The last record of her was her departure from Charleston for Port de Paix in 1795. It is quite likely that the tired old ship foundered in a gale in the West Indies soon after that date. In any event, she was clearly the last survivor of the original thirteen frigates authorized by Congress in 1775.

Her design, as approved by Congress, is said to have been modeled closely on a Philadelphia privateer frigate called *Hero* that fought successfully in the Seven Years' War in the 1760s, and this may explain the out-of-date beakhead bulkhead that appears to have been used in so many of the Philadelphia-designed warships of the Revolution. The official designs of the 28-gun frigates and the 32-gun frigates are said to have been merely scaled-up versions of *Delaware*'s plans. Since the plans of one each of the 28- and 32-gun frigates survive, we have scaled them down to the dimensions of *Delaware*, as recorded by the British, for the British apparently did not see fit to record her actual lines. The British used her as a 28-gun frigate, so we have made sure that her design had enough room for 28 guns.

Even if, as is assumed here, *Montgomery* and *Delaware* were built to identical designs, they were armed differently. *Delaware* was supposed to have had twenty-four 9-pounders, but, due to problems at the foundry, she was given larger guns that had been intended for the frigate *Washington*: twenty-two 12-pounders and six 6-pounders. *Montgomery*, on the other hand, was to have had only twenty 9-pounders and four 4-pounders.

DELAWARE/DAUPHIN/UNITED STATES, MONTGOMERY & HERO, 24

DATES	LENGTH HULL	LENGTH DECK	LENGTH KEEL	BEAM	DEPTH	DRAFT	TONNAGE B. M.
1776-ca. 1795	142	119	96	32	10	14	563
1776-1777							
ca. 1760-?							

Frégate

Frigate *Delaware*
Detail from a French map of the Delaware, 1778
Le Musée de la Marine, Paris

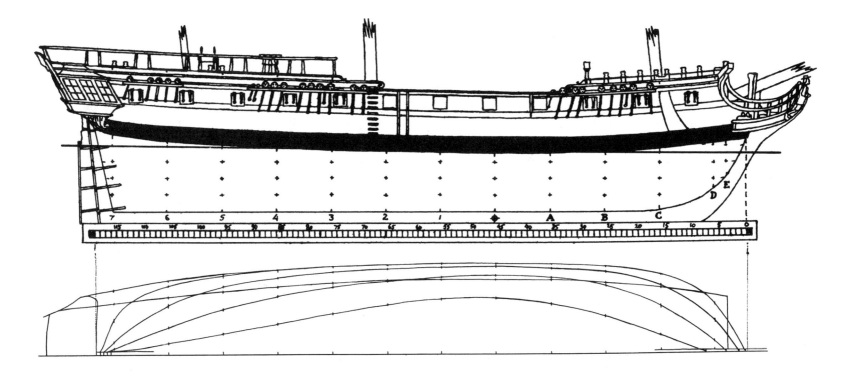

	DATES	LENGTH HULL	LENGTH DECK	LENGTH KEEL	BEAM	DEPTH	DRAFT	TONNAGE B. M.
	1739-?	ESTIMATED 79	66	57	18	8	10	90

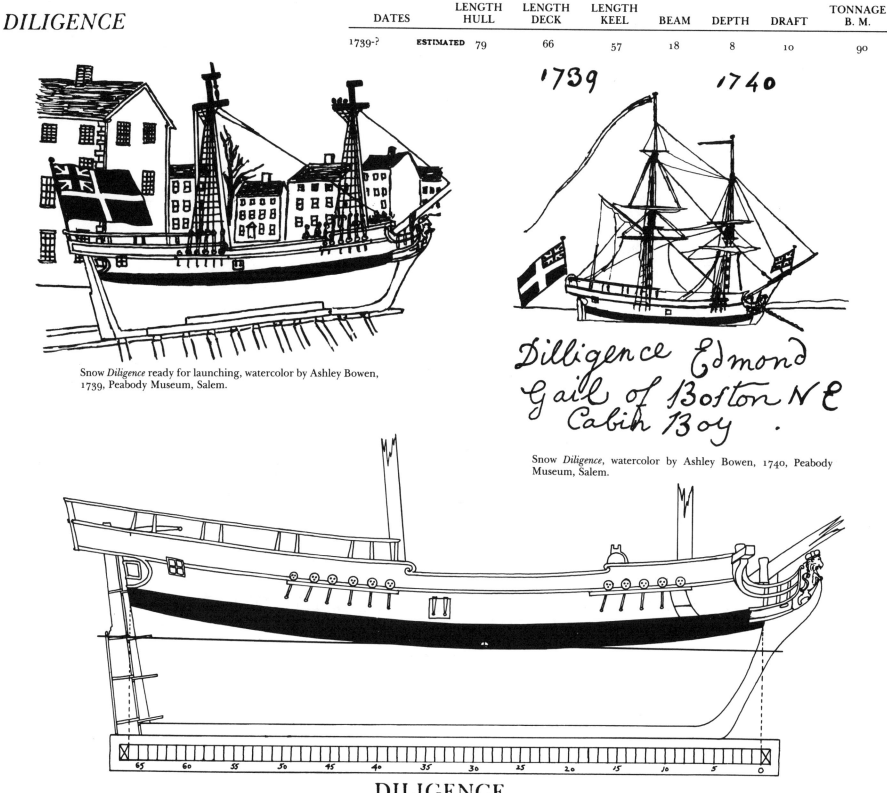

1739   1740

Snow *Diligence* ready for launching, watercolor by Ashley Bowen, 1739, Peabody Museum, Salem.

Dilligence Edmond
Gail of Boston N E
Cabin Boy .

Snow *Diligence*, watercolor by Ashley Bowen, 1740, Peabody Museum, Salem.

DILIGENCE

THE pink-sterned (not the color, but the shape!) snow *Diligence* was built in Boston in 1739, designed to be an all-purpose trading and fishing vessel. She was loaded with fish bound for Bilbao Spain, but news of the outbreak of hostilities between Britain and Spain (the War of Jenkins' Ear) arrived before she could set sail. Her cargo was taken off again and she was sent empty to the Cape Fear River, North Carolina, to load with tar for Bristol, England. At Bristol many of her crew were impressed into the Royal Navy. She then moved further down the Severn estuary to Swansea, Wales, where she took a load of coal back to Boston. That is about all we know of her history.

The Marblehead seaman Ashley Bowen, then aged eleven years, sailed on her during this time, and he recorded not only what happened but the appearance of the vessel. He even painted a watercolor picture of her before she was launched, which has served as the basis for our profile drawing. One useful feature that is prominent in her design is the loadingport in the stern, which would permit her to load large pieces of timber, some of which might be used for spars by a ship in some faraway port.

	DATES	LENGTH HULL	LENGTH DECK	LENGTH KEEL	BEAM	DEPTH	DRAFT	TONNAGE B. M.
	fl. 1777 ESTIMATED	63	56	47	19	10	11	90

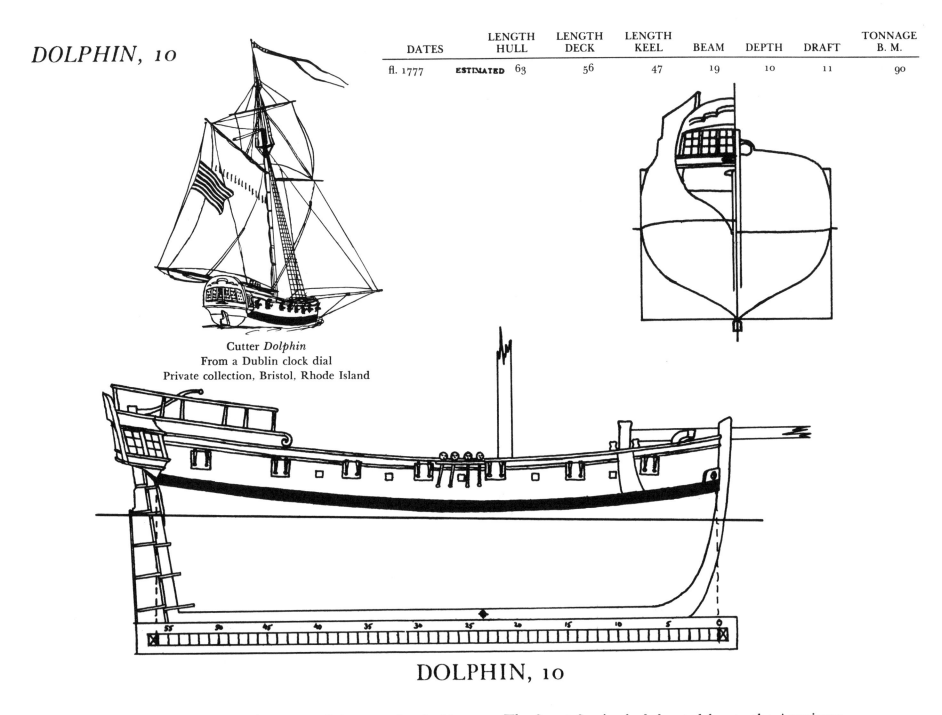

Cutter *Dolphin*
From a Dublin clock dial
Private collection, Bristol, Rhode Island

DOLPHIN, 10

Aℕ oil painting of a cutter flying a red-and-white-striped flag was executed on the revolving part of the dial of a tall-case clock that was made in Dublin, Ireland, about 1777. The clock is now in a private collection in the United States. Although the cutter appears to have 16 guns on its gun deck, the artist probably had heard exaggerated tales of the Yankee ship's strength. Her real strength was 10 carriage guns and 12 swivels, but she cruised brazenly off Dublin in 1777, and her name was *Dolphin*.

While Benjamin Franklin was American commissioner in Paris, he tried to stir up trouble between Britain and France and capture some British shipping at the same time by fitting out ships under American captains to raid British shipping from French ports. One of the vessels so fitted out was *Dolphin,* described as a Folkstone or Dunkirk cutter, and she had fallen into Franklin's hands courtesy of the British Secret Service.

The Secret Service had donated her to the Americans through an intermediary in the hope that they could catch her at sea with a precious cargo of Franklin's secret dispatches. But Franklin sent the dispatches another way and armed the cutter to sail with his little fleet. *Dolphin* was commanded by Samuel Nicholson. An attempt by *Dolphin* and her two consorts to capture the Irish linen fleet failed, but they did take about twenty British ships in a short period of time off the Irish coast. There is no record of *Dolphin*'s subsequent career, nor of her plans nor dimensions. Being an old vessel at the start of her American career, she was probably sold after a short time.

If the artist's conception is at all accurate, *Dolphin* was a most unusual cutter, for she had raised quarterdeck, quarter galleries, and a square-tuck stern. It is possible that the quarterdeck and quarter galleries were alterations made by the Americans.

Two warships were built at Philadelphia during the Revolution that were about the same size; although we have no evidence that they were identical, we have decided to give one plan for both of them. These are the Pennsylvania State Navy corvette *Montgomery* and the Continental Navy ship *Duc de Lauzun*. The drawing shown here is based on the official drawing for the 32-gun *Randolph*, which we know was a scaled-up version of *Delaware*, so *Montgomery* and *Duc de Lauzun* are drawn as if they were scaled-down versions of *Delaware*.

Duc de Lauzun was built at Philadelphia in 1781-2 for Captain Thomas Truxtun. She was named for the leader of the cavalry in Rochambeau's army, who was certainly the most flamboyant figure at the battle of Yorktown, if not the most useful. The Continental Navy purchased the ship in 1782 and put her under the command of John Green (who later commanded *Empress of China* on her epic voyage to Canton). In March 1783, she took part in the last naval battle of the Revolution: she left Havana in company with *Alliance*, both ships loaded with gold and military supplies. They were chased by three British frigates, but the appearance of a large French ship on the horizon caused the British to give up the chase and scatter. At that point, the Americans turned on them and heavily damaged the 28-gun *Sibyl*. When the Americans arrived at Newport, Rhode Island on 20 March, they learned that the war was over. *Duc de Lauzun* was sold in France later in the year in an effort to gain Congress some hard cash.

Ships of 18-20 guns were very popular with Americans in the Revolution. They were big enough to have real firepower and speed, and yet their cost to build and operate was relatively modest. They could also be used to advantage after the war as fast, long-range merchant ships. One such ship was being built on a creek near Sunbury, Georgia when she was burned by a landing party from the British frigate *Hind* in May 1776.

Montgomery's contract was awarded to Simon Sherlock's shipyard on 7 November 1775; she was supposed to be capable of mounting 20 eighteen-pounders for river service (smoother water and calmer winds than at sea allowed a much heavier armament than this size ship would normally have carried), and John Barry, deprived of his previous ship *Black Prince* when she was taken into the Continental Navy as *Alfred,* was put in charge of the construction. In March she was given the name of *Wallace,* but this was soon changed to *Montgomery* in honor of the general who had lost his life at Quebec a few months earlier. When she was launched she was fitted with only 14 eighteen-pounders, 16 small mortars, and 8 swivels after it was found that 20 big guns would have been both too heavy and too expensive. By May 1776 she was ready with about 120 men under command of Thomas Read to lead a number of galleys in repelling the advance up the river by the 44-gun ship *Roebuck* and the 28-gun frigate *Liverpool;* after an inconclusive action, the British left the river. In June, Samuel Davidson was made her commander,

and he had her armament altered to 16 twelve-pounders. He was replaced in October 1776 by Henry Dougherty, who was required by Commodore Seymour to take her up the river to Trenton to deter a possible British advance in December. Shortly thereafter, she was disarmed and her cannons given to the other forces in the area. However, when Dougherty resigned in May 1777, she was quickly rearmed with 16 nine-pounders, and command was given to William Allen; Commodore John Hazlewood made her his flagship, but it was very difficult to find more than half enough men to man her.

Montgomery came downriver at the end of September in company with the frigate *Delaware* in hopes of preventing a British fleet from proceeding up the river to meet the British army that had already taken Philadelphia. *Delaware* was captured when she ran aground and *Montgomery* was dismasted in the same action. In November, just below Philadelphia, she was destroyed to prevent capture.

Commodore John Hazelwood, Pennsylvania Navy.

DATES	LENGTH HULL	LENGTH DECK	LENGTH KEEL	BEAM	DEPTH	DRAFT	TONNAGE B. M.
1782-? 1775-1777	ESTIMATED 109	94	77	27	13	13	300

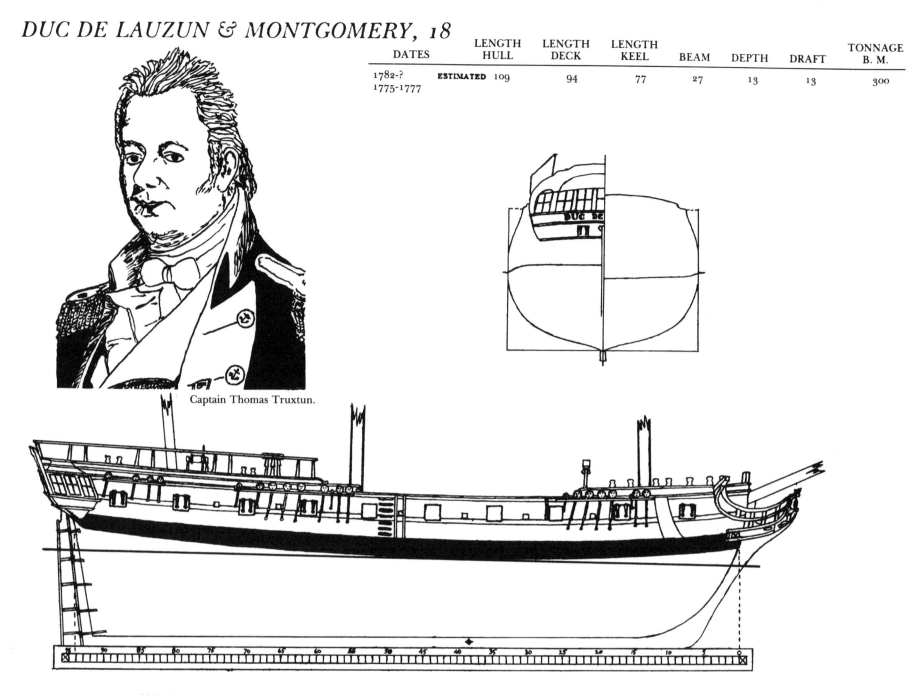

Captain Thomas Truxtun.

EMPRESS OF CHINA (ex-ANGELICA)/EDGAR/CLARA, 18

BEFORE the Revolution, the only legal way for Americans to buy goods from China, India and the East Indies was to purchase them through the East India Company in London, which had a monopoly for British subjects. This was both slow and expensive (the tax on East India Company tea was the cause of the Boston Tea Party), and even more so after the Revolution when the British could rightfully place high tariffs on some of their exports to America.

The answer was to send American ships to the Far East directly. They would not be welcome in British India, where the East India Company had a monopoly, but they could trade at Mauritius and at Canton, as well as a few other places. Robert Morris of Philadelphia and a few others resolved to give it a try.

The first such try was with a newly-built 360-ton privateer ship of 18 guns. This was *Angelica*, built at Boston by the maverick designer, John Peck. He had apparently been

asked to build her as a scaled-down version of his ship *Belisarius*, and so that is how she is shown here. She had a square stern and coppered bottom, and some of her dimensions are known. A Philadelphia syndicate bought her and built a roundhouse (term for poop cabin on the stern). She left New York in February, 1784 with a new name, *Empress of China*, and arrived in Canton 28 August with a cargo that included thirty tons of ginseng. Her captain, John Green, who had formerly commanded the privateer *Duc de Lauzun*, was not much of a navigator for he missed the Sunda Strait by miles, but he eventually arrived at Whampoa by trial and error and saluted the town with thirteen guns. *Empress of China* was warmly received by the British, French and Danish ships already there. Major Shaw of Massachusetts served as her supercargo before becoming America's first consul at Canton.

The ginseng was surprisingly not a success, but other items in her cargo sold well so that she was able to buy 200 tons of tea. She arrived in New York on 11 May

1785. The tea, spices, silks, and chinaware that she had brought home realized Morris a thirty percent profit, which was not regarded as terribly good, but good enough to encourage other merchants to try the China trade.

Empress of China made a second voyage to Canton under Green in 1786-7. Upon her return, she was sold and renamed *Edgar*. On a voyage to France she was badly mauled by a storm. She was put into the New York—Belfast trade, and renamed *Clara* in 1790. She was sunk off Dublin in 1791. Much of this information on her career was assembled by Philip C. F. Smith for his book, *The Empress of China*.

There is only one known authentic portrait of *Empress of China,* and this is a painting on a Chinese fan brought home by Captain Green, and now the property of the Historical Society of Philadelphia. We have based our reconstruction mostly on this portrait, and on the known appearance of other American merchant ships of her size and date. She probably originally had about nine gunports per side on her gun deck, but the fan portrait shows no ports at all, and it is obvious that she would not have had the capacity to carry all her cargo if there had been cannons in the way. The thirteen-gun salute at Whampoa could easily have been fired by the four guns on the quarterdeck, whose position is indicated on our drawing. There is a punchbowl at the New Jersey State Museum that belonged to Captain Green which shows a picture of a ship flying the American flag and the caption *Empress of China;* this ship shows a number of guns. Experts are convinced that it is a portrait of a British ship called *Hall,* whose portrait was used for any ship that visited Whampoa with only the flag and name changed; *Grand Turk* of Salem is among the ships awarded a portrait of *Hall.*

In any case, the gunports were probably planked over before she left for China to make the ship better able to withstand the heavy weather likely to be encountered on a long voyage. At the same time, the high poop was probably fitted to make her a more comfortable ship for her officers and supercargo for traveling in the tropics.

The first ship from the port of Philadelphia to sail to Canton was named *Canton.* She sailed in 1785-6. A modern model of her, once displayed at the Philadelphia Commercial Museum, is not believed to be accurate.

EMPRESS OF CHINA (ex-ANGELICA)/EDGAR/CLARA, 18

DATES	LENGTH HULL	LENGTH DECK	LENGTH KEEL	BEAM	DEPTH	DRAFT	TONNAGE B. M.
1781-1791	**ESTIMATED** 121	100	83	28	13	14	360

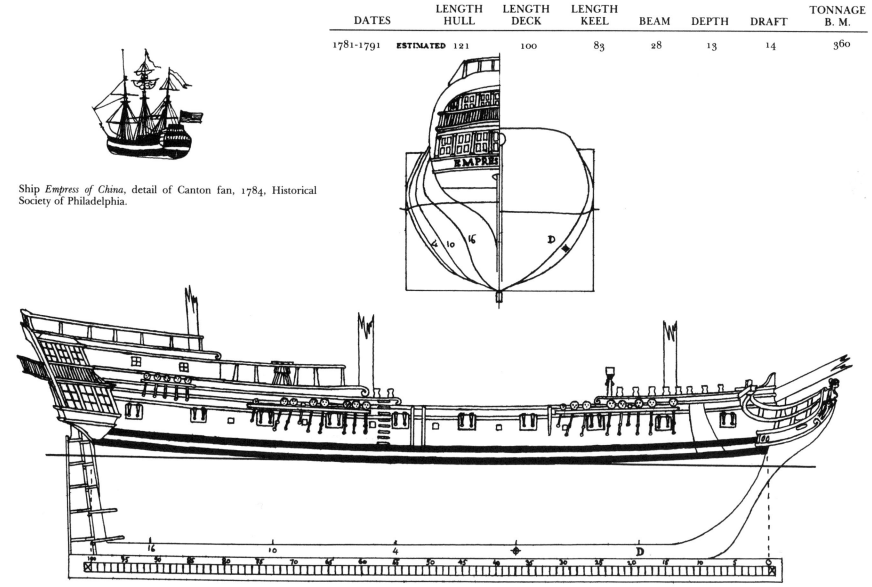

Ship *Empress of China,* detail of Canton fan, 1784, Historical Society of Philadelphia.

EXPERIMENT

DATES		LENGTH HULL	LENGTH DECK	LENGTH KEEL	BEAM	DEPTH	DRAFT	TONNAGE B. M.
1783-?	ESTIMATED	66	58	50	19	9	9	85

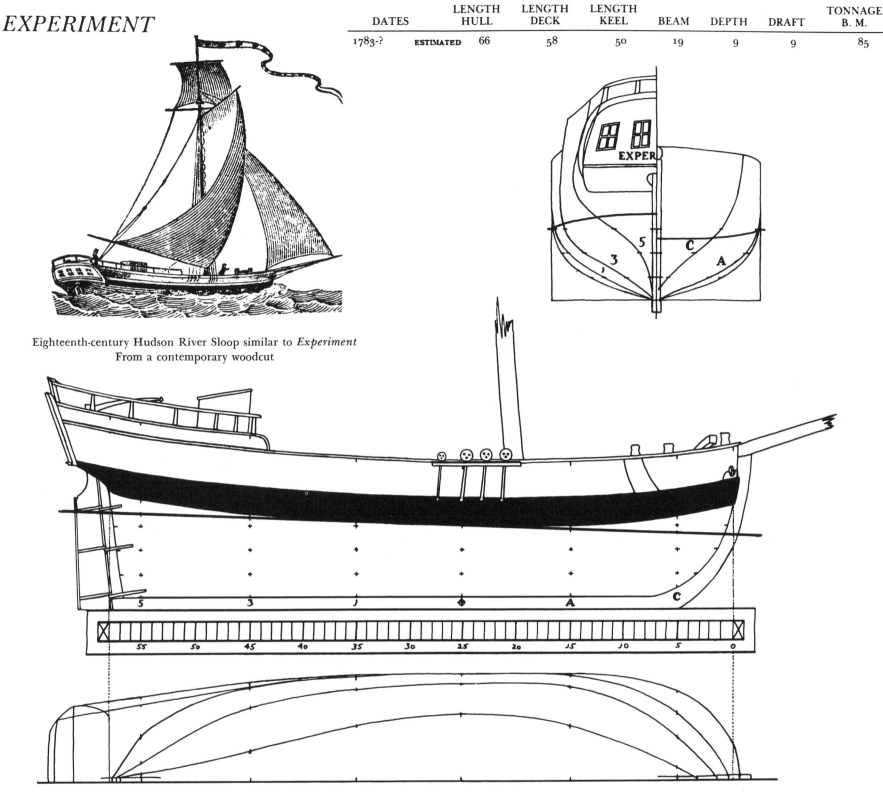

Eighteenth-century Hudson River Sloop similar to *Experiment*
From a contemporary woodcut

EXPERIMENT

THE 360-ton ship *Empress of China* was the first American ship to arrive in China, but she was not the first to leave for China. The first to leave for China was the tiny 55-ton sloop *Harriet,* of Hingham, Massachusetts, which left in December 1783 under the command of Captain Hallet. However, *Harriet* never reached China, for she found a ready market for her goods at Capetown, South Africa, and returned home.

Another sloop that entered the China trade was the New York sloop *Experiment,* built in 1783 on the Hudson near Albany. She left New York for Canton on 15 December 1785 with a crew of seven men and two boys under Captain Stewart Dean.

The wide, shallow-draft sloop was a Dutch legacy to New York that has continued in one form or another up to the twentieth century. More than a few people have seen the Hudson River sloop *Clearwater,* a 1960s re-creation of the typical nineteenth-century Hudson River sloop; although *Clearwater* has a clipper bow, wider beam, shallower draft, and a centerboard, her family resemblance to *Experiment* is unmistakable.

Our drawings of *Experiment* are loosely based on plans that appeared in the September 1932 *Yachting* in an article by C. G. Davis about Hudson River sloops.

There is no statement in the article as to whether these are copies of original plans that are now lost or whether Davis used his own imagination. Many models have been built from the Davis plans, including one that is exhibited at Mystic Seaport, Connecticut.

EXPERIMENT/THORNTON

DATES		LENGTH HULL	LENGTH DECK	LENGTH KEEL	BEAM	DEPTH	DRAFT	TONNAGE B. M.
fl. 1788	ESTIMATED	68	60	55	13	2	4	50

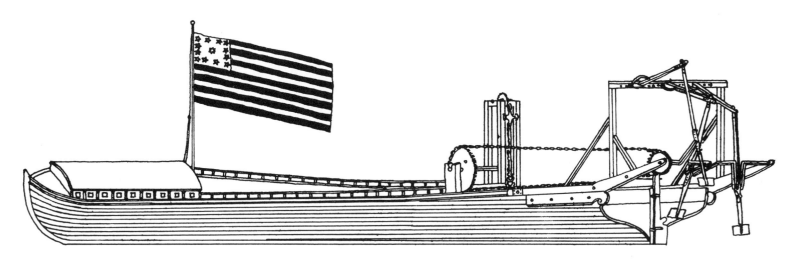

Patent drawing of *Experiment* steamboat, by John Fitch and Henry Voight, 1790, New Jersey Patent Office.

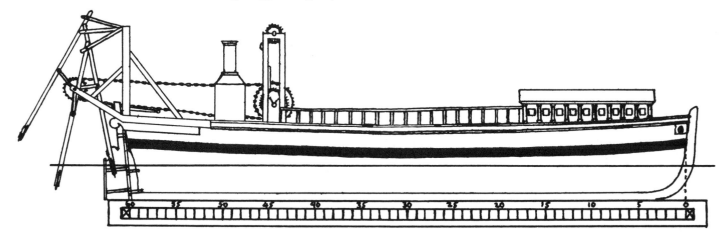

EXPERIMENT/THORNTON

Surprising as it may seem, the period covered by this book contains a great many of the advances in maritime affairs that were not actually to bear fruit until much later. For example, fast sailing vessels, with sharp lines were being produced in the 1770s and 1780s, long before the clipper ships; one of the greatest improvements in gunnery, the carronade, was introduced in 1779; the first American ship to circumnavigate the globe was *Columbia;* the first vessel to be built by English-speaking people on the West Coast was the *Northwest America* of 1788; centerboards were invented by Lieutenant Schank on Lake Champlain in 1776; *Turtle,* the first practical submarine, was built in Connecticut in 1775. Another advance of the period was the harnessing of steam power.

Denis Papin of France first proposed a steam-powered boat in 1700, but steam engines of the day were not powerful enough to use, and jealous contemporaries destroyed his boat before he could try it out. John Hull in England built a functional stern-wheeler powered by steam in 1732, but it had problems. After the invention of Watt's improved steam engine of 1770, the comte de Follenay and the comte d'Auxiron collaborated to build a steamboat, but it too was sabotaged and sunk in the River Seine. In 1783 Comte Jouffrey d'Abbans operated his *Pyroscaphe* on the Saône River for fifteen minutes against the current, but the Academy of Sciences, which was more interested in Montgolfier's balloon projects, forced him to drop his experiments.

But all this work in Europe had not gone unnoticed in America. As early as the 1760s industrialist William Henry tried to launch a steamboat on the Conestoga River, and in 1783 John Fitch of Philadelphia began a series of experiments that would lead to several steamboats. His first design was for a boat with twelve paddles, in two banks of three on each side of the boat; the boat was to be about 34 feet long, but he first built an 18′ model which worked satisfactorily on the Delaware in 1786. The full-size version, to be named *Perseverance*, was delayed while he built a larger vessel to a different design, launched in 1788.

This vessel, 60 feet long, had its paddles arranged like ducks' feet aft of the stern. He named the craft *Experiment*, but sometimes referred to her as *Thornton* as a compliment to one of his financial backers. He operated this boat as a packet between Philadelphia and Trenton for about four months in 1790, but operations were never resumed again, perhaps a reflection on the excessive maintenance required for such crude machinery. Remarkably, Fitch had enough confidence in his machinery that he did not install an auxiliary sailing rig, so *Experiment* was one of the very few early steamboats to have no provision for sails. Fitch built another boat in 1790 on the duck-feet principles, but it was wrecked before its trials and never repaired. Fitch was unstable and always in trouble; he committed suicide in 1798 in the midst of great poverty, but others followed after him and made the United States a leader in the development of steam.

At the same time as Fitch's experiments, James Rumsey of Berkeley Springs, Virginia, was developing his own steamboat. He began it in 1787 (some say 1784, but they are confusing it with a manual-powered vessel)

and ran it in the Potomac River in 1788. It had a high-pressure "flash" boiler (very dangerous when one considers how little was known about metal strengths at that time), and the steam engine operated a water pump that sent a stream of water out of the stern—the first water-jet boat. The boat was considered a success, so Rumsey went to England to build another boat there, but he died before it was finished. His backers completed it and ran it in the Thames, but it was not impressive enough to continue the experiments. Not enough reliable information exists about either of Rumsey's boats to justify a drawing in this book.

In 1792, engineer Elijah Ormsbee took a steamboat against a strong current from Providence, Rhode Island, to Pawtucket, and he was followed by Oliver Evans, John Stevens, and Robert Fulton in Philadelphia and New York.

In 1793, Samuel Morey of Connecticut operated a small steamboat at Orford on the Connecticut River, its engine mounted on the bow. The following year, he built a stern-wheel steamboat and ran it from Hartford, Connecticut to New York City. He did further demonstrations on the Delaware and on the Hudson, but never obtained financial backing.

FAIR AMERICAN, 14

At the museum of the U.S. Naval Academy at Annapolis, Maryland, is a contemporary, large-scale model of a brig, complete with sails. Tradition says that she represents the 14-gun American brig *Fair American* which was captured by the British in the Revolutionary War, and that an admiring new owner commissioned the model so that he would have a reminder of the sleek lines of the ship long after the actual vessel had been broken up. Since there were many American ships of that name, it is difficult to identify which one is represented by the model. One was owned by Blair McClenahan of Philadelphia, and accompanied the celebrated privateer *Holker* on cruises in 1781; one was captured by the British frigate *Vestal* in 1780. However, the most likely candidate for the identity of the model has been uncovered by research by Merritt A. Edson, Jr., Dr. Clayton A. Feldman and Erik A. Ronnberg, Jr.: she was built in Bermuda about 1776 and commanded by Charles Morgan as both a privateer and as a South Carolina Navy ship under charter. She accompanied the Continental frigate *Randolph* on her last fateful cruise in March 1778 but avoided capture herself until the end of 1778. Early in 1779 she was sold at New York and became a Loyalist privateer. In 1782 she

cruised in company with the British frigate *General Monk* (formerly the American privateer *General Washington*) at the mouth of the Delaware. When Joshua Barney on *Hyder Ali* cleverly captured *General Monk*, he was unable to reach *Fair American*, which had accidentally run aground on a shoal, so she escaped and continued to make a fortune for her owner. The owner apparently ordered the model constructed upon his return to England at the end of the war. She appears in the painting of the battle that hangs at the U. S. Naval Academy.

The brig is variously described as carrying 16 or 14 guns—eight 4-pounders and six 6-pounders. Her hull is notable for its large beam and steep deadrise, both typical of fast American designs for small ships. The deadrise is reminiscent of that of the frigate *Loyal American* designed by Loyalist scientist Benjamin Thompson, but never built. Her tafferel projects prominently from the plane of the topsides, allowing an extra window to be painted on each end of the stern. Until 1985, it was said that the presence of a dolphin-striker on this model proved that such a spar existed before 1794, but an old photograph recently discovered shows that the model lacked such a spar when first built.

FAIR AMERICAN, 14

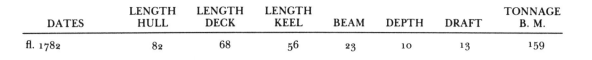

DATES	LENGTH HULL	LENGTH DECK	LENGTH KEEL	BEAM	DEPTH	DRAFT	TONNAGE B. M.
fl. 1782	82	68	56	23	10	13	159

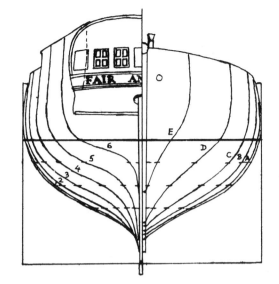

Brig *Fair American* aground in the Delaware, 1782, detail of oil painting by Crépin, U. S. Naval Academy, Annapolis.

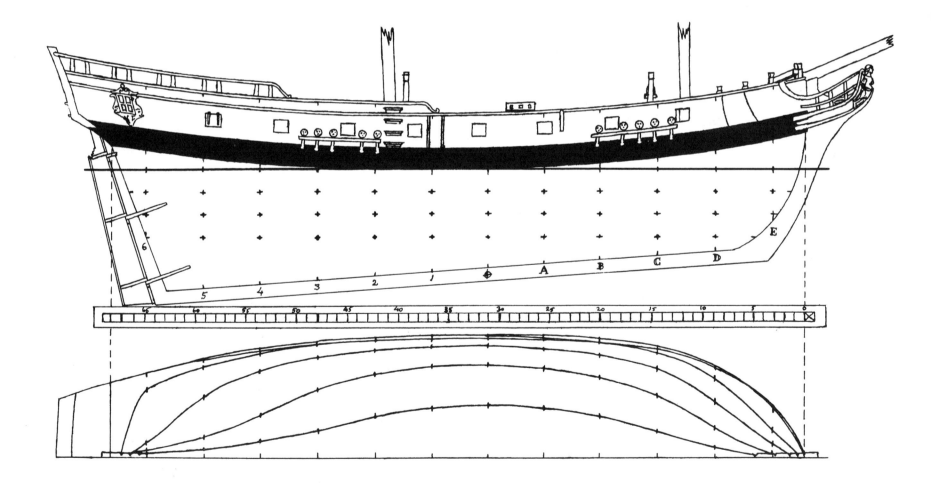

FAIR AMERICAN, 12

Oᴺᴇ of the many vessels in the Revolution with the name of *Fair American* was a privateer brig from Connecticut, built about 1780, and mounting 12 or 14 guns. Judging from the sketch of her that is preserved at the Connecticut Historical Society she was a very fast ship, and she carried all her guns on a spar deck, rather like the Salem privateers *Mohawk* and *Jack* (although they also had gun decks under their spar decks). The unusual arrangement may have been chosen because the owner wished to use her as a merchant ship after the war and he therefore would not have to contend with any gunports. An obvious disadvantage to this arrangement, however, is that there was

no cover for the men working the guns. It could be that the owner intended for her to fight only with unarmed or lightly armed vessels, trusting that she would be fast enough to escape from a ship of equal or superior force. She was owned by Jabez Perkins & Co. of Norwich, Connecticut, and was commanded first by Samuel Champlin and later by Peleg Eldred. She was commissioned on 18 July 1781, and had 90 men in her crew. She captured at least eight enemy ships before the end of the year, but there is no record of her after that time.

No lines or dimensions survive for her.

FAIR AMERICAN, 12

DATES	LENGTH HULL	LENGTH DECK	LENGTH KEEL	BEAM	DEPTH	DRAFT	TONNAGE B. M.
fl. 1781 ESTIMATED	87	69	—	21	—	—	135

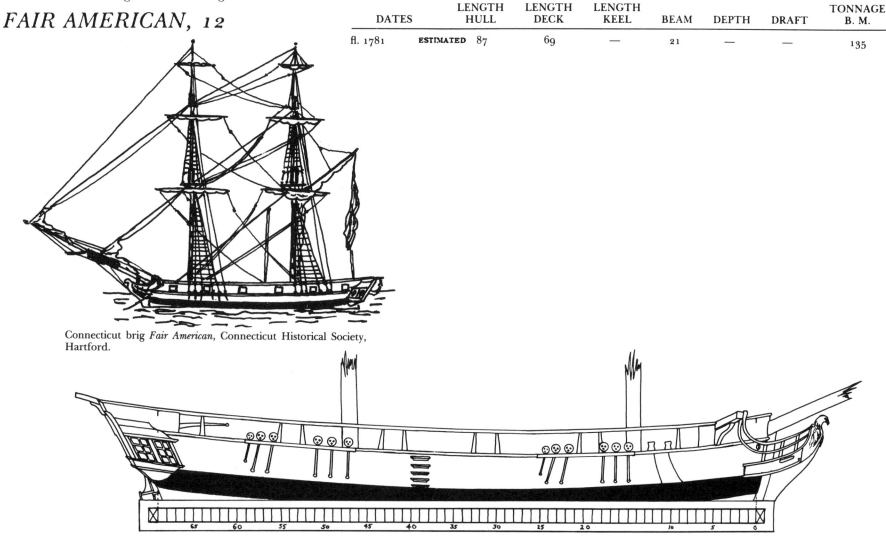

Connecticut brig *Fair American*, Connecticut Historical Society, Hartford.

FALKLAND, 44

Tʜᴇ first large ship built on the North American continent, and the first American-built ship to be taken into the Royal Navy, was the 44-gun ship *Falkland*. She was built at Holland's shipyard at New Castle (a section of Portsmouth), New Hampshire, about 1690. She had been ordered by John Taylor, a London mast and lumber merchant, as a speculation; he hoped to sell her to the Royal Navy if she could pass their rigid inspection standards, and if she failed he could still use her profitably to transport masts from Maine and New

Hampshire to England. For some reason or other, she was not actually taken into the navy until 1696. By 1701, it was noticed that she was rotten in places, and thirty-three frames had to be replaced. After service without incident, mostly in the English Channel, she had to be extensively rebuilt in 1720.

At the time of this rebuilding her lines were taken off and recorded, and these lines are preserved at the National Maritime Museum at Greenwich. These lines, however, reflect the way she was rebuilt in 1720, not the way she looked when she arrived at the dockyard. In this rebuilding, the stern appears to have been altered to bring it up to date with the current styles, and the elaborate carving that was typical of late seventeenth-century ships, such as wreaths around the gunports, was removed. In our drawing we have attempted to reconstruct the stern and the wreaths, based on other ships of the period. Apart from these details, it is believed by experts that very little change was made to the overall shape and size of the ship in 1720.

Falkland appears to have lasted for a long time after this, for the records say that she was not transferred out of active service until as late as 1768. This is actually misleading, for she was rebuilt in 1744 at Bursledon, Hampshire, so extensively that she had increased her tonnage from 638 to 974; in other words, she was almost completely replaced at that time, but in order to get the necessary funds for a new ship from Parliament the navy had to pretend that they were only repairing an older ship. The new ship took part in the first battle of Finisterre in 1747, the battle of Quiberon Bay in 1759, and the capture of Martinique in 1762. In 1768 she was turned into a victualing hulk, one of those infamous purveyors of rotten and maggot-infested salt beef and pork. There is no record of her after that.

The purchase of *Falkland* by the navy was enough of a success for Taylor that he immediately ordered another ship, *Bedford Galley,* of 34 guns, to be built at Holland's shipyard.

There is a beautiful Admiralty-type model of *Falkland,* built by Robert V. Bruckshaw of Toledo, Ohio, on display at the Smithsonian in Washington, D.C., but it looks a little strange in that it combines the *Falkland*'s original seventeenth-century rig with the simplified hull design of the 1720 rebuilding. The ship appears in various oil paintings and prints of the battles she took part in after the 1744 replacement, but these pictures would be of absolutely no use to anyone studying the American *Falkland*.

FALKLAND, 44

DATES	LENGTH HULL	LENGTH DECK	LENGTH KEEL	BEAM	DEPTH	DRAFT	TONNAGE B. M.
ca. 1690-1744	146	129	109	33	14	16	638

FANCY

I^N the celebrated engraving by Burgis of New York Harbor in 1717 is a little yacht under sail. Her name was *Fancy*, and she belonged to Colonel Morris. We know little about her except what can be seen in the picture. There had been other yachts in New York at an earlier date, but they were all Dutch in style while the lineage of this little sloop is clearly English.

FANCY

	DATES	LENGTH HULL	LENGTH DECK	LENGTH KEEL	BEAM	DEPTH	DRAFT	TONNAGE B. M.
	fl. 1717 ESTIMATED	38	35	—	10	—	—	25

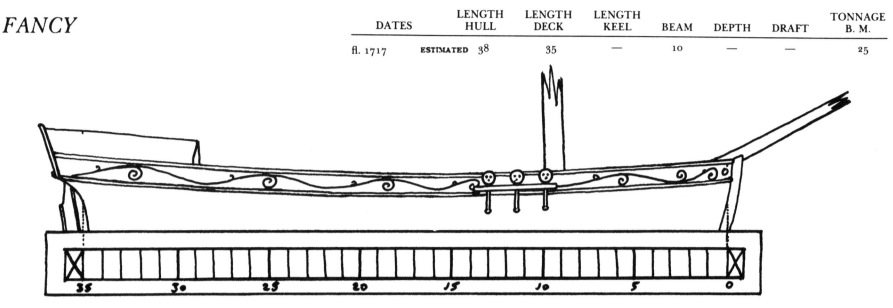

FENIX (ex-SAN ALEJANDRO)/GIBRALTAR & SAN PEDRO/RAYO, 80

I^T is tantalizing to think that a number of large warships were built out of Cuban mahogany at Havana in the eighteenth century, but it is practically impossible to find out anything about them because of the total lack of cooperation accorded to researchers in this field both by the Spanish and Cuban authorities. Perhaps some enterprising scholar will break through the red tape in the next few years.

The 80-gun ship *San Alejandro* was built at Havana in 1749 and later renamed *Fenix* (Spanish for *Phoenix*). She was built on the same lines as *San Pedro*, later renamed *Rayo*, that had been built there the previous year. These sisterships were probably the largest ships built in the Americas up to this date. Owing to the difficulties involved in consulting Spanish records, we know little about the careers of either ship. *Rayo*, by then rotten, was the only ship at Trafalgar in 1805 not to fire a gun; she was commanded by a colorful Irishman, who called himself Don Enrique Macdonel, and she was dismasted and wrecked after the battle. In January 1780, *Fenix* was the flagship of a fleet under Admiral Don Juan de Langara, and her captain was Don Francisco Melgareso. At that point, she was captured by Admiral Sir George Rodney's fleet that had been sent to relieve Gibraltar. She was taken into the Royal Navy and renamed *Gibraltar*.

She was sent to the West Indies and served as Rear Admiral F. S. Drake's flagship, under Captain C. Knatchbull, in Hood's fleet in the unsuccessful attempt to dislodge de Grasse's fleet from its hold on Martinique in April 1781. She returned to England shortly afterward

and was fitted out to be sent as a reinforcement for Hughes in India. When she arrived in India, she was the largest ship in either of the opposing fleets out there, but she only had time to take part in one battle before the war ended, Cuddalore, on 20 June 1783. In the French wars that began a few years later she was again in the thick of the fighting, taking part in the so-called Glorious First of June, 1794, the battles of Basque Roads in 1801 and Aboukir Bay (Egypt) in 1801. As the naval side of the war diminished she was converted into a powder hulk at the end of 1813, and later into a lazaretto in 1824. She was finally broken up at the end of 1836 at Pembroke Dock. She had a career of eighty-seven years and apparently required no major rebuilding in her whole career. Not only is this a tribute to her construction, and particularly to the Cuban mahogany, but also to her design, for it is hard to believe that a ship designed at the end of the War of Jenkins' Ear could still have been a useful and competitive ship for Nelson at the Nile in 1801.

Gibraltar appears in a number of oil paintings and prints of the various battles in which she took part. Her lines, as taken off by the British, are on file at the National Maritime Museum at Greenwich, where there is also a half-model of her. Her design looks very English, a fact that is probably explained by the presence in the Spanish dockyards of a number of British shipwrights. Whether the design was sent out from Spain or drawn in Havana is not known.

FENIX (ex-SAN ALEJANDRO)/GIBRALTAR & SAN PEDRO/RAYO, 80

DATES	LENGTH HULL	LENGTH DECK	LENGTH KEEL	BEAM	DEPTH	DRAFT	TONNAGE B. M.
1749-1836 1748-1805	211	179	145	53	22	26	2157

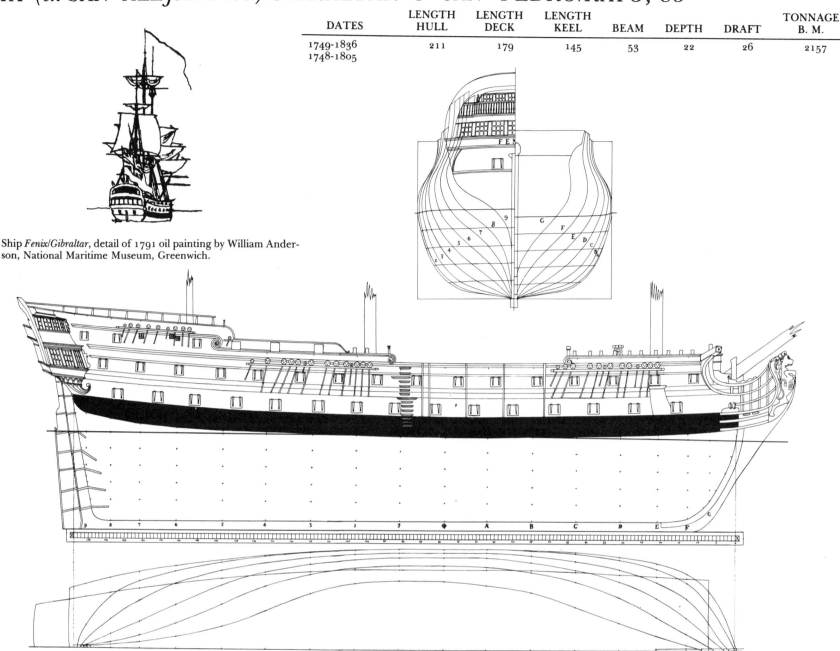

Ship *Fenix/Gibraltar*, detail of 1791 oil painting by William Anderson, National Maritime Museum, Greenwich.

FLORA (ex-LA VESTALE)/LA RECONNAISSANCE, 32

HARDLY any ship that fought on the American side in the Revolution had a more interesting career than the frigate *Flora*, and yet few people have ever heard of her. She was built in France in 1756 with the name of *La Vestale*, and was intended to carry 26 eight-pounder cannons. She took part in the battle of Quiberon Bay in 1759, where a British observer said she carried 34 guns. She was captured by the British frigate *Unicorn* in January 1761, and was recorded as carrying 32 guns. Since there was already a *Vestal* in the Royal Navy, her name was changed to *Flora*, and her eight-pounders were replaced by twelve-pounders. In the American Revolution, she was still described as a 32-gun frigate, and under Captain John Brisbane she was responsible for the recapture from the Americans of the British frigate *Fox* in June 1777. In August 1778, Brisbane, then commodore of a small British fleet at Newport, Rhode

Island, found himself surrounded and trapped by d'Estaing's powerful fleet and ordered the destruction of all his ships. Either because he was fond of her, or because she was anchored next to the town and he wished the town no harm, he merely scuttled *Flora* while all the other British frigates were blown up.

The British continued to occupy Newport for another year, but no attempt was made to raise *Flora* from the bottom of the harbor. In July 1780 the Americans raised her, made temporary repairs at a Newport wharf, and then towed her to Providence where she would be safer from possible British raids while repairs were made (apparently the Americans still did not trust the French, who had just occupied Newport with a large force of both army and navy). She must have been exceptionally well built in order to have withstood, after twenty-two years of regular service, two years on the bottom of the harbor and then be so easily be made serviceable once more. She was owned by Jacob and Griffin Greene of Providence in August 1781 and commanded by Captain Henry Johnson of Boston. At various times she mounted anywhere from 26 to 32 guns. On 28 June 1782 she captured the London merchant ship *Industry*, and by August of that year she was based in Boston. The entertaining book, *The Revolutionary Adventures of Ebenezer Fox* (Boston, 1838), recounts how she lay amid the combined French and Spanish fleets at Cap François, Haiti later in 1782, before those fleets were destroyed by Rodney, and *Flora*'s crew had to keep their wits about them to avoid being pressed by the French who were short of men.

At the end of the war, she sailed to Bordeaux, and her owners decided that their best profit could come from selling her back to the French. The French Navy, probably embarrassed by the blunt proposition, agreed to purchase her, subject to survey. She evidently passed the survey and she was briefly called *La Flore* until it was found that another ship already bore that name in the French Navy. She was renamed *La Reconnaissance* and armed with twenty-six 8-pounders. She was employed in cruising off Africa from 1787 to 1789, and her captain reported that she steered well and heeled less than any warship in Europe in

a breeze, although she did not go well to windward in light airs.

In 1792 the French navy had no further use for her, even though a war had just begun. However, there was still life in the old ship, for she was purchased by the Sieur Fauré de Rochefort for use as a privateer. What success she had as a privateer we do not know, but she was not captured by the British until 1798 when she encountered the 38-gun British frigate *Phaeton*. She was sold immediately.

Her lines have not survived, but the British recorded her dimensions, which show that she was almost an identical sistership to *La Brune* that was built in the same shipyard only a few months apart, so the plans given here are those of *La Brune* as modified in the light of the set of four oil paintings of her by Francis Holman at the Peabody Museum, Salem, Massachusetts. A beautiful contemporary model of a French frigate with a flush deck at the Musée de la Marine, Paris is entitled, *"La Flore," dite Américaine*, but it is quite different in both size and shape from any known French frigate, including *Flora*; it is believed to represent no more than an experimental design that was never executed.

FLORA (ex-LA VESTALE)/LA RECONNAISSANCE, 32

DATES	LENGTH HULL	LENGTH DECK	LENGTH KEEL	BEAM	DEPTH	DRAFT	TONNAGE B. M.
1756-1798	153	132	117	35	15	15	698

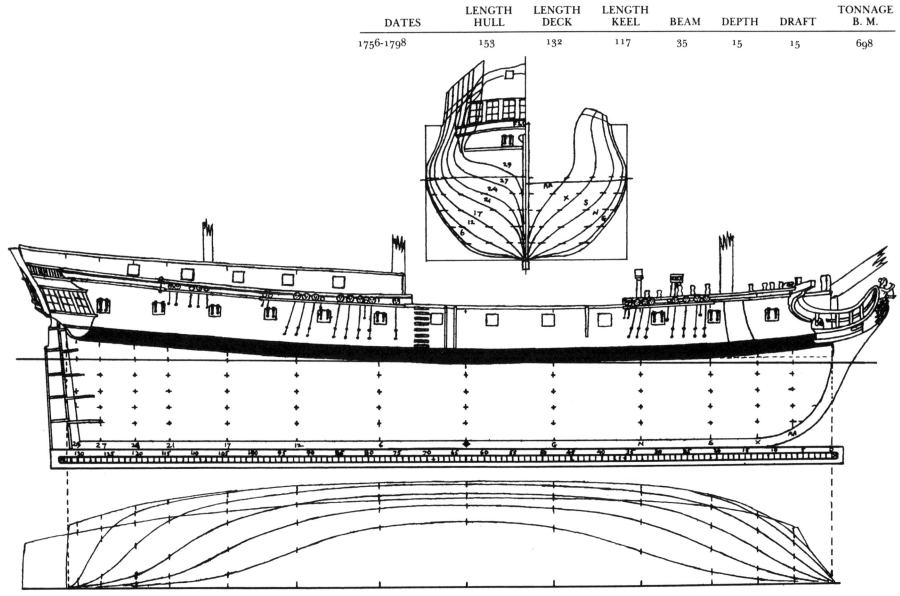

Frigate *Flora* from two of a set of four oil paintings by Francis Holman, 1779, Peabody Museum, Salem.

FOX, 28

Fox seems to have been an unlucky ship; she was captured three times in her short career. The 28-gun frigate was built at Calhoun's shipyard at Northam, Hampshire, and taken into the Royal Navy in 1773. While she was cruising under Captain Fotheringham not far from the New England coast she was captured by the American frigates *Hancock* and *Boston* on 7 June 1777 in a battle that was characterized by the appearance of considerable chivalry; whenever hot wadding could be seen to have set the opposing ship on fire, the respective captains ordered a cease-fire until the fires had been extinguished, and then recommenced hammering away at each other. Stephen Hills, First Lieutenant of *Hancock*, was made captain of *Fox*. *Fox* cruised for a while with *Hancock* and *Boston* until the British ships *Rainbow*, 44 guns, and *Flora*, 32 guns, attacked them. *Boston* turned and fled, leaving *Hancock* to be taken by the aged *Rainbow* and *Fox* to be retaken by *Flora*. While the three American frigates theoretically should have been a match for their opponents they were short of men to handle the guns. The battle took place on 8 July 1777.

Late in 1778 (the exact date is uncertain), *Fox* hauled down her colors once more. *Fox* had been cruising near Ushant off the French coast under the command of Captain Windsor when she encountered the 32-gun French frigate *La Junon*. After having her main and mizzen masts shattered in several places she surrendered, having apparently done her adversary little harm. She was taken into the French Navy and was shipwrecked on 21 March 1779.

The lines of *Fox* do not survive, although she appears in four contemporary oil paintings by Francis Holman of the action with *Flora* and in a French engraving of the fight with *Junon*. Based on these five pictures and on her known dimensions we have reconstructed her. She appears to have an unusually long waist and a short quarterdeck. We think that her figurehead may have represented the politician Charles James Fox, who had been active in the administration of the British Admiralty starting in 1770 (at age 21).

DATES	LENGTH HULL	LENGTH DECK	LENGTH KEEL	BEAM	DEPTH	DRAFT	TONNAGE B. M.
1773-ca. 1778	140	121	104	34	11	15	585

Frigate *Fox* being captured by *La Junon*, 1779 engraving, Musée de la Marine, Paris.

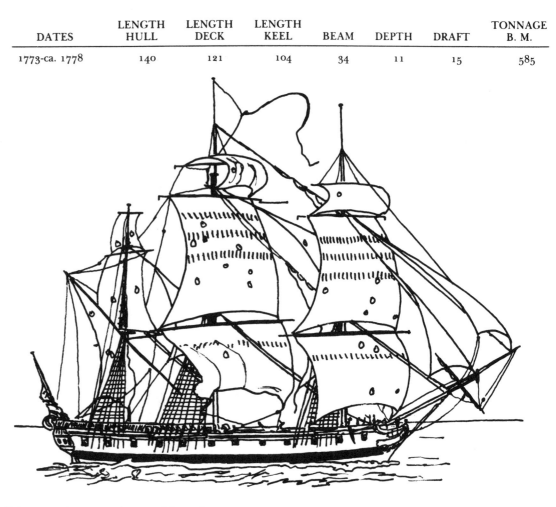

Frigate *Fox* from two of a set of four oil paintings by Francis Holman, 1779, Peabody Museum, Salem.

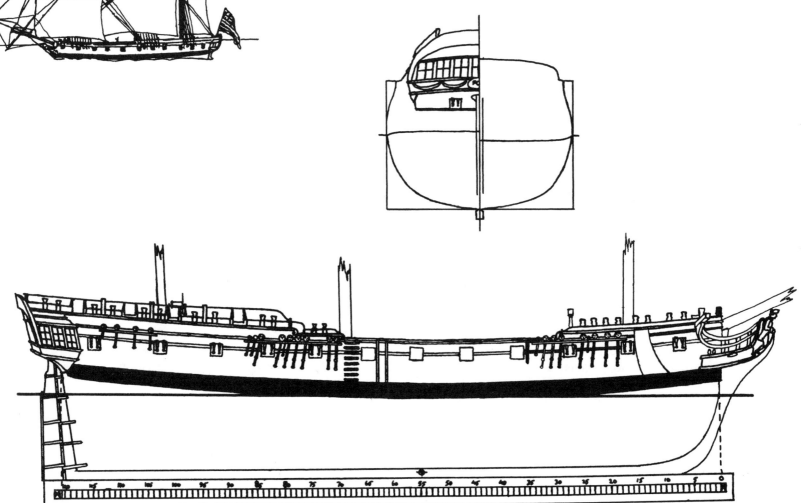

FURY, 6

When the British were trying to force their way up the Delaware River to build a supply line for their garrison in Philadelphia, they encountered difficulties from a number of forts built by the Americans in the mud banks and on islands in the river. The waters around these positions were frequently quite shoal, so the British fitted out two ships to deal with the batteries. They took a retired East Indiaman called *Grand Duchess of Russia,* renamed her *Vigilant,* cut her down to make her as light as possible, fitted her for oars, and gave her a battery of 24-pounder cannons. She was accompanied by an American-built sloop that the British had been using to transport horses, which they fitted with three 24-pounders and named *Fury.* Naturally, *Fury* would not have been safe at sea with three guns of such large size, but anchored on spring cables in the river she would be an effective floating battery. Both ships were used in the attack on Fort Mifflin in November 1777, and a wash drawing of them in this operation was made by John Hunter in an inset on his map of the Delaware that is now at the Library of Congress. After the river was cleared all the way to Philadelphia one assumes that *Fury* was either converted back to a transport or was scrapped, for we find no further record of her.

FURY, 6

DATES		LENGTH HULL	LENGTH DECK	LENGTH KEEL	BEAM	DEPTH	DRAFT	TONNAGE B. M.
fl. 1777	ESTIMATED	62	54	—	18	—	—	85

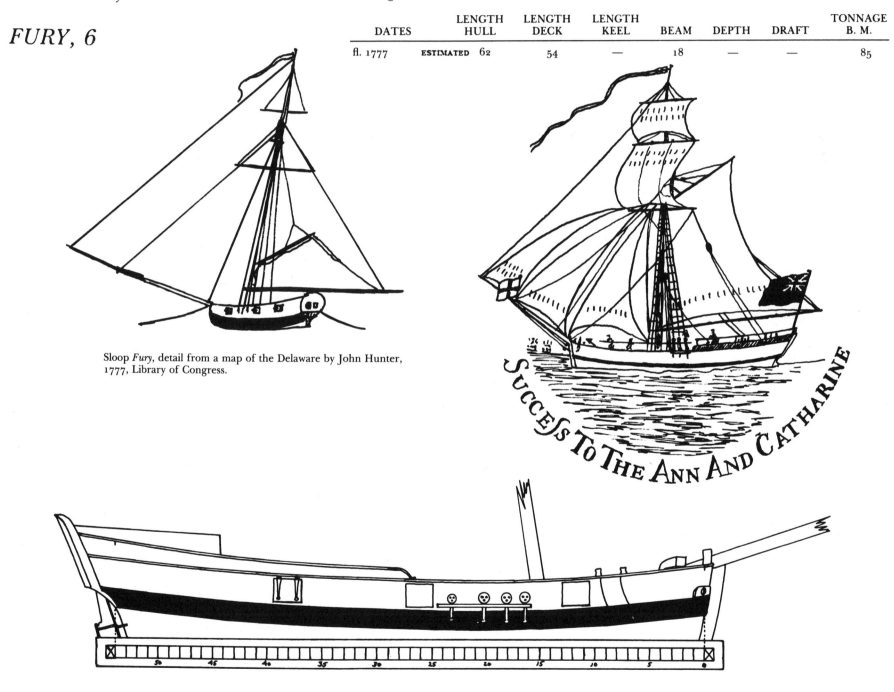

Sloop *Fury,* detail from a map of the Delaware by John Hunter, 1777, Library of Congress.

Success To The Ann And Catharine

GASPEE & SAINT JOHN, 8

DATES	LENGTH HULL	LENGTH DECK	LENGTH KEEL	BEAM	DEPTH	DRAFT	TONNAGE B. M.
ca. 1763-1772	68	62	49	20	8	9	102
ca. 1763-1771							

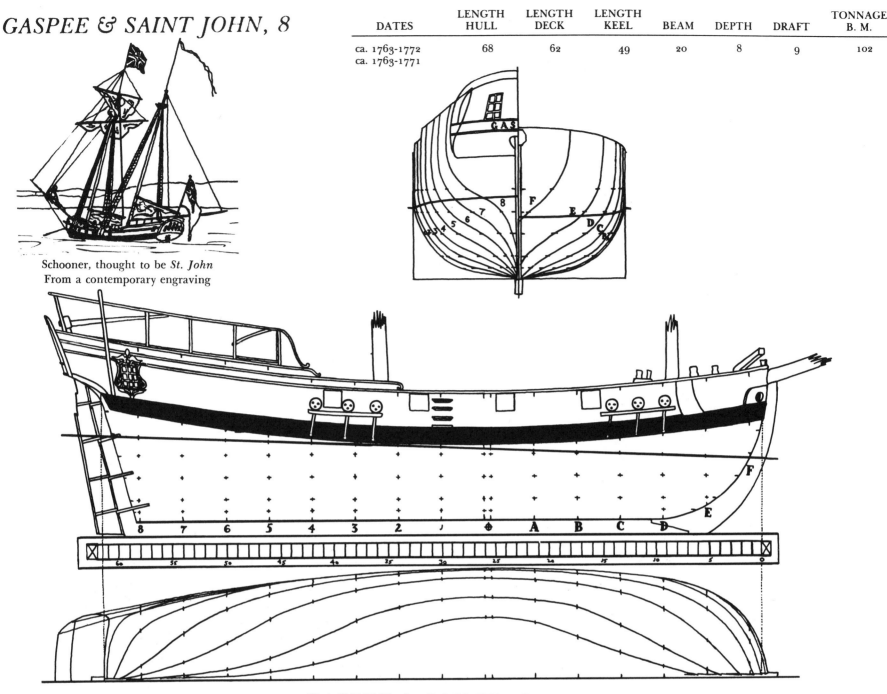

Schooner, thought to be *St. John*
From a contemporary engraving

GASPEE & SAINT JOHN, 8

THE 8-gun schooner *Gaspée* played an important part in the excitement that led to the American Revolution, but there are no contemporary pictures of her, nor do her lines survive. She was probably built in Canada about 1763 (her name is French for "Girl from the Gaspé Peninsula"), and she was purchased by the Royal Navy in North America in 1770 for use in the enforcement of Customs duties. Under the command of Lieutenant William Dudingston she was assigned to eliminate smuggling in Rhode Island. Since smuggling was Rhode Island's major industry (they had previously fired on and burned three other Customs vessels from 1764 to 1769), Rhode Islanders looked for a chance to destroy *Gaspée*. The chance came when she ran aground off Warwick, Rhode Island, on 9 June 1772 on a falling tide. Several open boats from Providence and Bristol converged on her in the middle of the night and set her on fire, wounding Dudingston. The Royal Enquiry

into this incident trampled so severely on Rhode Island's charter and on other Colonial rights that the Committees of Correspondence were formed between the various Colonies; this was an important step on the road to independence.

The lines that we show here are similar to those drawn up by naval architect and historian William A. Baker when a Rhode Island group was considering building a full-sized copy of the *Gaspée*. Baker based his lines of those of the similar schooner *Chaleur,* using the known dimensions of *Gaspée*.

Another schooner almost exactly the same size as *Gaspée* was purchased for the Royal Navy in 1763 at the same time as *Gaspée* and for the same purpose; her name was *St. John*. Some Rhode Islanders link the name of *St. John* with "the first shots of the American Revolution." The incident in question, which occurred on 9 July 1764, almost exactly twelve years before independence, happened as follows: Newport, Rhode Island, then the second most prosperous city in America, had gained her wealth by smuggling French and Spanish goods, especially molasses, from the West Indies and then reexporting them duty free to other British colonies in North America. *St. John*'s job, under the command of Lieutenant Thomas Hill, was to stop this, and she did such a good job that the elected governor, Stephen Hopkins, and members of the General Assembly ordered the chief gunner at Fort George in Newport Harbor to fire his eighteen-pounder cannons at *St. John* until she pulled up her anchor and left. Fortunately, his aim was not as good as it might have been, and *St. John* fled from Newport after suffering only moderate damage. She was apparently sold out of the navy in 1771 or earlier.

GENERAL PICKERING, 16

DATES	LENGTH HULL	LENGTH DECK	LENGTH KEEL	BEAM	DEPTH	DRAFT	TONNAGE B. M.
fl. 1780	106	83	—	25	—	—	200

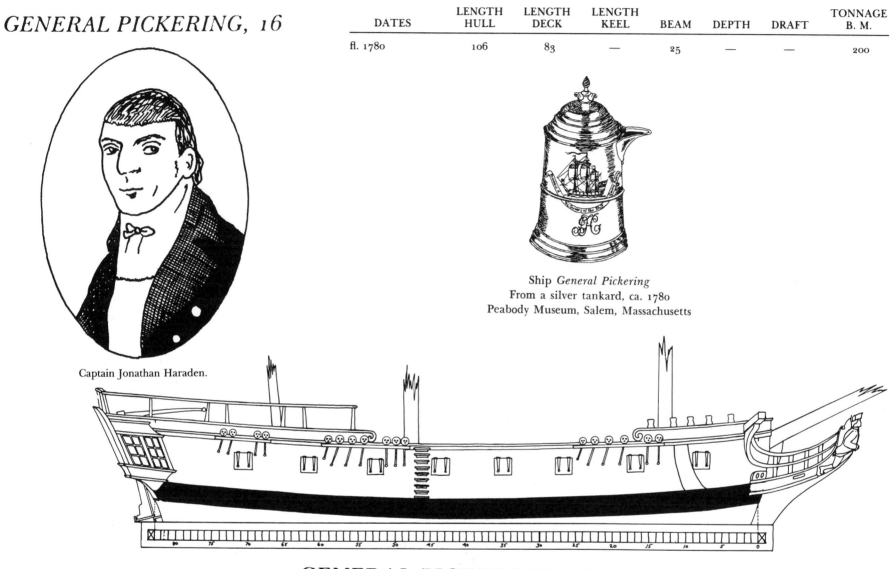

Captain Jonathan Haraden.

Ship *General Pickering*
From a silver tankard, ca. 1780
Peabody Museum, Salem, Massachusetts

GENERAL PICKERING, 16

CAPTAIN Jonathan Haraden of Salem, Massachusetts, had established a good reputation for himself as captain of the ship *Tyrannicide* by the time he was given command of the 16-gun Salem letter-of-marque ship *General Pickering* in 1780; she had been named after Timothy Pickering of Massachusetts, who was adjutant general and later quartermaster general of the Continental Army. On her way to Spain laden with sugar, she fended off a Royal Navy cutter of 16 guns and captured the 14-gun schooner *Golden Eagle*. On her arrival off Bilbao, Spain, she was attacked by the armed British merchant ship *Achilles* of 40 guns and 130 men, which was either a former East Indiaman or a former two-decker warship. When Haraden ran out of cannonballs he ordered the guns loaded with crowbars, and eventually *Achilles,* much damaged, broke off the engage-

ment. Haraden had his ship repaired and set off for home again. After a three-day chase she escaped from a fleet of pursuers and arrived back in Salem on 14 September 1780, followed by two brigs she had captured. Haraden took *General Pickering* on a number of trading voyages to France before the end of the war and his luck continued. He had a narrow escape from a large British battleship and then captured three British ships at the same time, armed with a total of 42 guns. At another time he captured three more British ships within sight of each other with a total of 44 guns. This kind of capturing must have been hard on his crew, which numbered a scant 45 men and boys, hardly enough to man one additional ship, let alone three. At still another time he disguised his ship so as to lure two British privateers within range and then captured them. All this time he was ferrying munitions and supplies from France back to the United States, and the privateering was merely incidental. Presumably *General Pickering* returned to being a regular merchant ship at the end of the war.

No lines or dimensions survive for *General Pickering*, which is not surprising for she was built as an ordinary armed merchant ship. However, after her exploits had made her famous, her owners presented a silver tankard and two silver canns to Haraden, each piece carefully engraved with a picture of the *General Pickering* under sail, and from these engravings we have managed to reconstruct her appearance. The silverware is now at the Peabody Museum at Salem. Unusual features of her design were the especially long head, and the position of the mizzenmast, which looks as if it had been added to a brig rig as an afterthought (perhaps it had).

GENERAL PUTNAM & OLIVER CROMWELL, 18

THE 16-gun privateer ship *General Putnam* was built in Connecticut in 1778. She was named after the unflappable Connecticut farmer Israel Putnam, who left his plough in midfurrow to walk to the aid of Massachusetts as soon as he heard the news about the battles of Concord and Lexington in 1775.

She was built at Winthrop's Neck, New London, at the shipyard belonging to Nathaniel Shaw, who also became the owner of the ship. Her first captain was Thomas Allen, and she was reported ready to sail on 13 May 1778. On 18 September she returned to New London, after taking six brigs. Early in 1779 she went out under the command of Nathaniel Saltonstall and captured at least three enemy vessels. By June 1779 she had put into Boston and changed commanders once more, this time taking on John Harmon. Harmon took her on a cruise off the coast of Maine in which she took about four prizes, and narrowly missed being taken herself by a British frigate off Saco. When she returned to Boston she changed captains again.

In 1779 the Continental Navy sold the corvette *General Gates* because she had become unserviceable. This left her captain, Daniel Waters, without a ship, so he returned to privateering. The first job offered to him was as captain of *General Putnam*. She became part of the fleet that Massachusetts was sending to the Penobscot Bay to dislodge the weak British garrison at Castine, Maine. The whole operation was bungled by the land and sea forces alike, resulting in the loss on 13 August of the whole fleet of ships that had sailed there with such high hopes. *General Putnam* was blown up along with the other ships. At that time, she was reported to have mounted 20 guns, and no doubt some of these were mounted on the quarterdeck, whose rail would have had to be altered to accommodate them.

A contemporary sketch of the ship can be seen at the Connecticut Historical Society, and it is from this that we have reconstructed our drawing of her. Dimensions, as scaled from the drawing, are: length overall, 107' 3"; length on the deck, 90'; tonnage, about 275. One document from the Penobscot expedition claims that this ship measured about 350 tons; if this is so, then her length could have been up to five feet greater, but it is possible for her to have measured 350 tons with the length we have drawn, given the widely differing measurement practices of the day. Unusual features of her design include the double wale and the marked lack of sheer.

From all the existing information, it seems that the Connecticut State Navy ship *Oliver Cromwell* (not to be confused with other ships of that name) was similar in size and appearance to *General Putnam*. She was built at Uriah Hayden's shipyard at Essex, Connecticut. She was ordered by the General Assembly in January 1776, launched on 13 June, damaged by lightning on 1 August, and away at sea under Captain William Coit (formerly of Washington's little fleet) by 18 August. She measured 80' on the keel, 27' beam, and 12' depth in hold, and her tonnage was about 300. Her first cruise was only to New London, where she was finished under the direction of Nathaniel Shaw (the owner and builder of *General Putnam* in 1778). She mounted 18 nine-pounders, plus two two-pounders and six swivels. Later, her armament was altered to sixteen 9-pounders plus a few 6-pounders.

Coit was fired in April 1777 and replaced by Captain Seth Harding, later captain of the frigate *Confederacy*. Harding got her to sea immediately and soon captured a number of prizes. He put his prisoners ashore at the Kennebec River in Maine, but being ill himself, he proceeded over land to Boston and Lieutenant Timothy Parker took over command. Parker was later confirmed as captain. On 15 April 1778, while cruising with the Connecticut state ship *Defence*, *Oliver Cromwell* fought a fierce battle with the 18-gun privateer *Admiral Keppel* and captured her just as *Defence* captured the 16-gun *Cyrus*; aboard the *Keppel* was Governor Henry Shirley of Jamaica. The prizes went to Boston while *Defence* and *Oliver Cromwell* went to Charleston, South Carolina, for repairs. Then Parker sailed for Nantes, France, although he seems to have changed his plans en route and *Oliver Cromwell* stayed on this side of the Atlantic. In the spring of 1779 she left New London for the last time, captured a few more prizes, and was then herself caught by the 24-gun British frigates *Daphne* and *Delaware* (formerly the Continental frigate *Delaware*) and the privateer *Union*. *Oliver Cromwell* was taken into New York and sold. One source says that she was bought by a New York Loyalist as a privateer, and was renamed *Restoration*.

DATES	LENGTH HULL	LENGTH DECK	LENGTH KEEL	BEAM	DEPTH	DRAFT	TONNAGE B. M.
1778-1779 1776-?	ESTIMATED 114	96	80	27	12	13	300

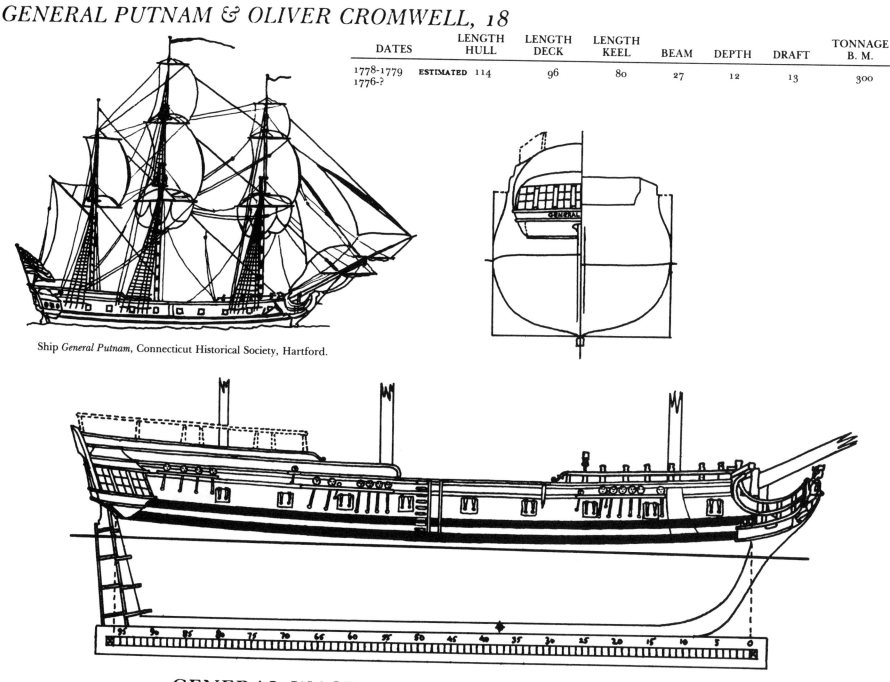

Ship *General Putnam*, Connecticut Historical Society, Hartford.

GENERAL WASHINGTON/GENERAL MONK, 20

IN 1779, John Brown, a rich merchant of Providence, Rhode Island, had a 20-gun privateer ship constructed which he called *General Washington*. She was almost exactly equivalent in size and type to the three Continental corvettes *Ranger*, *General Gates*, and *Saratoga*. Her first captain was James Munro, who made some moderately successful cruises on her including capturing a ship called *John Barrington*, before he left her to be captain of the larger ship *Belisarius*. In the summer of 1780 the command of *General Washington* was given to Silas Talbot, who held commissions as a captain in the Continental Navy and a colonel in the Continental Army at the same time. Soon after Talbot got her to sea, she captured a valuable British merchant ship that was on her way from Charleston, South Carolina, to London. Not long after, *General Washington* captured another British ship bound from the West Indies to Ireland, but she was retaken before she could reach port. Talbot's luck had changed.

Just as a fierce storm descended on him, Talbot was chased by several British warships. In the strong winds, the larger ships could sail faster than the little *General Washington*, so Talbot reluctantly had to surrender. The date of this action differs wildly, depending on the source, and some sources claim that she was captured by *Culloden*, 74 guns, while others say by *Chatham*, 50 guns. In any event, Talbot was shamefully treated on his way to prison in England, and his old ship, renamed *General Monk*, was taken into the Royal Navy.

Under Captain Rogers, *General Monk* inflicted considerable damage to American shipping. In August 1781, she assisted the 32-gun frigate *Iris* (formerly the American frigate *Hancock*) in capturing the 28-gun Continental frigate *Trumbull*. On 8 April 1782 she was patrolling the mouth of the Delaware with the frigate *Québec* when she captured one or two ships of an American convoy. The convoy guard ship, a converted merchant ship called *Hyder Ali* (named after the prince who was fighting the British in India at that time), was her next target. Although they were almost evenly matched in terms of cannons, *Hyder Ali*'s young captain, Joshua Barney, was sure he would be captured because of the weakness of his ship. Nonetheless, he tried a trick that enabled him to board *General Monk* and capture her.

She was immediately given back her old name, *General Washington,* and was chartered by Robert Morris, who was more or less in charge of the Continental Navy at that time. He sent her to the West Indies and she fought a sharp action with a British privateer off Cap François (now Cap Haitien in Haiti), and captured another ship before arriving in Havana, Cuba. In Cuba she loaded a large shipment of gold to bring back to Philadelphia. She returned to Philadelphia on 17 July 1782, after clearing the Delaware of some small British craft.

In September she was purchased by the Continental Navy, and departed for France on 7 October with letters for Franklin. She made a very fast passage (she was regarded as a particularly fast ship anyway), arriving at l'Orient in under three weeks. She left l'Orient in January 1783, returning to Philadelphia on 12 March, only a few days before news arrived from Britain announcing the end of hostilities. She left once more for France on 10 November 1783 with Joshua Barney still her captain and with John Paul Jones as a passenger. Jones wished to go ashore in England for some business, so *General Washington* put him ashore at or near Plymouth, making her the first ship of the American navy to visit Britain in peacetime. Barney took the occasion to give a sumptuous dinner party for all the people in the area who had assisted him in his escape from the dreaded Mill Prison two years earlier. Then he took the ship on to France and thence back to Philadelphia. By summer 1784, all the ships of the Continental Navy had been sold except *General Washington* and *Alliance,* and then the *General Washington* was put up for auction in midsummer. The successful bidder was none other than John Brown, the Providence merchant who had had her built five years earlier. Brown fitted her out as an East Indiaman and she left for China in 1787 under the command of Jonathan Donnison, the first Rhode Island ship to do so. When she returned to Providence in 1789, Brown loudly proclaimed that he had lost £500 on the voyage, but his biographer, James Hedges, discovered that Brown had "fiddled" the books in order to discourage competition; he had actually made a $20,000 profit! It was small wonder, then, that Brown sent her back to India and China in a few weeks. He also built two other ships for the China trade, the 950-ton *President Washington* in 1790 and the 624-ton *George Washington* in 1793 while *General Washington* was still sailing to China; when one considers that Brown had owned a sloop called (plain) *Washington* in 1775, historians must take special care not to be confused by Brown's shipping activities.

Chapelle gives her dimensions as those of a large ship, but he later admitted that he was confusing her with the privateer *Congress.* The British never recorded her dimen-

sions, as they had put her into service before she could be measured and drawn. Three portraits of *General Washington* have been identified. The earliest is a 1779 primitive oil painting of her at anchor in the background of a portrait of a Rhode Island black sailor. Another is a postwar painting by Crépin done under Barney's direction of *General Monk* being taken by *Hyder Ali*; the former is in a private collection, while the latter is at the U. S. Naval Academy at Annapolis. The third portrait is on an English linen handkerchief of about 1785 at the Henry Francis DuPont Winterthur Museum in Delaware; it shows a cartouche with an allegorical picture of Washington and Franklin offering Independence and Commerce to America seated under a palm tree, and behind Franklin is the stern of this ship, bearing no name but a plaque of the Commander-in-Chief's emblem.

We feel that *General Washington* was probably built by the same builder as the privateer *Oliver Cromwell* whose draft is preserved at the National Maritime Museum at Greenwich. Hence, we have simply enlarged the Greenwich draft for our drawing, with few alterations.

Corvette *General Washington*
From an anonymous oil painting, ca. 1780
Private collection, Kingston, Rhode Island

Corvettes *Hyder Ali* and *General Washington*
From an oil painting by Louis-Philippe Crépin, ca. 1800
U.S. Naval Academy Museum, Annapolis, Maryland

GENERAL WASHINGTON/GENERAL MONK, 20

DATES	LENGTH HULL	LENGTH DECK	LENGTH KEEL	BEAM	DEPTH	DRAFT	TONNAGE B. M.
1779-ca. 1794 ESTIMATED 117	98	81	30	14	14	340

Captain Joshua Barney.

Captain Silas Talbot.

Robert Morris

Ship *General Washington*, detail from English printed linen handkerchief of ca. 1785, H. Francis DuPont Winterthur Museum, Delaware.

GEORGE/ENTERPRISE, 10

DATES		LENGTH HULL	LENGTH DECK	LENGTH KEEL	BEAM	DEPTH	DRAFT	TONNAGE B. M.
1775-1777	ESTIMATED	51	46	40	18	6	6	55

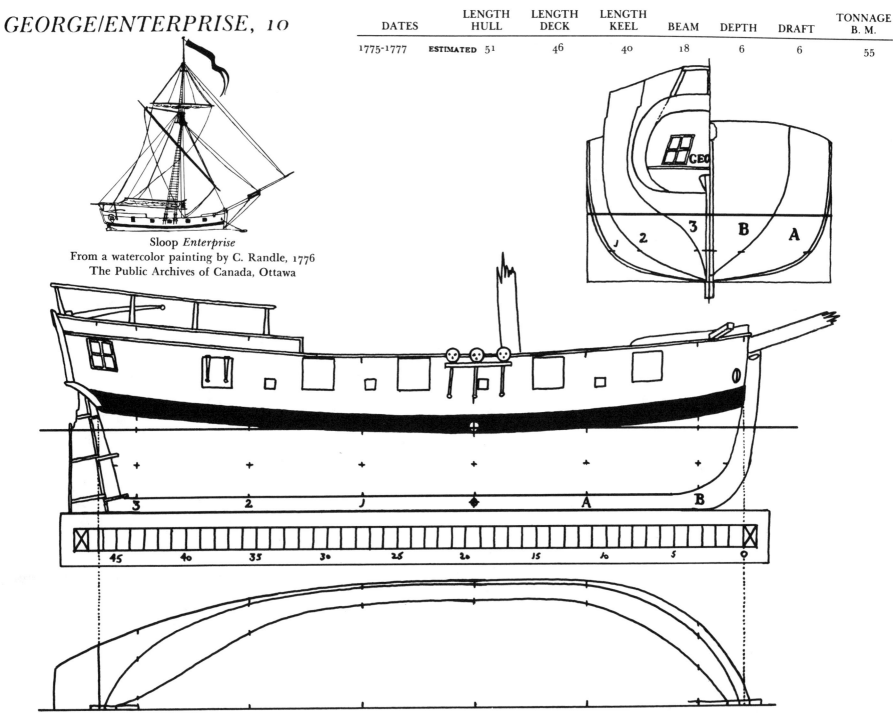

Sloop *Enterprise*
From a watercolor painting by C. Randle, 1776
The Public Archives of Canada, Ottawa

GEORGE/ENTERPRISE, 10

THE British had long understood the strategic importance of Lake Champlain, for it could be used as an invasion route in either direction between Canada and what is now the United States. Therefore, they began a program of building some small warships to protect their interests on the lake. Their base and shipyards were at St. John on the Richelieu River at the northern end of the lake. Benedict Arnold arrived there with the armed ketch *Liberty* on 18 May 1775 and the base surrendered without a shot. Already built and ready for launching was the schooner *Royal Savage*, and already launched was the sloop *George*, capable of mounting ten guns.

Arnold renamed her *Enterprise* and took her into his growing naval force on the lake. She was involved in the battle of Valcour Island in October 1776, and appears to have been among the ships that Arnold burned

in 1777 to avoid their capture by the powerful British fleet that had miraculously materialized on the lake.

She had a shallow draft and almost a flat bottom, which was ideally suited to navigating the shallower parts of the lake, but she was a dull sailer. She was equipped with oars or sweeps for rowing when the wind was either unfavorable or dead.

Her lines and dimensions are unrecorded, although there are a few contemporary paintings of her, and we have drawn her lines based on the pictures and on an enlargement of the lines of the cutter *Lee,* which was being built at St. John's at the same time. Although she was pierced for ten guns she is reported to have carried 12 four-pounders, so the other two must have been mounted on the quarterdeck. Her crew numbered 50 men.

GLORIOSO (ex-NUESTRA SEÑORA DE BELEN), 70

MORE information is available about ships built in Cuba when British shipwrights were in the ascendency than when French builders were in charge. No plans are known to have survived from the French period, but we have perhaps the next best thing: an engraving of the 70-gun ship *Glorioso* by Richard Short, who was one of the most accurate in an age of accurate marine artists. *Glorioso* was built at Havana in 1738. Her original name was *Nuestra Señora de Belem*, but that was soon changed. She was captured by the British in 1747. Perhaps because the war was nearly over or because they thought her design inferior to comparable British ships. British officials neither bought her into the Royal Navy nor even had her lines taken off in drydock (or if the lines were taken off they have since been lost). Her profile was typical of French designs from the early part of the century.

Ship *Glorioso*, engraving after Richard Short, 1747.

GLORIOSO (ex-NUESTRA SEÑORA DE BELEN), 70

DATES	LENGTH HULL	LENGTH DECK	LENGTH KEEL	BEAM	DEPTH	DRAFT	TONNAGE B. M.
1738-1747	**ESTIMATED** 204	166	142	45	25	25	1600

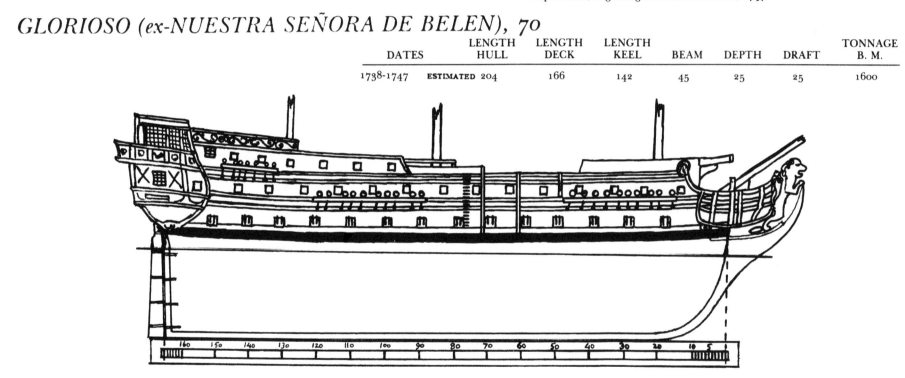

HALIFAX, 10

THE best eighteenth-century route, either for trade or for military invasion, between the Hudson River and the St. Lawrence River was along Lake George and Lake Champlain, and the shores of both these lakes were heavily fortified. We have included a number of Lake Champlain vessels in this book, but we have only found enough information on one vessel from Lake George to include her. This was the sloop *Halifax,* apparently built in 1759.

During the Seven Years' War, Captain Joshua Loring* of the Royal Navy was sent into the mountains of New York to put together and operate a naval force on Lake George. This force, which was assembled around Fort William Henry and Fort George, consisted of the sloop *Halifax,* the radeau *Invincible,* and a number of "whaleboats" and bateaux. Loring is said to have maintained good discipline and morale, but little is known of the ships themselves or their histories.

---

* Loring's son of the same name was married to the lady who became General Sir William Howe's mistress during the Revolution, giving many satirical poets the golden opportunity of rhyming "snoring" with "Mrs. Loring."

According to an engraving on display at Fort Ticonderoga Museum on Lake Champlain, the sloop *Halifax* looked like any saltwater sloop. She was armed with about ten carriage guns and a few swivels. The big (and successful) French offensive down Lake George had taken place in 1757, so the sloop *Halifax* saw little action, and it seems likely that she was either broken up or sold as a merchant vessel as soon as the British took possession of Canada from the French, thus eliminating any military threat along Lake Champlain. As we see her, she measured 69 feet in overall length and about 60 feet in length between perpendiculars.

Archaeologists have recently found the remains of three vessels of the same period as *Halifax* a few miles away from Lake George at the bottom of Lake Champlain. Two of these vessels were built by the British at Fort Ticonderoga and the third had been captured from the French. As this book goes to press, no further information is available, but further development of the project bears watching; these vessels are among the most important underwater discoveries in America.

HALIFAX, 10

DATES		LENGTH HULL	LENGTH DECK	LENGTH KEEL	BEAM	DEPTH	DRAFT	TONNAGE B. M.
fl. 1759	ESTIMATED	69	60	—	19	—	—	90

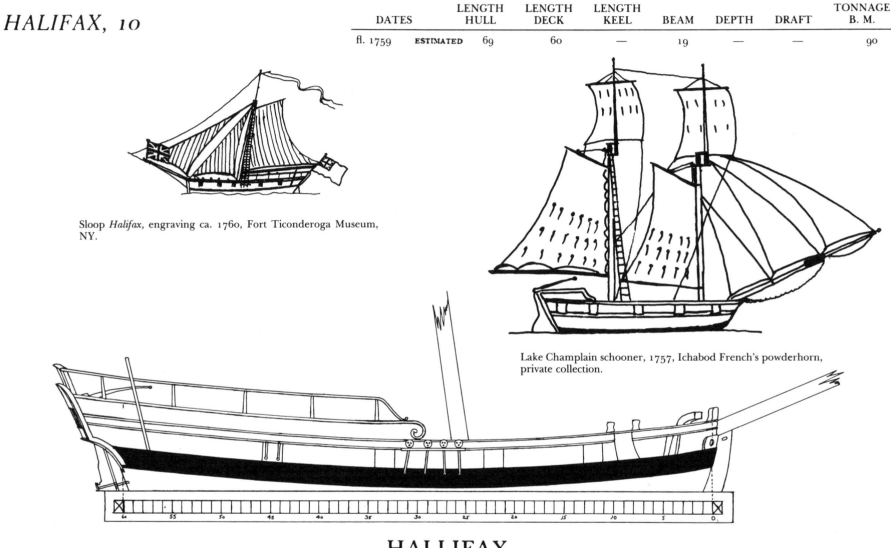

Sloop *Halifax*, engraving ca. 1760, Fort Ticonderoga Museum, NY.

Lake Champlain schooner, 1757, Ichabod French's powderhorn, private collection.

HALLIFAX

THE schooner *Hallifax* [sic] was purchased in New England by the Royal Navy in 1768, presumably to assist with enforcement of the Customs laws. Although her full hull lines indicate that she would have been too slow to catch the smugglers, she was fitted out with a few small carriage guns. She may have been employed briefly as a troop transport. She seems to have visited England at one time, for two sets of lines (one showing "improvements" made by the navy) survive at the National Maritime Museum at Greenwich. She was wrecked on the coast of Maine in February 1775; Chapelle says that she took part in the infamous raid on Falmouth (now Portland), Maine, in October 1775, but that was another vessel of the same name. Her figurehead is not recorded, but the lines do show a finely carved mermaid on the headrails; we have drawn a woman for the figurehead.

She should be compared with the slightly smaller schooner *Sultana*.

DATES	LENGTH HULL	LENGTH DECK	LENGTH KEEL	BEAM	DEPTH	DRAFT	TONNAGE B. M.
ca. 1765-1775	68	57	47	18	9	8	83

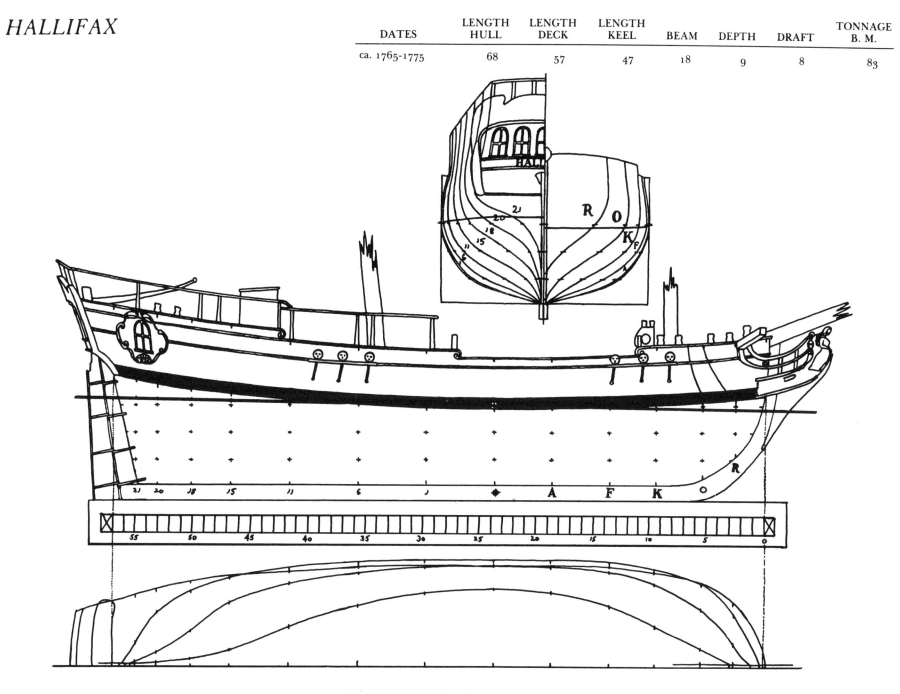

HANCOCK/IRIS, 32

IN December 1775, Congress passed the second half of the Rhode Island Navy Bill; this called for the construction of thirteen frigates, including five of 32 guns. One of these, later known as the *Hancock,* was to be built at the yard of Greenleaf & Cross at Newburyport, Massachusetts. Congress approved a design for the 32-gun ships, but it was so long in getting to New England that the builders had the ship half built to their own design when it arrived. Their own design resulted in a ship slightly bigger than the other 32s, and much prettier. When she was captured by the British she was described as the "finest and fastest frigate in the world."

She was launched in July 1776, but did not set sail until the spring of 1777. She left Boston on 21 May in company with the 24-gun frigate *Boston,* which had been built in the same shipyard. Early in June they captured the 28-gun British frigate *Fox* in an action characterized by chivalry on both sides. Early in July the three frigates were cruising in company when they were chased by the

44-gun ship *Rainbow* and the 32-gun frigate *Flora.* If they had stood and fought they would quite likely have taken both their adversaries, but they split in three directions. *Boston* escaped, her captain much criticized for having deserted the others; *Fox* was quickly recaptured by *Flora;* and *Hancock* was taken by *Rainbow* after a long chase. She should have been fast enough to escape from the aging *Rainbow,* but for some reason her captain, John Manley, had shifted her ballast so that she was trimmed heavily down by the head.

Hancock was taken into the Royal Navy and was renamed *Iris,* her previous name not being exactly popular with the British. She was taken to England, where her lines were recorded in drydock, and they survive today at the National Maritime Museum at Greenwich. She was sent back to the American station and captured her share of Allied shipping. In 1780, she fought a duel with the French frigate *La Hermione* and was on the point of capturing her when another French warship appeared on the scene. *Iris* escaped. In August 1781, she and the 20-gun *General Monk* (formerly the Rhode Island privateer *General Washington*) captured the already-disabled 28-gun Continental frigate *Trumbull* in an "all-American" battle.

But *Iris*'s days as a British ship were coming to an end. De Grasse's powerful French fleet left their mooring in the Chesapeake early in September 1781 to do battle with a British fleet off the coast. Almost like naughty schoolboys, *Iris* and another frigate went around the anchorage cutting all the moorings of the French ships, but the French came back from the battle before the frigates could escape, so they were taken into the French navy on 11 September. Iris remained in the French navy until 1793, when the French Royalists asked the British to occupy Toulon as a base against the Republicans. When the Republican artillery under Na-

poleon forced its way through the British lines, the British and French Royalists evacuated Toulon on 18 December 1793, taking thousands of refugees with them on ships formerly of the French navy, and blowing up other French ships. One of these latter was *Iris,* which was then being used as a gunpowder storage hulk; she was the next-to-last survivor of the original frigates of the Continental Navy, the last being *Delaware.*

An unusual feature about *Hancock* was her rig. Like *Boston* and *Raleigh,* she used her ensign staff as a fourth mast, setting on it a small lateen sail for balance. This clearly shows up in the four oil paintings (at the Peabody Museum of Salem) by Francis Holman of the engagement with *Rainbow* and *Flora.* In addition to these four pictures, there is a possibility that she can be identified in one or more of the pictures of the evacuation of Toulon.

HANCOCK/IRIS, 32

DATES	LENGTH HULL	LENGTH DECK	LENGTH KEEL	BEAM	DEPTH	DRAFT	TONNAGE B. M.
1776-1793	162	137	116	35	11	17	762

Frigate *Hancock*
From one of a set of four oil paintings by Francis Holman, 1779
Peabody Museum, Salem, Massachusetts

MANLY

Captain John Manley.

HANNAH, BALTICK & FRANKLIN, [4]

A T the Peabody Museum in Salem, Massachusetts, are two interesting contemporary paintings of the Salem merchant schooner *Baltick,* built in the late 1760s. She was fairly typical of schooners of her size from New England, there being many like her among the sketches of Ashley Bowen.

When George Washington decided to commission a naval force in his Continental Army in 1775, it was to vessels like these that he turned. The first to be commissioned was the fishing schooner *Hannah,* on 2 September 1775. She was exactly the same tonnage (and therefore the other dimensions would have been almost identical) and date as the schooner *Baltick.* Washington chartered *Hannah* from Nicholas Broughton and hired Broughton as captain. For crew, he used soldiers from John Glover's Marblehead regiment, and he armed *Hannah* with four small carriage guns poked through hastily cut gunports in her waist. She set sail on 5 September and returned on the seventh after capturing a vessel called *Unity.* The crew was mutinous, Broughton was surly, and the vessel did not sail very well, so the first ship chartered by Washington was quickly dropped and replaced by others of the same type, called *Lynch, Franklin, Lee, Warren, Washington,* and *Harrison.*

The schooner *Franklin,* in company with another schooner called *Hancock,* made what appeared to be a remarkable capture on 6 August 1776: the 305-ton ship *Nelly Frigate,* armed with 18 guns. When they boarded her they found that twelve of her guns were mere wooden "Quakers."

The Peabody Museum also has a modern sketch of the *Franklin,* which, it is hopefully suggested, is based on an original that is now lost. Allowing for obvious distortion in the sketch, *Franklin* looks much the same as *Baltick* and *Hannah,* although she was a little smaller. She had been the 60-ton schooner *Eliza,* and was chartered from Archibald Selman of Marblehead. Under the command of Selman, she disobeyed orders and raided Charlottetown, Prince Edward Island, much to Washington's disgust. Her next captain, Samuel Tucker, was relieved by James Mugford in April 1776. A few days after Mugford had captured a rich British transport, *Franklin* ran aground in Boston Harbor and was attacked by the British. The schooner was saved, but Mugford was killed. *Franklin* continued in army service for a few more months until Congress ordered Washington's little fleet disbanded.

Washington

113

Reuben Dyer 1777
His horn

Captain James Mugford.

Armed American schooner and sloop, powderhorn engraving, 1777, private collection.

Schooner *Baltick*
From a watercolor painting, 1766
Peabody Museum, Salem, Massachusetts

Schooner *Baltick* in heavy weather off Cape Fear, NC, 1766, watercolor, Peabody Museum, Salem.

American fishing schooner captured by a British privateer, oil painting by Francis Holman, ca. 1778, National Maritime Museum, Greenwich.

Schooner *Franklin*
From a watercolor painting of uncertain date
Peabody Museum, Salem, Massachusetts

HANNAH, BALTICK & FRANKLIN, [4]

DATES		LENGTH HULL	LENGTH DECK	LENGTH KEEL	BEAM	DEPTH	DRAFT	TONNAGE B. M.
fl. 1775	ESTIMATED	61	56	45	17	8	8	78
fl. 1765								
fl. 1775								

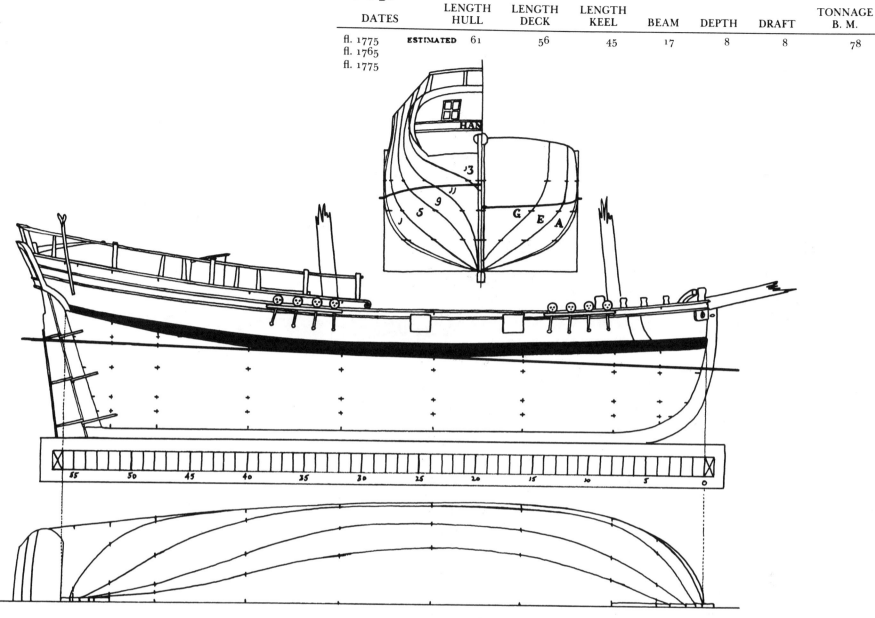

HARLEQUIN/PORTO, 12

THE 12-gun ship *Harlequin* was built in America about 1778, and was purchased by the French for use as a fast mail packet in the West Indies. She was captured by the brand-new 32-gun British frigate *Cerberus* off Martinique on 6 June 1780. Commodore George Johnston wrote to his superiors in July, praising his new acquisition and saying that she was extremely swift. However, her shape was such that she could easily be overloaded, and when that was coupled with the unusual square-tuck stern with its high drag she was a disaster. Naval officials not being noted for a keen eye for the finer points of a ship, *Harlequin* was overloaded and Johnston's superiors reprimanded him for his poor choice of a purchase; they ordered her sold on 19 June 1782. While in British service she was named *Porto* because Johnston expected she would be used on the coast of Portugal. One of the most unusual features about this pretty design was her small amount of freeboard even when she was light.

	DATES	LENGTH HULL	LENGTH DECK	LENGTH KEEL	BEAM	DEPTH	DRAFT	TONNAGE B. M.
	ca. 1778-1782	91	80	67	20	9	11	141

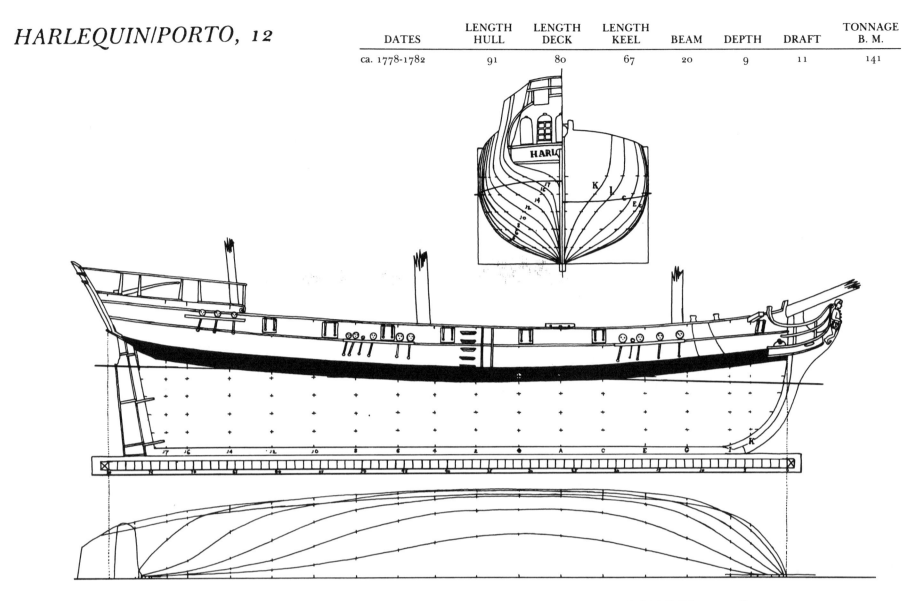

HERO (ex-GENERAL GATES) & GRAND TURK, 18

LATE in 1776, Congress authorized the construction of a number of new ships for the Continental Navy, including three corvettes of 18 guns apiece (although the actual bill has not been found). These were subsequently named *Ranger* (built at Portsmouth, New Hampshire), *Saratoga* (built at Philadelphia), and *General Gates* (built at Boston). *General Gates* was launched in 1777 and taken into the navy in 1778 and named after the supposed hero of the great victory at Saratoga in 1777, General Horatio Gates. However, the ship that was constructed at Newburyport, Massachusetts for the order of the Congress was apparently abandoned by Congress due to lack of money; late in 1777, Congress decided that the name *General Gates* should go to a newly-built prize brig of 160 tons, formerly named *Industrious Bee*. Before the construction project had been abandoned, Stephen Cleveland, who had been appointed as one of her lieutenants, commissioned the engraving of personal bookplates bearing his signature under a portrait of the ship under sail; presumably, he was familiar with her plans. The bookplate, a surviving example of which is in the Essex Institute, Salem, Massachusetts, shows her flying the Grand Union Ensign. What happened to the ship begun to the account of Congress?

Captain James Tracy and the privateer brig *Yankee Hero* were captured by the British frigate *Milford* in June 1776. Tracy was exchanged in December 1776 and soon began looking for a new ship to buy. It seems that he took over the project that had been started for Congress. The new ship was launched on 2 June 1777 and named *Hero*. She departed Boston in August and ran into a severe hurricane; she was overwhelmed and lost with all hands.

Another ship that may have been built to a similar design was the 18-gun privateer *Grand Turk*. She was built for Salem merchant prince Elias Haskett Derby in 1780-1 at Hanover, Massachusetts (several miles up the North River, near Plymouth). She was successful as a privateer; one of her prizes was *Pompey* which was later renamed *America of Charleston*. In 1786, Derby sent her to the French island of Mauritius in the Indian ocean under the command of Ebenezer West, and there she was chartered by French merchants to take their goods to Canton. Derby was so impressed at the rewards of this voyage that he sent the ship out again the following year under the command of his own son, Elias, Jr., who had just graduated from Harvard. Young Derby had an astute eye for a profit, so he accepted the offer of a French merchant to buy the battered ship for twice her book value in 1788. On her first visit to Canton, she brought back porcelain bowls showing a ship under full sail flying the stars and stripes with the caption "Grand Turk." In fact, the picture was adapted from the frontispiece of Hutchinson's *Naval Architecture* (1777) depicting a British ship called *Hall*; this same picture was amended and used over and over by Canton artists. Thus, it is not an accurate portrait of *Grand Turk*.

The plans of these ships shown here are based on the engraving in the Stephen Cleveland bookplate and on the assumption that they were scaled-down versions of the frigates *Hancock* and *Boston*, although Massachusetts had other capable designers working at that time.

HERO (ex-GENERAL GATES) & GRAND TURK, 18

DATES	LENGTH HULL	LENGTH DECK	LENGTH KEEL	BEAM	DEPTH	DRAFT	TONNAGE B. M.
1777-1777 1780-?	ESTIMATED 111	94	80	27	11	12	300

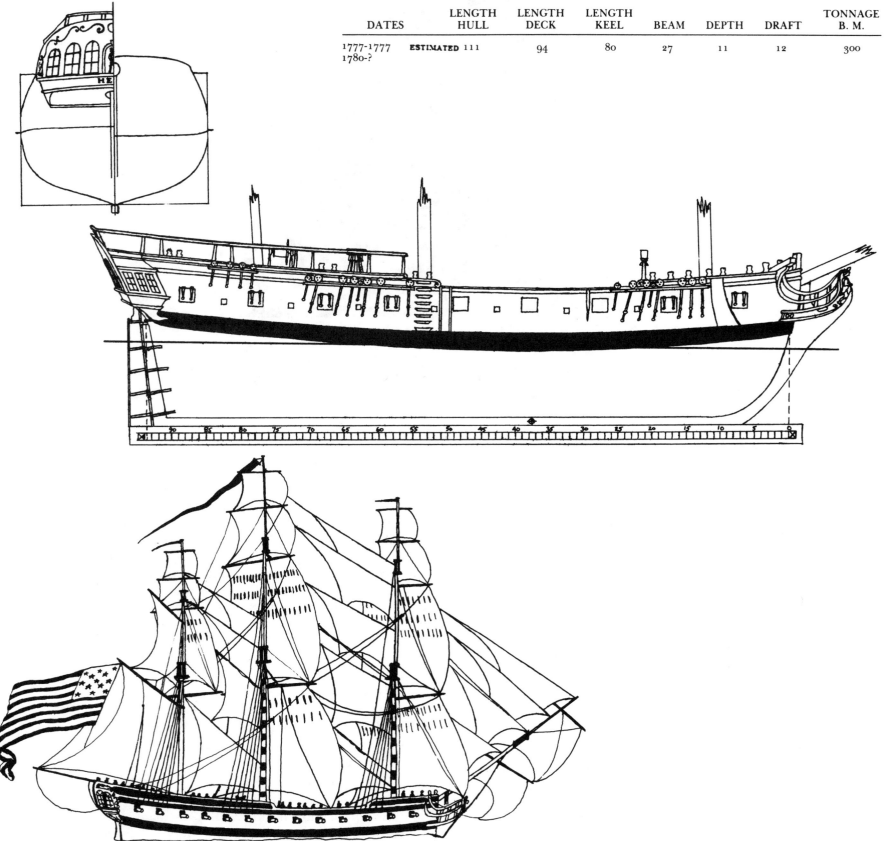

Canton porcelain punchbowl decoration purporting to represent the ship *Grand Turk*, but actually copied and adapted from an engraving in Hutchinson's *Naval Architecture* of the British ship *Hall*; *Hall* was the same size as *Grand Turk*, and both had nine gunports, not the thirteen shown on the punchbowl; 1786.

Ship *Hero*, bookplate of Stephen Cleveland, Essex Institute, Salem.

HORNET (ex-FALCON), 10

O NE of the members of the first fleet of the Continental Navy was the little 10-gun sloop *Hornet* from Maryland. Originally named *Falcon,* she was purchased in the autumn of 1775 from William Stone and he was then made her captain. She sailed with the fleet for Nassau in February 1776, but got separated from them in a storm and collided with the sloop *Fly.* *Hornet*'s damage was far greater than *Fly*'s, and she limped back to Philadelphia by early April, having carried away her boom and the top of her mast.

Several months later she was given a new captain, John Nicholson, the younger brother of James Nicholson. He attempted to get her to sea in company with the frigate *Randolph* around Christmas 1776, but British patrols at the mouth of the Delaware thwarted their plans. They did get out in February, guarding a tobacco convoy that was bound for France, but once the convoy was a safe distance from the coast *Hornet* teamed up with *Fly* and headed for Martinique.

They returned from Martinique with some valuable military supplies, but soon found themselves trapped in the Delaware by the British fleet that was forcing its way upriver to open a supply line to Philadelphia. It has for long been reported that *Hornet*, along with others, was burned in the Delaware to avoid capture. In fact, she and some of the smaller vessels (including *Sachem, Fly, Wasp,* and probably *Mosquito*) managed to escape to the open sea. In February 1777, *Hornet* sailed to Charleston to pick up a load of rice and indigo to exchange in Martinique for military supplies, but she never reached Martinique; she was captured by the British schooner *Porcupine*. She was sold in Jamaica, where she was described as Bermuda-built. Her sailing-master was the young Joshua Barney, who took the job at age sixteen.

We have reconstructed *Hornet*'s lines from an existing picture of the sloop (in the background of a portrait of William Stone, painted by Peale) and from knowledge of other Chesapeake Bay sloops. Her rig, according to the painting, included a gaff topsail, very rare on sloops of this period; this may have been an invention from the Chesapeake Bay, as there are gaff topsails in a primitive painting of a Maryland shipyard from before the Revolution.

HORNET (ex-FALCON), 10

DATES	LENGTH HULL	LENGTH DECK	LENGTH KEEL	BEAM	DEPTH	DRAFT	TONNAGE B. M.
ca. 1774-1777 ESTIMATED	64	56	39	18	7	10	75

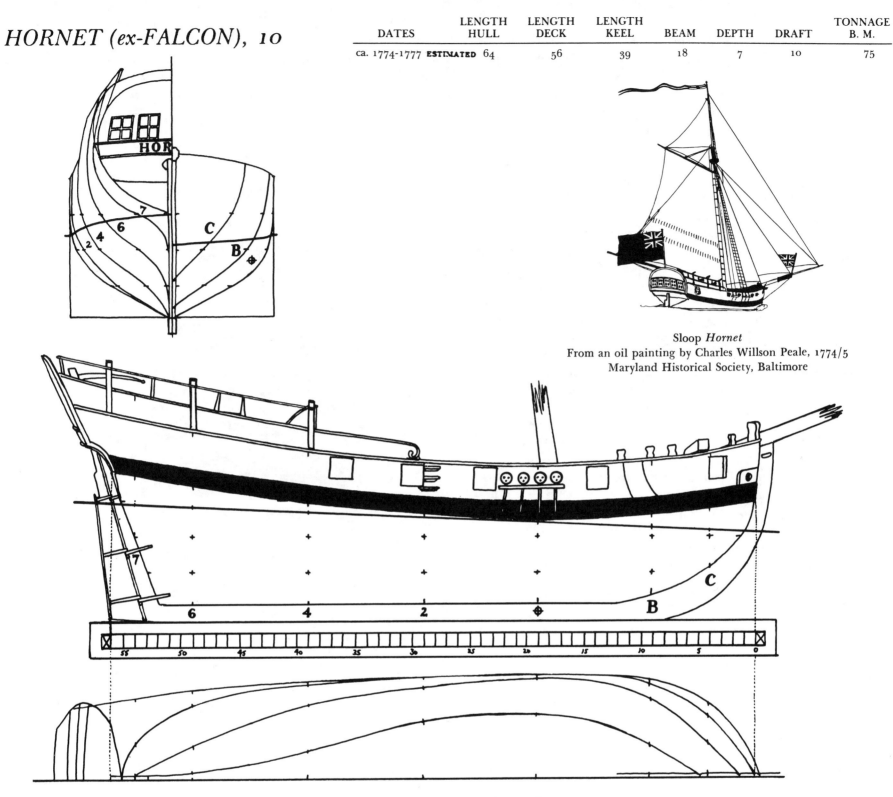

Sloop *Hornet*
From an oil painting by Charles Willson Peale, 1774/5
Maryland Historical Society, Baltimore

INFLEXIBLE, 18

In the summer of 1776, British forces in Canada were building an 18-gun corvette on the St. Lawrence near Quebec City. They had been stung by the American expedition to Quebec the previous year (led by Montgomery and Arnold) and had decided to build this powerful rivercraft with ship rig and shallow draft to make sure Arnold did not show himself on the St. Lawrence again. Suddenly Sir Guy Carleton, the British commander, realized where the real danger lay; Arnold was not planning to come to Quebec, but he was building a fleet on Lake Champlain to prevent Carleton from making a fast attack along the lake into the heart of the infant United States. The corvette would thus be much more useful, in fact almost vital, on the lake.

Carleton immediately ordered the corvette dismantled and the pieces dragged overland to St. John's. There the ship was reassembled in only twenty-eight days by a team working day and night under the direction of Lieutenant John Schank of the Royal Navy; Schank had recently invented the drop-keel or centerboard, but his superiors refused to allow him to use it on the lake even though it would have given the British vessels a marked superiority with the shoal-draft flat-bottomed boats on the lake.

The ship was named *Inflexible* and mounted 18 twelve-pounders on her gun deck, which made her one of the most powerful warships yet built on America's inland waters. Unfortunately, she was quite unable to work to windward, a handicap that Arnold soon perceived. She was placed in commission on 1 October 1776 and immediately set sail with the British fleet toward the south. Arnold's fleet was hiding behind Valcour Island, and the British had gone two miles past him before they saw him. This meant that they would have to tack to windward, and it caused them to be strung out. The schooner *Carleton*, the most weatherly of the British fleet, was able to exchange fire with the Americans as early as noon, but *Inflexible* did not get to the scene of the battle until sunset, at which time the firing ceased. Arnold's fleet slipped away in the foggy night and was a few miles to windward toward Crown Point by the time the British saw them. *Inflexible* and the other British ships were able to catch up to Arnold's rearguard after several hours. They captured the galley *Washington*, and *Inflexible*'s fire so heavily damaged the galley *Congress* (Arnold's flagship) that Arnold was forced to run her ashore and burn her. When he saw that he had destroyed the bulk of the American fleet Carleton withdrew his fleet to St. John for the winter, but that extra winter of time was exactly what Arnold had been trying to buy. Carleton figured that he could have crushed American forces in New York if only he had had an extra four weeks of good weather; four weeks was the time it took to build *Inflexible*, which the British needed to have clear superiority over Arnold's fleet, and four weeks was all Arnold needed to ensure American independence.

Inflexible was used on the lake the following year,

but she had no opposition. Presumably she was broken up at the end of the war. She appears in a number of contemporary paintings and prints of the activities on Lake Champlain, and we have used these as the basis for our reconstruction of her. The only measurement recorded was that she was 180 tons. She had quarter galleries but no head.

Ship *Inflexible*, engraving published by Sayer & Bennett, 1776, National Maritime Museum, Greenwich.

INFLEXIBLE, 18

DATES	LENGTH HULL	LENGTH DECK	LENGTH KEEL	BEAM	DEPTH	DRAFT	TONNAGE B. M.
1776-1783	97	88	75	28	10	9	180

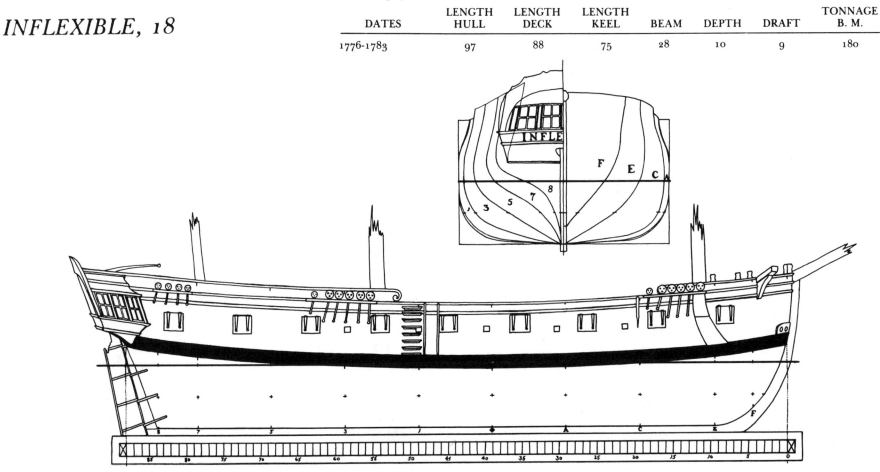

JACK, 14

THERE is a painting by Robert Dodd, from which prints were made, of a battle between the British brig *Observer* and the Salem privateer *Jack*. Both ships were precisely drawn in the picture, which helps in reconstructing them. *Observer* herself had previously served as the Salem privateer *Amsterdam*. During the battle, *Jack*'s captain, listed variously as David or John Ropes, was killed by a shot from *Observer*, and so all resistance crumbled shortly afterward. This was quite fortunate for *Observer*, for *Jack* appears to have been much the stronger ship. *Jack* was taken into Halifax, Nova Scotia, which was only a few miles away. The battle took place on 28 May 1782. *Observer* had almost three times as many crew as *Jack* at the time of the battle.

Jack's design is closely allied to that of the Salem privateer *Mohawk*. The idea of having the gun deck completely covered by a flush spar deck on which more cannons could be placed was an idea that was developed further in the 1790s with the construction of the frigate *Constitution*.

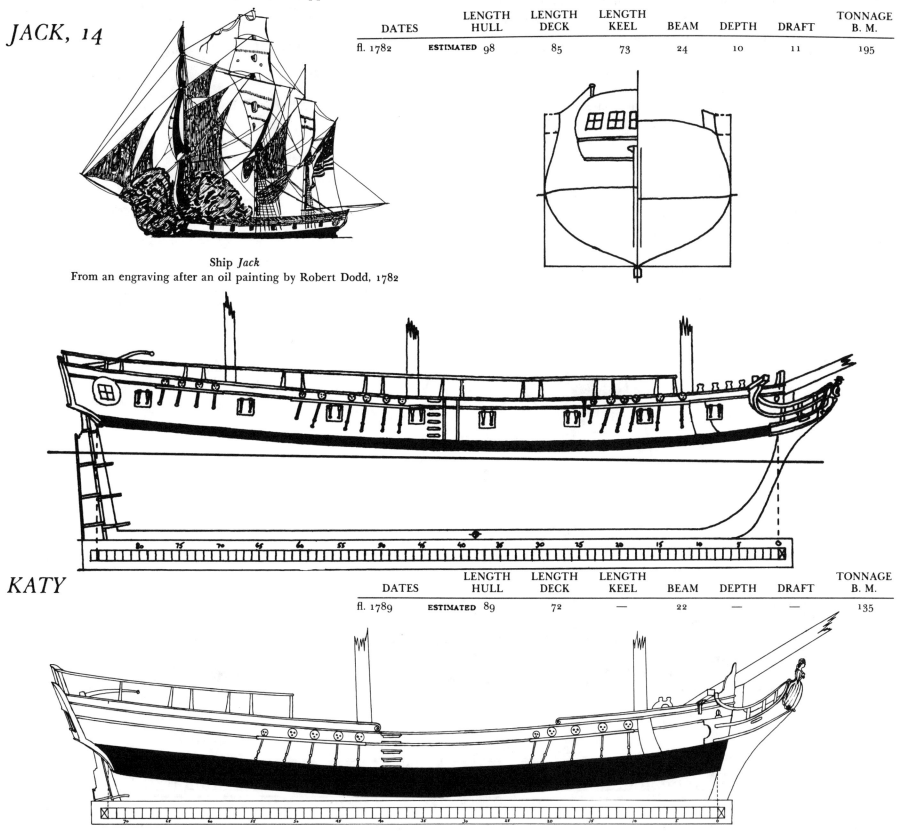

JACK, 14

DATES		LENGTH HULL	LENGTH DECK	LENGTH KEEL	BEAM	DEPTH	DRAFT	TONNAGE B. M.
fl. 1782	ESTIMATED	98	85	73	24	10	11	195

Ship *Jack*
From an engraving after an oil painting by Robert Dodd, 1782

KATY

DATES		LENGTH HULL	LENGTH DECK	LENGTH KEEL	BEAM	DEPTH	DRAFT	TONNAGE B. M.
fl. 1789	ESTIMATED	89	72	—	22	—	—	135

KATY seems to have been a relatively common name for American ships in the eighteenth century, with the result that it is often difficult to find reliable information about the history of any specific vessel of that name. One of these was the merchant brig from Boston that is shown in a fine watercolor painting belonging to the Bostonian Society at the Old State House, Boston. Its owners know no more about the ship than is written on the painting, that her captain was Martin Pease and that she is shown in the painting sailing out of the French port Havre de Grâce. She has no dolphin striker and she is flying an American ensign with thirteen stars and thirteen stripes, so one might date the picture slightly before 1790. Her head was unusually long, and the planking of the bow was reinforced in the manner of some French ships just below the hause hole.

A few words about her color scheme might be helpful, not that it was unusual. Her off-white bottom extended past the waterline to the bottom of the wale. The black paint of the wale itself was extended a few inches above and below the wale. The sheer planks above the ochre of the topsides were painted a light bluish-green, while the planks under the forecastle and quarterdeck rails were bright red, and the canvas or light planks that formed a bulwark around the quarterdeck were painted plain black.

Brig *Katy*
From an anonymous French watercolor painting in the style of
Antoine Roux, ca. 1790
The Bostonian Society, Boston

KING GEORGE, 24

DATES	LENGTH HULL	LENGTH DECK	LENGTH KEEL	BEAM	DEPTH	DRAFT	TONNAGE B. M.
1756 -? ESTIMATED	130	110	90	30	13	14	450

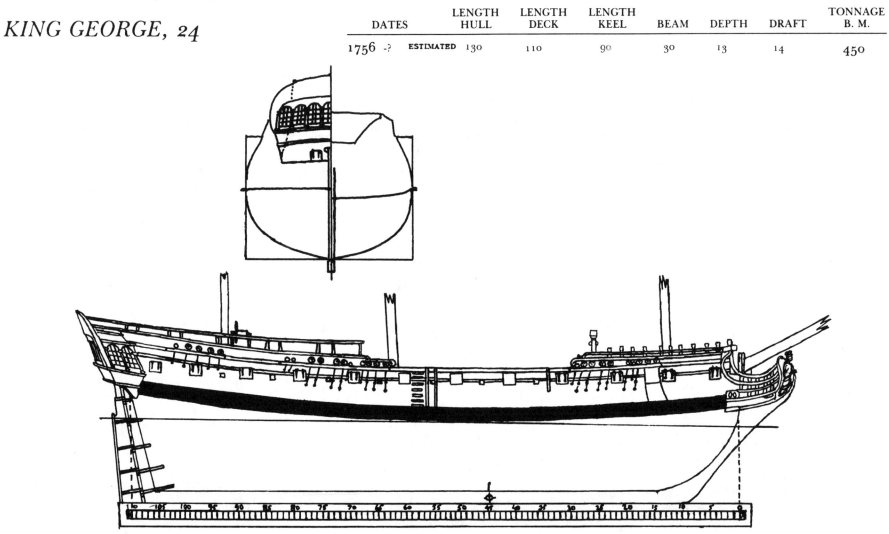

KING GEORGE, 24

About three years after the Province of Massachusetts had sold its 24-gun frigate *Massachusetts*, war with France broke out again in 1756. Governor William Shirley asked the Legislature to build another frigate to protect the province's coasts, fisheries and trade. The 24-gun frigate *King George* was ordered on 14 October at £7000 from John Ruddock, and she was launched the following April 18th. She was placed under the command of Benjamin Hallowell, Jr., who was himself a shipbuilder. She was taken on a number of almost uneventful cruises as far afield as Louisbourg and Newfoundland to the north and New York to the south. The new governor, Francis Pownall, was fond of her and spent much time aboard her, both for military and social reasons. The Legislature wanted to send her to England in 1760, but the merchants scuttled that plan; when the merchants wanted to send her south for the winter of 1761–2 to guard New England commerce in the Caribbean, the Legislature refused, possibly because there was no way to see that other colonies paid for their fair share of the protection.

With the British capture of Louisbourg and Quebec in 1759, French threats to New England coasts and shipping essentially ended. Similarly, opportunities to capture French prizes in New England waters dwindled. If prosecuting the war as vigorously as possible had been the Massachusetts aim, *King George* should have been sent south after 1759, but she was not, and hence a great opportunity to gain experience for future officers of the Continental Navy was lost — although 13-year-old Samuel Tucker served on her for a few months in a position equivalent to midshipman (no such actual rank existed in her crew). At the end of the war, *King George* was sold at auction on 28 April 1763 to Boston merchant Andrew Hall. She must have needed some repairs, for she did not sail for six months. She sailed for Lisbon with a cargo of lumber and barrel staves and so passes out of the historical record. Very little is known about her; she is described as measuring about 450 tons (the British 24-gun frigate *Rose*, built the same year, measured 444 tons), and so the plan shown here is necessarily speculative, being an adaptation of the plans of the earlier (and larger) 24-gun frigate *Boston*.

LADY HAMMOND, 10

DATES	LENGTH HULL	LENGTH DECK	LENGTH KEEL	BEAM	DEPTH	DRAFT	TONNAGE B. M.
ca. 1788-?	70	64	51	20	10	10	119

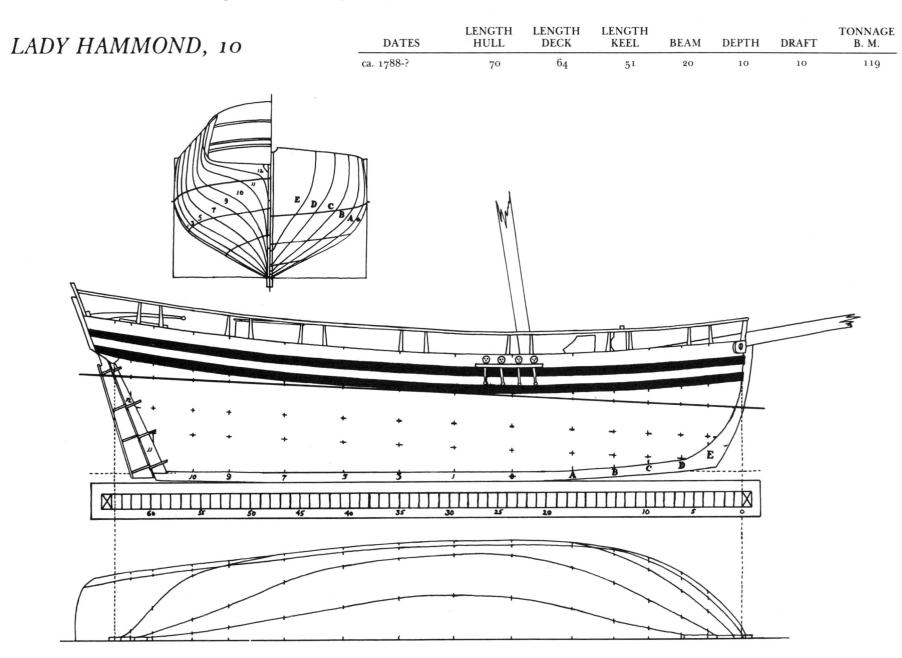

LADY HAMMOND, 10

THE 10-gun sloop *Lady Hamond* was built in Bermuda about 1788. She was measured in Britain and her lines taken off in both 1792 and 1804, and one of these drafts is now on file at the Science Museum in London. The scale is badly drawn, but the drawing is good enough to be interpreted reasonably accurately. At one time or another she was rigged as a schooner, or at least such a change was contemplated. In 1804, the Admiralty ordered twelve sloops or cutters built to her design in Bermuda, but for some reason the Bermudans thought her design to be out of date and used a completely different design, which was probably nowhere near as fast.

She had a flush deck, somewhat like some European cutters and luggers. She had a double wale, which was unusual for this late date, and a fairly sharp deadrise. Her keel, which was rockered at the forward end, had quite a bit of drag.

LADY WASHINGTON

DATES	LENGTH HULL	LENGTH DECK	LENGTH KEEL	BEAM	DEPTH	DRAFT	TONNAGE B. M.
ca. 1786-1798 **ESTIMATED** 74		58	46	19	10	9	90

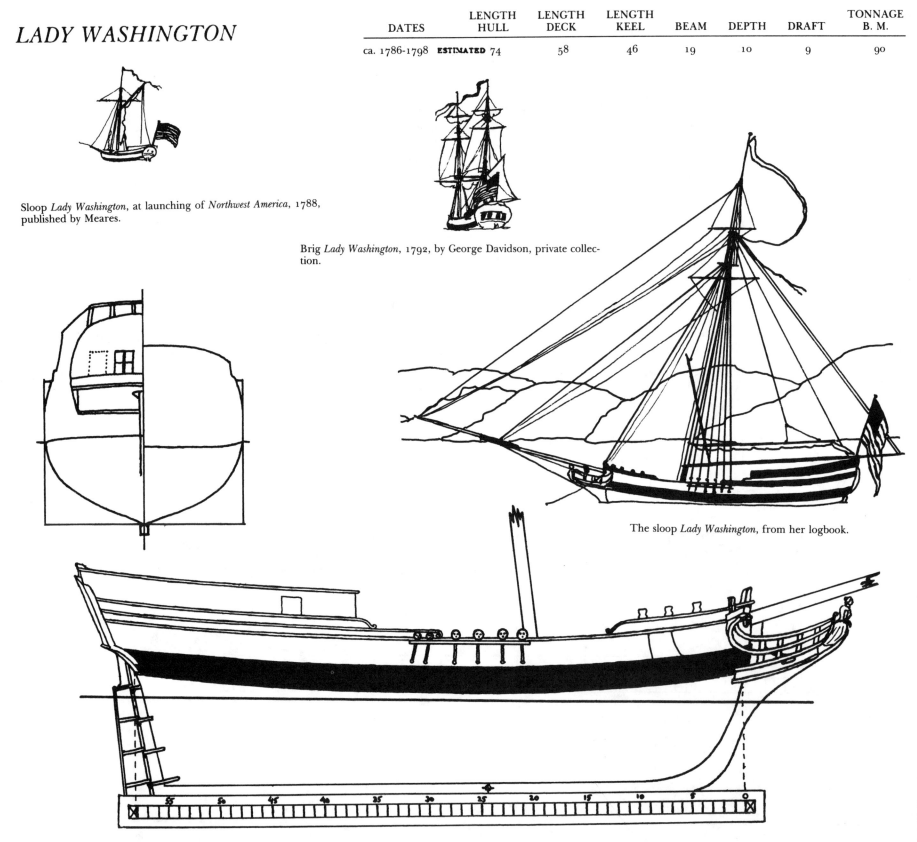

Sloop *Lady Washington*, at launching of *Northwest America*, 1788, published by Meares.

Brig *Lady Washington*, 1792, by George Davidson, private collection.

The sloop *Lady Washington*, from her logbook.

Two sketches of sloop *Union* from her logbook by John Boit, 1794, Massachusetts Historical Society.

Sloop off Boston Light
From a mezzotint dated 1717

American sloop at Louisbourg, French manuscript drawing, 1758.

LADY WASHINGTON

WHEN the ship *Columbia* departed on her epic voyage around the world in 1787, she was accompanied by a tiny 90-ton sloop. The sloop is sometimes known as *Washington* in the records, but more often called *Lady Washington* (the new republic frowned on titles, but Martha Washington seems to have been called Lady Washington on many occasions), just as the ship *Columbia* is also known as *Columbia Rediviva*.

The sloop's captain was Robert Gray of Tiverton, Rhode Island, who was an enterprising man. When the two vessels were parted from each other in a storm off Cape Horn, Gray managed to get his sloop to the rendezvous at Nootka Sound before Kendrick could get *Columbia* there, so *Lady Washington* became the first American vessel to reach the West Coast. Gray explored and traded (mostly for sea otter skins, which he would

sell in China for a high price) along the coast from Oregon to a point far up in Alaska. He then amicably arranged with Kendrick that they should swap commands. Gray took *Columbia* back home, via China, and Kendrick took *Lady Washington* to China. Then he sold the sloop to himself, never actually sending the money back to the owners, and wandered around the Pacific dabbling in trade. In December 1794, Kendrick was killed in a freak accident: the sloop had arrived at Honolulu and Kendrick asked the captains of British ships present to salute his American flag. They cheerfully complied, but the powder in one cannon was damp so the gunner fired the next cannon in line—which was loaded with a ball that killed Kendrick. She was the first vessel to fly the American flag in Alaska and in Japan.

Kendrick had converted her to a brig at Macao in 1790.

Later, she was sold at Canton and sent back to northwest America and returned with otterskins and sandalwood in December 1795. She is known to have been at Manila on 28 May 1798, but she was wrecked either on the Chinese coast or near Malacca shortly thereafter.

Three sketches of *Lady Washington* are known, two of her as a sloop and one as a brig. She was a simple New England sloop with a square topsail to be set only downwind. Curiously enough, she had a long head, seldom found on sloops, but probably a necessity on long voyages.

A sloop of remarkably similar appearance, *Union*, sailed from Rhode Island to northwest America and back in 1794-6, under the command of John Boit who started the voyage at the age of only nineteen.

LEE, 8

DATES	LENGTH HULL	LENGTH DECK	LENGTH KEEL	BEAM	DEPTH	DRAFT	TONNAGE B. M.
1775-ca. 1783	48	44	34	16	5	4	48

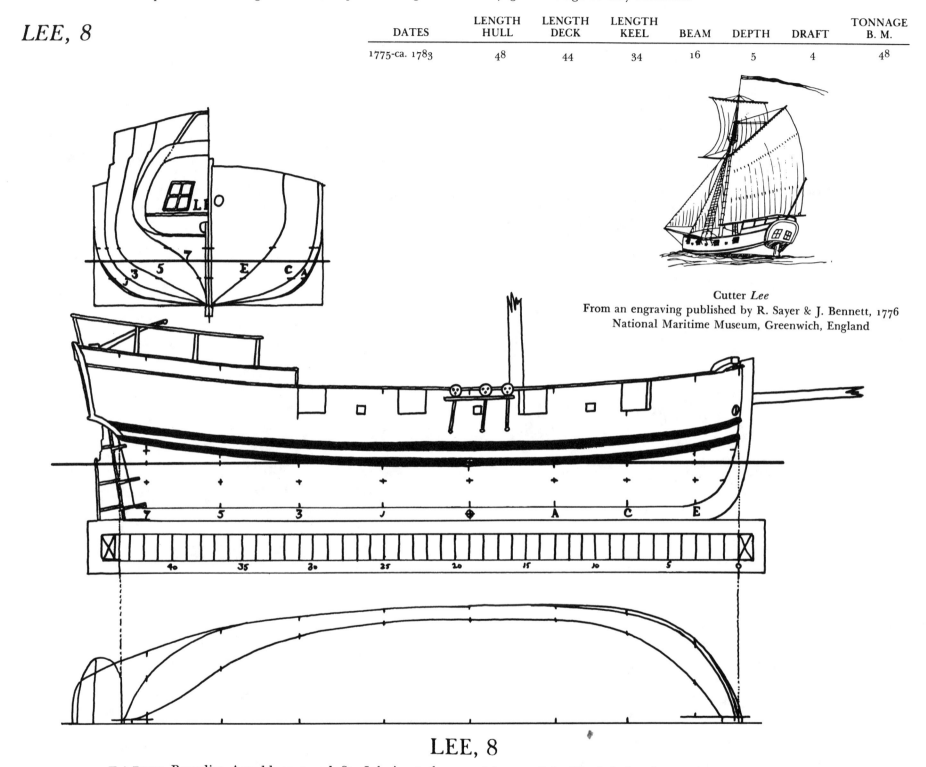

Cutter *Lee*
From an engraving published by R. Sayer & J. Bennett, 1776
National Maritime Museum, Greenwich, England

LEE, 8

WHEN Benedict Arnold captured St. John's at the northern end of Lake Champlain in May 1775, he took possession of two vessels that had recently been built by the British: the sloop *George* (which he renamed *Enterprise*) and the schooner *Royal Savage*. The British had also begun construction of a cutter, but all they had built to that date was the frames. Arnold took these over and had his men complete the vessel, which he named *Lee* (after General Charles Lee, or possi-bly one of the Virginia Lees).

She served under Arnold at the battle of Valcour Island in October 1776, but was captured by the British shortly after the battle and was incorporated into their fleet. The British take-off of her lines following her capture survives at the National Maritime Museum at Greenwich and a number of contemporary pictures of the fleets on Lake Champlain portray her. With her blunt lines and flat bottom she seems not to have been

a good sailer, but she had ports for three large oars or
sweeps per side so as to be able to row when the wind
was foul or calm.

LEXINGTON (ex-WILD DUCK), 14

DATES	LENGTH HULL	LENGTH DECK	LENGTH KEEL	BEAM	DEPTH	DRAFT	TONNAGE B. M.
ca. 1773-1777	94	86	74	25	10	11	210

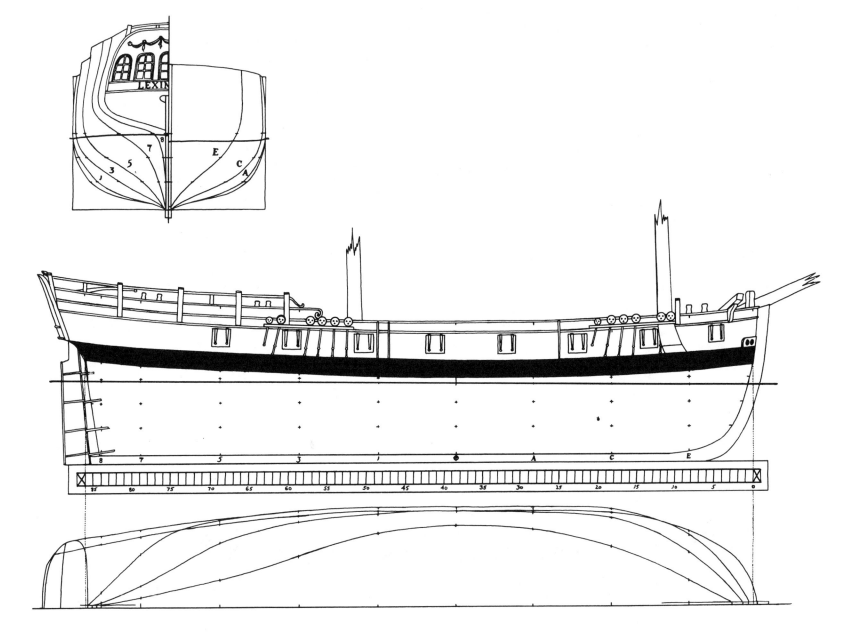

Brig *Lexington*
From an oil painting, probably by Francis Holman, 1777
Private collection, New Haven, Connecticut

Brig *Lexington*
From an anonymous watercolor painting, 1777
National Maritime Museum, Greenwich, England

LEXINGTON (ex-WILD DUCK), 14

A LARGE merchant brig called *Wild Duck,* probably built in Philadelphia, was purchased in the Caribbean by the Maryland Committee of Safety in 1775, fitted with guns, and then sold to the Continental Navy in the fall. She was fitted with 14 four-pounders, 2 six-pounders, and 12 swivels, and given the name of *Lexington.* Joshua Humphreys was given the job of converting her into a warship, and John Barry was made captain. On 7 April 1776 she captured the small armed sloop *Edward* (tender to the frigate *Liverpool*) which was the first capture of the war by a Continental Navy ship in a single-ship action (it is because of this capture, and because of the fact that Barry was the first officer to receive a commission in the reconstituted United States Navy in the 1790s, that many Philadelphians and Americans of Irish descent consider John Barry to have been the "founder of the Navy," whatever that means). *Lexington* was careful to stay close to the coast to avoid capture by British patrols, which could not match her shallow draft. On 29 June she helped the gunpowder brig *Nancy* escape from six enemy ships off Cape May. Then Barry was relieved by William Hallock of Maryland.

Hallock took her to the West Indies and back, but was captured at the mouth of the Delaware by the 32-gun British frigate *Pearl.* Hallock and his officers were taken onto the frigate, but the rest of the crew stayed on the brig under her prize crew of six men. In the night the 70 Americans rose up, overpowered the prize crew, and brought the brig back to Philadelphia.

Her next captain was Henry Johnson, a Massachusetts privateersman who had already been captured and had escaped from a British prison. He set sail for France on 27 February 1777 from Baltimore. After taking two prizes he arrived at Bordeaux on 3 April and delivered some important dispatches from Congress to Paris. He was ordered to take *Lexington* a few miles up the coast to Nantes, and narrowly escaped from the 80-gun ship *Foudroyant.* At Nantes he joined the squadron of Lambert Wickes with the cutter *Reprisal* and the lugger *Surprise,* and together they set out to attack the Irish linen fleet. They missed the linen fleet, but took eighteen prizes between them. Then they were chased by a British squadron and sought sanctuary in different French ports on 27 June.

Lexington left France with dispatches for Congress on 17 September 1777, but two days later she met the British cutter *Alert. Alert,* under Lieutenant John Bazely, had only ten guns, but she had a copper bottom, which made her the faster vessel. They fought each other on and off for nine and a half hours, doing damage to the rigging on both sides. Finally, Johnson decided to surrender after running out of ammunition (or, as one report said, when the French members of the crew refused to man the guns any more). Fortunately, Johnson had the presence of mind to throw the dispatches overboard in a weighted bag first. *Alert* suffered three killed while *Lexington* lost seven.

The appearance of the *Lexington* is known to us through a fine oil painting by either Francis Holman or one of the Cleveley brothers, showing her in the act of surrendering to *Alert,* and from a contemporary watercolor of the same scene. At that time, she was apparently setting royals on both masts, and two spritsails. From British records after her capture we know her length and breadth, and from the report of a British spy in Philadelphia we know that she had a "square-tuck stern painted yellow, and a low, rounded stem painted lead colour, black sides and yellow mouldings." From the watercolor we know that she had no head (the stem is hidden in the oil painting), and we can see from the painting that her foremast was stepped very far forward. (The real *Lexington* clearly bears no resemblance at all to the model plans bearing her name that have been in wide circulation for many years. The model plans appear to represent a vessel of the 1815 period.)

LIBERTY

DATES		LENGTH HULL	LENGTH DECK	LENGTH KEEL	BEAM	DEPTH	DRAFT	TONNAGE B. M.
fl. 1768	ESTIMATED	64	55	—	18	—	—	85

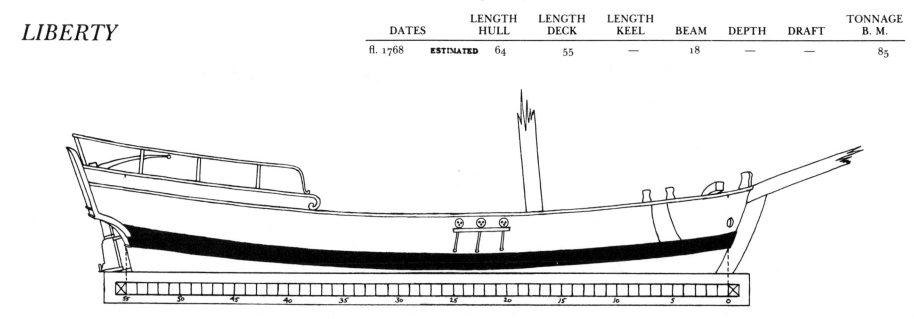

LIBERTY

On 9 May 1768 John Hancock's little sloop *Liberty* arrived in Boston with a cargo of wine and other goods. The amount of wine that was declared to the Customs was considerably less than such a vessel could carry, so the Customs officials suspected that she had actually carried far more wine and had smuggled it off during the night. When they found a witness to the smuggling, they seized the hapless sloop, using seamen and marines from the 50-gun ship *Romney* for protection. Boston radicals rioted, seriously injuring some of the Customs commissioners and publicly burning a yacht that belonged to one of the commissioners. Although the seizure took place on 10 June, the court procedure lasted all the following winter. Hancock eventually lost the sloop, and she was given to the Customs Service to assist them with their patroling.

Under the command of Lieutenant Reid, *Liberty* (what a bizarre name for a Customs vessel!) was sent to Newport, Rhode Island. Presumably she was outfitted with a handful of carriage guns, and she did such a good job at interfering with the smugglers (smuggling was Rhode Island's major industry at that time) that the local mob found a slim pretext and boarded the sloop when she came alongside the dock. They forced the crew ashore, pillaged the sloop of all her contents, cut down her spars with axes, and set her adrift in the har-bor, whereupon she grounded less than a mile away at Goat Island. In the meantime, they took her longboat and dragged it to a prominent spot and publicly burned it. The next night, "persons unknown" boarded the sloop and finished the destruction by burning her to the waterline. This was 19 July 1769, five years before independence.

Liberty's appearance is known to us through watercolors by Christian Remick, showing her in Boston Harbor protected by British warships from being retaken by the Boston mob.

Sloop *Liberty*
From a watercolor painting by Christian Remick, 1768
Massachusetts Historical Society, Boston

LIBERTY (ex-KATHARINE), 8

Philip Skene was a prosperous gentleman who lived at the southern end of Lake Champlain in New York, at a place he immodestly called Skenesborough (most atlases call the place Whitehall today, but local inhabitants renamed it Skenesborough at least for the period of the Bicentennial). Skene had a yacht built for him, and he named her *Katharine* after his wife. This yacht had two masts, and some accounts called her a schooner while others said she was a ketch. Based on the pictorial evidence (it has been suggested that even this one picture of her, entitled *God Bless Our Armes,* is actually a forgery dating only from the 1930s) she seems to have been a ketch, with a single yard on the mainmast on which could be set a square sail when the wind was fair. The rail of the quarterdeck projected out over the stern in the manner of a pink.

In May 1775 Ethan Allen and his Green Mountain Boys captured Fort Ticonderoga on the shores of Lake Champlain. A few days earlier, another group of New England troops seized the yacht *Katharine,* armed her with eight small carriage guns, and set sail for St. John's at the other end of the lake, with Benedict Arnold at the tiller. St. John's put up no resistance and Arnold was able to add the sloop *George* and the schooner *Royal Savage* to his fleet; both had been recently built at St. John's. The date was 18 May 1775, and some enthusi-asts claim that this was the first naval battle of the Revolution, even if there was no actual resistance by the British. *Liberty* missed the battle of Valcour Island since she had been sent on a mission elsewhere, but she was burned to avoid capture in 1777.

Ketch *Liberty*
From the sketch "God Bless Our Armes," 1776
Fort Ticonderoga Museum, Fort Ticonderoga, New York

LIBERTY (ex-KATHARINE), 8

DATES	LENGTH HULL	LENGTH DECK	LENGTH KEEL	BEAM	DEPTH	DRAFT	TONNAGE B. M.
ca. 1770-1777	**ESTIMATED** 48	41	—	14	—	—	40

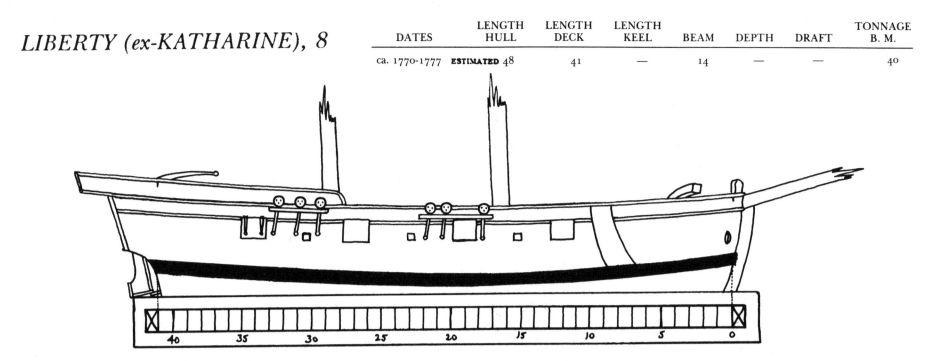

LONDON/GRASSHOPPER/BASILISK, [14]

DATES	LENGTH HULL	LENGTH DECK	LENGTH KEEL	BEAM	DEPTH	DRAFT	TONNAGE B. M.
ca. 1770-1783	112	93	69	27	11	16	282

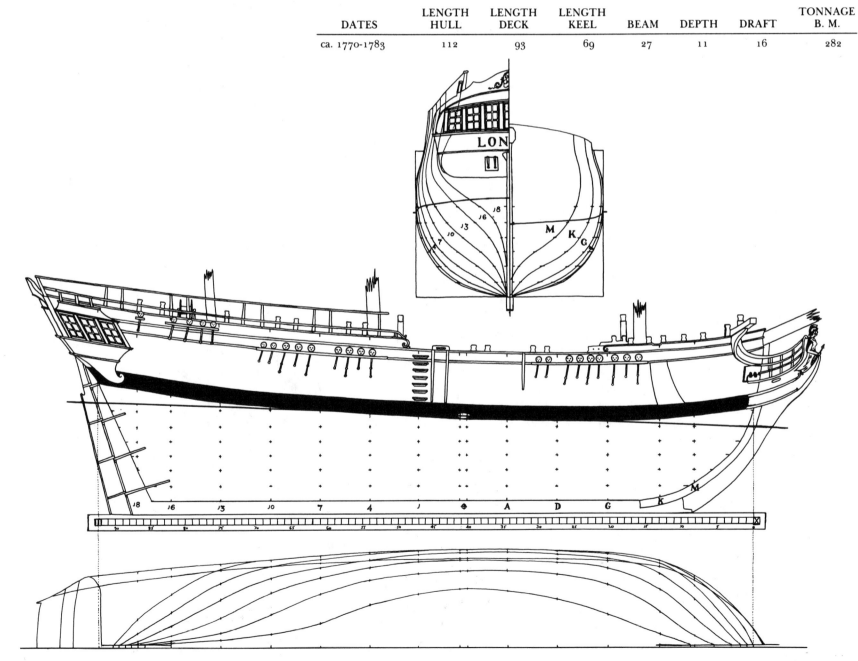

LONDON/GRASSHOPPER/BASILISK, [14]

THE merchant ship *London* was built in New York in 1770 or 1771, and was presumably used in the transatlantic trade. About 1775 she was chartered by the Admiralty for use in transporting troops to America, and in 1776 she was surveyed at Deptford with a view to purchasing her for the navy. She was purchased in 1777 and fitted with 14 guns; there is no existing plan of the location of her gunports, but they must have been very close to the water. Her new name was *Grasshopper,* and she was used as a guard for the con-voy that was unsuccessfully attacked by the Continental ships *Alfred* and *Raleigh* on 3 September 1777.

On 27 August 1779 she was renamed *Basilisk* and was fitted out as a fireship; this entailed, among other things, rehinging the gunport lids so that they opened downward instead of upward in order to prevent them from closing and snuffing out the fire. She was never used as a fireship, and was finally sold at Plymouth (England) in April 1783. Her plans survive at the National Maritime Museum at Greenwich. She appears to have carried an unusually large sail area.

LORD CAMDEN/VULCAN

THE merchant ship *Lord Camden* (this ship and the city of Camden, New Jersey, were both named after the lord Chancellor of Britain in the 1760s) was built in Philadelphia and registered there in March 1775. She was purchased for the Royal Navy not long after and was fitted to be a fireship under the name of *Vulcan*. For this, several ports with hinges at the bottoms of the lids had to be cut in her side, and her plans, together with these alterations, survive at the National Maritime Museum at Greenwich. Unfortunately, the records of the many ships called *Vulcan* and *Volcano* have been much confused over the years so it is not presently possible to know exactly what happened to this ship during the first half of the Revolution. However, it is fairly certain that she was one of the four fireships used by the British against the French fleet in the Chesapeake just as the siege of Yorktown began in 1781. According to one source, she was the last to catch fire and, while the other three went wide of their marks, she very nearly set a French battleship on fire. The Royal Navy used quite a number of American-built ships as fireships in the various wars of the eighteenth century.

As far as we know, *Lord Camden*'s appearance was almost identical to the two other Philadelphia merchant ships of the same date that were later converted into the warships *Alfred* and *Drake,* and it is from her plans that we have reconstructed the plans of those other two ships. Their dimensions were almost exactly the same.

Philadelphia merchant ship *Providence,* 18th century, Elliott family crystal goblet recently on the art market.

Philadelphia merchant ship, detail of an oil portrait of Robert Gilmor by C. W. Peale, 1788, DeWitt Wallace Gallery, Colonial Williamsburg Foundation.

DATES	LENGTH HULL	LENGTH DECK	LENGTH KEEL	BEAM	DEPTH	DRAFT	TONNAGE B. M.
1775-1781	110	92	72	28	12	15	296

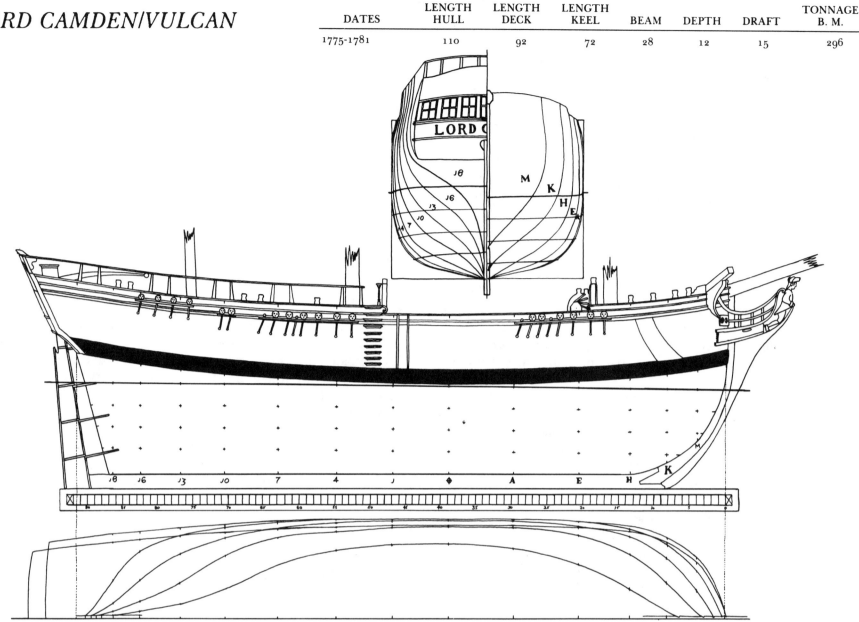

LOVELY LASS/SYLPH/LIGHTNING, [14]

ONE of the many American merchant ships purchased for use in the Royal Navy at the time of the Revolution was built in Philadelphia in 1774 and named *Lovely Lass*. She had the standard Philadelphia pattern of decks and otherwise her shape was fairly similar to *Lord Camden*, except that she was a few feet shorter in length and she had quarter galleries in the stern. The British purchased her in 1776 and renamed her *Sylph*. They outfitted her with 14 carriage guns and perhaps 12 swivels, and fitted her for use as a convoy guard. Experts disagree as to whether all these guns were mounted on the weather deck or whether ports were cut in her sides to receive them; if the former, she would have been quite top-heavy, and if the latter, the ports would have been dangerously close to the waterline, as on *Alfred, Drake,* and others. If she had not been fitted with ports for her guns in 1776, she was definitely fitted with them in 1779, with the lids hinged to open downward, because her new job was to serve as a fireship with the new (and appropriate) name of *Lightning*. She was not actually used as a fireship, and was sold out of the navy when peace came in 1783. Her lines are preserved at the National Maritime Museum at Greenwich.

LOVELY LASS/SYLPH/LIGHTNING, [14]

DATES	LENGTH HULL	LENGTH DECK	LENGTH KEEL	BEAM	DEPTH	DRAFT	TONNAGE B. M.
1774-1783	102	85	68	28	12	14	274

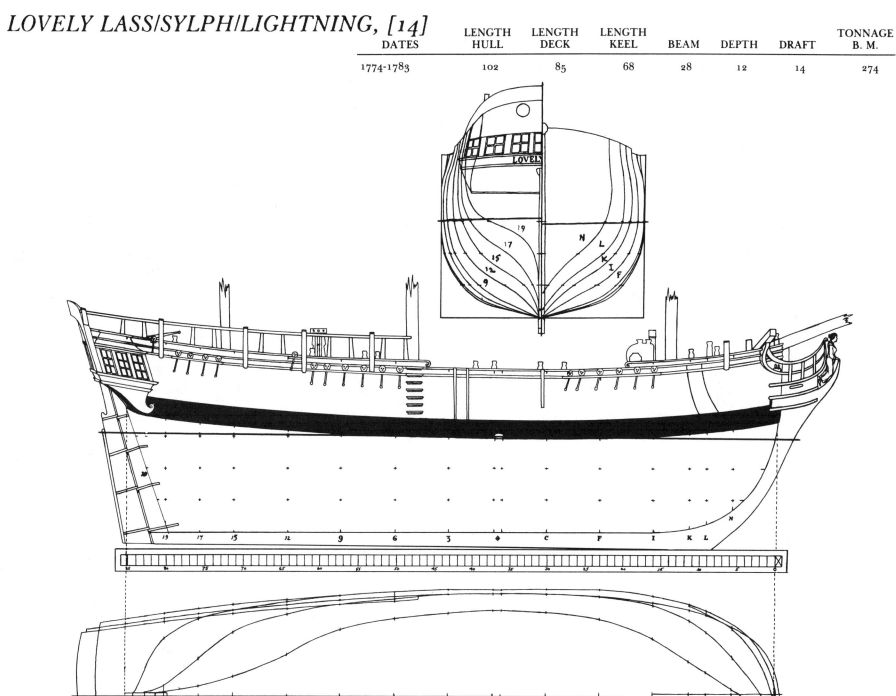

Woodcut of a Philadelphia packet ship, ca. 1785.

Philadelphia merchant ship armed during the War of Independence, from the Captain Robert Niles punchbowl, ca. 1792, Connecticut Historical Society, Hartford.

133

Philadelphia merchant ship, oil painting ca. 1790, Philadelphia Maritime Museum; note crescent moon in canton of flag.

Two views of a Philadelphia merchant ship, oil painting by a British artist (Dominic Serres?), ca. 1790, H. Francis DuPont Winterthur Museum, Delaware.

LOYAL AMERICAN, 38

DATES	LENGTH HULL	LENGTH DECK	LENGTH KEEL	BEAM	DEPTH	DRAFT	TONNAGE B. M.
1781	169	145	121	40	11	17	1000

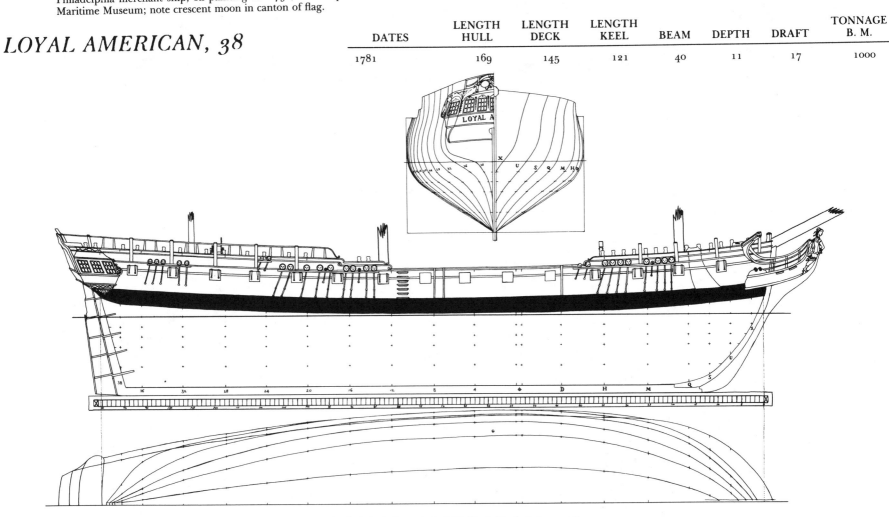

LOYAL AMERICAN, 38

Iᴛ has been customary to compare scientists of the Colonial period with Benjamin Franklin, and to say something like "He was almost another Benjamin Franklin." If the British had won the War of Independence, we might have found ourselves saying "Franklin was almost another Benjamin Thompson." Thompson, who was raised in Massachusetts, was not popular with his contemporaries, who did not care for his undisguised ambition ("He never lost an opportunity to kick an underdog," said one of his biographers). He applied for a commission in the Continental Army, but was turned down when some of his personal enemies spoke out against him. He therefore, with little conviction, became a Loyalist, working first as a spy, then in the government in Britain, and, late in the war, as a cavalry officer in the South.

In 1781, to amuse himself he drew designs for a 38-gun frigate that he hoped the Royal Navy would build for service in American waters, and he won the approval of many senior officials of the navy. However, the war was almost over, so the frigate was never built. Above the water she looked much the same as any other British frigate of her size and date, but below the water she was very sharp, with straight floors and steep deadrise, almost like a Chesapeake Bay privateer schooner. There never had been a design for a large vessel with such deadrise, and it would have been interesting to see how she performed. Chapelle says that she would have been very fast with the right rig, but one suspects that she would have been restricted to carrying only small caliber guns (or carronades?) and stores for only short cruises. Whether or not her specific design influenced

Humphreys when he conceived the *Constitution* almost fifteen years later, the *Constitution* had significantly more deadrise than earlier frigates had; this has often been attributed to a French influence of some sort, but although French theory influenced some American frigates (such as *New York* of 1799, for example) no real French connection can be traced to *Constitution*.

Thompson had the design for his frigate printed in Marmaduke Stalkaart's *Naval Architecture,* published in 1784, and it is from that source that we have obtained her lines. Thompson gave no name for the frigate—that, after all, would have been the province of the navy—but it has been suggested that he intended that she be called *Loyal American,* so that is what we have called her.

MANDA, 24

DATES	LENGTH HULL	LENGTH DECK	LENGTH KEEL	BEAM	DEPTH	DRAFT	TONNAGE B. M.
fl. 1779	ESTIMATED 132	115	100	32	15	14	510

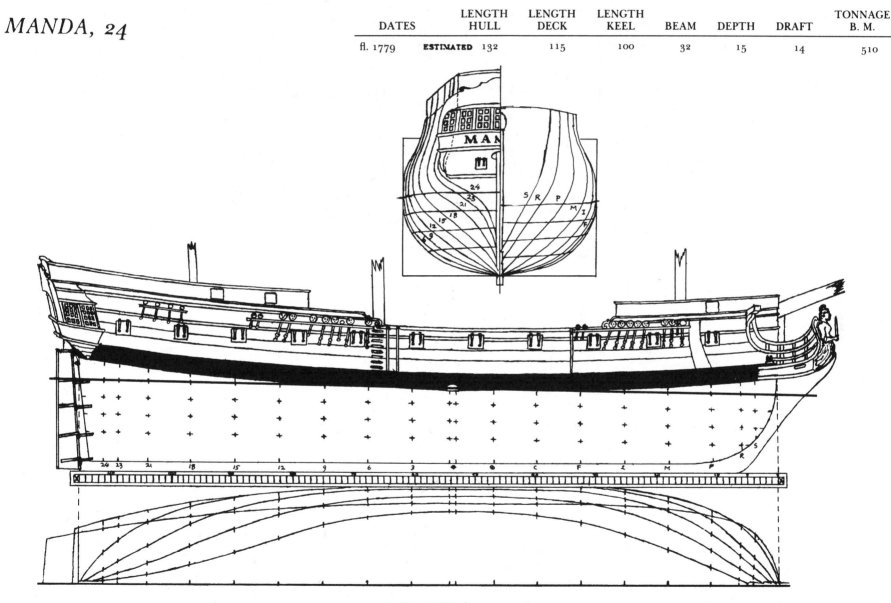

MANDA, 24

THE Abby Aldrich Rockefeller Folk Art Collection at Williamsburg, Virginia has a primitive watercolor by a seaman-artist called (appropriately enough) David Jones. The painting bears the caption in the artist's hand, "Philadelphia July 20th, 1779 The lovely Manda Frigate setting sail." No reference to any such ship by that name or description can be found in records in England and

America, but a certain amount of information can be gathered from the picture itself. The hull resembles closely some of the earliest British 20-gun frigates from the late 1740s, but with the addition of bulwarks on quarterdeck and forecastle. Therefore, the plan shown in this book is a modification of a British plan of about 1750 from the Science Museum, London. *Manda* flies an American, nongovernment ensign with a red fly and thirteen (the artist actually painted fewer than thirteen) red, blue and white horizontal stripes in the canton. The deduction is that *Manda* had once been a frigate in the Royal Navy, had been sold about 1763, rebuilt by private owners for trading and finally reconverted into a warship to serve as a privateer. It is remarkable that such an important ship should otherwise be totally unknown.

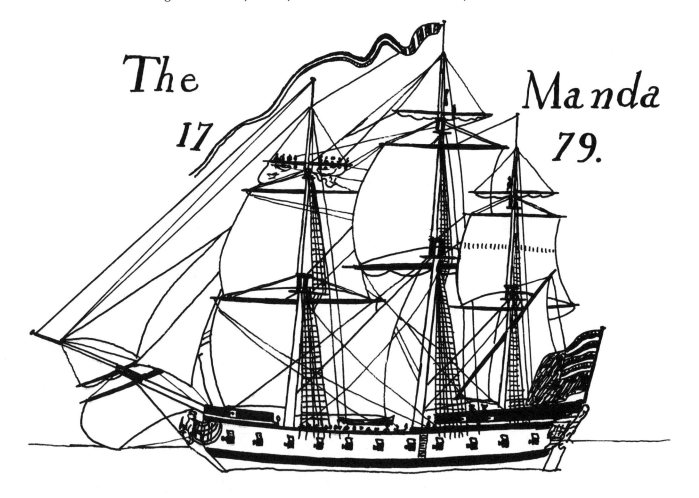

David Jones *Philadelphia July 20.*th *1779 The lovely Manda Frigate setting sail*

Privateer frigate *Manda*, watercolor by David Jones, 1779, Abby Aldrich Rockefeller Folk Art Collection, Williamsburg.

MARIA, 14

WHEN the British decided to launch an invasion into New York from Canada in 1776 there was one small obstacle: Benedict Arnold had hastily built and assembled a fleet of warships on Lake Champlain on the main route southward. The British countered by building an even larger fleet, but the time it took them to do this was just long enough to force them to postpone the invasion until 1777, when the Americans would be readier for them. One of the vessels in the British fleet on the lake was the schooner *Maria,* armed with 14 six-pounders. She had been built in Quebec out of a kit that had been sent over from England in the hold of a large merchant ship, and she was named after Guy Carleton's wife. The plan was to sail her to the Richelieu River and roll her ten miles over logs until she had bypassed the rapids, all the way to St. John's on Lake Champlain. Unfortunately, it rained and rained, which rendered the rollers useless. Lieutenant Schank, the in-

ventor of the centerboard, was directed to dismantle her once more and cart the pieces to St. John's, where they were assembled again.

As soon as the fleet was ready in October 1776, Carleton and Pringle boarded *Maria* and led the way south to Valcour Island. *Maria* somehow totally failed to get into the action, but redeemed herself in the next action when she outstripped all the other British ships in catching up to the American rearguard and helping capture the galley *Washington.* Her design, which is preserved at the National Maritime Museum at Greenwich, shows that she would have been faster than most of the other vessels on the lake. A number of paintings of her also survive. Presumably she was broken up at the end of the war in 1783.

MARIA, 14

DATES	LENGTH HULL	LENGTH DECK	LENGTH KEEL	BEAM	DEPTH	DRAFT	TONNAGE B. M.
1776-1783	79	66	52	22	8	7	128

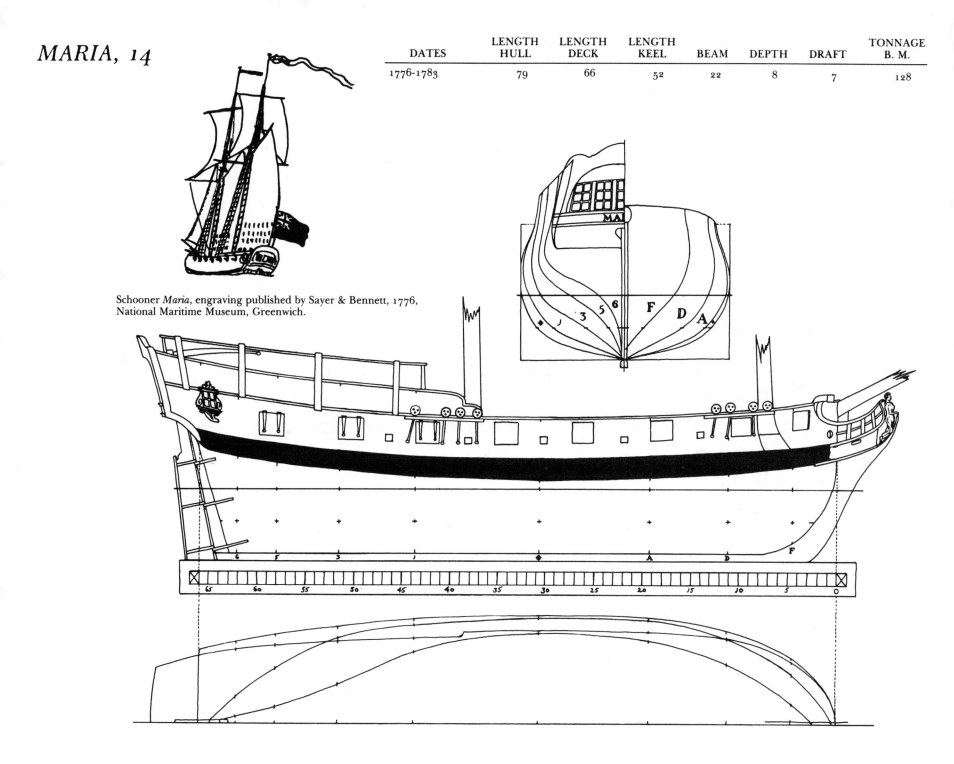

Schooner *Maria*, engraving published by Sayer & Bennett, 1776, National Maritime Museum, Greenwich.

MARIA WILHELMINA, 36

ALMOST nothing has been found about the ship *Maria Wilhelmina*, 1000 tons, that was launched from Thomas Cheeseman's shipyard on the East River in New York City in 1774. She was almost certainly the shape and size of ship known as an East Indiaman, but she was never used by the British East India Company. A number of other nations, such as Sweden, Denmark and the German Baltic ports, used such ships in their trade to India and China, and the Germanic name that she bore suggests that she was built for their account. Since she was probably the largest merchant ship built in America through the end of the eighteenth century she has been included here. For her plans, the general shape of other New York-built ships has been extrapolated to the size and configuration of an East Indiaman.

DATES	LENGTH HULL	LENGTH DECK	LENGTH KEEL	BEAM	DEPTH	DRAFT	TONNAGE B. M.
1774-? ESTIMATED	173	145	114	41	21	21	1000

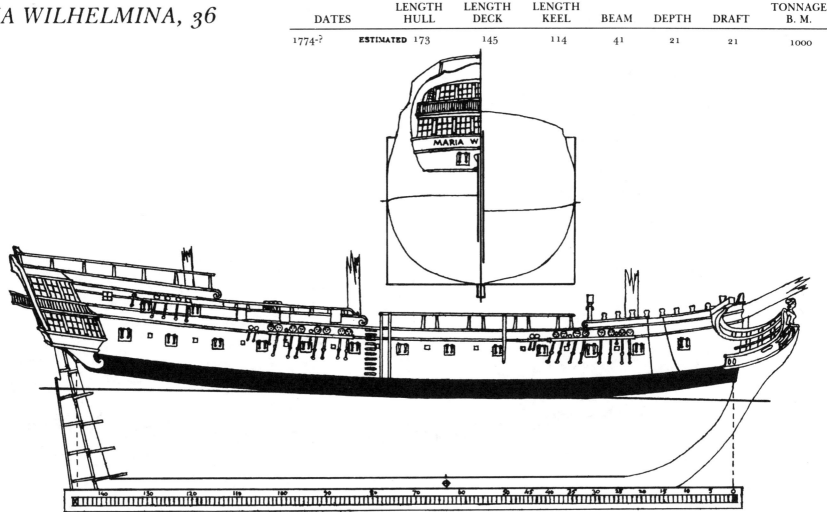

MARQUIS DE VAUDREUIL/RACEHORSE/THUNDER/LE SÉNÉGAL, 18

ONE of the most extraordinary careers of any American-built ship was that of the ship *Marquis de Vaudreuil* (or *Vandrevil*, as it mistakenly appears in some records). No record has been found of her construction, but since the Marquis de Vaudreuil was a much-beloved governor of French Canada and his family remained resident in Canada, it is reasonable to assume that a ship of that name was built along the Saint Lawrence, perhaps about 1756. She was captured by the British in 1757 and the Royal Navy renamed her *Racehorse*. When originally built, she was pierced for twenty guns, and she was of stout enough construction and large enough beam that she could have carried that many with ease. However, the Royal Navy had other plans for her; they cut down her topsides more than five feet, cut ports for ten guns on her new weather-deck and installed beds for two mortars.

In 1773, she was sent with another bomb vessel, *Carcass*, on a voyage of exploration into the Arctic under the command of C. J. Phipps (with Horatio Nelson and Nicholas Biddle among the midshipmen). On the way, she measured an ocean depth of 683 fathoms, which remained a record for many years. When she returned, her topsides were repaired and ports were cut for sixteen guns. At that point, she was renamed *Thunder*, a more appropriate name for a bomb ship. As a bomb, she took part in Sir Peter Parker's ill-fated attack on Charleston. She had a 13-inch mortar and an 11-inch mortar, one of which cracked its bed at Charleston. She was captured by D'Estaing's French

fleet at Newport, Rhode Island in 1778. The French named her *Le Sénégal* and sent her to Africa. The British recaptured her in a five-hour battle on the Gambia River on 11 November, 1780; eleven days later, *Senegal* blew up inexplicably, killing all of her 23 British crew.

Because she looked so different after being cut down, two different profiles are shown here, based on the three sets of plans of her at the National Maritime Museum, Greenwich.

Ship *Racehorse* in the Arctic, 1773, John Cleveley, National Maritime Museum, Greenwich.

MARQUIS DE VAUDREUIL/RACEHORSE/THUNDER/LE SÉNÉGAL, 18

DATES	LENGTH HULL	LENGTH DECK	LENGTH KEEL	BEAM	DEPTH	DRAFT	TONNAGE B. M.
ca. 1756-1780	115	97	81	30	18	14	350

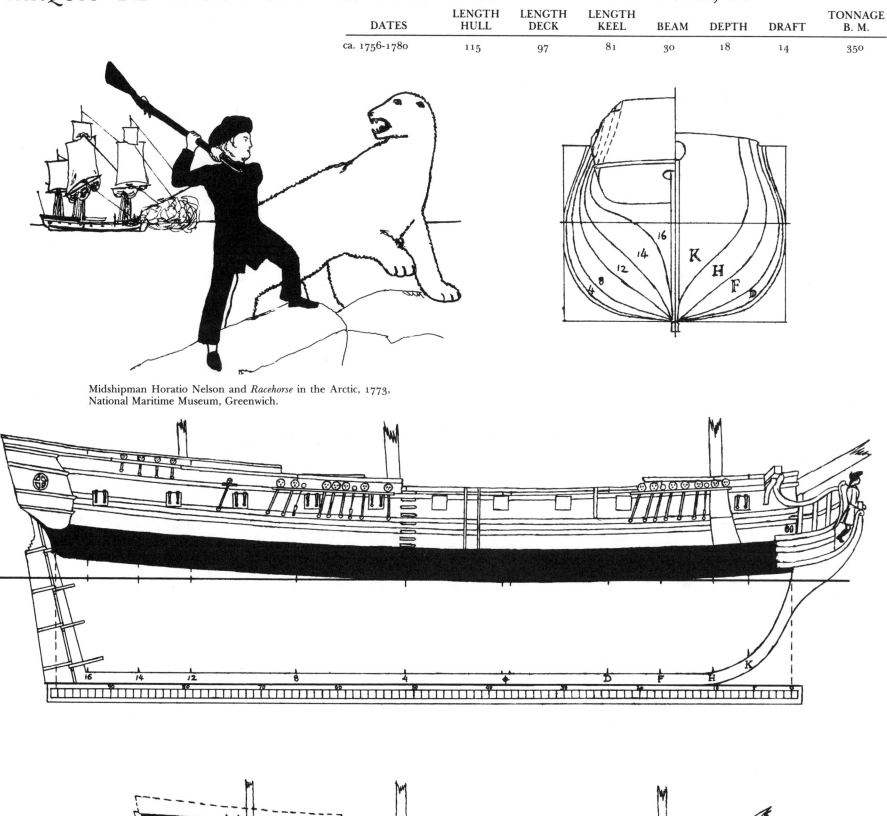

Midshipman Horatio Nelson and *Racehorse* in the Arctic, 1773, National Maritime Museum, Greenwich.

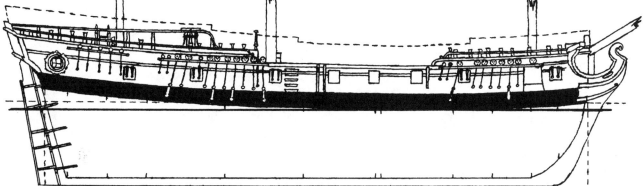

DATES	LENGTH HULL	LENGTH DECK	LENGTH KEEL	BEAM	DEPTH	DRAFT	TONNAGE B. M.
1789-ca. 1792 **ESTIMATED**	160	137	116	38	11	17	820

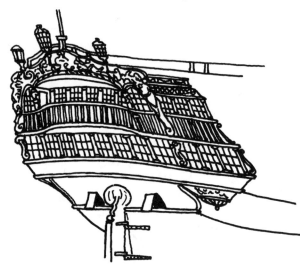

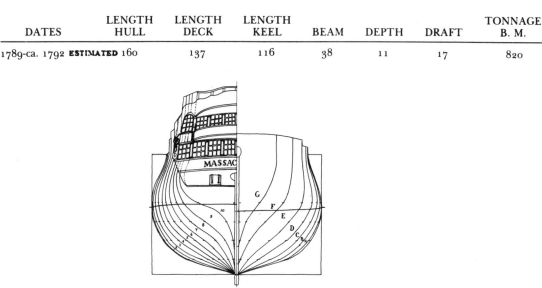

Stern of East Indiaman *Massachusetts*, S. Skillin, 1789, New York Public Library.

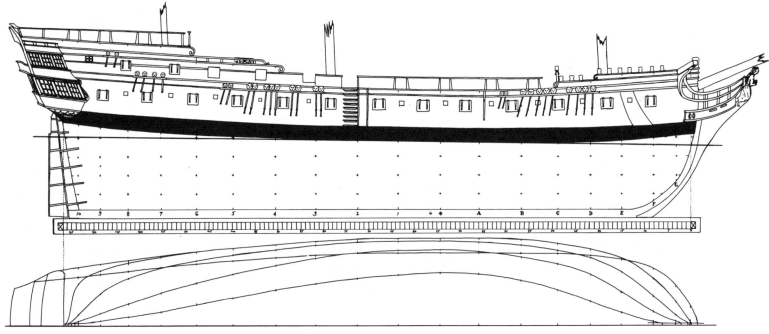

MASSACHUSETTS, 36

I N 1786, Major Shaw of Massachusetts was sent to China to become America's first consul ever sent there, because it was thought that trade with China would increase considerably in the next few years. In 1788, Shaw ordered a fine ship to be built in Quincy, Massachusetts, by the same Hackett family who had previously built the warships *America, Alliance, Raleigh, Ranger,* and *Hampden.* Named *Massachusetts,* she was launched in 1789.

Local mystics declared that *Massachusetts* would be an unlucky ship, so the crew deserted. A second crew also deserted, but she departed for China with a third crew under Captain Job Prince. Her planks and the barrels in her hold were made of green wood and quickly began to rot. Consequently, the meat in her hold spoiled before she had sailed far. She carried no chronometer, so it was a miracle that she reached her destination at all.

The outward voyage was a financial failure for Shaw.

He sold the ship at Canton and died himself on the way home a few months later, aged only thirty-nine. What happened to the ship after that is not recorded, but it is unlikely that she lasted more than another year or two. We know little enough about her appearance. She measured 820 tons, and there is a detailed pen-and-ink sketch of her elaborate stern preserved at the New York Public Library, showing the fine carvings wrought by S. Skillin. There are also a number of pieces of Chinese export porcelain decorated with a portrait of an East Indiaman of her size and date flying American colors. Using this information, and bearing in mind what British and French ships of her size and type looked like, plus remembering the designs of the New England frigates such as *Hancock, Alliance,* and *Raleigh,* we have reconstructed her lines. She was evidently a handsome ship, and it is a pity that she was not more soundly built. The little ports we have indicated in between the gunports are not oarports; they are for ventilating the ship in the tropics, although one assumes that they could have been used as oarports if the ship were attacked by the legendary pirates of the Straits of Malacca in a calm. Although most ships of this period had an odd number of windows across the stern, such as five or seven, *Massachusetts* had eight, a number that was to be echoed in the *Constitution* a few years later.

Ship *Massachusetts*, decoration on a Canton porcelain plate, 1789.

MEDIATOR, 12

IN April 1745, the Royal Navy purchased a "Virginia-built" (meaning anywhere in the Chesapeake Bay, not necessarily Virginia) sloop in the West Indies and named her *Mediator*. She was fitted out with 10 four-pounder carriage guns and no fewer than 18 swivels. She was sent off immediately to England where her lines were taken off, and they are on file at the National Maritime Museum at Greenwich. She had been built in 1741. On 29 July 1745, she was captured by a French privateer off Ostende, and reportedly was sunk there shortly afterward.

She was built in the style of the so-called Bermuda sloop, a form that was popular in the Chesapeake and in Jamaica. These were fast vessels with fairly sharp lines, and they were useful for smuggling, among other things. The master's cabin was almost invariably in the stern under a rounded coach roof. An unusual feature of *Mediator*'s design was the backward-sloping stem. She was steered with a wheel, like most of the Bermuda sloops, while virtually all other sloops of her size were steered with a tiller.

DATES	LENGTH HULL	LENGTH DECK	LENGTH KEEL	BEAM	DEPTH	DRAFT	TONNAGE B. M.
ca. 1741-1745	67	61	44	21	10	11	105

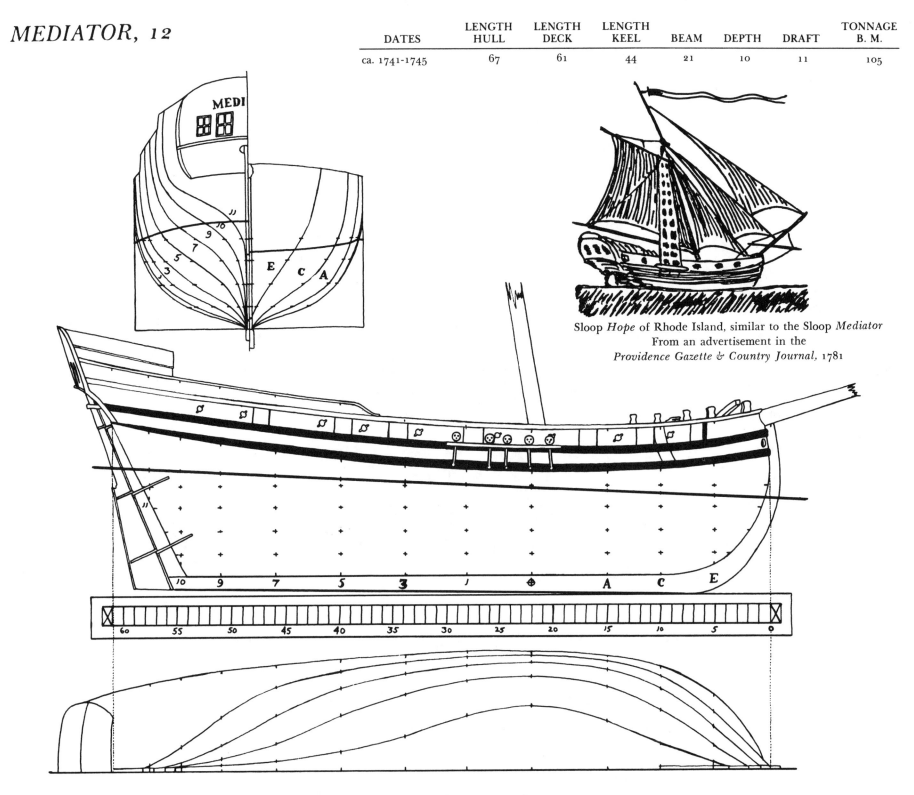

Sloop *Hope* of Rhode Island, similar to the Sloop *Mediator*
From an advertisement in the
Providence Gazette & Country Journal, 1781

MERCURY, 8

THE Continental Navy commissioned a number of different ships in the Revolution with the name of *Mercury,* and it is not always clear which one was which. As might be expected from the name of the mythological messenger of the gods, all these ships were intended to be fast packets to take important messages to and from Paris for Congress. One packet *Mercury* was captured by the corvette *Fairy* and the frigate *Vestal* near the Newfoundland Banks on 10 September 1780; this packet was reported to be a ketch, but it now seems that this was a clerical error, for she was a brig. Her dimensions were recorded, and she was said to have mounted eight guns. A schooner packet called

Mercury was built a few months later at Plymouth, Massachusetts, to a design by John Peck.

The brig *Mercury* was built by Wharton & Humphreys at Philadelphia around 1776. Apart from her dimensions we know little about her. However, it was thought worth attempting to reconstruct her, since there are a number of nicely built models (including one at Mystic Seaport in Connecticut) that purport to represent her, but which were actually built to plans of a British ketch of the *Speedwell* class of a much earlier period, and it would be useful to put the record straight. The Wharton & Humphreys design for the frigate *Randolph* was an influence on our reconstruction.

MERCURY, 8

DATES	LENGTH HULL	LENGTH DECK	LENGTH KEEL	BEAM	DEPTH	DRAFT	TONNAGE B. M.
ca. 1776-?	84	73	60	21	11	10	135

MEXICANA & SUTIL

DATES	LENGTH HULL	LENGTH DECK	LENGTH KEEL	BEAM	DEPTH	DRAFT	TONNAGE B. M.
1790-?	ESTIMATED 63	51	46	14	8	6	40

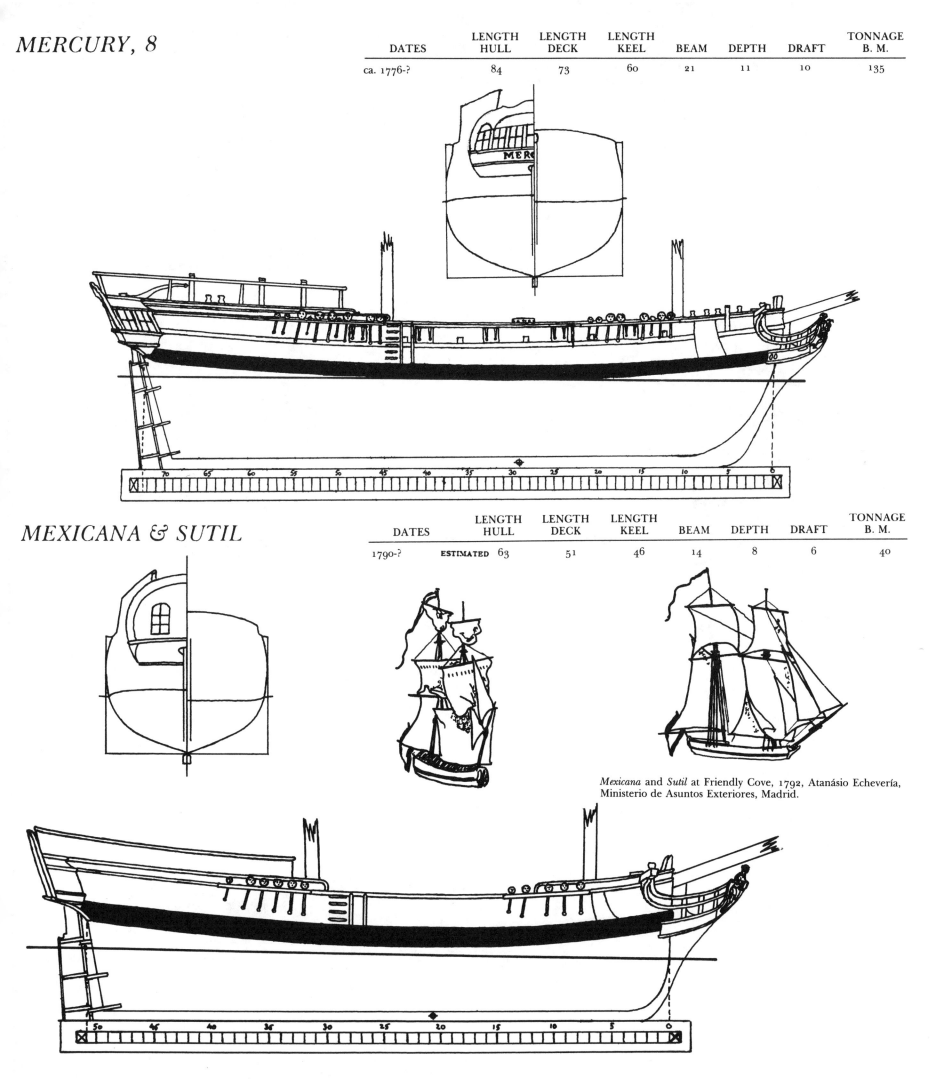

Mexicana and *Sutil* at Friendly Cove, 1792, Atanásio Echevería, Ministerio de Asuntos Exteriores, Madrid.

MEXICANA & SUTIL

IN 1790, the Spanish authorities in Mexico ordered the construction of two identical two-masted vessels at Acapulco, to be named *Mexicana* and *Sutil*. Owing to an accident with the rigging, the two vessels had to be rigged differently: *Mexicana* was a brig and *Sutil* was a topsail-schooner. They were used for exploring and patrolling the west coast of North America, including Alaska. Their subsequent history has not come to light. At least three pictures of the pair were painted along that coast, one of which was reproduced on a Spanish postage stamp of 1967.

Mexicana and *Sutil* off the Pacific Northwest coast, ca. 1792, Spanish National Archives; this engraving was reproduced on a Spanish postage stamp.

Mexicana and *Sutil* off Maguaa, 1792, José Cardero, Museo de America, Madrid.

MOHAWK, 18

DATES	LENGTH HULL	LENGTH DECK	LENGTH KEEL	BEAM	DEPTH	DRAFT	TONNAGE B. M.
1759-1764	95	77	—	24	—	—	140

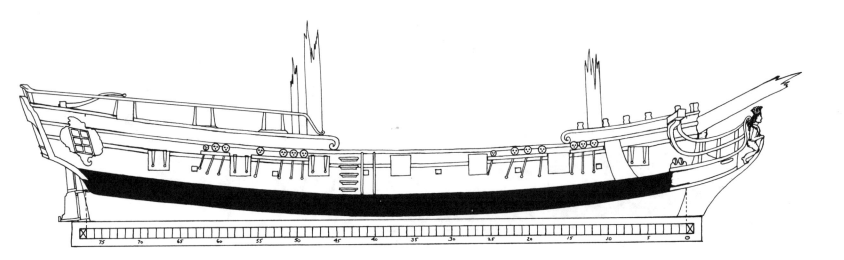

URING the Seven Years' War from 1756 to 1763, the British and the French built a number of small and medium-size warships on the Great Lakes. The first group of British vessels was built in 1756, including a 16-gun brig and a 22-gun snow that were sent out from England as kits; all were captured by the French that same year. The next group of three included the 22-gun snow *Onondaga* and the 18-gun snow *Mohawk;* these were built in 1759–60, and both were lost in an accident in 1764 after the war ended. There is a wash drawing of these two vessels in front of Oswego, New York, on Lake Ontario with Fort Ontario in the background, but the picture of *Onondaga* is not distinct enough for a reconstruction. Five more schooners and two snows were built between 1763 and 1771, and of these, the 18-gun snow *Seneca* was still going strong in 1788.

Judging from what little we know of her, the snow *Mohawk* had a fairly shallow draft with a bottom that was nearly flat. Naturally, this configuration assisted navigation in shallower or uncharted sections of the lake, but it was also adopted for another good reason: ships in the ocean had to carry several tons of drinking water, which in turn made the ships more burdensome; ships on lakes did not have to carry water because the water they were sailing in was drinkable then (will the Great Lakes ever be that pure again?), and they did not have to carry much food because they were never far from land and wild game.

Snows *Onondaga* and *Mohawk* off Oswego, NY, ca. 1763.

MOHAWK, 16

DATES	LENGTH HULL	LENGTH DECK	LENGTH KEEL	BEAM	DEPTH	DRAFT	TONNAGE B. M.
1779–?	112	96	79	26	10	12	285

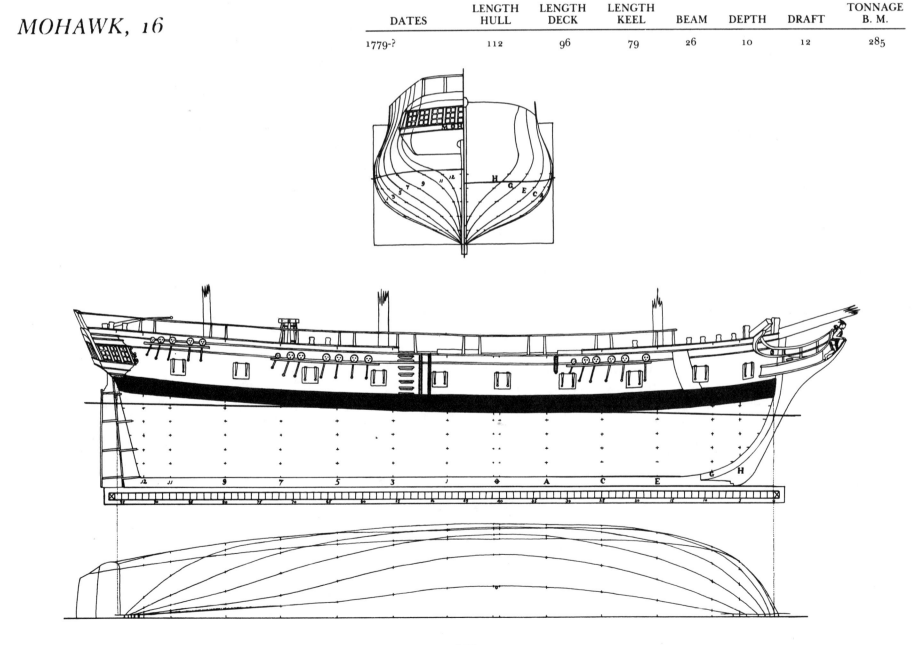

MOHAWK, 16

IN 1779 a neat little privateer ship was built at Salem, Massachusetts, to a design that was most unusual for her early date. She was placed under the command of John Carnes, but he lost her to a British ship that was not much larger. A much later picture of the engagement can be seen in the background of a portrait of Carnes in the 1790s at the Peabody Museum at Salem. The British used her in the New York area for wages and sea victualing "in conformity with Admiral Pigot's establishment" of 18 October 1782. In September 1783 she was measured at Deptford Dockyard and her lines recorded (they can be seen at the National Maritime Museum at Greenwich), and she was then prepared for sale.

She mounted up to 18 guns, probably six-pounders, on her gun deck, with provision for another 18 guns (they must have been small if fitted at all) on a flush spar deck. This is an arrangement that looks forward several years to the design of the frigate *Constitution,* and is only seen in one or two other ships in the Revolution. She had relatively steep deadrise, and was presumably a fast ship. Her bottom is known to have been copper sheathed.

Ship *Mohawk*
From an oil painting, ca. 1800
Peabody Museum, Salem, Massachusetts

Captain John Carnes.

NASSAU, 30

THE story of the dashing pirates who operated in the Caribbean and the Indian Ocean in the period 1680–1725 is an exciting one, and has been told often. Many Americans were among the early pirates. The first Americans to enter the Indian Ocean were two pirates from Newport, Rhode Island, Thomas Tew and William Mayes, Jr. (probably no relation to the baseball player!). They were soon followed by others from New York and elsewhere, and they found that life on Madagascar was most congenial. A New York ship of' some size, the 30-gun ship *Nassau,* was one of those fitted out to go to Madagascar. She left New York in 1697 under Captain Giles Shelley. One may well imagine what happened to her men when they arrived at their destination, but we can leave that for another book.

All we know about the appearance of *Nassau* is from a fine portrait of her that was engraved on the lid of a silver tankard. Judging from the shape of her quarter galleries and the design of her head, she was built to a Dutch design, but whether she was built at New York or in Holland is unknown.

	DATES	LENGTH HULL	LENGTH DECK	LENGTH KEEL	BEAM	DEPTH	DRAFT	TONNAGE B. M.
	fl. 1697	ESTIMATED 117	96	78	28	11	12	350

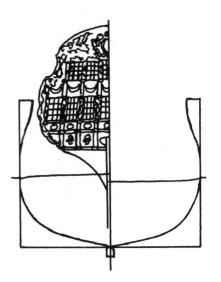

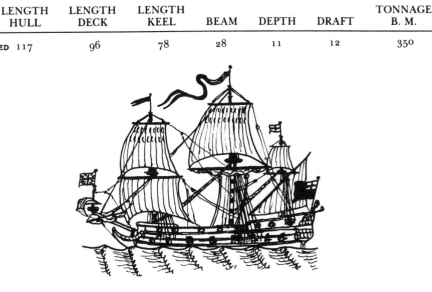

Ship *Nassau*
From an engraving on the lid of a silver tankard, ca. 1700

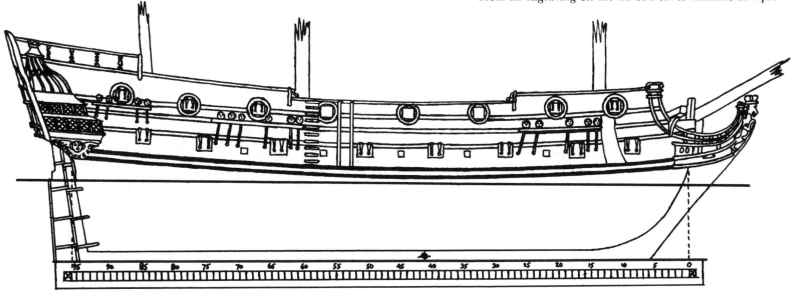

NORTHWEST AMERICA/SANTA GERTRUDIS LA MAGNA, 8

THE British explorer-adventurer John Meares is said to have been one of the less savory characters of his day. Nevertheless, he is responsible for building the first vessel on the west coast of North America constructed by English-speaking people. Meares first arrived on the Oregon coast in 1786 on his ship *Nootka* in an effort to circumvent the British East India Company's trade monopoly. When 23 of his crew died of scurvy over the winter, Meares promised never to return to the coast, in return for assistance from the ship *King George*. In fact, he did return in May 1788 with two ships, *Felice Adventurer* (possibly *Nootka* renamed) and *Iphigeneia Nubiana* and fake Portuguese papers. He made his base at Friendly Bay in Nootka Sound, British Columbia, where he built a house and the vessel, *Northwest America*. She was originally supposed to be a sloop but she was fitted with a lugger rig (mistakenly called a schooner by some), and although she was small she was capable of mounting ten guns to defend against unpredictable attacks by the Indians. Such a small vessel would be useful for exploring and charting the coast, as well as for gathering sea otter skins for sale at Canton.

Northwest America was launched bow-first after the Dutch fashion. She shot down the ways at high speed and, since no one had thought to tie a line to her, she continued some distance out into the Pacific before longboats could catch up with her. On her deck, Kaiana, a Hawaiian prince who had been travelling with Meares, danced excitedly as she slid through the water. Meares departed for China four days later aboard *Felice*, never to return, but *Iphigeneia* remained. Robert Funter commanded *Northwest America* on several coasting voyages over the next year until angry Spanish authorities confiscated all British vessels trading on that coast in July 1789. In Spanish hands, she was renamed *Santa Gertrudis la Magna* and she was sent south to San Blas, Mexico, after which she disappears from the records. The matter of Spanish sovereignty in the area was not settled for another sixteen months with the arrival of Don Juan Francisco de Bodega y Cuadra and George Vancouver (it was finally resolved in Britain's favor).

Before Cuadra arrived, Meares sent another British ship from Canton; *Argonaut* arrived at Nootka on 3 July, 1789, but the Spanish seized her the day after her arrival. They found that she carried in her hold a kit to build a 30-ton sloop for further exploration of the coast, so the Spanish assembled the kit, rigged her as a schooner and called her *Santa Saturnia*. No pictures or further records of this vessel have been found.

DATES	LENGTH HULL	LENGTH DECK	LENGTH KEEL	BEAM	DEPTH	DRAFT	TONNAGE B. M.
1788-?	ESTIMATED 56	50	43	16	7	8	40

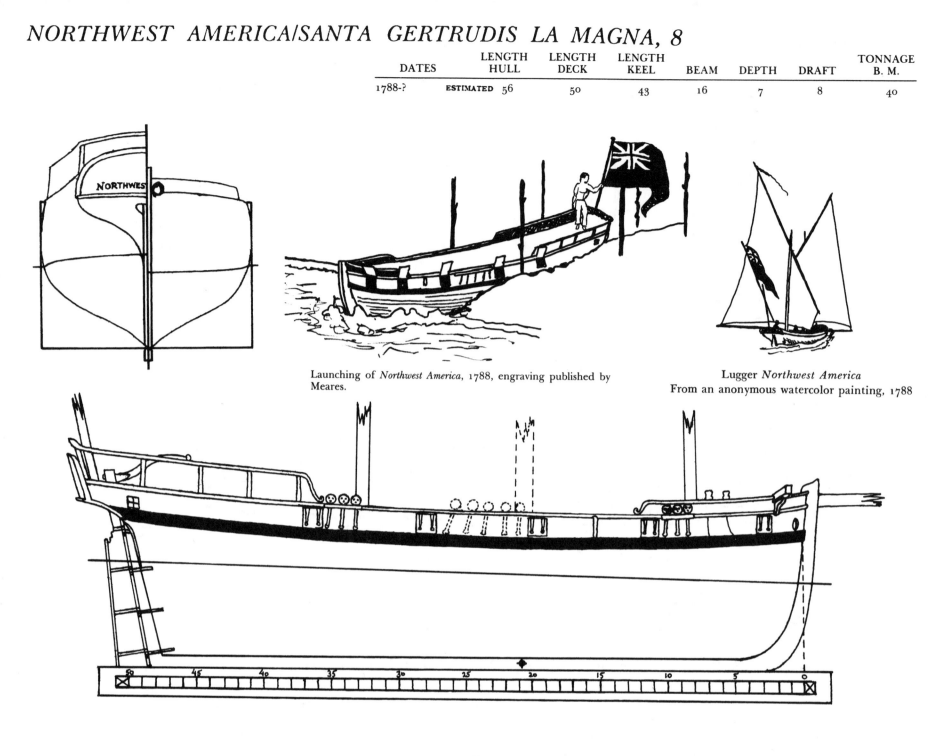

Launching of *Northwest America*, 1788, engraving published by Meares.

Lugger *Northwest America*
From an anonymous watercolor painting, 1788

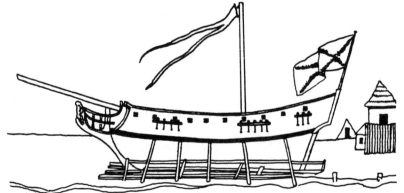

Russian merchant ship *Feniks* shortly before launch in Alaska, 1794, James Shields, Library of Congress.

NUEVA ESPAÑA (ex-NUESTRA SEÑORA DEL ROSARIO), 64

THE National Maritime Museum at Greenwich has a beautiful model of a 60-gun Spanish ship of about the period 1740-1745. Her name is unknown, but since she bears on her stern the arms of the province of Mexico she has to be *Nueva España*, 64 guns, built at Havana, Cuba in 1743 under the original name of *Nuestra Señora del Rosario*. She would have been constructed of long-lasting Cuban mahogany.

Nueva España followed the general lines of Spanish ships of her day designed by hired British shipwrights, with several vertical boat-fenders on her topsides. Her figurehead had the head and upper body of a horse with the scaly lower body of a fish. Her channels were set low, after the custom of the day, a custom that caused considerable damage to many ships in serious storms. Her lower gundeck had a row of oarports interspersed between the gunports; one wonders how effective a few oars could be to move such a large and heavy ship.

NUEVA ESPAÑA (ex-NUESTRA SEÑORA DEL ROSARIO), 64

DATES	LENGTH HULL	LENGTH DECK	LENGTH KEEL	BEAM	DEPTH	DRAFT	TONNAGE B. M.
1743-?	167	142	115	41	16	19	1000

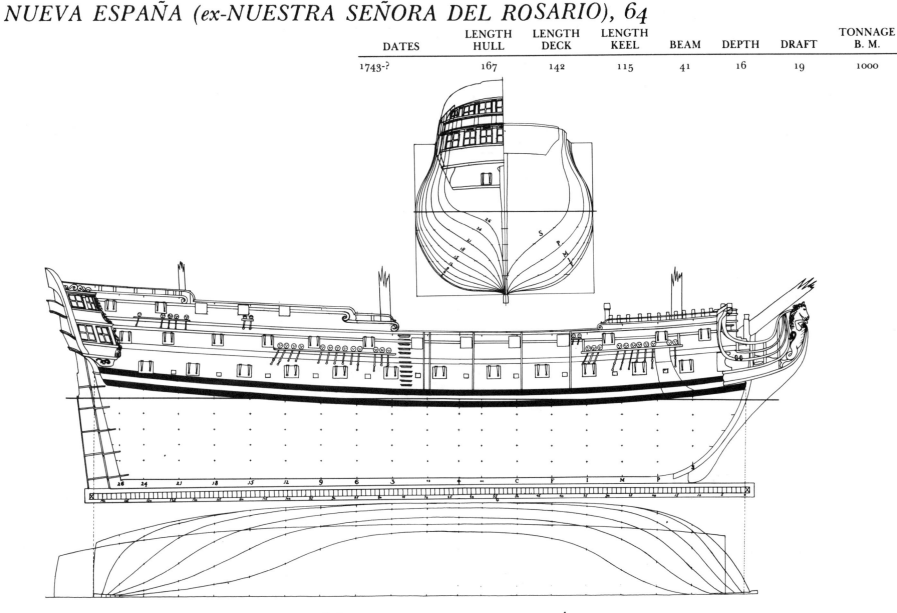

OLIVER CROMWELL/BEAVER'S PRIZE, 16

A CONSIDERABLE amount of oratory has been expended over the years concerning various ships in the American Revolution with the name of *Oliver Cromwell*. The most famous of these ships is undoubtedly the Connecticut State Navy ship, while another came from Beverly, Massachusetts, and still another, which belonged to Nicholas Brown and William Russell of Providence, was destroyed in August 1777. The ship shown here, however, was a smart-looking privateer of about 16 guns that was captured by the British corvette *Beaver* on 19 May 1777. She was subsequently renamed *Beaver's Prize*, which was not a terribly imaginative

name; she could not have retained her earlier name, of course, while serving in the Royal Navy, for the name of the regicide Cromwell was anathema to George III at a time when he was reaching for absolute power for the British crown in the same manner as Charles I had done.

Harold Hahn has done impressive research on this ship, published in both *Model Shipwright* and *Nautical Research Journal*. The earliest record he has found of her shows that she was bonded as a Philadelphia privateer on 7 February 1777. Her principal owners were John Bayard and James Caldwell; her captain was

Harmon Courter, and she carried 150 men in her crew. The late Marion Brewington has suggested that she had previously been a Philadelphia merchant ship called *Juno,* while V. R. Grimwood suggests that she was formerly a Rhode Island ship by the name of *Ye Terrible Creture.* The figurehead of a lady could represent either of those former names, the latter being of course the first owner's wife, a joke entirely in keeping with humor of the Colonial period.

Our own opinion, and it is no more than that, is that she was built at Providence about 1774. At the end of 1776, Narragansett Bay was occupied by a powerful British garrison and fleet at Newport which would have made it too difficult to sail her in or out of Providence, so she was transferred to Philadelphia ownership and renamed *Oliver Cromwell* at that time. One piece of circumstantial support for this theory is that ship design,

particularly for major vessels, can be as easily identified with a particular region as can furniture design or the architecture of buildings. We know the general characteristics of ships of her size and type from Charleston, the Chesapeake, Philadelphia, New York, and New England, as well as from Great Britain. Only Rhode Island, a major center of shipbuilding, is left blank in the documented and recorded designs of ships. This *Oliver Cromwell* is completely different in many ways from ships of all the areas mentioned above. It seems likely that she represents the Rhode Island type, especially since her stern closely resembles the stern of the Providence privateer *General Washington*. It is because of this that the author has gone out on a limb and reconstructed the appearance of four important Rhode Island ships (*Warren, Providence* frigate, *General Washington* and *President Washington*) with no more than their dimensions and

OLIVER CROMWELL/
BEAVER's PRIZE, 16

DATES	LENGTH HULL	LENGTH DECK	LENGTH KEEL	BEAM	DEPTH	DRAFT	TONNAGE B. M.
ca. 1774-1780	102	86	69	26	12	13	248

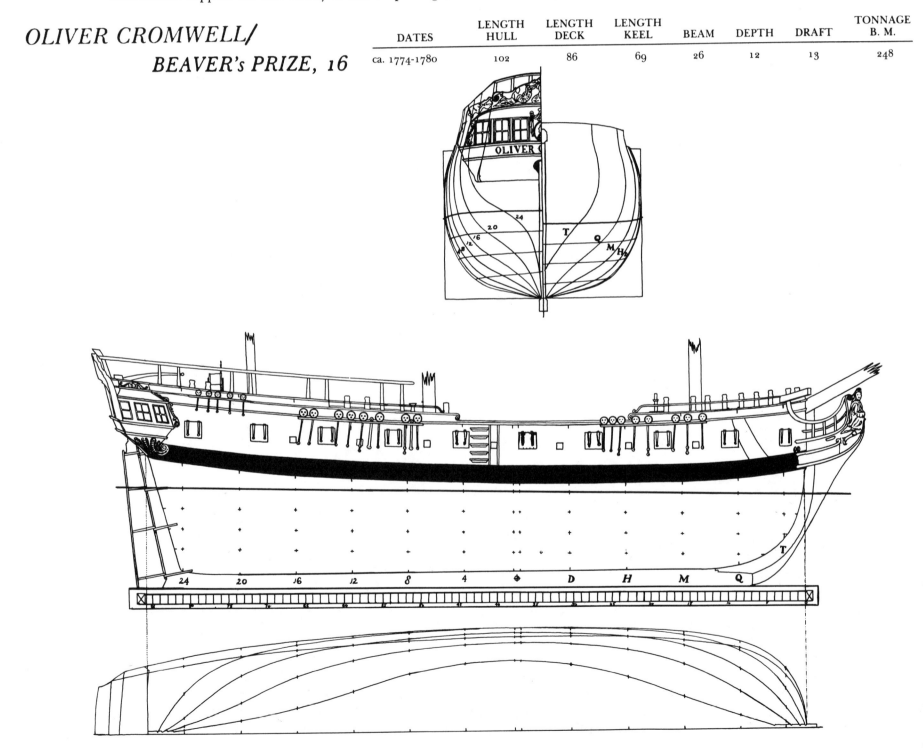

some crude pictures to go by, other than the lines of *Oliver Cromwell*.

Oliver Cromwell's lines, among the handsomest ever recorded by the British Admiralty, are on file at the National Maritime Museum at Greenwich. We have reconstructed portions of her rail that we believe was shot away and never replaced after her capture. She was probably originally steered only with a tiller, but a wheel was added later, which we show. Her rudder post was so close to her tafferel that the center window of the stern was omitted, and a bust, possibly of Cromwell, was placed there in its stead. Her capstan was located in the waist, so the British added a second one (a two-decker) in their favorite place on the quarter-deck. She was fitted with port lids for all her gunports, even in the waist. She had a full-bodied hull for carrying a lot of cargo or supplies, but her ends were fine enough to give her a moderate turn of speed (British records say that she was slow, but she also had a foul bottom at that time). An unusual feature was the extra decorative rail in the head, also found on *Cupid* and a few others. At the time of her capture she was obviously overloaded, for she is reported to have been mounting a total of 24 carriage guns in addition to a number of swivels and cohorns; the carriage guns were 12 nine-pounders, 6 six-pounders, and 6 four-pounders. The British, who stated that her guns were worthless, refitted her with first 12 six-pounders and eventually 16 six-pounders.

This miniature frigate, for so she was, sailed from Philadelphia in 1777 to cruise in the West Indies. She captured a number of prizes there, but was herself captured off the island of St. Lucia a few weeks later. Her unruly crew, composed largely of foreigners, was blamed for her capture. She was taken to England where she served as a convoy guard, and was temporarily assigned to the convoy guarded by *Serapis* and *Countess of Scarborough* that was so notably attacked by John Paul Jones, but she had been reassigned just before that incident. She was sent to Goree, Senegal, in Africa, with a convoy, and then found her way back to the West Indies where she was wrecked in a terrible hurricane on 11 October 1780. The location of her wreck, recently discovered by an underwater archaeological team, is close to Vieux-Fort, St. Lucia, less than ten miles from the scene of her capture some three years earlier.

ONTARIO, 16

DATES	LENGTH HULL	LENGTH DECK	LENGTH KEEL	BEAM	DEPTH	DRAFT	TONNAGE B. M.
1780-1780	95	80	68	24	8	8	187

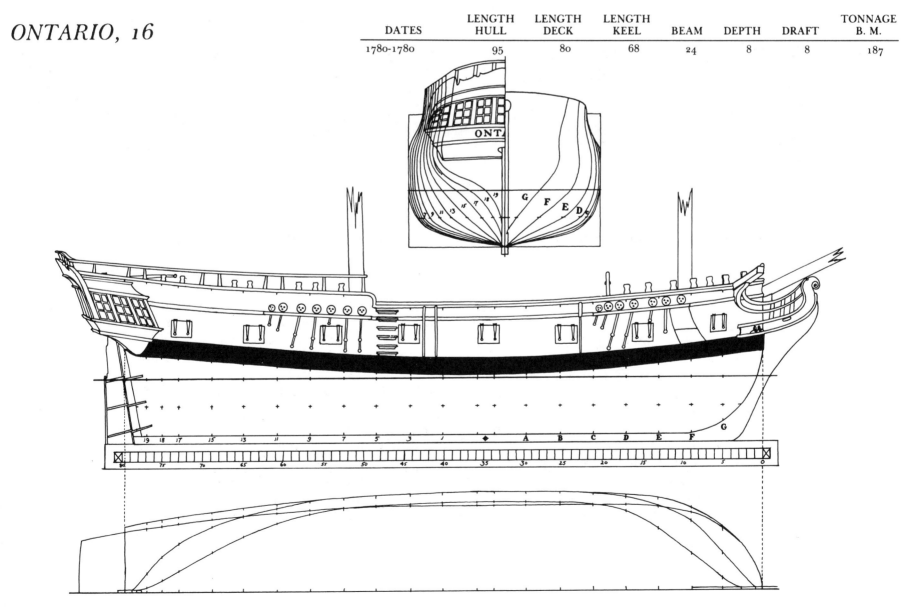

151

ONTARIO, 16

URING the American Revolution the British felt it necessary to strengthen their forces on the Great Lakes by building a 16-gun brig called *Ontario*. She was launched at Carleton Island on the Canadian side of Lake Ontario on 10 May 1780. She did not last long, for she foundered on 1 November 1780 in one of those sudden Great Lakes winter storms. She had the shallow draft common to all lake vessels. Her stern was unusual for such a small vessel in having quarter galleries, and her bow was unusual for the period in that it had only a billet head instead of a figurehead. Her lines are preserved at the National Maritime Museum, Greenwich.

L'ORIGINAL, 70

DATES	LENGTH HULL	LENGTH DECK	LENGTH KEEL	BEAM	DEPTH	DRAFT	TONNAGE B. M.
1750-?	**ESTIMATED** 197	166	152	45	20	21	1600

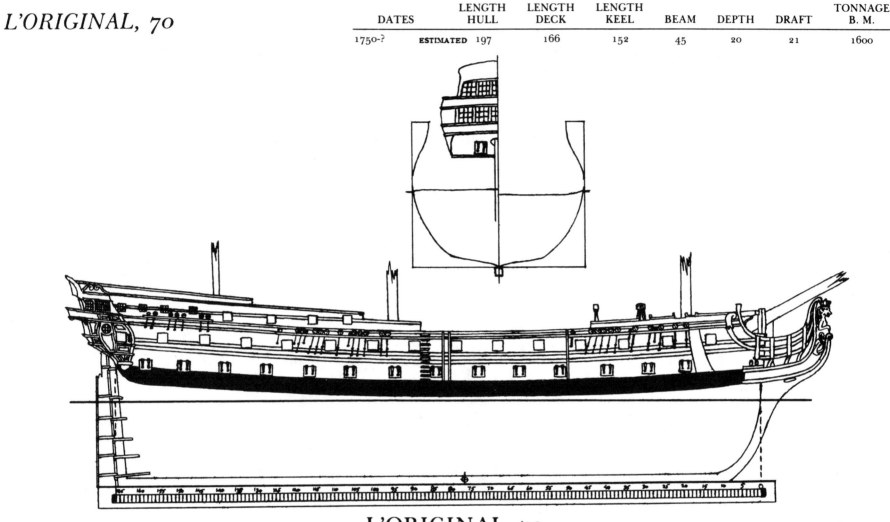

L'ORIGINAL, 70

IT is not generally known that the French built some substantial warships in Quebec in the 1740s and 1750s (for a complete list of these ships, see the description of the frigate *L'Abenakise*). Of all these ships, however, very little in the way of descriptive records remains: a partial drawing of the lines of *L'Abenakise* at the National Maritime Museum at Greenwich, England, and a list of the names and types of the other ships. Monsieur Jean Boudriot of Paris, the world's leading authority on eighteenth-century French ships, writes "I am very embarrassed to have to say that information on these warships constructed in Canada is non-existent, at least as far as my research in the French Archives is concerned."

We know that *L'Original* was built at Quebec in 1750 and that she mounted 70 guns, but we know nothing more. Accordingly, because this ship is so important

to the history of American ships of this period, we have reconstructed her appearance by taking the dimensions and designs of other French 70-gun ships of this period and crossing them with various "local" features from the design of *L'Abenakise,* and we have done the same thing with two other French-Canadian ships, *Le Saint-Laurent* and *Le Québec*.

Notice that the upper gun deck has no gunport lids; this was a typical French feature, and one wonders what they did in the winter. Also, notice the row of windows just forward of the Great Cabin; the French were very particular about the comfort of their officers, and these windows, which were never used as gunports, represent the location of "l'État Major" or "officers' country."

L'OUTAOUAISE, 18

	DATES		LENGTH HULL	LENGTH DECK	LENGTH KEEL	BEAM	DEPTH	DRAFT	TONNAGE B. M.
	ca. 1757-?	ESTIMATED	99	84	—	26	—	—	180

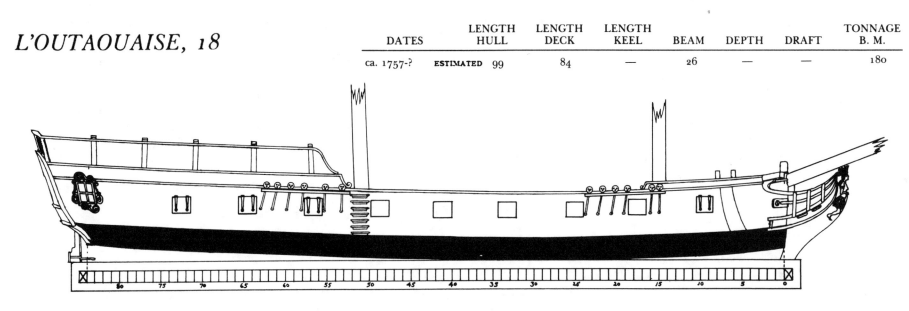

L'OUTAOUAISE, 18

THE French and the British both built a number of small warships for service on the Great Lakes, Lake Champlain, and the St. Lawrence River in the mid-eighteenth century. One such craft was presumably built at Quebec shortly before 1760 and fitted with 18 carriage guns, probably four-pounders or six-pounders. Her name was *L'Outaouaise,* which means "girl from the Ottawa tribe," one of the lesser Algonquin tribes. She was rigged as a brig, or possibly as a snow, and was stationed in the St. Lawrence about a third of the way from Lake Ontario to Montreal near Fort La Galette (now Ogdensburg, New York) in 1760 in an effort to block Major General Jeffery Amherst's advance toward Montreal from the west. Amherst had cleverly built at least four galleys each armed with a twelve-pounder, and he used their superior mobility to capture the French warship, thus leaving the way open to Montreal. A painting of the battle by British military artist Thomas Davies can be seen at the National Gallery of Canada in Ottawa. No record of what happened to the brig after her capture seems to have survived, nor do we know her dimensions. However, judging from the painting, she appears to have been about 98' 6" in length overall and 84' in length between perpendiculars. Her shallow draft and flat bottom would have made her suited for only inland waters such as the St. Lawrence, so she may have continued on guard duty in the Montreal area under a new nationality.

French Brig *l'Outaouaise* being captured by British galleys
in the St. Lawrence River in 1760
From a watercolor by Thomas Davies
National Gallery of Canada, Ottawa

PERSEVERANCE

	DATES		LENGTH HULL	LENGTH DECK	LENGTH KEEL	BEAM	DEPTH	DRAFT	TONNAGE B. M.
	1786ff	ESTIMATED	38	35	32	10	4	3	—

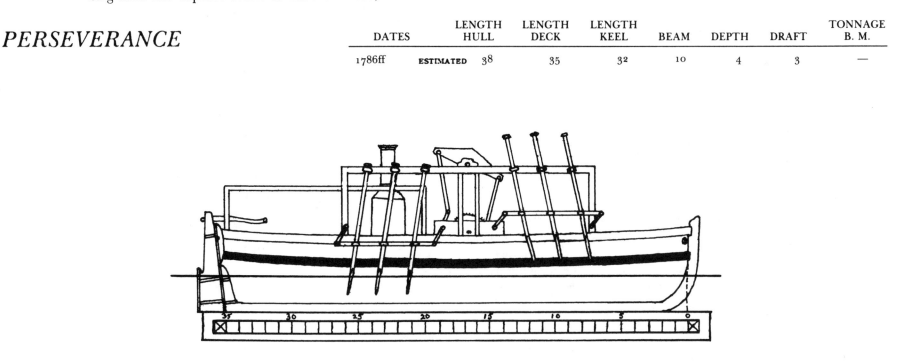

PERSEVERANCE

JOHN Fitch's pioneering work with steamboats has been described in the text for the vessel *Experiment/Thornton*, the steamboat whose paddles resembled ducks' feet. Fitch's first design was for a boat with twelve paddles, in two banks of three on each side of the boat. He intended to name this 34-foot boat *Perseverance* and use it to carry passengers. In 1786, he built a half-size model of it which worked satisfactorily on the Delaware. At that point, his overactive mind worked out the details of the ducks' feet paddles and started building *Experiment*. *Perseverance* was to have been put into a passenger service on the Delaware in 1791, but he was using her engine in *Experiment*, so *Perseverance* was never completed. In the mean time, Fitch had also built a larger version of *Perseverance*, 45 feet long and eight feet wide, begun in August 1786, but this, too remained unfinished.

PHILADELPHIA *et al.*, 3

WHEN Benedict Arnold put together an American fleet on Lake Champlain in the summer of 1776, he used sloops, schooners, cutters, ketches, and galleys. In addition to these larger craft, he also constructed gondolas or gundaloes as they were sometimes called. These had flat bottoms, flaring topsides, and double ends. They were propelled by oars except when the wind was astern, at which time they could set a square course and square topsail. They mounted three carriage guns, one twelve-pounder in the bow and one six- or nine-pounder on each side (staggered) amidships. They had a raised deck aft, under which it was possible to sleep and to stow gear, and the topsides could have their height augmented in battle by the addition of branches and other impedimenta to guard against bullets and flying splinters. The crew numbered as many as forty-five men.

It seems that all the gondolas were built at Skenesborough to the same plans, and they are said to have been painted barn-red. *Boston* was sunk in action on 12 October 1776. *Connecticut* survived the battle of Valcour Island, but no history after that is recorded. *Jersey* was captured by the British on 13 October and taken into their forces. *New Haven* was burned to avoid capture on 13 October. *New York* was probably captured by the British in October, but there is no record. *Philadelphia* was sunk at the battle of Valcour Island, and raised again in the 1930s; she has been carefully preserved and is on display at the Smithsonian Institution in Washington, D.C. *Providence* was sunk on 12 October, and *Spitfire* was burned on 13 October to avoid capture. *Success* seems not to have been present at the battle of Valcour Island, and to have had her name changed not long afterward, but there is no record of her new name nor of her ultimate fate.

Benedict Arnold is thought to have designed all the gondolas, and they are believed all to have been built from the same plans. However, Arnold's written description of them does not exactly fit *Philadelphia*, the only one presently existing. For example, Arnold called for a small keel, which no doubt would have been a help in steering, particularly when the gondola was under sail, but no keel was fitted. The dimensions are also a little different. We suspect that Arnold had to modify his original plan based on certain realities that he faced, but of which we are ignorant.

Here are the dimensions, based on Arnold's descriptions: length overall, 56′ 2″; length between perpendiculars, 51′ 6″; length of keel, 48′; breadth, 16′; depth, 3′ 6″; draft, 1′ 6″. Here are the dimensions as built (other dimensions remain the same): length of keel, 48′ 9″; breadth, 15′ 6″; depth, 3′ 10″; draft, 1′8.

Gondola *Philadelphia*
From a watercolor by C. Randle, 1776
The Public Archives of Canada, Ottawa

Benedict Arnold

DATES	LENGTH HULL	LENGTH DECK	LENGTH KEEL	BEAM	DEPTH	DRAFT	TONNAGE B. M.
1776-1777	56	52	49	16	4	1	—

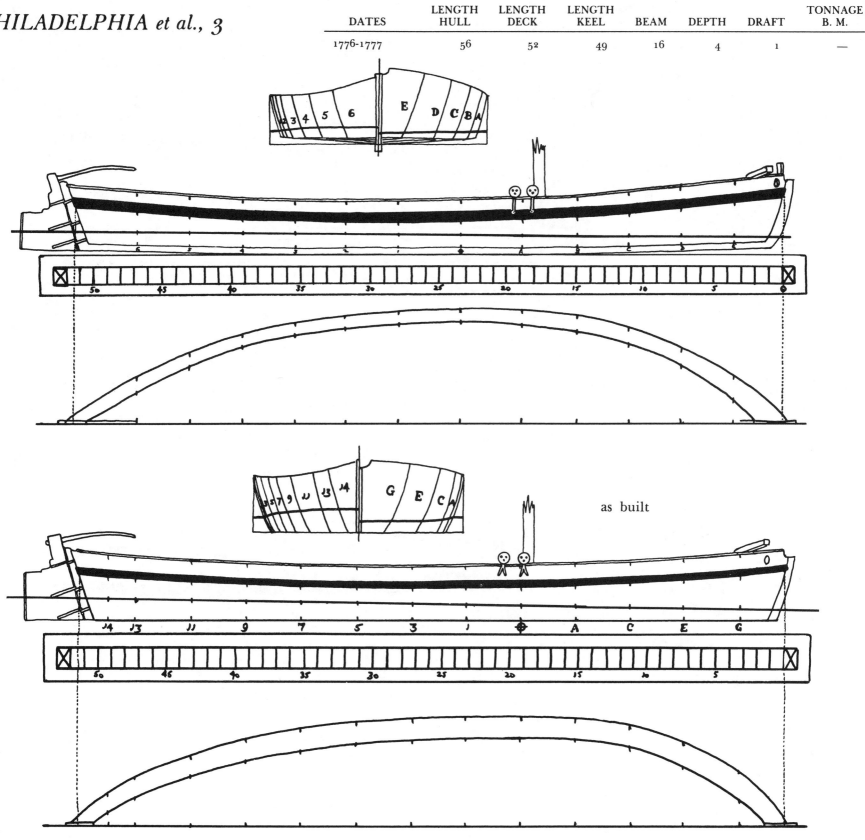

as built

PLACENTIA & TREPASSEY

In 1790, the Royal Navy had two small cutters constructed in Newfoundland, presumably from designs sent from London. They were rated at six guns apiece, but it is difficult to see how any carriage guns could have been used on them to advantage. *Placentia* was built by Jeffery & Street, and *Trepassey* was built by Lester & Stone. *Placentia* was wrecked on the Newfoundland coast on 8 May 1794, but *Trepassey* survived to be sold at the end of 1803.

DATES	LENGTH HULL	LENGTH DECK	LENGTH KEEL	BEAM	DEPTH	DRAFT	TONNAGE B. M.
1790-1794 1790-1803	48	44	35	15	8	7	42

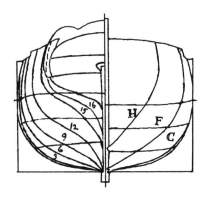
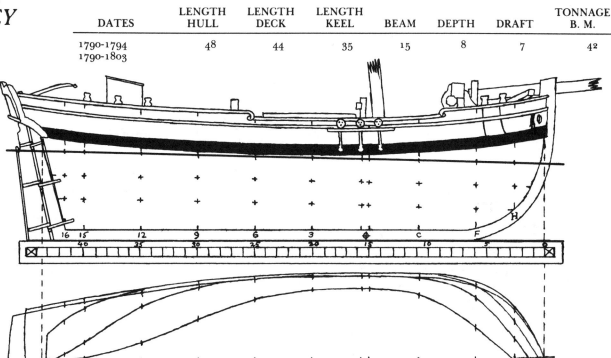

PLEASANT MARY/DUCHESS OF MANCHESTER

DATES	LENGTH HULL	LENGTH DECK	LENGTH KEEL	BEAM	DEPTH	DRAFT	TONNAGE B. M.
ca. 1757-ca. 1782	85	71	56	21	8	10	137

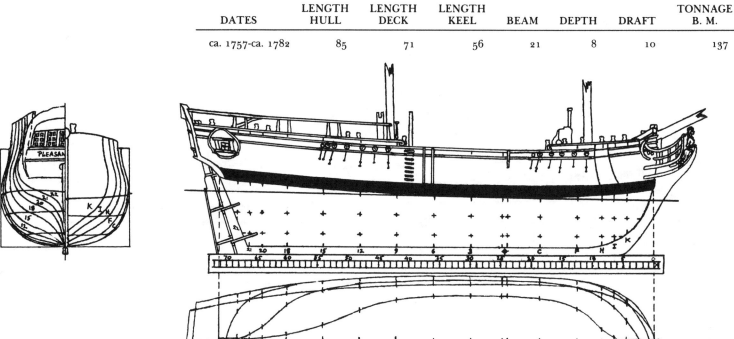

PLEASANT MARY/DUCHESS OF MANCHESTER

T HE snow was a popular rig in the eighteenth century, but few drawings survive of snows built in America. The snow *Pleasant Mary* is believed to have been built in America in 1757. She was apparently rebuilt in 1767. Her name was changed in 1776 to *Duchess of Manchester*, at which time she may have been rebuilt again. The following year, the Royal Navy purchased her and had her lines taken off at Deptford. A proposal was made to rerig her as a brig, which involved moving the mainmast four feet further aft, but if the work was done it was not recorded. She was used for surveying the British coasts.

Near the northeasternmost point of Maine is a village (now it is larger than a village) called Machias. The people of Machias proudly believe, as do inhabitants of many other communities, that their town was the location of the first naval battle of the Revolution. These claims will no doubt be debated for years to come, but here is what happened. A tiny (although some say she was 100 tons, she was actually 35 tons) British armed schooner called *Margaretta* had come to Machias to escort some large sloops loaded with lumber to Boston or Halifax. News of Concord and Lexington had excited the inhabitants and they resolved to capture the schooner. They set off on two sloops, *Unity* and *Polly,* after the fleeing *Margaretta;* the British schooner was armed with some small cannons while the American sloops had a few muskets, pitchforks, and scythes, and a lot of courage. *Polly* ran aground, leaving *Unity* to catch the schooner. Jeremiah O'Brien led the boarding party, and *Margaretta* was captured on 12 June 1775. The schooner being both small and slow, the citizens of Machias decided to take the cannons off her and mount them on *Polly,* renaming *Polly* for the occasion *Machias Liberty* (some accounts say that it was *Unity* that was so used, but recent evidence indicates that it was *Polly*).

Polly was immediately used to capture two small British craft called *Diligent* and *Tattamagouche* that were being used to make measurements for a new atlas of North America. Fearing British reprisals after these bold captures, Machias sent representatives to the Massachusetts General Court (Maine was then part of Massachusetts) to petition for support. At the end of August the legislature voted to accept *Machias Liberty* and *Diligent* as the first commissioned ships of the Massachusetts Navy.

Evidence as to the appearance of any of these vessels is scant, but one contemporary portrait of *Polly* survives; the prisoners captured at Machias were taken for arraignment at the Pownalborough Court House in Dresden, and either one of the prisoners or one of the guards took a penknife and scratched a crude picture of *Polly* on the wall paneling. It shows that she was a standard lumber sloop, having a square-tuck stern with a large port in it to one side of the rudder for loading timber. She is shown flying a striped flag for a jack and another striped flag for an ensign at the top of the mast. She set a square topsail for going downwind. We also know that she measured 90 tons.

Sloop *Polly*
From a primitive carving on wood
Pownalborough Court House, Dresden, Maine

POLLY

DATES		LENGTH HULL	LENGTH DECK	LENGTH KEEL	BEAM	DEPTH	DRAFT	TONNAGE B. M.
fl. 1775	ESTIMATED	66	58	—	19	—	—	90

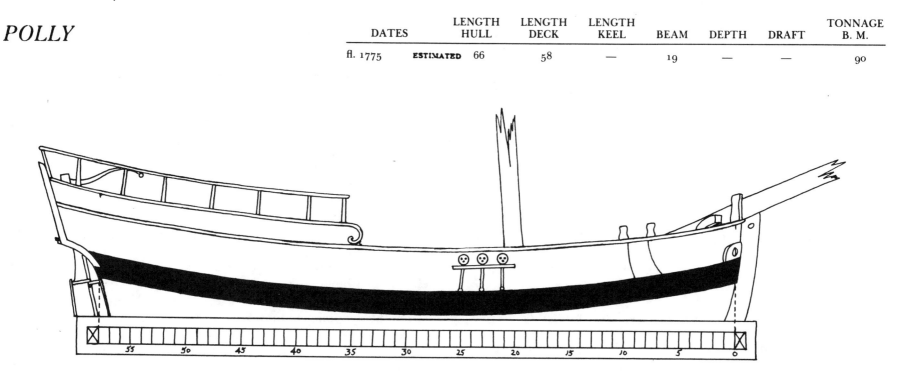

POSTILLION, 12

Among the watercolor sketches of various ships that Ashley Bowen of Marblehead executed during the course of his travels is a series showing the ship *Postillion* of Salem, Massachusetts. *Postillion* was a merchant ship built about 1780 and armed with 12 guns. We know very little about her except that on 28 January 1781 she ran into a serious storm. Her masts and rigging were cut away, but it was too late. She capsized and later sank, but her crew were fortunate and were able to row to safety. The paintings are on file at the Peabody Museum at Salem.

She seems to have been a typical armed merchant ship of the period. Our reconstruction was naturally based on the paintings, and for that reason we may have placed the main and mizzenmasts too far forward for good balance.

POSTILLION, 12

DATES	LENGTH HULL	LENGTH DECK	LENGTH KEEL	BEAM	DEPTH	DRAFT	TONNAGE B. M.
1780-1781	ESTIMATED 80	66	—	20	—	—	120

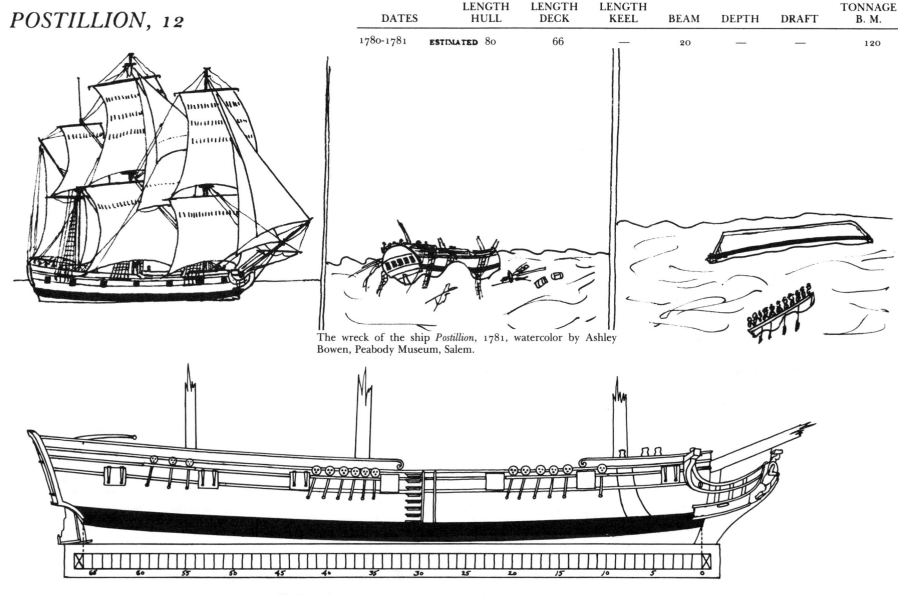

The wreck of the ship *Postillion*, 1781, watercolor by Ashley Bowen, Peabody Museum, Salem.

PRESIDENT WASHINGTON, 36

In 1779, wealthy Rhode Island merchant John Brown proposed to build a 38-gun privateer frigate of 1000 tons, but when he was unable to find enough other investors for the project he decided to settle instead on the 20-gun *General Washington* of just over a third of the tonnage. *General Washington* was captured first by the British and then by the Americans and taken into the Continental Navy, but Brown bought her back at the end of the war and used her in the Canton trade. Before she had returned from her second voyage there, Brown started to build his earlier dream, the 950-ton *President Washington*. While she could carry 38 guns, his intention this time was to put her in the Canton trade. Brown's favorite builder, Colonel Benjamin Talman, found such a large ship more difficult to build than his previous projects, so she was not launched until the first days of the new year of 1791, several weeks behind schedule. The *Providence Gazette* of 8 January 1791 reported the launch of "a most elegant coppered ship called the *President*, allowed to be the best ship ever built in New England."

It seems, however, that Brown had not counted on the expense of equipping and properly manning such a large ship. It is probably for that reason that he gave his agents authority to sell her on the voyage if they found the right opportunity. She was sold, along with her cargo, as soon as she reached Calcutta in 1792. The *Providence Gazette* of 14

September 1793 reported the arrival of a "Waggon, with between 50 and 60,000 Dollars in Specie," proceeds from the sale in Calcutta, to make a deposit at a Providence bank—just in time, for ship-insurance rates were shooting upwards due to the French Revolution. Brown then hired Talman to build him a 28-gun frigate called *George Washington*, which he used in trade to the Orient and then conned the United States Navy into purchasing for an unreasonable price; the Secretary of the Navy in vain warned his agent to be wary of Brown and "let the public be Screwed as little as possible."

Nothing further is known about the East Indiaman *President Washington* and her career subsequent to 1792. Only one Chinese primitive portrait of her is known, so the drawing shown here is highly speculative, based on scaling up the plans of the privateer *Oliver Cromwell*. Nevertheless, such an important ship deserves to be represented.

PRESIDENT WASHINGTON, 36

DATES	LENGTH HULL	LENGTH DECK	LENGTH KEEL	BEAM	DEPTH	DRAFT	TONNAGE B. M.
1790-?	ESTIMATED 172	144	122	39	21	20	950

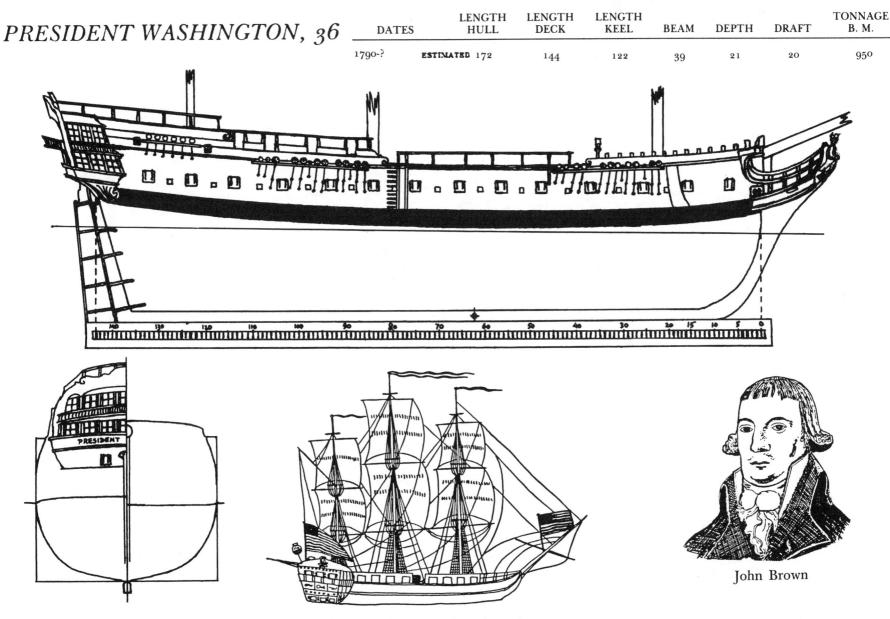

Ship *President Washington*, primitive decoration on Canton porcelain, ca. 1792, private collection.

John Brown

PRINCE CHARLES, 24

Because so little is known about American ships during the War of Jenkins' Ear in the 1740s, it is perhaps worth inserting a mention of the privateer *Prince Charles*. She had been a French privateer measuring 380 tons and mounting 24 carriage guns, mostly nine-pounders, and was captured by Americans close to the beginning of the war. Captain Tingley of New York managed to squeeze a crew of 200 into this little ship that should have had hardly more than 100. Her name, incidentally, contained a dose of irony: during the course of the War of Jenkins' Ear against Spain and France, the British found they also had to contend with a large rebellion from Scotland in 1745 led by Prince Charles Stuart, "Bonnie Prince Charlie," who had allied himself with the French. When the ship was captured, the name remained unchanged, and so the ship *Prince Charles* found herself fighting against Prince Charles' side in the war. Her most important capture in 1746 was the massive French East Indiaman *Le Soleil Levant* (Rising Sun); Tingley accomplished this by dressing some of his crew in grenadier caps, which persuaded the French that they faced a Royal Navy ship rather than a privateer. For the drawing here, the known plans of the French privateer *La Panthère* (captured 1745) have been slightly adapted to fit the smaller size of *Le Prince Charles*.

PRINCE CHARLES, 24

DATES	LENGTH HULL	LENGTH DECK	LENGTH KEEL	BEAM	DEPTH	DRAFT	TONNAGE B. M.
1745-?	113 ESTIMATED	100	91	29	8	13	380

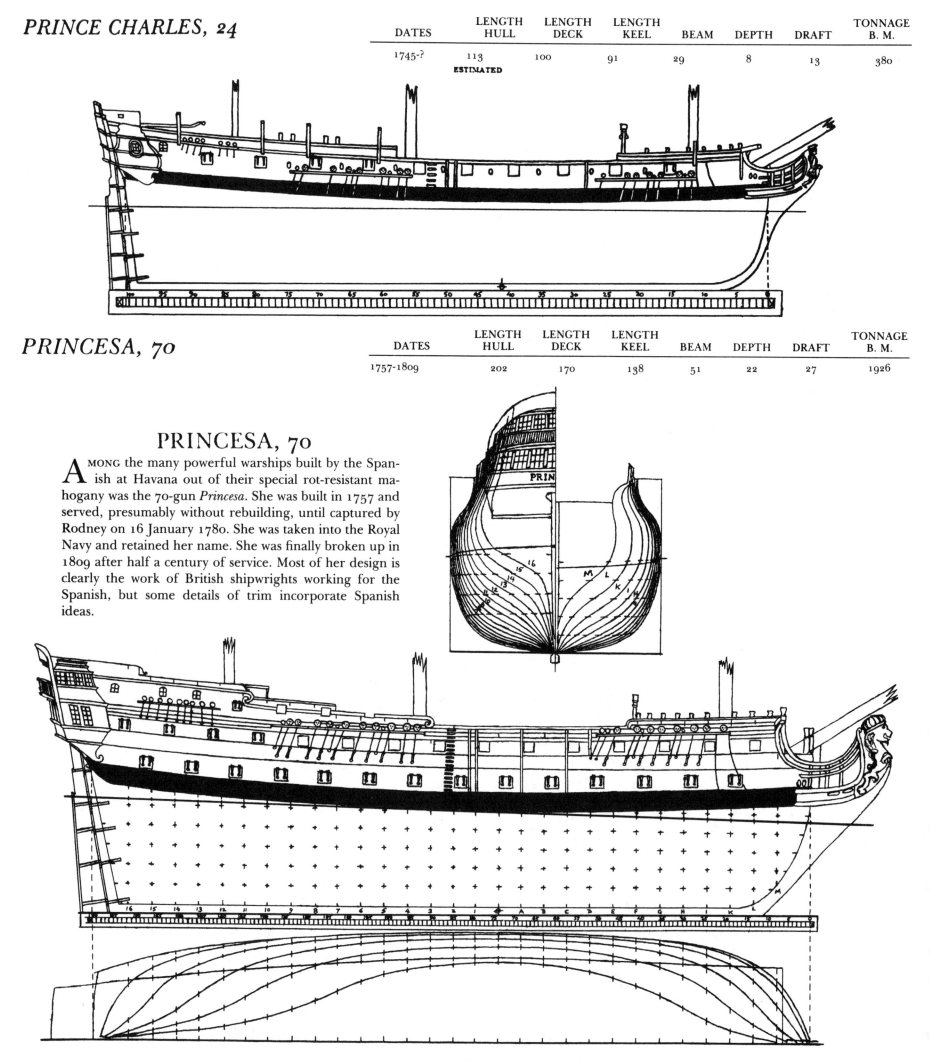

PRINCESA, 70

DATES	LENGTH HULL	LENGTH DECK	LENGTH KEEL	BEAM	DEPTH	DRAFT	TONNAGE B. M.
1757-1809	202	170	138	51	22	27	1926

PRINCESA, 70

Among the many powerful warships built by the Spanish at Havana out of their special rot-resistant mahogany was the 70-gun *Princesa*. She was built in 1757 and served, presumably without rebuilding, until captured by Rodney on 16 January 1780. She was taken into the Royal Navy and retained her name. She was finally broken up in 1809 after half a century of service. Most of her design is clearly the work of British shipwrights working for the Spanish, but some details of trim incorporate Spanish ideas.

DATES		LENGTH HULL	LENGTH DECK	LENGTH KEEL	BEAM	DEPTH	DRAFT	TONNAGE B. M.
1720-? 1723-? 1724-? 1725-?	ESTIMATED	172	147	128	42	17	18	1000

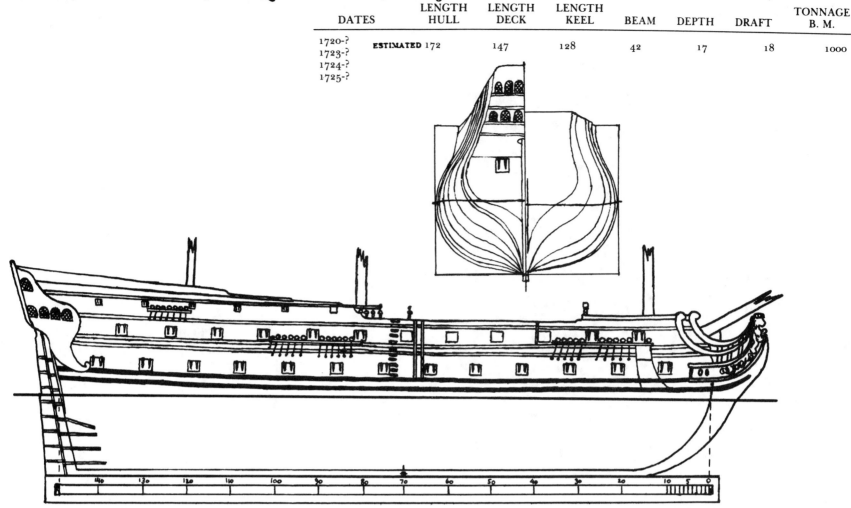

PRINCIPE DE ASTURIAS, CONQUISTADOR, SAN JUAN BAUTISTA & SAN ANTONIO, 60

In the days of Columbus, the conquistadors and the gold fleets, Spain was widely respected as a maritime nation. However, by the end of the seventeenth century, the Spanish Navy was pathetically out of date. While the British understood that the purpose of warships was to defeat enemy ships and hold sea-power, the French thought that the primary purpose of warships was to enable French armies to land on whatever coast they desired. The Spanish lagged even behind the French, for they thought that warships should reflect the design of merchant ships—the wider the better. Wide ships were stable gun-platforms, but they lacked speed and ability to maneuver.

Early in the eighteenth century, Bernardo de Tinajera, Secretary of the Council of the Indies, gave the king a plan to build many warships in the Americas to designs by Admiral Antonio Gaztañeta. A few warships had been previously built at Havana and Veracruz, but this plan considerably enlarged the operations.

The plan was approved, but action was postponed. A few ships to Gaztañeta's designs were built in Spain, and Spain purchased a number of fully-equipped warships from France and Italy, but many of these were lost to the British at the Battle of Cape Passaro in 1718.

The Tinajera plan was revived in 1720, and four 60-gun ships were built at Havana to Gaztañeta's designs: *Principe de Asturias* in 1720, *Conquistador* in 1723, *San Juan Bautista* in 1724, and *San Antonio* in 1725. To eyes used to the neater British designs of the period, the Gaztañeta design looks extremely old-fashioned with its square-tuck stern and narrow poop and no quarter-galleries, but it was up-to-date in its beam-to-length ratio, which was a beginning. A few years later, the much-enlarged shipyard at Havana imported French constructors to give the benefit of French theory, and then replaced them with a permanent array of British constructors, who gave Spanish battleships from about 1740 onwards a British look. Of course, the greatest advantage enjoyed by ships produced in the Havana shipyards was the unique Cuban mahogany out of which the hulls were constructed, the finest ship-building timber then known anywhere in the world.

This book was just going to press when a wealth of information on Spanish ships built in Havana and Veracruz was supplied by Dr. Douglas Inglis of Seville, Spain and formerly of the Texas State Archives. Without his assistance very little of the Spanish-American content of this book would have been possible. However, much more information remains to be uncovered.

The subsequent histories of the four 60-gun ships shown here are still unknown, except that *Conquistador* (not to be confused a later Havana-built ship of the same name that was captured by the British) was scuttled by the Spanish at Cartagena, Colombia to avoid capture by a British fleet in 1741. The British also managed to destroy a ship called *San Juan Bautista* at about the same date, but she is thought to be a smaller ship than the ship of that name that mounted 60 guns.

PROSPER, 20

DATES	LENGTH HULL	LENGTH DECK	LENGTH KEEL	BEAM	DEPTH	DRAFT	TONNAGE B. M.
1775 ESTIMATED	106	87	74	27	11	13	250

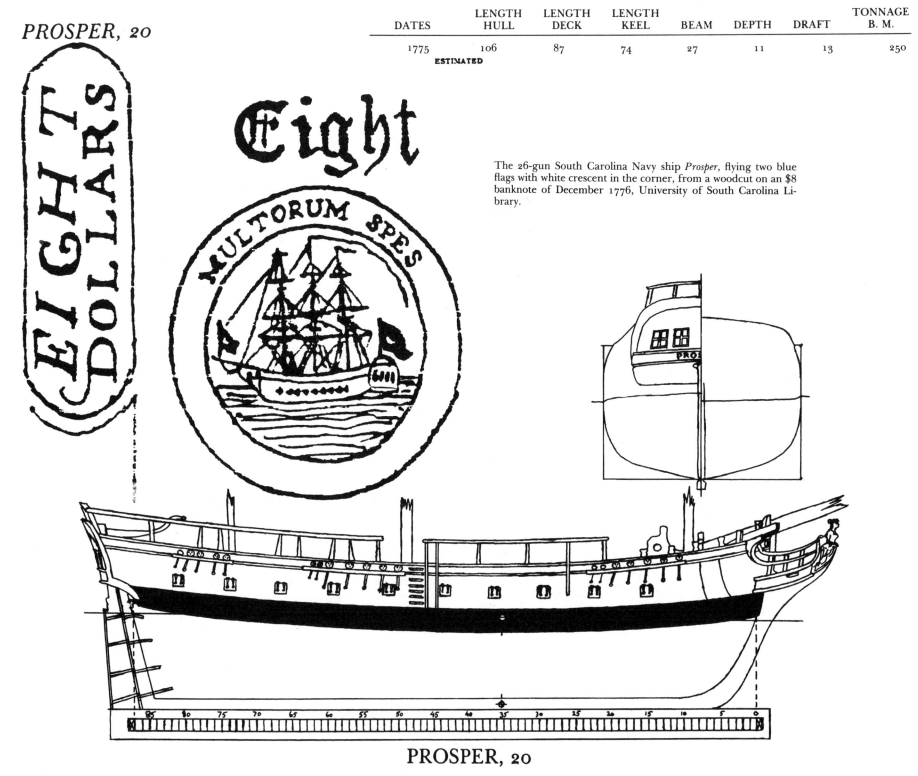

The 26-gun South Carolina Navy ship *Prosper*, flying two blue flags with white crescent in the corner, from a woodcut on an $8 banknote of December 1776, University of South Carolina Library.

PROSPER, 20

In the spring of 1775, the Province of South Carolina worried that British forces might invade and occupy Charleston and give her a taste of the medicine then being swallowed by Boston. Therefore, orders were given to seize the 250-ton merchant-ship *Prosper*, lately arrived from Bristol, England. In November, she was valued at £2000 British money (£15,400 local money) and that amount was offered to Captain Smith to give her owners, but he declined.

The province appointed Simon Tufts her captain after Clement Lemprière turned down the job, but Tufts resigned after a few weeks in favor of Justice William H. Drayton. Drayton placed the ship in position to guard the harbor entrance in December, after she had been armed with 26 guns arranged on her quarterdeck and through twenty holes hastily cut in her topsides. One report states that all 26 guns were 12-pounders, which would have been such a heavy armament for such a small ship that she would have been limited to harbor service, but another report says that she mounted eight 12-pounders, eight 6-pounders and from four to ten 4-pounders. When the British invasion did come in June 1776, the Americans were able to repulse Sir Peter Parker's fleet, but *Prosper* played no direct part in the struggle: her guns were all given to the shore batteries. A few weeks earlier, Drayton had resigned and been replaced by the reluctant Lemprière. By late summer, it was obvious that the ship could be of no further use to South Carolina, so she was ordered sold on 16 September. A single portrait of her survives on the $8 banknote issued by South Carolina in December 1776, a copy of which is owned by the library at the University of South Carolina.

PROVIDENCE (ex-KATY), 12

DATES	LENGTH HULL	LENGTH DECK	LENGTH KEEL	BEAM	DEPTH	DRAFT	TONNAGE B. M.
ca. 1769-1779	67	59	49	20	7	9	95
ESTIMATED							

Captain Samuel Nicholas, Continental Marines.

Sloop *Providence*
From an oil painting by Francis Holman, 1777
Private collection, Providence, Rhode Island

Sloop *Providence*, detail of grisaille of capture of *Mellish*, Roosevelt Collection, Hyde Park, NY.

THE sloop *Katy* was built at Providence, Rhode Island about 1768 for wealthy merchant John Brown. He used her briefly for whaling, and may have used her in the slave trade. When the Rhode Island General Assembly voted to found the first navy of any of the Colonies during the Revolution on 12 June 1775, *Katy* was chartered as the flagship of the Rhode Island Navy, and her captain, Abraham Whipple, was appointed commodore. Three days later, on 15 June, she captured the British sloop *Diana* in what must be considered the first act of war committed by any American Colony against Great Britain on the water. At this time, she was armed with 10 four-pounders, all on the main deck.

Her main job was to harass the 24-gun British frigate *Rose,* that had effectively put an end to Rhode Island's main industry of smuggling. But August, the General Assembly concluded that it needed outside help to get rid of the *Rose,* and on 26 August it voted to instruct its delegates at the Continental Congress to introduce a bill to create the Continental Navy. The bill passed on 13 October 1775, and written into the bill was authorization by Congress to purchase *Katy* and one other vessel. The other vessel was not available, so *Katy* was thus the first vessel authorized for the Continental Navy, even though she was not actually commissioned until December. In the meantime, she was sent to Bermuda on a fruitless mission to seize some gunpowder.

When she was taken into the navy, she was renamed *Providence.* (There were three vessels in Continental service in 1776 by the name of *Providence:* the sloop, the 28-gun frigate, and a gondola on Lake Champlain. No doubt this caused great confusion to friend and foe alike, as it does to historians.) *Providence* was rearmed and given 12 carriage guns, some or all of them being six-pounders, and 10 swivels; she had 8 carriage guns on the maindeck and 4 on the quarterdeck. Her new captain was John Hazard of Philadelphia. She took part in the expedition against Nassau in March 1776, and since she had a shallower draft than the rest of the fleet she was able to get close enough to the beach to land the marines in their first amphibious landing. After her return to Rhode Island she became the first command of John Paul Jones, on 10 May 1776; Hazard had been dismissed.

Jones used her aggressively, capturing over sixteen prizes in six months before he was promoted to captain of *Alfred.* Her next captain was Hoysted Hacker of Rhode Island, and he cruised for a while in company with Jones before returning to Providence just in time to be bottled up by the British occupation of Newport a few days later.

Her command then passed to John Peck Rathbun of Rhode Island, and the nimble *Providence* dodged British patrols and escaped to Charleston. From there Rathbun took her to Nassau, which the *Providence* captured once more, but this time single-handedly with 50 men in her crew. She also released American prisoners held there and captured nearly a ton of gunpowder along with five ships and a big supply of muskets; the date was 28 January 1778. In 1779 she was once more commanded by Hacker, and on 7 May she captured the 12-gun British navy brig *Diligent* off Newfoundland. She was then assigned to the expedition to the Penobscot Bay in Maine. When a British force appeared off the bay, the American vessels all fled up the bay and their crews set fire to them when they could go no further. That could be the end of the story of the "lucky" sloop *Providence,* for her crew reported that they had indeed set her on fire on 15 August, but one record of the Royal Navy states that she was captured and taken into the Royal Navy for a few months; if this is so, perhaps the fire went out without doing her much damage.

The only pictorial descriptions of the sloop *Providence* are in an oil painting, dated 1777, by Francis Holman (it is from that painting, now in a private collection, that we have reconstructed her lines), and in a grisaille in the Franklin D. Roosevelt Collection at Hyde Park. New York, that purports to be *Alfred* capturing *Mellish;* the artist, who obtained his information from a primitive sketch presumably made on the scene, mistakenly transposed the flags on the two vessels, thus leading to the incorrect identification of the scene. Before World War II, a ship model club, of which Howard Chapelle was a member, developed a speculative set of plans of her from which many models were made. There is one of these models at each of the following (not a complete list): the Mariners Museum, Newport News, Virginia; the Boston Museum of Fine Arts; the Phillips Andover Academy Museum, Andover, Massachusetts; the Rhode Island Historical Society, Providence; the Bristol Historical Society, Rhode Island. The model turns out to be quite inaccurate in the stern and quarterdeck, but otherwise acceptable except for the dolphin striker, which was not invented until the 1790s. We know that she was a fast ship, which is partly attributable to her design and partly to the fact that she had a copper bottom, a rarity among American ships.

A "biography" of the sloop *Providence,* called *Valour Fore & Aft,* by Hope Rider, was published by the Naval Institute Press in 1976. This book appeared at the same time as a full-sized copy of the sloop *Providence* was launched in Newport. The new *Providence* has proved to be a fast sailer.

PROVIDENCE, 28

DATES	LENGTH HULL	LENGTH DECK	LENGTH KEEL	BEAM	DEPTH	DRAFT	TONNAGE B. M.
1776-?	144	124	103	34	10	16	632

Frigate *Providence*
From a powderhorn engraving made for Charles Hewitt, 1777
Private collection, New Jersey

Frigate *Providence* at Charleston, SC, 1780, with Commodore Abraham Whipple, oil painting by Edward Savage, 1786, U.S. Naval Academy, Annapolis.

Details from Sir Henry Clinton's map of the capitulation of Charleston, South Carolina, 1780:

the corvette *Ranger* and the frigates *Boston* and *Providence*. Next is a row of ships sunk to block the harbor entrance, including *Queen of France*, *La Bricole* and *La Truite*. Further out in the roadstead, the British fleet includes two former American frigates captured earlier, *Raleigh* and *Virginia*.

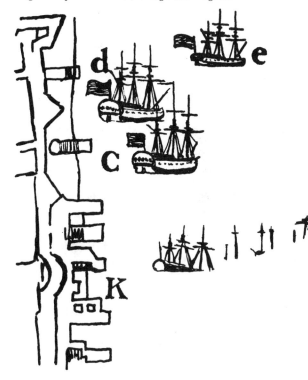

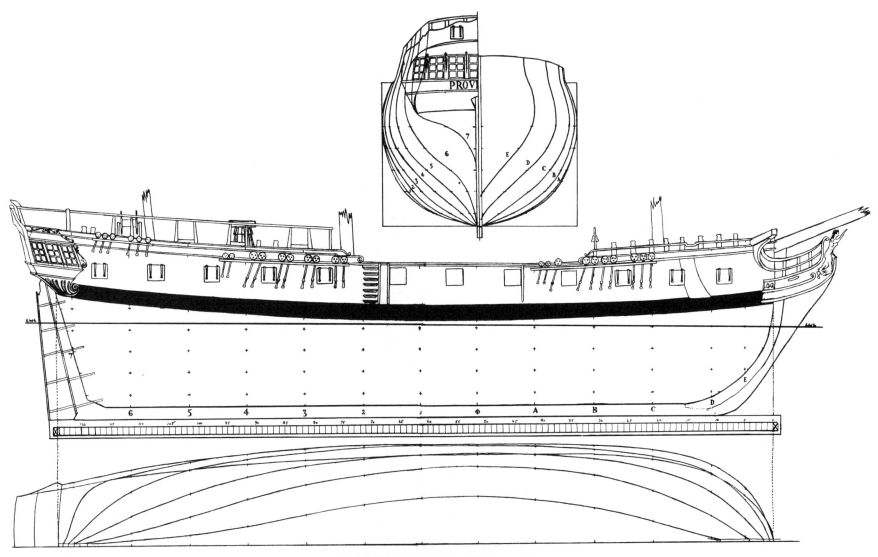

PROVIDENCE, 28

THE 28-gun frigate *Providence* was built at Providence, Rhode Island, in 1776 as one of the original thirteen frigates ordered by Congress late in 1775. She was built by Talman and Bowers, and in spite of the accuracy of the charge made by Esek Hopkins that the supervisory committee had diverted supplies for the frigates *Providence* and *Warren* to equip the privateers belonging to members of the committee, the two frigates were launched before those in any of the other Colonies. *Providence* was launched second, on 18 May 1776, and the ever-generous committee voted to appropriate $50 for the entertainment of the shipwrights.

Abraham Whipple, one of Rhode Island's favorite sons, was made her captain, and she was armed with a mixture of twelve-pounders and eighteen-pounders, which made her more powerful than any other frigate of her rate in the world. Nevertheless, she did not get to sea for almost a year after her launching because a British fleet had occupied the mouth of Narragansett Bay. Whipple made a run for it on the night of 30 April 1777 with 170 men in the crew (not quite full strength), and escaped after a damaging battle with the 32-gun frigate *Lark*. Whipple arrived at Nantes, France, on 26 May, joining *Boston* and *Ranger*.

The three of them finally left St. Nazaire, France, on 26 September 1778, arriving at Boston before Christ-mas. There they and three other frigates sat for several months with no crew and few supplies. In the summer *Providence* left on a cruise with *Queen of France* and *Ranger*. On 18 July 1778, while in a thick fog off Newfoundland, they had the good fortune to run into a sixty-ship convoy from Jamaica bound for London, and guarded by one two-decker and some smaller ships. They carefully surprised and cut out eleven transports (of which three were later recaptured). The prize money realized from this escapade came to over $1 million, which made it the most lucrative cruise made by the Continental Navy in the whole war.

In 1780, *Providence* was ordered to Charleston, South Carolina, in company with *Boston*, *Ranger* and the rotten *Queen of France*. Their job was to assist the South Carolina Navy ships *La Bricole* and *La Truite* in defending Charleston against a massive British invasion. *Queen of France* and the two South Carolina ships were sunk in an attempt to block the entrance of the harbor, but the others were captured when the city had to capitulate on 12 May 1780. *Providence* was taken into the Royal Navy with no change of name and was sold out of the service after the war on 11 March 1784.

The British recorded *Providence*'s dimensions, but if her lines were taken off, they have not been found. There is one crude engraving of her on a powderhorn, dated 1777, and she is also possibly the ship in the background of Savage's portrait of Whipple (dated 1786), which means little since Savage probably never saw her. Our reconstruction, then, is based on the British dimensions and on an enlargement of the plans of the privateer *Oliver Cromwell* which we believe to have been designed by the same man.

The frigate *Providence* was not built to the official design that was approved by Congress because those designs did not arrive in time to start construction. She is not to be confused with another *Providence* that served in the Royal Navy from 1782 to 1784 as a storeship; the latter was slightly smaller, and her plans survive at Greenwich.

LE QUEBEC, 32

DATES		LENGTH HULL	LENGTH DECK	LENGTH KEEL	BEAM	DEPTH	DRAFT	TONNAGE B. M.
1757-?	ESTIMATED	152	130	122	35	16	15	700

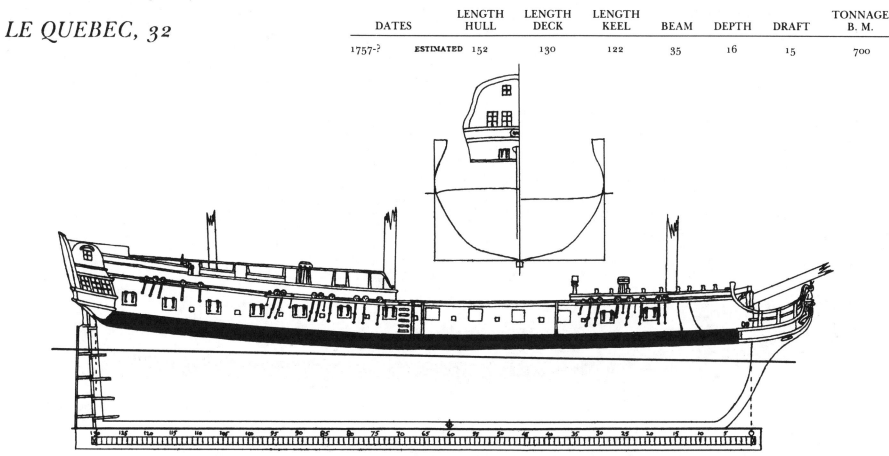

LE QUEBEC, 32

A NUMBER of warships of different sizes were built in Quebec for the French navy in the 1740s and 1750s (for a list of these, see the descriptive text for the frigate *L'Abenakise*), but unfortunately Monsieur Jean Boudriot, the greatest expert on eighteenth-century French ships, can find absolutely no information about any of these ships in the French Archives.

One of them was the 32-gun frigate *Le Québec;* all we know about her is that she was built in Quebec in 1757. Because of her obvious importance to the history of American ships in the eighteenth century, we have at-

tempted to reconstruct her appearance, based on the lines of other French frigates of the same date and based on the known appearance of the larger frigate *L'Abenakise,* which had been built in the same shipyard the previous year. *L'Abenakise* had a double-decked stern, like an East Indiaman, and although this was virtually never seen on British or American frigates it seems to have been fairly common on French frigates of this period, so we have given *Le Québec* the same kind of stern. The French were quite particular about the comfort of their officers, and this kind of stern added to their comfort.

QUEEN OF FRANCE (ex-LA BRUNE), 28

E ARLY in the War of American Independence, efforts were made to obtain assistance, especially from the French. The French government was officially neutral, but individual Frenchmen found ways to help, as did the French royal family. For example, Louis XVI channeled great quantities of military supplies to America through a bogus company called Hortalez & Cie., run by Pierre Caron de Beaumarchais (the author of such plays as the *Barber of Seville* and the *Marriage of Figaro*). In 1777 Queen Marie Antoinette bought a small privateer frigate called *La Brune* (which means brown-haired girl; not to be confused with the French Navy frigate of the same name that was

captured by the British in 1761), since she could not very well take a ship from her husband's navy, and presented it to Congress. Congress was delighted and renamed the ship *Queen of France*, but the value of the gift was limited. The ship was old and somewhat rotten, and she mounted no more than twenty-four 6-pounders—hardly more than pop-guns. It was evident that Marie Antoinette had not dug any deeper into her purse than she had to in order to place Congress in her debt.

All that to the contrary not withstanding, *Queen of France* was well used by the Continental Navy, for she acted in concert with the frigates *Providence* and *Warren* and the corvette *Ranger* on a number of occasions to take scores of rich prizes from British convoys. In 1780, she was sent to Charleston, South Carolina, but when the threatened British invasion came, there was no use offering opposition to such superior forces, so *Queen of France* was sunk along with *La Bricole* and *La Truite* in a vain attempt to block the harbor entrance.

No pictures, plans or dimensions survive of *Queen of France*, so the drawing shown here is speculative. It is based on the known appearance of the 24-gun French privateer *Le Tygre*, captured by the British in 1747.

QUEEN OF FRANCE (ex-LA BRUNE), 28

DATES	LENGTH HULL	LENGTH DECK	LENGTH KEEL	BEAM	DEPTH	DRAFT	TONNAGE B. M.
ca. 1757-1780 ESTIMATED	137	118	98	34	15	17	581

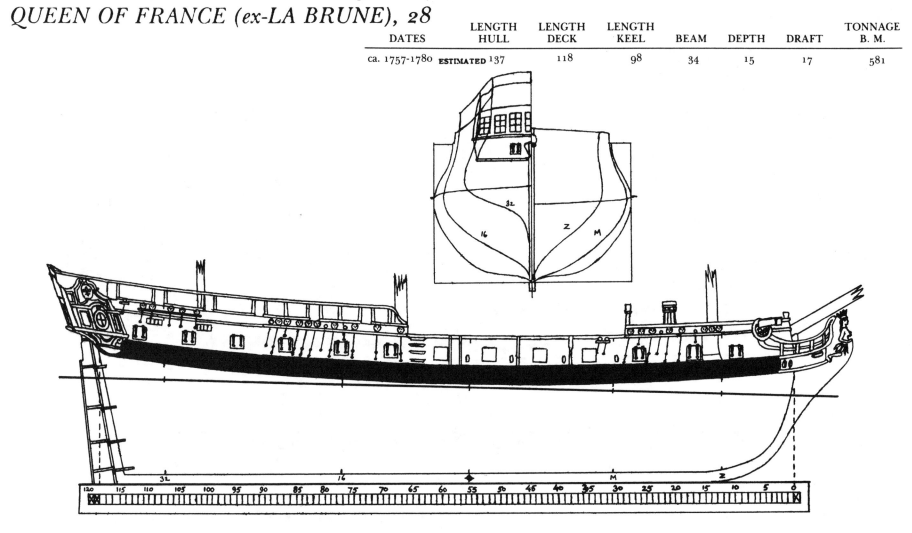

RALEIGH, 32

THE 32-gun frigate *Raleigh* was built by the Hackett family at Portsmouth, New Hampshire. She was named after the Elizabethan sea dog and launched on 21 May 1776 after the incredibly short time of only sixty days. She was one of the original thirteen frigates authorized by Congress in 1775, but the official plans approved by Congress did not reach the wilderness of New Hampshire in time, so she was built to plans drawn by the local shipwrights. Due to shortages of men and material she did not get to sea until 1777, when she was commanded by Captain Thomas Thompson. Although short of cannons, she left in mid-August in company with *Alfred,* and they soon ran into a British convoy guarded by a group of converted merchantmen, including *Druid* and *Grasshopper* (both American built). *Raleigh* made a poor showing in her attack on the convoy, and the two ships arrived at Lorient, France, on 7 October.

As soon as she had acquired all the cannons she needed in France, *Raleigh* set sail for home again, still in company with *Alfred*. On 9 March 1778 they engaged two British warships of very small force near the West Indies, and *Raleigh* ignominiously fled, leaving *Alfred* to be taken. Thompson was relieved of his command as soon as he arrived in Boston in April, and John Barry was made her new captain. *Raleigh* left Boston on 25 September 1778, but only a few hours out she was chased by the 20-gun frigate *Unicorn* and the 50-gun ship *Experiment*. *Raleigh* quickly lost parts of her fore- and mainmasts, so Barry ran her onto the rocks of the Maine coast and escaped with a third of his men. The next day the British pulled the ship off and sent her to England. She was taken into the Royal Navy, and her plans were drawn in a royal dockyard; these plans survive today at the National Maritime Museum at Greenwich. She took part in the British expedition to Charleston, South Carolina, in 1780, and remained in the Royal Navy until the end of the war, when she was sold on 17 July 1783.

Raleigh had a round bow with no trace of a beakhead bulkhead. Her wale was unusually low, and she had no moldings along her topsides above the gunports as other frigates usually did. Like *Hancock* and *Boston*, she had a small lateen sail set on the ensign staff for steadying her. An engraving by the French artist Baugean is one of only two known contemporary por-traits of her; Baugean was only fourteen years old when *Raleigh* was in France, so he must have made his engraving later in life from a sketch made in 1778 either by him or by another artist. The other portrait is a watercolor by Nicolas Ozanne.

RALEIGH, 32

DATES	LENGTH HULL	LENGTH DECK	LENGTH KEEL	BEAM	DEPTH	DRAFT	TONNAGE B. M.
1776-?	154	131	111	34	11	17	697

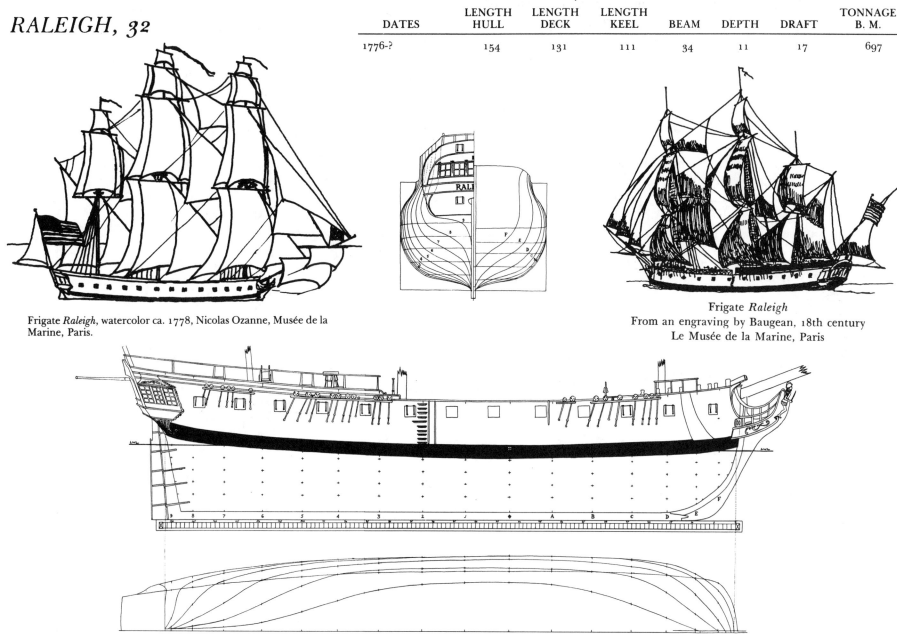

Frigate *Raleigh*, watercolor ca. 1778, Nicolas Ozanne, Musée de la Marine, Paris.

Frigate *Raleigh*
From an engraving by Baugean, 18th century
Le Musée de la Marine, Paris

RANDOLPH & WASHINGTON, 32

Two of the original 32-gun frigates authorized by Congress for the Continental Navy in 1775 were constructed at Philadelphia: the *Randolph* was built by Wharton & Humphreys and the *Washington* was built by the Eyre shipyard, both to the official design approved by Congress. *Washington* was launched in November 1776, and most accounts say that she was not completed before the British occupied the Delaware River area; her captain was Thomas Read of Pennsylvania. She is reported to have been scuttled in the river just above Philadelphia about 20 November 1777, without ever having been used. However, a French map of British operations on the Delaware clearly shows "*Le Washington*, frégate" at anchor just above the point where the Schuylkill joins the Delaware, which

may indicate that she was used briefly to confront a possible British breakthrough on the river early in the campaign.

She was scuttled with the 28-gun frigate *Effingham* at Bordentown Creek, but both were raised again to serve as floating barracks for 400 men. When the British made a raid up the river in May 1778, the two frigates were burned to prevent capture.

As for *Randolph*, her career was more interesting but hardly less tragic. She was launched on 16 July 1776 and assigned to Captain Nicholas Biddle of Philadelphia; Biddle had served as a midshipman in the Royal Navy with Horatio Nelson on the *Racehorse-Carcass* Arctic expedition of 1773. On 13 January 1777 she escaped through the British blockade of the Delaware with only half her complement of crew to go on a cruise with *Fly* and *Hornet*. However, she was seriously damaged by a storm off Cape Hatteras, so she put into Charleston, South Carolina for repairs. In July she was ordered to sail in search of a convoy from Jamaica and returned in September with but three prizes. She was hove down to clean the bottom and then departed for France, arriving at Lorient in December.

Early in 1778 she returned to Charleston, and then set sail on 12 February with a small squadron into the West Indies. Around 8:00 P.M. (after dark) on 7 March they were engaged by the 64-gun ship *Yarmouth* off Barbados. *Randolph* gave a good accounting of herself for about twenty minutes, apparently inflicting considerable damage on her much larger adversary. Suddenly, a spark got into her magazine and she blew up with a tremendous explosion. There were only four survivors, and they were miraculously picked up five days later by *Yarmouth* as she cruised through the same waters once more. One of the biggest tragedies of this incident was the loss of Nicholas Biddle, who probably had better qualifications than any other captain in the Continental Navy; among other things, he had served in the Royal Navy as a midshipman, and had been a messmate of the young Nelson.

Randolph's plans are the only original plans approved by Congress to survive of any of the first frigates. The plans were not followed exactly, for accounts were written of the alterations that were made. Our plans reflect these alterations as far as possible, as set down by the late Howard Chapelle. We have also added the upper wale to conform with what we know about the 28-gun frigates that apparently came from the same drawingboards. Interesting features about her design are the out-of-date beakhead bulkhead (probably retained from the connection of this design with that of the privateer *Hero* that had been built during the Seven Years' War), and the sharp rake to the transom.

RANDOLPH & WASHINGTON, 32

DATES	LENGTH HULL	LENGTH DECK	LENGTH KEEL	BEAM	DEPTH	DRAFT	TONNAGE B. M.
1776-1778	156	133	108	34	11	16	700
1776-1778							

Frigate *Washington*, detail from French map of the Delaware, 1778, Musée de la Marine, Paris.

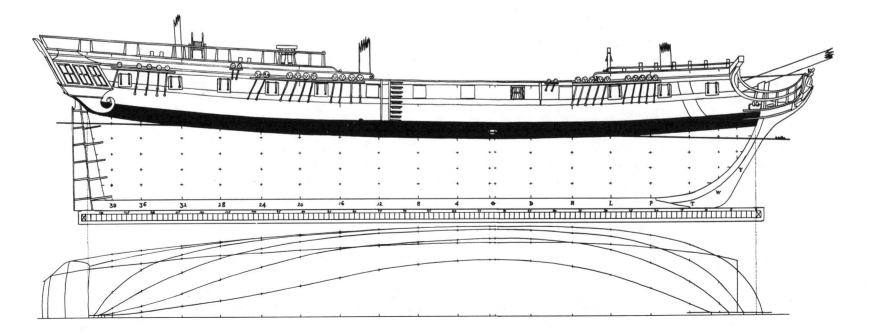

Explosion of frigate *Randolph*, 1778, engraving published 1786.

Captain Nicholas Biddle.

RANGER (*ex*-HAMPSHIRE)/HALIFAX, PORTS-MOUTH & HAMPDEN, 18/20

DATES	LENGTH HULL	LENGTH DECK	LENGTH KEEL	BEAM	DEPTH	DRAFT	TONNAGE B. M.
1777-1781 1776-? 1778-1779	116	97	82	29	13	12	308

American Brig leaving Portsmouth, N.H.;
very likely the *Hampden*
From a grisaille by Pierre Ozanne, 1778
Le Musée de la Marine, Paris

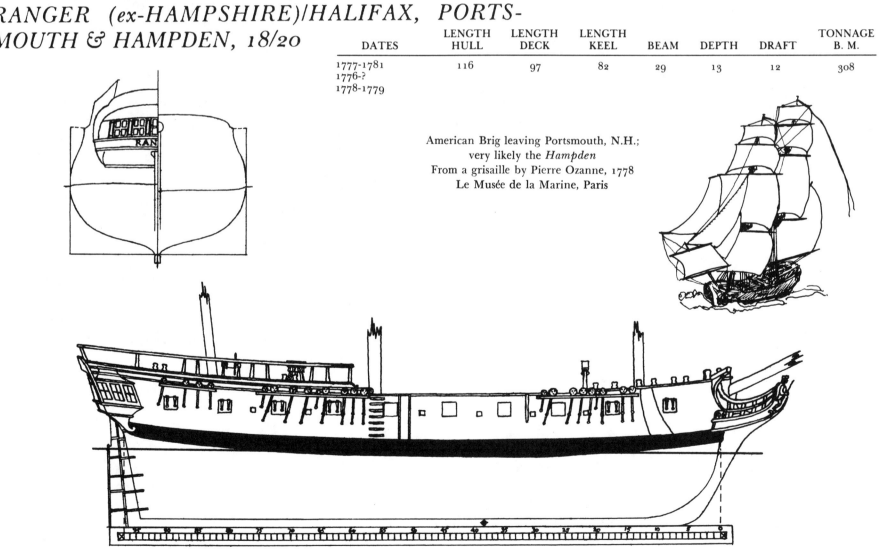

ONE of the best-known ships in the Continental Navy was the 18-gun corvette *Ranger*, to which fame accrued because of her connection with John Paul Jones. However, the story of *Ranger* properly begins with the construction at Portsmouth, New Hampshire of the 20-gun privateer ship *Portsmouth*, for *Ranger* was built as a copy of her. *Portsmouth* was built at the Hackett shipyard (where the Continental frigate *Raleigh* had been built earlier that year) to the order of John Langdon, and launched on 20 December 1777. In spite of a ban on privateers until *Raleigh* should be fully manned, *Portsmouth* departed on her first cruise to the West Indies under the command of Robert Parker in February 1777. She was armed with twenty "small" cannons, probably 6-pounders. By April, she sent in four or five prizes and returned home in May by way of Boston. On 7 June she received a new captain, John Hart, and set sail for France. In November and December she was reported at Bordeaux and then Lorient. A spy noted that she was remarkably fast. At the time of writing, no further information about this interesting ship was available.

In October 1776 Congress authorized construction of three 18-gun corvettes (although the actual bill has never been found). When these ships were commissioned in 1777 and later they were named after various aspects of the great victory over the British at Saratoga in October 1777: *Saratoga*, built at Philadelphia; *General Gates*, which was to have been built in Massachusetts but was replaced by the prize brig *Industrious Bee* renamed; and *Ranger*, named after the riflemen who had contributed so much to the war effort. The Continental Marine Committee wrote to John Langdon directing him to build them a brig of eighteen 6-pounders; he replied that they would save time and money by building a copy of *Portsmouth*, which could carry twenty 9-pounders if required. He also warned against using the brig rig for such a large ship. The new ship was launched in May 1777 and apparently named *Hampshire* but soon renamed *Ranger*. She mounted twenty 9-pounders, but two of them were soon removed, partly because Jones thought they made the ship too heavy in the bow, and partly because a 20-gun ship would have required a captain with more seniority than Jones.

Ranger was given to John Paul Jones to command on 14 June 1777. He sailed for France on 1 November, capturing two brigs on the way. He arrived at Nantes on 2 December and began to have the ship rerigged and rebalasted. On 14 February 1778 he contrived to have a French warship return his salute while he was flying the new stars-and-stripes flag, and this is thought to be the first time that flag was officially recognized by a foreign government. On 10 April he left Brest on a cruise in the Irish Sea. He captured a few prizes and sank others, raided the town of Whitehaven, allowed his crew to plunder the mansion of the absent earl of Selkirk, and then captured the 20-gun ship *Drake* near Carrickfergus. *Drake* was not a proper warship, so the victory was not really all that it was publicized as being; she was a converted Philadelphia merchantman and a sister ship of *Alfred*. While Jones remained in France,

Corvette *Ranger*
From the printed broadside
"Great Encouragement for Seamen . . ," No. 1, 1777

Corvette *Ranger*
From the printed broadside
"Great Encouragement for Seamen . . ," No. 2, 1777

Ranger was placed under command of the mutinous Lieutenant Thomas Simpson on 27 July, and on 26 September she set sail for New England from St. Nazaire, in company with the frigates *Providence* and *Boston*.

Still under the command of Simpson, the following July *Ranger* accompanied the frigates *Providence* and *Queen of France* on a cruise off the Newfoundland coast in which they captured eleven members of a British convoy; the prize money came to over $1 million, the richest cruise of the Continental Navy during the entire war. Towards the end of 1779, *Ranger* was sent to Charleston, South Carolina, along with *Providence*, *Queen of France* and *Boston*. Unfortunately, the city was overwhelmed by superior British land and sea forces on 12 May 1780, and one of the terms of the surrender was that the surviving ships (*Queen of France* had been sunk) be turned over to the British intact. Ranger was taken into the Royal Navy and renamed *Halifax*. The hard usage to which she had been put in her short life obviously began to tell, for she was sold out of the service on 13 October 1781.

Shortly after the construction of *Ranger*, some New Hampshire citizens ordered a brig of the same size from the same shipyard. They named her *Hampden* after the member of Parliament who had stood up to the arbitrary and absolutist taxation policies of Charles I. She is not to be confused with another brig of the same name that served briefly in the Continental Navy early in the war. *Hampden* was about as large a vessel as was then thought practical to rig as a brig, and there were few as big as she. It is reasonable to assume that her hull was identical to *Ranger*'s.

Hampden mounted twenty cannons on her gundeck, probably 6-pounders, and more on the quarterdeck, which, having no mizzen mast, had more room than

Ranger's. Under Captain Thomas Pickering, *Hampden* had a successful cruise in European waters during the winter of 1778-9 (not a pleasant time to be cruising in that area), and sent in at least four substantial prizes. On her way home in the spring, she encountered a former East Indiaman armed with twenty-six 9-pounders and eight 4-pounders. In a long battle, the two wrecked eachother's rigging. When Pickering was killed, *Hampden* turned away and left her adversary totally disabled. In June 1779 the brig was chartered or sold to the New Hampshire State Navy under Captain Salter, and was sent on the ill-fated Penobscot expedition in Maine. *Hampden* was one of the last to flee upriver, and, after receiving the broadsides of three British frigates, was obliged to surrender. She was one of only two or three ships captured, as the rest were burned by their crews. What happened to her in British hands is not recorded.

No plans survive for *Portsmouth*, *Ranger* or *Hampden*. The contemporary portraits of the latter two are crude and small. The British noted down *Ranger*'s dimensions, but Chapelle made an error in copying them; he wrote that she was 116 feet on the gundeck with a 34-foot beam, but measuring only 308 tons. The tonnage figure is correct, but the others are too large. *Ranger* was described as a fast ship, but the British thought her "overhatted," and they cut down her rig accordingly. The appearance of the three vessels that has been reconstructed here is based on scaling down the known plans of the frigate *Raleigh* to fit the known dimensions.

RATTLESNAKE/CORMORANT/? *LE TONNANT*, 16

DATES	LENGTH HULL	LENGTH DECK	LENGTH KEEL	BEAM	DEPTH	DRAFT	TONNAGE B. M.
1780-? ca. 1795	106	89	75	22	9	11	199

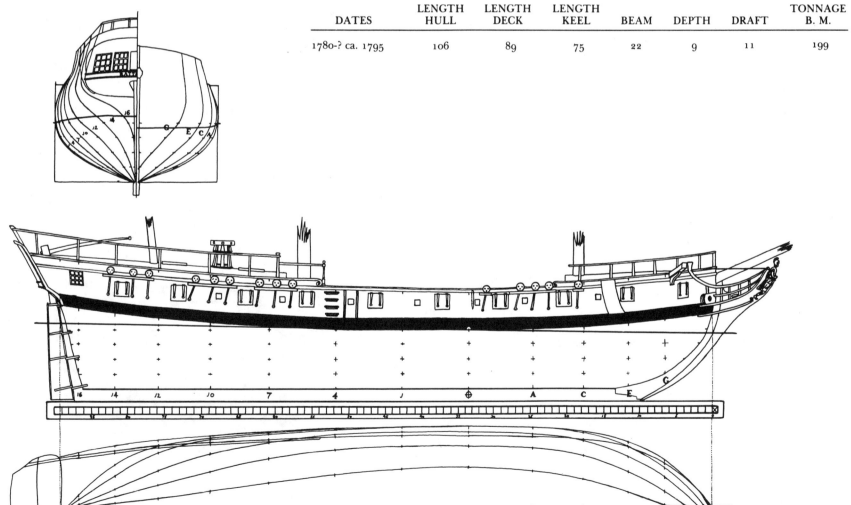

RATTLESNAKE/CORMORANT/? LE TONNANT, 16

THE 16-gun privateer ship *Rattlesnake* was built at Plymouth, Massachusetts, in 1779 or 1780 allegedly to designs by the maverick designer John Peck. She was owned by John Andrews and others of Salem, and her captain was Mark Clark. She mounted anywhere from 14 to 20 carriage guns at various times, and she usually carried about 85 men. The earliest commission found for her is dated 12 June 1781, but she may have been commissioned earlier. One privateer with the name of *Rattlesnake* is reported to have captured more than $1 million worth of British shipping on a single cruise in the Baltic, but whether it was this *Rattlesnake* or not we do not know.

Our *Rattlesnake* was captured off the American coast in 1781 by the brand-new British 44-gun ship *Assurance* and was renamed *Cormorant*. She was taken to England and her lines were drawn (her lines survive on file at the National Maritime Museum at Greenwich). It took the British bureaucracy a long time to realize that they already had a ship called *Cormorant* in the Royal Navy, so she was renamed *Rattlesnake* once more in August 1783, after the war was over. Chapelle says she was sold out of the service in 1784, but British records indicate she was not sold until 10 October 1786.

What happened next is partly conjecture, but it seems she passed into French hands during the period of the French Revolution, for there was a French privateer called *Le Tonnant* in the 1790s that had *Rattlesnake*'s exact lines. These lines have been issued as part of a European model kit of *Le Tonnant*.

Rattlesnake was extremely sharp and had moderate deadrise; she must have been very fast. For a time the British Admiralty contemplated building a corvette to her lines but to a larger scale; however, this plan was dropped.

A modern adaptation of *Rattlesnake*'s design has recently been built in Ontario for charter.

REAL CARLOS, SAN HERMENEGILDO, CONDE DE REGLA & SAN HIPOLITO/MEXICANO, 104

IN the late 1780s, the Spanish Navy began a flurry of major ship construction at Havana and produced, among others, four ships of 112 guns. These were *San Hipolito* later renamed *Mexicano* (1786), *Conde de Regla* (also 1786), *Real Carlos* (1787), and *San Hermenegildo* (1789). They were constructed out of the superb local mahogany, which unfortunately is extinct with the possible exception of a few isolated trees in Haiti. They were built basically in the British style, which indicates the presence of British shipwrights at Havana or in Spain, where the design may have originated. Principal differences from a British ship of their size include their lion figurehead (British ships of this size never had a lion, which was reserved for smaller ships in the first half of the eighteenth century and abandoned almost entirely by the 1780s) and the two fender bars at the forward part of the waist. When completed, these four ships must have been the finest in the world.

We have not been able to trace the careers of the first two ships, but the end of the other two is known. When Spain was forced to throw in her lot with Napoleon against Britain, *Real Carlos* and *San Hermenegildo* became important elements in the combined Franco-Spanish fleet. French Admiral Linois anchored with his battered fleet in Algeciras Bay near Gibraltar and called for reinforcements from Cadiz. Six ships of the line, including these two, and three frigates joined the French on 9 July 1801. On 12 July, the combined fleet got under way and headed for Cadiz, but a British fleet under Saumarez of less than half the force came out from Gibraltar to do battle with them as the sun was setting. Saumarez detached Captain Keats in the 74-gun *Superb* to chase the Spaniards, and Keats completely surprised *Real Carlos* in the dark. Keats fired several broadsides at the flagship from within pistol-shot range while the Spaniards were in confusion. A chance shot in the right place set the huge ship afire. *Real Carlos* then began firing wildly in all directions, particularly at *San Hermenegildo*. The latter, mistaking *Real Carlos* for the enemy, fired back at her and then collided with her. Both ships were by then heavily on fire in a strong wind on an otherwise black night. Shortly after midnight both ships blew up as the fires reached the magazines. About 2000 lives were lost. Sir James Saumarez became a hero for his

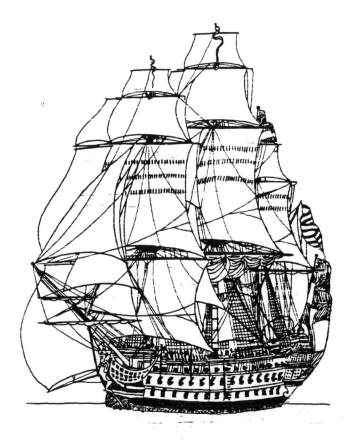

Ship *Real Carlos*, aquatint, ca. 1790, Don Alejo Berlinguero de la Marcay Gallego, Museo Naval, Madrid.

part in winning the battle of Algeciras Bay, although the Spanish really did it all to themselves; one other French ship was captured in the action.

The source for our plans is an outstanding model of *Real Carlos* at the Museo Naval in Madrid. *Real Carlos,* once the pride of the Spanish navy, was also depicted in a number of pictures, including a horrifying scene by Breton of the two ships on fire at night. According to the model and some of the pictures, she had two sprit-sail yards and still had a lateen yard on the mizzen, although this had been replaced by a gaff on British ships many years before.

REAL CARLOS, SAN HERMENEGILDO, CONDE DE REGLA &
SAN HIPOLITO/MEXICANO, 104

DATES	LENGTH HULL	LENGTH DECK	LENGTH KEEL	BEAM	DEPTH	DRAFT	TONNAGE B. M.
1787-1801	232	189	161	53	22	25	2300
1789-1801							
1786-?							
1786-?							

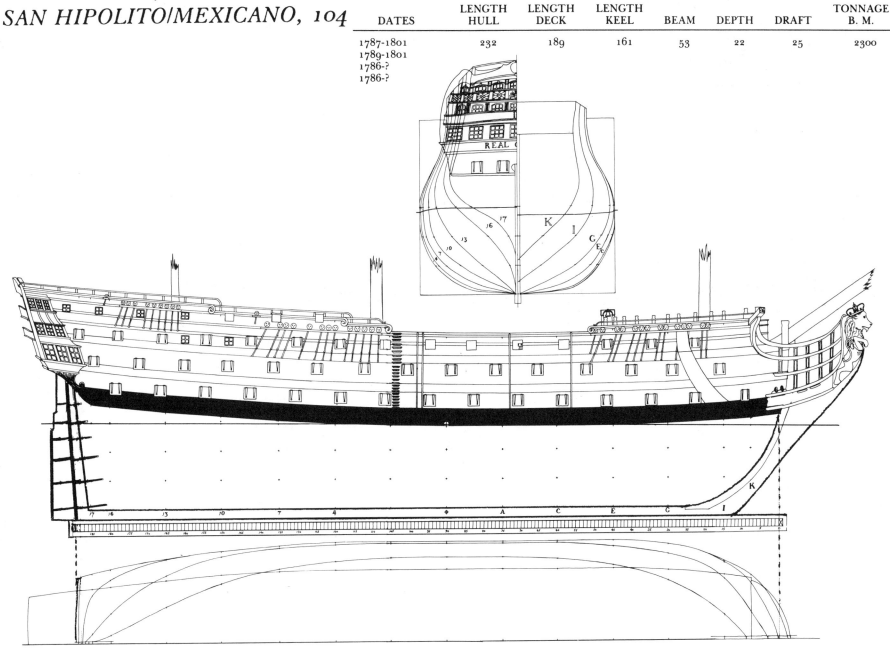

REVENGE, 8

WHEN Benedict Arnold set about building a fleet on Lake Champlain in the summer of 1776 to slow down the expected British attack, most of his fleet was built at Skenesborough. However, he did order one small schooner, called *Revenge,* built further along the lake at Ticonderoga. She mounted 4 four-pounders and 4 two-pounders, in addition to a few swivel guns, and carried 50 men. At her bow was a raised rail which may have been only a splashboard of sorts, but it may actually have been there to support a forecastle, which would have been an unusual feature for a vessel so small.

She was in Arnold's fleet at the battle of Valcour Island, but escaped serious damage in that action and in the flight that followed. However, the following year, when the British fleet had been reinforced, she was captured and burned in the summer of 1777. She was included in a number of pictures of the various vessels on the lake, and it is on these that we have based our reconstruction. Otherwise, we know virtually nothing about her.

REVENGE, 8

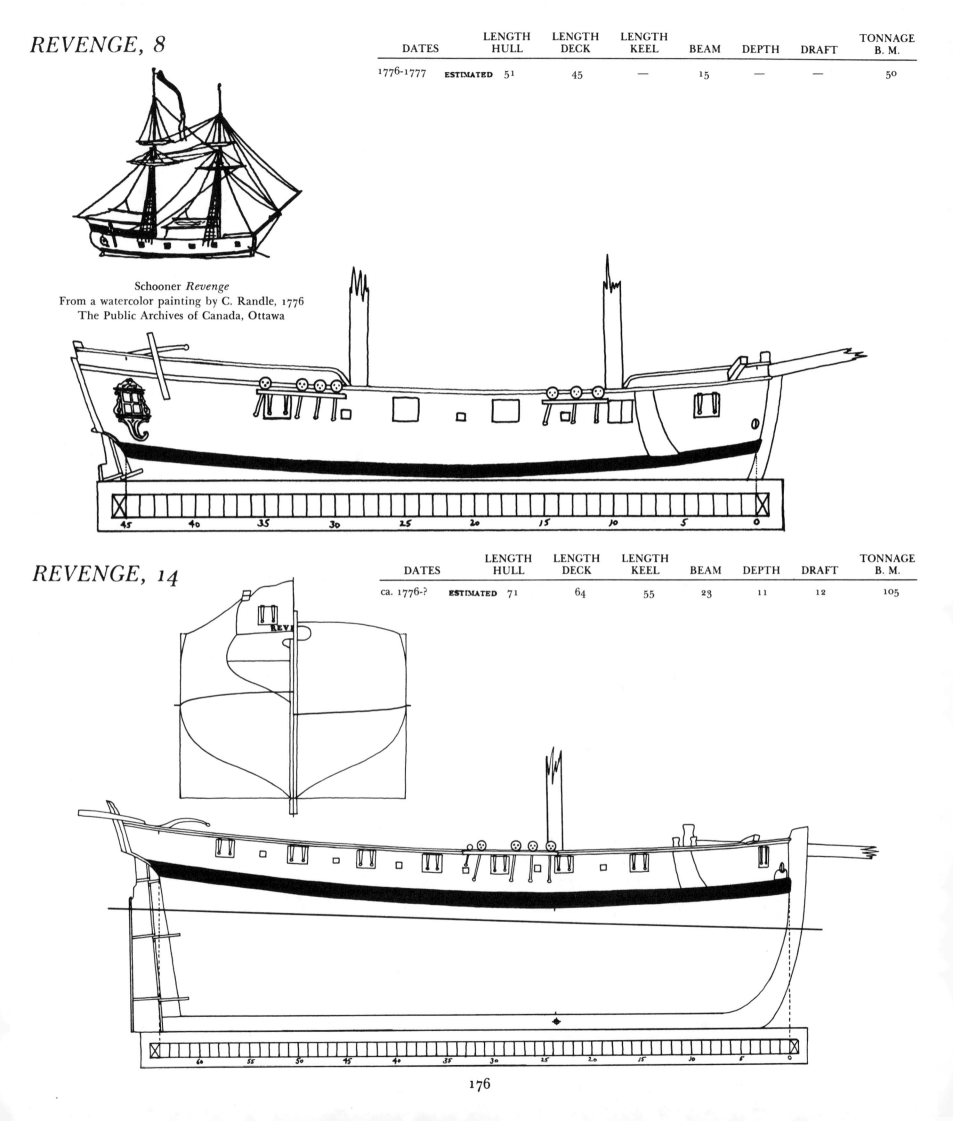

DATES		LENGTH HULL	LENGTH DECK	LENGTH KEEL	BEAM	DEPTH	DRAFT	TONNAGE B. M.
1776-1777	ESTIMATED	51	45	—	15	—	—	50

Schooner *Revenge*
From a watercolor painting by C. Randle, 1776
The Public Archives of Canada, Ottawa

REVENGE, 14

DATES		LENGTH HULL	LENGTH DECK	LENGTH KEEL	BEAM	DEPTH	DRAFT	TONNAGE B. M.
ca. 1776-?	ESTIMATED	71	64	55	23	11	12	105

REVENGE, 14

BENJAMIN FRANKLIN was so pleased with the results of the first ships he had commissioned to raid the British in their home waters that he tried to add more vessels to his fleet. One of these was a cutter of 14 six-pounders and 22 swivels that was lying at Dunkirk. She was named *Revenge* after Sir Richard Grenville's heroic ship from Elizabethan days, and was purchased for Continental service by William Hodge. She set off on 2 May 1777, manned by 106 men, including 66 Frenchmen. Since the French were not officially at war with Britain, the British protested loudly and caused French ports to be off-limits to *Revenge*. The restrictions were apparently unimportant to her intrepid captain, Gustavus Conyngham, who cheerfully took many British prizes within sight of their own coast, and even held the town of King's Lynn, Norfolk, for ransom (he failed to collect when the wind shifted).

Next, he made his base in a number of Spanish ports, where he was very popular. Once more the British protested to the then-neutral Spanish government, which looked the other way until Conyngham's rapacious crew insisted on capturing a Spanish-owned ship, contrary to orders. With Spanish ports closed, he took her back to Philadelphia via Martinique, arriving 21 February 1778 with a heavy load of weapons for the Continental Army. She was then sold to some Philadelphia merchants as a privateer, but Conyngham remained in command. During a cruise to the West Indies she was captured by the 20-gun frigate *Galatea*, and Conyngham was carried off in heavy chains. He had captured over seventy British ships with the sturdy cutter.

No plans, dimensions, or portraits of *Revenge* survive. However, since she was such an important vessel in the story of American ships we have reconstructed her appearance by following the lines of a number of typical cutters of her size and date.

ROYAL GEORGE, 20

DATES	LENGTH HULL	LENGTH DECK	LENGTH KEEL	BEAM	DEPTH	DRAFT	TONNAGE B. M.
1777-ca. 1783	113	97	78	31	10	9	386

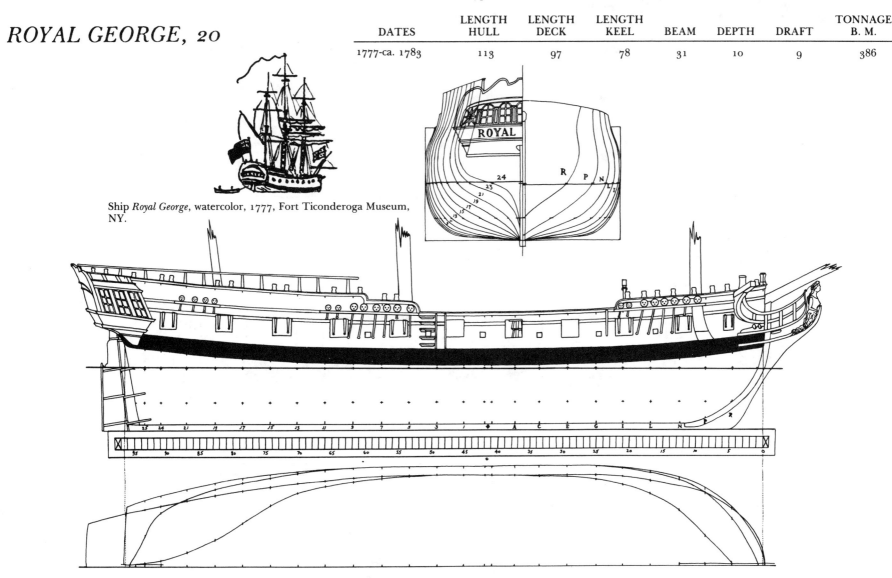

Ship *Royal George*, watercolor, 1777, Fort Ticonderoga Museum, NY.

ROYAL GEORGE, 20

LATE in 1776, the British, impressed by the usefulness of the 18-gun corvette *Inflexible* in defeating Benedict Arnold's fleet on Lake Champlain, began to build another 18-gun corvette at St. John's at the northern end of Lake Champlain. While *Inflexible* had been hastily reassembled from the pieces of a river patrol ship that had been under construction near Quebec City, *Royal George* was designed and built with care for service on Lake Champlain. She was quite a bit larger than *Inflexible* and could mount 20 nine-pounders if called on to do so. In 1777 she became the flag-ship of the British squadron on the lake, and the squadron had no trouble in capturing or destroying the remnants of Arnold's fleet. In fact, Arnold had not reinforced his fleet, knowing that the advantage in time that he had hoped to obtain by first building the fleet in 1776 had already been obtained, and that there was nothing further to gain by pouring more money and men into building yet another fleet on the lake. Presumably *Royal George* was broken up at the end of the war, but records about her are scanty.

(There was also another ship in the Royal Navy with the name *Royal George* at the same time; she mounted 120 guns, and she capsized and sank during cleaning operations at Portsmouth, England, on 29 August 1782 with the loss of about 800 lives.)

Royal George had the shallow draft, flat bottom, and wide beam that was characteristic of most lake vessels. It must be remembered that lake vessels did not need a huge displacement for carrying drinking water or food, for in those days one could drink the lake water and put ashore for a few hours to scrounge some food. Her plans are on file at the National Maritime Museum at Greenwich, and there are a number of distant pictures of her among the various lake scenes painted and drawn in 1777.

ROYAL SAVAGE, 12

DATES	LENGTH HULL	LENGTH DECK	LENGTH KEEL	BEAM	DEPTH	DRAFT	TONNAGE B. M.
1775-1776 ESTIMATED	66	60	53	21	7	7	100

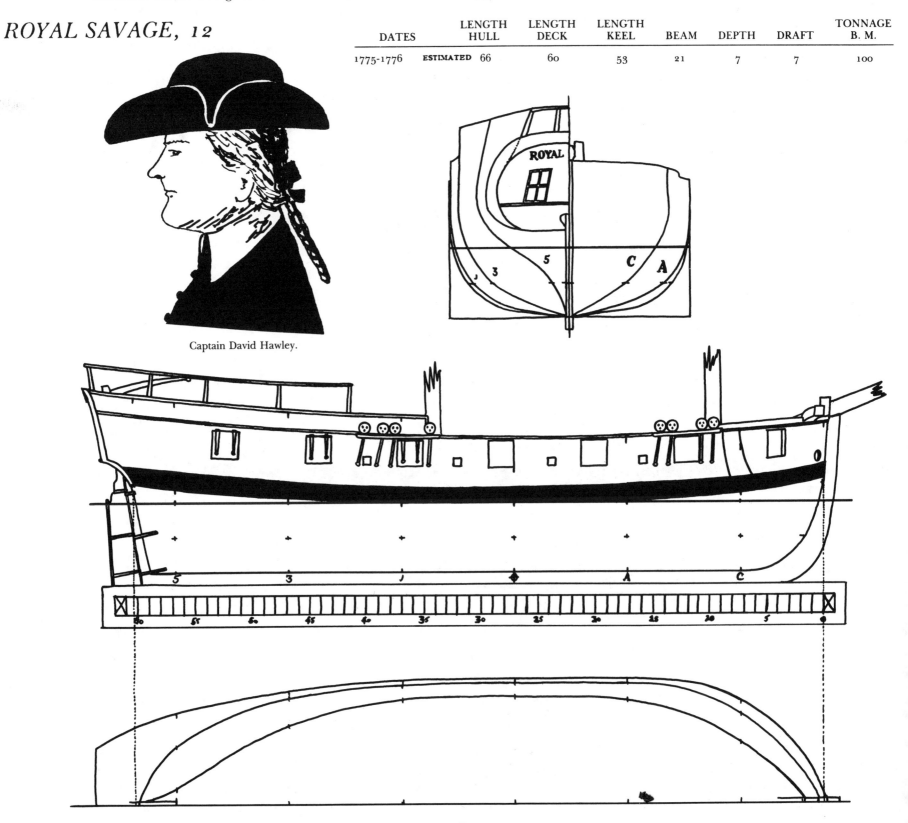

Captain David Hawley.

Schooner *Royal Savage*
From an anonymous sketch in the Schuyler Collection, ca. 1776
New York Public Library

Schooner *Royal Savage*, engraving published by Sayer & Bennett,
1776, National Maritime Museum, Greenwich.

Schooner *Royal Savage*
From a watercolor painting by C. Randle, 1776
The Public Archives of Canada, Ottawa

ROYAL SAVAGE, 12

WHEN Benedict Arnold captured St. John's, the British post at the northern end of Lake Champlain, for the Americans in May 1775, he found that the British had been busy building a few small armed vessels there. The sloop *George* was completed, the cutter *Lee* was only in frame, and the schooner *Royal Savage* had been sunk by American shore cannons. He changed *George*'s name to *Enterprise,* took *Lee*'s frames to Skenesborough for eventual completion, and raised *Royal Savage,* letting her keep her original name. She was a poor sailer, as were most of the shallow-draft, flat-bottomed, blunt vessels of the lake, but she mounted 12 guns, so Arnold made her his flagship before the battle of Valcour Island in the early fall of 1776.

At Valcour Island, the British fleet overshot the American position and had to claw their way back against the wind. To delay them a little further, *Royal Savage* went out to harass them, but soon turned back when it was realized that she would have equally as much trouble going against the wind. Unfortunately, she ran aground just short of the American position behind the island, and was abandoned as soon as the concentration of British fire made her untenable. The British boarded her and set her on fire to prevent Arnold's men from retaking her during the night.

No plans or dimensions survive of *Royal Savage,* but it is thought that in many respects she was merely a larger version of *Lee,* whose lines do survive. In addition, there are a number of portraits of *Royal Savage,* which were helpful in reconstructing her. A model at the Mariners Museum, Newport News, Virginia, that has her name bears no likeness to her at all.

SAINT ANDREW

THE Corning Museum of Glass, Corning, New York, owns a German glass goblet engraved with the picture of a small brig with topgallant masts housed and flying a British ensign. It bears the legend, "Success to the St. Andrew of New York, Captain Robert Donaldson." According to research by Jane S. Spillman, *Saint Andrew* was built in 1752 and measured only 50 tons. With a crew of five, she was sailed on trading voyages between New York, Leith (Scotland) and the Caribbean. She was owned by Joseph Haynes and William Donaldson of New York and is listed in New York records for 1753-1755; customhouse records are missing for 1756-1762, and the brig does not appear later.

Perhaps surprisingly, this small brig was fitted with a full head with figurehead, but she carried no visible cannons. She had quartergalleries under a raised quarterdeck that was protected by a rail and some netting. It is fortunate to find an illustration of a specific vessel of such diminutive size, for such tiny craft carried much of America's cargo, both coastwise and all over the Atlantic trading world.

New York brig *Saint Andrew,* from a crystal goblet ca. 1755, Corning Museum of Glass, Corning, NY.

A New York snow, engraving, late 18th century.

American merchant brig, detail of a view of Sint Eustatius, ca. 1788, Library of Congress.

Two American brigs captured by a British privateer, details from oil painting by Francis Holman, ca. 1778, National Maritime Museum, Greenwich.

The BRIG
INDUSTRY,
JOSEPH ROSE,
MASTER;
NOW lying at Murray's wharf,
bound for the West-Indies,
Musqueto shore, and the Bay of Honduras, will sail in
10 or 12 days. For freight or passage apply to said master
on board; who has for sale, a quantity of choice
MAHOGANY and LOGWOOD;
And a FEW
SPANISH HIDES,
Which he will sell on reasonable terms.

SAINT ANDREW

DATES	LENGTH HULL	LENGTH DECK	LENGTH KEEL	BEAM	DEPTH	DRAFT	TONNAGE B. M.
1752-ca. 1760 ESTIMATED 61		50	43	16	10	8	50

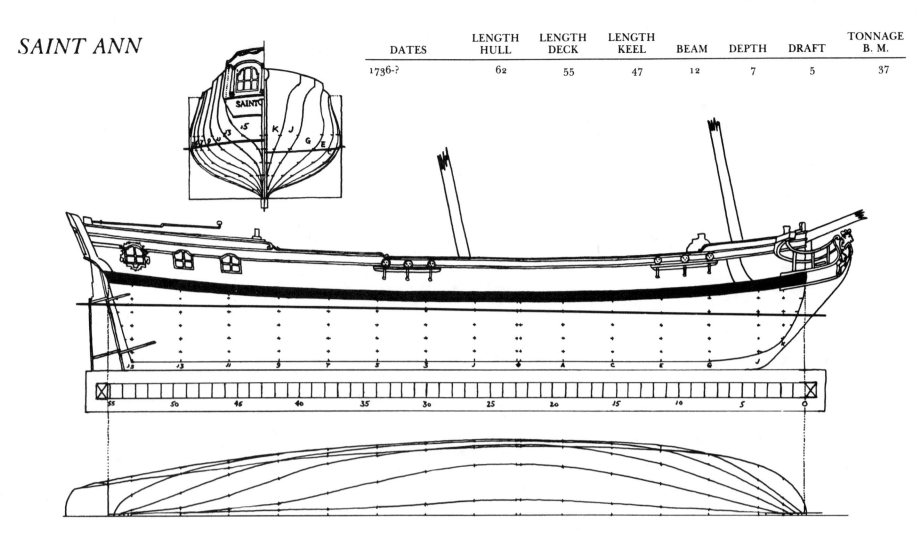

	DATES	LENGTH HULL	LENGTH DECK	LENGTH KEEL	BEAM	DEPTH	DRAFT	TONNAGE B. M.
	1736-?	62	55	47	12	7	5	37

SAINT ANN

THE schooner *St. Ann* was apparently built somewhere in America before 1736, and was possibly originally intended as a yacht. She was bought by the Portuguese and used as a dispatch boat in 1736, and visited Portsmouth, England, that same year. At that time she was taken into the dock and her lines were taken off. Chapman, the great Swedish naval architect, took a copy of the lines home with him about 1753, and they can now be found at the Statens Sjohistoriska Museum in Sweden. Apart from *Falkland,* which was altered in part before her plan was drawn, this is the earliest plan of an American vessel that is known.

According to her spar and sail dimensions (tantalizingly incomplete) she had two pole masts and set a square topsail and topgallant on the foremast, and possibly the same on the mainmast, for downwind sailing only; these were furled whenever the wind came ahead of the beam. This delightful vessel was extraordinarily narrow and shallow draft for her length, which would indicate that she could not carry much sail in a blow, nor was she intended to carry cargo. However, this, combined with her relatively sharp lines (including moderately sharp deadrise), probably meant that she was very fast in a medium breeze. Nothing further is known about her history or sailing characteristics.

SAINT HELENA

At the Science Museum in London is a rather fancy portrait of a ship built in Charleston, South Carolina, called *St. Helena.* The picture is one of those bombastic exaggerations that are intended to make owners happy. The ship is depicted with royals on main and fore, topgallant and top-studding sails on main and fore, two spritsails, three jibs, three staysails between each set of masts, a fore-course studding sail, and a ringtail. An unexpected quality of this ship is that she apparently carried no armament, which gives no indication that the date of her construction was 1776; she would be fair game for any privateer or warship whose politics differed from her owner's. Although the profile of her hull gave the appearance of having a regular waist, by showing a raised quarterdeck and forecastle, the place where the waist would have been was actually decked over, thus providing more covered space for cargo. The British Navy Board employed a ship called *St. Helena* to carry ordnance supplies to the Caribbean in March 1777, but it is not known whether this was the same ship.

No plans for this ship survive, and the only dimension we know is her tonnage.

SAINT HELENA

DATES		LENGTH HULL	LENGTH DECK	LENGTH KEEL	BEAM	DEPTH	DRAFT	TONNAGE B. M.
ca. 1775-?	ESTIMATED	103	86	—	26	—	—	240

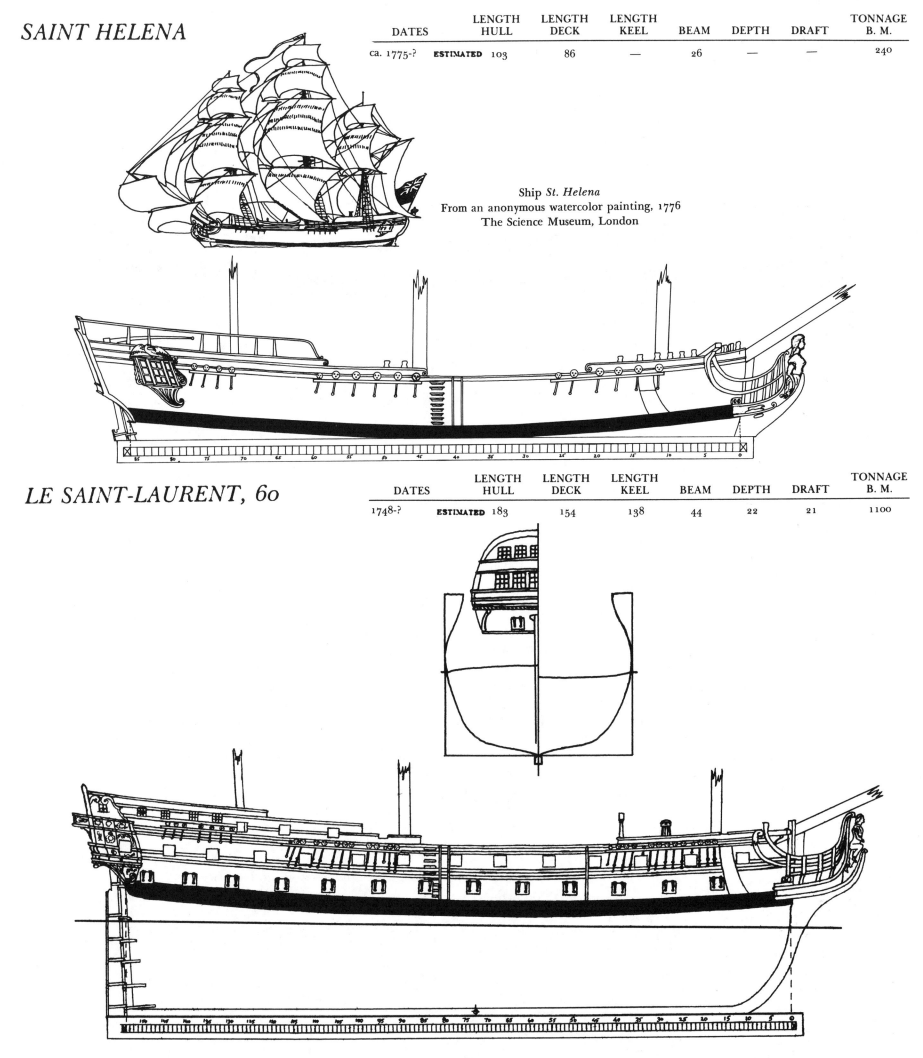

Ship *St. Helena*
From an anonymous watercolor painting, 1776
The Science Museum, London

LE SAINT-LAURENT, 60

DATES		LENGTH HULL	LENGTH DECK	LENGTH KEEL	BEAM	DEPTH	DRAFT	TONNAGE B. M.
1748-?	ESTIMATED	183	154	138	44	22	21	1100

LE SAINT-LAURENT, 60

Monsieur Jean Boudriot of Paris reports that he can find no information on ships built in Canada for the French navy before the British captured the country in 1759. A list of all these ships can be found in the text describing the frigate *L'Abenakise*. From this list, we know that a ship called *Le Saint-Laurent* was built in Quebec in 1748, and that she mounted 60 guns. Because this ship is so important to the history of American ships in the eighteenth century, we have attempted to reconstruct her appearance, based on the known lines and dimensions of French warships of the period and on certain details of *L'Abenakise*.

It is indeed a pity that we know so little about these ships, how they performed, and how long they lasted. Perhaps someday researchers will turn up information from the Canadian archives.

Two interesting features should be pointed out: the French almost never placed gunport lids on the upper gun deck, which must have made that deck very cold in winter. Also, they were very particular about the comfort of their officers, and the cabins for "l'État Major" or "officers' country" had a row of window ports leading forward from the Great Cabin; these ports never had cannons in them, and were actually situated too high off the deck for a cannon to reach anyway.

SANTÍSIMA TRINIDAD, 120/144

DATES	LENGTH HULL	LENGTH DECK	LENGTH KEEL	BEAM	DEPTH	DRAFT	TONNAGE B. M.
1769-1805	238	202	170	53	25	28	2600

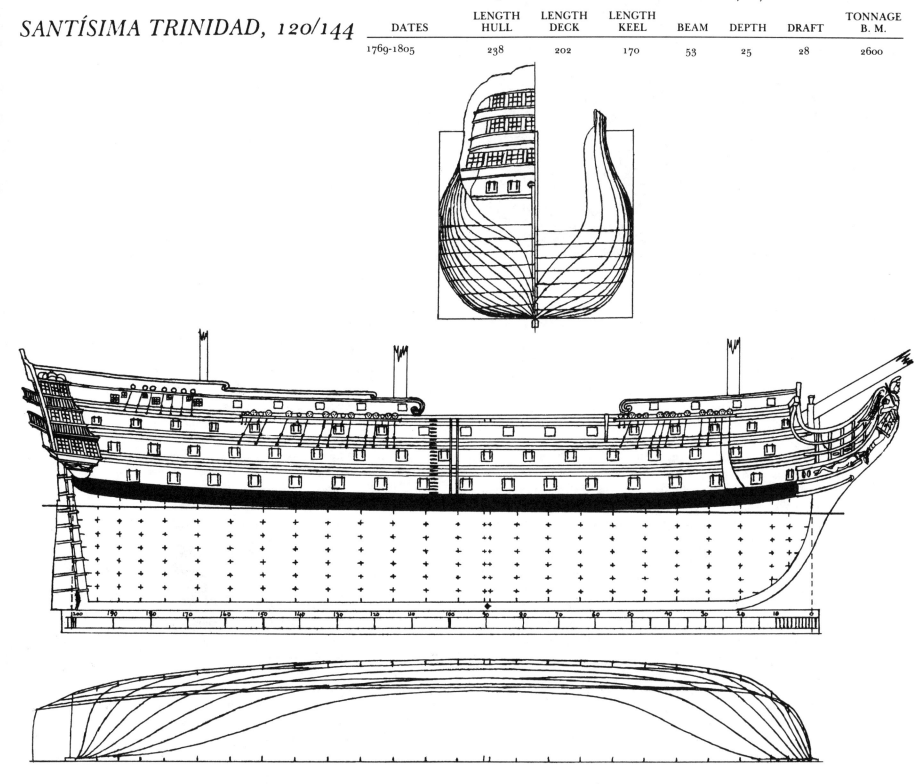

Ship *Santísima Trinidad*, aquatint ca. 1790, Don Alejo Berlinguero de la Marca y Gallego, Museo Naval, Madrid.

Many people interested in the history of the sailing navies know that the Spanish ship *Santísima Trinidad* was the largest ship ever built in the world at the time when she sank in 1805, but few know that she was built in America. She was contructed of Cuban mahogany at Havana in 1769. Her English appearance suggests that a British naval architect in Havana designed her, and in fact a strong tradition holds that the English designer Matthew Mullan was responsible, for he died in Havana of a fever three months before the ship was launched. She was designed to have 120 guns on three decks, but early in the nineteenth century her waist was decked over and given a bulwark so she could have four complete gundecks with a total of 144 guns. Throughout the eighteenth century the Spanish industrial economy was in a disastrous state. One result of this was that there were almost never enough cannons of the right calibre to arm the splendid warships that the Spanish Navy was having built (about a third of them in Havana). Thus, many of the cannons on these ships were of much smaller size than authorized for such ships. By the nineteenth century, however, *Santísima Trinidad* would probably have received her proper armament, if not before.

Santísima Trinidad (which means Most Holy Trinity) was the flagship of the Spanish fleet that blockaded the British at Gibraltar 1779-1782. She fought at the battle of Cape Saint Vincent in 1797 and would have been captured by Horatio Nelson were it not for a daring maneuver by a 27-year-old captain named Valdez. At Trafalgar in October 1805, she was the flagship of Admiral Cisneros but she was outfought and forced to surrender. Not long after the battle she sank in a violent storm. When first built, she was painted the standard ochre with a black wale, but at Trafalgar she was cream with four broad red stripes, according to an eyewitness aboard the British ship *Neptune*, 98 guns, that engaged her. She carried 1200 men.

Of the 221 larger warships built for the Spanish Navy in the eighteenth century, 74 were built at Havana, thanks to the outstanding properties of Cuban mahogany. Dr. G. Douglas Inglis of the Texas State Archives has done the research necessary to compile a list of all the Havana-built ships, from which the following list of the more important ships has been excerpted.

1701, *Santa Rosa*, 50; 1701, *Rubí*, 50; 1714, *San Francisco*, 50; 1718, *San Juan Bautista*, 60 and *Victoria*, 60; 1720, *Príncipe de Asturias*, 64; 1723, *Conquistador*, 60; 1724, *San Juan Bautista*, 60; 1725, *San Antonio*, 60 and *San Lorenzo*, 50; 1726, *Incendio*, 58; 1727, *San Jeronimo/El Retiro*, 54, *Santa Rosa*, 56 and *Santa Barbara*, 22; 1728, *Nuestra Señora de Guadalupe/El Fuerte*, 60 and *San Dionisio/El Constante*, 60; 1729, *Conquistador*, 70; 1730, *Gallo Indiano*, 66, *Nuestra Señora del Carmen*, 64 and *Volante*, 52; 1731, *San Cristobal/Constante*, 66; 1732, *San Jose/Africa*, 70; 1734, *Nuestra Señora del Pilar/Europa*, 64, *Nuestra Señora de Loreto/Asia*, 64 and *Santo Cristo de Burgos/Castilla*, 58; 1735, *Santísima Trinidad/Esperanza*, 50 and *San Cristobal/Triunfo*, 24; 1736, *Nuestra Señora de Belen/America*, 64; 1737, *Santa Rosa de Lima/Dragon*, 64 and *Santa Barbara/Astrea*, 24; 1738, *Nuestra Señora de Belen/Glorioso*, 70; 1739, *San Ignacio/Invencible*, 70 and *Nuestra Señora de Guadalupe/Bizarro*, 50; 1740, *Soberbio*, 66; 1743, *Nuestra Señora del Rosario/Nueva España*, 64; 1744, *San Jose/Invencible*, 70 and *Reina*, 70; 1745, *Jesus, Maria y Jose/Conquistador*, 70; and *Santa Teresa de Jesus/Dragon*, 64; 1746, *Santo Tomás/Vencedor*, 74 and *San Francisco de Asis/Africa*, 70; 1747, *Castilla*, 60 and *Santa Rosalia/La Flora*, 24; 1748, *San Pedro/Rayo*, 80 and *San Lorenzo/Tigre*, 70; 1749, *San Alejandro/Fenix*, 80; 1750, *San Luis Gonzaga/Infante*, 74 and *Santiago el Mayor/Galicia*, 74; 1753, *Triunfo*, 30; 1754, *Volante*, 20; 1755, *Tetis*, 22 and *Tetis II*, 44; 1757, *Princesa*, 74; 1758, *Santa Barbara/Fenix*, 18 and *San Carlos/Cazador*, 18; 1759, *Asia*, 64 and *San Eustaquio/Astuto*, 60; 1761, *San Genaro*, 70, *San Antonio*, 64 and *Nuestra Señora de Guadalupe/Fenix*, 22; 1762, *Caiman/San Francisco*, 30; (British capture of Havana, 1762, closed shipyard for a few years) 1756, *San Carlos*, 98 and *San Fernando*, 94; 1766, *Santiago/America*, 60; 1767, *San Luis*, 94; 1768, *Cecilia*, 34; 1769, *Santísima Trinidad*, 120/144, *San Francisco de Paula*, 70 and *San Jose*, 70; 1770, *Caiman*, 30; 1771, *San Rafael*, 80, *San Pedro Alcantara*, 68 and *Santa Lucia*, 34; 1772, *Santa Ana*, 26; 1773, *San Miguel*, 74; 1775, *San Ramon*, 68; 1776, *San Leandro*, 64 and *San Isidoro*, 64; 1777, *Santa Cecilia*, 46; 1778, *Santa Matilde*, 46, *Nuestra Señora de la O*, 34 and *Santa Agueda*, 32; 1780, *San Cristobal/Bahama*, 74, *Santa Clara*, 40, *Santa Maria de la Cabeza*, 34 and *Santo Cristo*, 30; 1786, *San Hipolito/Mexicano*, 112, *Conde de Regla*, 112, *Nuestra Señora de Guadalupe*, 36 and *Nuestra Señora de las Mercedes*, 36; 1787, *Real Carlos*, 112 and *Catalina*, 34; 1788, *San Pedro de Alcantara*, 64 and *Santa Matilde*, 34; 1789, *San Hermenegildo*, 112, *San Jeronimo/Asia*, 64, *Nuestra Señora de Atocha*,

40 and *Minerva*, 40; 1790, *Soberano*, 74.

Havana-built 22-gun frigates *Fenix* (ex-*Nuestra Señora de Guada-lupe*), 1761, and *Tetis*, 1755, details from engraving of their capture by the British frigate *Alarm*, 32 guns, in 1762, after Dominic Serres; private collection.

SARATOGA, 16

DATES	LENGTH HULL	LENGTH DECK	LENGTH KEEL	BEAM	DEPTH	DRAFT	TONNAGE B. M.
1777-1781	100	85	68	25	13	13	240

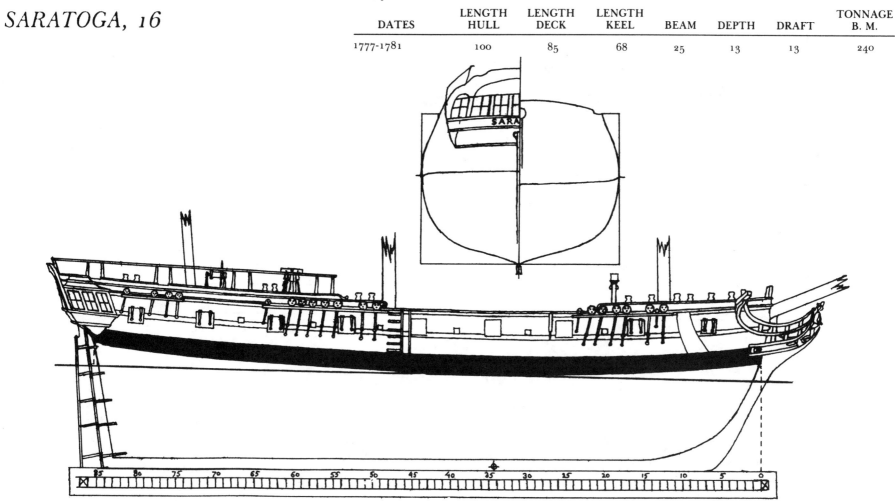

SARATOGA, 16

CONGRESS decided in October 1776 to order three warships of 18 guns each, which subsequently became *Ranger, General Gates* and *Saratoga*. *Saratoga* was built by Wharton & Humphreys in Philadelphia, but because of the British occupation of the city she was not actually begun until July 1779, at which point it was suggested she should be a brig of only sixteen 6-pounders. However, she was completed as a ship-rigged vessel with sixteen 9-pounders and two 4-pounders. Her dimensions are recorded in detail in the Humphreys Papers from the private collection of M. V. Brewington. In May 1780, she lay at anchor in the Delaware and was put under the command of John Young, who picked 20-year-old Joshua Barney as his lieutenant. On a cruise off the New Jersey coast in October 1780, she captured three brigs and the large, heavily-armed letter-of-marque *Charming Molly*, which had been on its way from Bristol to New York. Barney was put in charge of the prize crew of the latter, which was recaptured before she could get to Philadelphia by *Intrepid*, 64 and *Iris* (ex-Continental frigate *Hancock*), 32 guns.

Saratoga next headed south and cruised in the Caribbean until March 1781 when she was loaded with war supplies along with *Confederacy* and *Deane,* and the three ships began to escort a convoy back to the United States but the ships were separated in a storm in April. After the storm, *Confederacy* was captured and *Deane* arrived safely at Boston, but *Saratoga* had foundered with all hands during the storm; presumably she had been overloaded. The plan shown here is based on the known dimensions and is a scaled-down version of the frigate *Randolph*. No contemporary pictures of *Saratoga* are known.

SCOURGE/BARBADOES, 16

DATES	LENGTH HULL	LENGTH DECK	LENGTH KEEL	BEAM	DEPTH	DRAFT	TONNAGE B. M.
ca. 1779-?	116	98	82	25	11	13	270

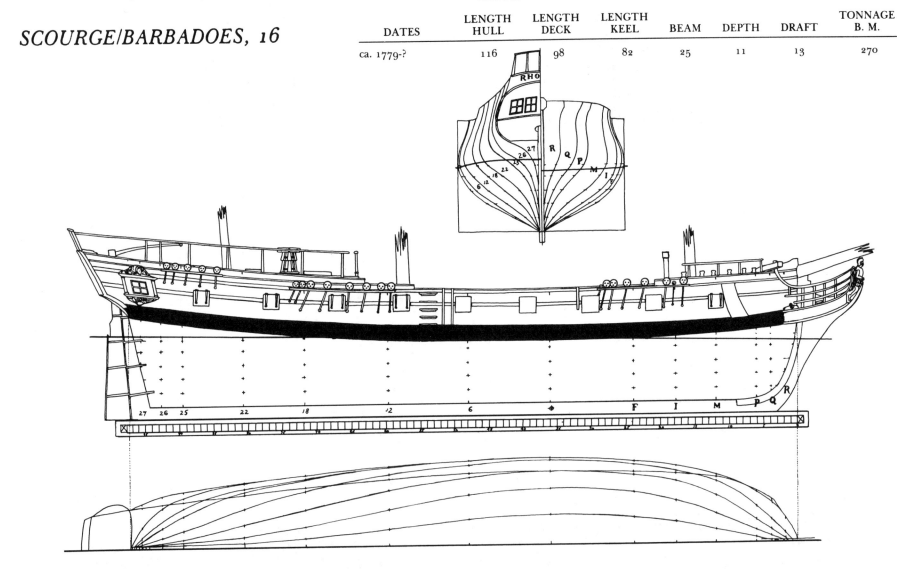

SCOURGE/BARBADOES, 16

IN February 1782, the British 64-gun ship *Prothée* captured two Massachusetts privateers, the brand-new 20-gun *Scourge* and the slightly smaller *Rhodes* (spelled *Roade* in the survey report) of 22 guns. Both were taken into the Royal Navy as 16-gun corvettes, the former as *Barbadoes* and the latter as *Stormont*. Chapelle misread the documents and claimed that *Rhodes* became *Barbadoes*, and Colledge says nothing about either ship. The surveys of these ships have been published in the *Letter-Book of Admiral Lord Rodney*. Both ships were sold a few months later when the war ended.

Scourge was described as "very well fitted and built of New England oak," and a weatherly ship, although she could obviously not carry a great deal of armament or stores because of her steep deadrise. In fact, in American service she mounted 18 six-pounders (with an additional four six-pounders stored as spares in the hold) and two 18-pounder carronades. Since carronades had been invented only two or three years earlier, this may be the first instance of their use on an American ship; presumably they had been captured from a British ship. While *Scourge's* lines (taken off by the British and preserved at Greenwich) were sharp, following the trend of fast-ship design in America, she displayed the classic British balance of "cod's head & mackerel tail" with her maximum beam well forward.

SERAPIS, 44

DATES	LENGTH HULL	LENGTH DECK	LENGTH KEEL	BEAM	DEPTH	DRAFT	TONNAGE B. M.
1779-1781	164	140	116	38	16	19	886

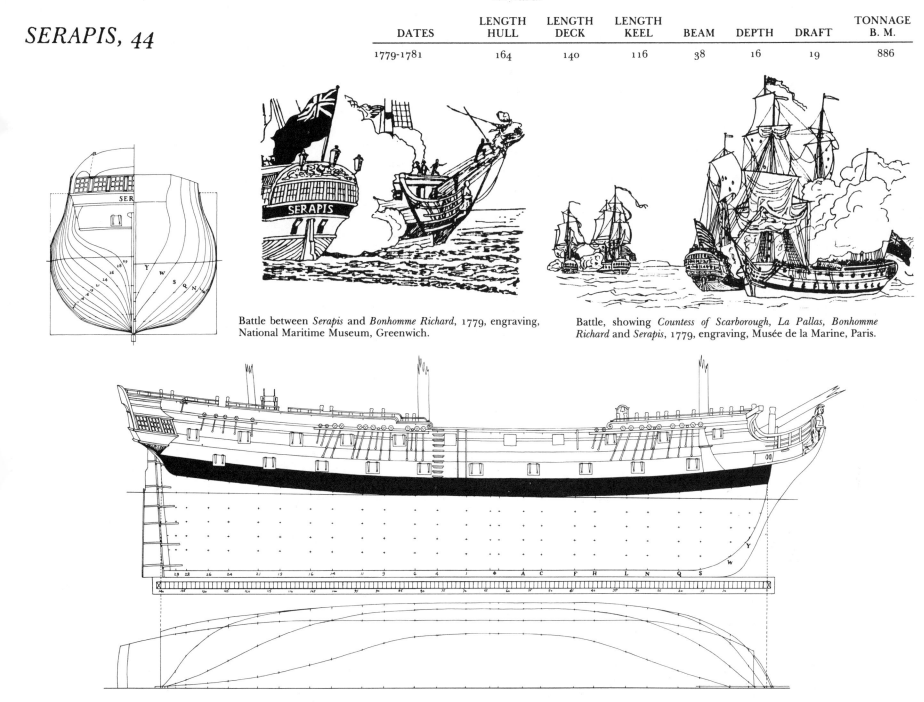

Battle between *Serapis* and *Bonhomme Richard*, 1779, engraving, National Maritime Museum, Greenwich.

Battle, showing *Countess of Scarborough, La Pallas, Bonhomme Richard* and *Serapis*, 1779, engraving, Musée de la Marine, Paris.

SERAPIS, 44

THE 44-gun ship *Serapis* was built for the Royal Navy at Randall's shipyard at Rotherhithe on the Thames early in 1779. She was placed under the command of Captain Richard Pearson and ordered to guard a convoy returning to England from the Baltic. On 23 September 1779, the convoy was spotted by John Paul Jones, who was cruising off Flamborough Head on board the 42-gun converted East Indiaman *Bonhomme Richard*, with his small fleet. *Serapis* left her convoy to engage the intruders and the convoy escaped to safety.

Serapis did rather more damage to *Bonhomme Richard* than she received back, but Jones was no ordinary captain. He survived a few wild broadsides fired by his supposed consort *Alliance* (the theory apparently was that if *Alliance* could sink *Bonhomme Richard*, she herself would be able to receive the surrender of the battered *Serapis*, but Jones held on). Finally, when he saw his ship was on fire, was dismasted, had been wracked by internal explosions caused by American hand grenades and could be attacked by the undamaged 36-gun frigate *Alliance* at any moment, Pearson surrendered to Jones. Pearson was soon exchanged and was knighted for having protected the convoy even at the expense of his own ship, to which Jones is reported to have said, "Let me fight him again and I will make him a lord."

Bonhomme Richard was too badly damaged to save, so Jones transferred his men and belongings to *Serapis* to watch his old ship sink. When he brought *Serapis* to France she was sold to the French navy, much to Jones's annoyance, for he wanted to use her himself. The French removed one deck of guns and sent her to the Indian Ocean, where she was destroyed by fire in 1781. Her dimensions but not her plans survive, but the plans of another ship of her dimensions that was built the same year do survive, so we have used them with changes indicated by the many portraits of the battle that are extant. She was unusual for her size and type in that her stern had only one deck of windows. Other important ships built to essentially the same design include *Roebuck*, that was one of the more successful British ships along the American coast, *Charon*, that was sunk in the York River at the battle of Yorktown, 1781, and *Guardian*, that was abandoned in 1790 near Capetown after being holed by an iceberg on her way to Australia with desperately-needed supplies for the starving new colony—her arrival at Cape-town is an extraordinary tale of heroism against over-whelming odds.

This is a convenient place to say a few words about the other ships involved in the action off Flamborough Head; their plans are not included in this book because they were never actually under American ownership or command. *La Pallas*, under the command of Denis-Nicolas Cottineau de Kerloguen, had been a privateer built in 1778 that had done so well in a battle against the British frigate *Brune* that the ship, officers and men were all taken into the French Navy as a unit. She mounted twenty-six 8-pounders. No plans survive. The cutter, *Le Cerf*, commanded by Ensign Joseph Varage, carried sixteen 6-pounders and two 8-pounder bow-chasers. She has been made the subject of an excellent monograph by Jean Boudriot available in both English and French with copious plans and illustrations. *La Vengeance*, probably a brig but possibly a cutter, was commanded by Lieutenant Philippe-Nicolas Ricot. She mounted twelve 4-pounders and took no active part in the battle. The British ship captured by *La Pallas* was the 20-gun frigate *Countess of Scarborough*, commanded by Thomas Piercy. She is not listed in Colledge as having been a Royal Navy ship, so she may merely have been under charter for that convoy. She was sold at Dunkirk to be used as a French merchant ship.

SIR EDWARD HAWKE & EARL OF EGMONT, 8

DATES	LENGTH HULL	LENGTH DECK	LENGTH KEEL	BEAM	DEPTH	DRAFT	TONNAGE B. M.
1768-?	65	58	46	18	7	10	100

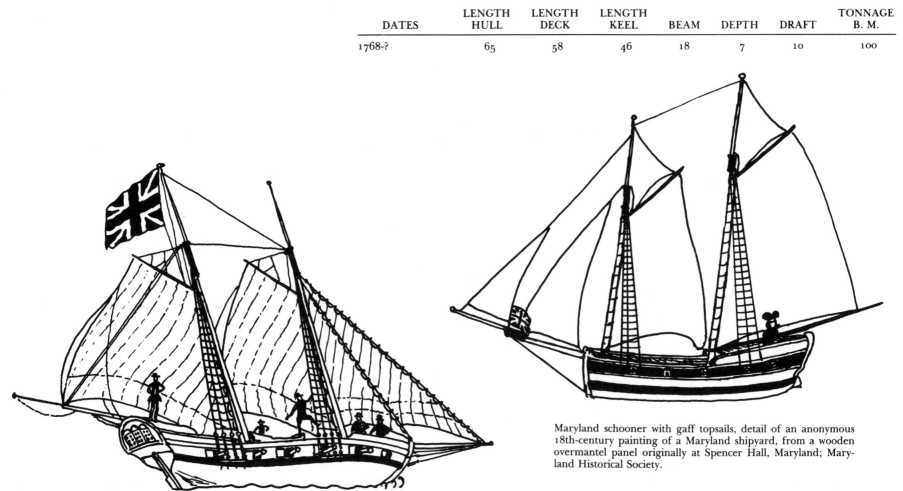

American-built armed schooner, from a 1785 British view of Curaçao.

Maryland schooner with gaff topsails, detail of an anonymous 18th-century painting of a Maryland shipyard, from a wooden overmantel panel originally at Spencer Hall, Maryland; Maryland Historical Society.

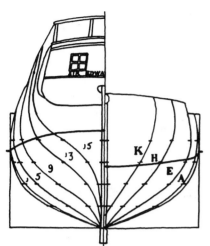

American armed schooner captured by a British privateer, detail of oil painting by Francis Holman, ca. 1778, National Maritime Museum, Greenwich.

Bermuda-rigged schooner, watercolor by Ashley Bowen, 1778, Peabody Museum, Salem.

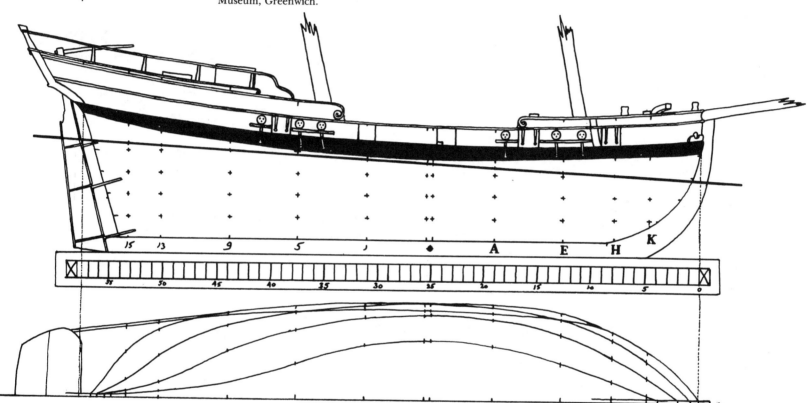

SIR EDWARD HAWKE & EARL OF EGMONT, 8

In the late 1760s the British attempted to acquire a number of fast, armed schooners for the purpose of eliminating the widespread evasion of the Customs laws. Since the Americans knew how to build such schooners better than anyone else in the world, and since these schooners would be used in America, the British either had these schooners built in America or purchased already existing American schooners.

Two or three of these schooners shared the same design. They were built in New York to what was described as a Marblehead design, meaning that they were similar to the so-called heeltappers that were produced in the area of Marblehead, Massachusetts. Two were called *Sir Edward Hawke* and *Earl of Egmont*. They were commissioned on 22 May 1768 for use on the

Jamaica station, and they carried eight small carriage guns apiece, in addition to a few swivels. Each carried a crew of thirty men. Their rigging plans have not been found, but it is believed that they had a square topsail on both masts in addition to the fore-and-aft sails. They were both sold out of the navy on 11 August 1773, so the *Hawke* that became the first British warship to be captured by the Continental Navy on 4 April 1776 was not one of these schooners. The lines for these schooners, drawn with slight imperfections, are on file at the National Maritime Museum at Greenwich.

DATES	LENGTH HULL	LENGTH DECK	LENGTH KEEL	BEAM	DEPTH	DRAFT	TONNAGE B. M.
1777-1782	198	164	147	44	18	23	1430

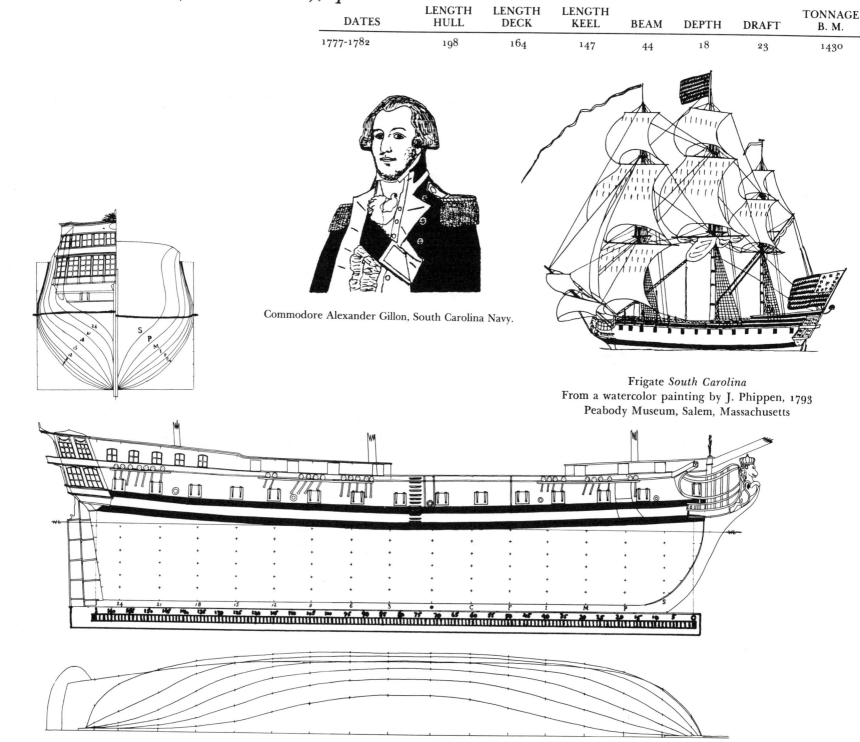

Commodore Alexander Gillon, South Carolina Navy.

Frigate *South Carolina*
From a watercolor painting by J. Phippen, 1793
Peabody Museum, Salem, Massachusetts

SOUTH CAROLINA (ex-L'INDIEN), 40

WHEN Benjamin Franklin arrived in Paris in 1776, he had authorization from Congress to buy, charter, or borrow a number of large warships from the French or from anyone else. However, since Europe, including France, was at least nominally neutral, this proved very difficult to achieve. Franklin ordered a large ship to be built at Amsterdam to French designs in 1776–77. Her name was *L'Indien,* but just as she was finished in November 1777 the British found out who the real owners were and told the Dutch to forbid the Americans to take possession of her. John Paul Jones tried to seize her, but in vain. She was then sold to the king of France.

In June 1778, Franklin wrote Jones that the way was clear to take command of *L'Indien* and Jones therefore relinquished command of *Ranger.* However, France was now at war with Britain, so the Dutch refused to allow the French king to send anyone to take possession of her. So she was sold again, this time to the duke of Luxembourg. In 1779 and 1780 the duke negotiated at great length with Commodore Alexander Gillon of the South Carolina State Navy, himself of French ancestry, and Gillon eventually chartered the ship for his state. He renamed her *South Carolina,* manned her with 250 American sailors who had recently been released from British prisons, and tried to sail out of Amsterdam in

June 1780. However, the water was too shallow most of the time, and the crew was practically mutinous. He did not get her out of Amsterdam until August 1781. She was manned with 250 sailors, some of whom had been aboard for well over a year, and no fewer than 300 French marines, who caused no end of trouble.

Her first cruise was in the North Sea, and she made her first capture on 25 August 1781. She sailed north around the Shetland Islands to Coruna, Spain, then left Spain in October and took more prizes. After a stop at Teneriffe, she headed for the West Indies. On 31 December, she was off enemy-occupied Charleston, South Carolina, but bore away for Havana, where she arrived on 12 January 1782. On 8 May she served as flagship for the ludicrously gigantic expedition of fifty-six Spanish and American ships and thousands of troops that captured Nassau for the third time in that war; the previous time, Nassau had fallen to the sloop *Providence* and her crew of but fifty men.

South Carolina arrived at Philadelphia on 28 May, at which point a representative of the duke of Luxembourg had Gillon removed from command for no stated reason. He was replaced by Captain John Joyner of the South Carolina State Navy. *South Carolina* left Philadelphia in November as guard of a small convoy that was bound for Europe. They anchored downriver for a few weeks and set sail again on 19 December. That very night she was chased by three British ships—*Diomede*, 44 guns, and *Astrea* and *Quebec*, both 32 guns. The chase lasted eighteen hours, and *South Carolina* put up very little resistance before surrendering; this is surprising, considering the fact that her broadside's weight matched almost exactly the sum of the weights of the broadsides of her three assailants. She was taken into New York and surveyed, but was found to be too lightly built and even a bit hogged from carrying her extraordinarily heavy armament, so she was sold instead of being taken into the Royal Navy.

One crude sketch of *South Carolina* by one of her crewmembers can be seen at the Peabody Museum at Salem, and a copy of her lines was included in French Admiral Paris's book *Souvenirs de Marine*, volume 5.

The dimensions on Paris' plan do not agree with those recorded by the British surveyor at New York. The reason for this is that Paris, who gave his figures in metres, converted the French *pieds* into metres as if they were English feet, which they are not. The two sets of measurements are close if Paris' figures are reconverted.

This ship was called a frigate by her contemporaries, but no frigate exactly like her had ever been built before. Her hull looked like a cross between that of a large frigate and an East Indiaman. She had a flush weather-deck from bow to poop, and had two decks of windows in the stern under a small poop or roundhouse. She carried twenty-eight 36-pounders (whether by French or British measure is not clear) and twelve 12-pounders, by far the heaviest armament to sail under the American flag during the war. However, she was weakly built like an Indiaman or a French frigate, and all that heavy armament combined with her unusual length and sharp lines caused her to "hog" (her bow and stern began to droop). Experts feel that her size and heavy armament were a direct inspiration for the large, flush-decked frigates *Constitution* and *United States* built 1794-7. These two ships, although slightly larger (deck length 173 feet, beam 44½ feet) than *South Carolina*, carried only 24-pounders in their main battery, but that was still more than British or French frigates were carrying at that time.

SULTANA

THE handsome little schooner *Sultana* was built at Benjamin Hallowell's yard in Boston in 1766-67. Hallowell had built the 24-gun ship *Boston* for the Royal Navy, but she had become rotten in a very short space of time. He also built a pole-masted sloop for the navy that was called *Bird*.

Sultana was purchased by the navy in 1768 as a dispatch boat and as a small transport, a duty for which her full lines made her quite suitable, if a little slow. She mounted a few swivels for protection and for signaling, but no carriage guns. She is not mentioned in Colledge's *Ships of the Royal Navy*, but research by D. L. McCalip shows that she was condemned at Bermuda in 1772, due to teredo worm damage. Her plans are kept at the National Maritime Museum at Greenwich. An attractive wooden model kit of her is available commercially.

DATES	LENGTH HULL	LENGTH DECK	LENGTH KEEL	BEAM	DEPTH	DRAFT	TONNAGE B. M.
1767	59	49	38	16	8	8	53

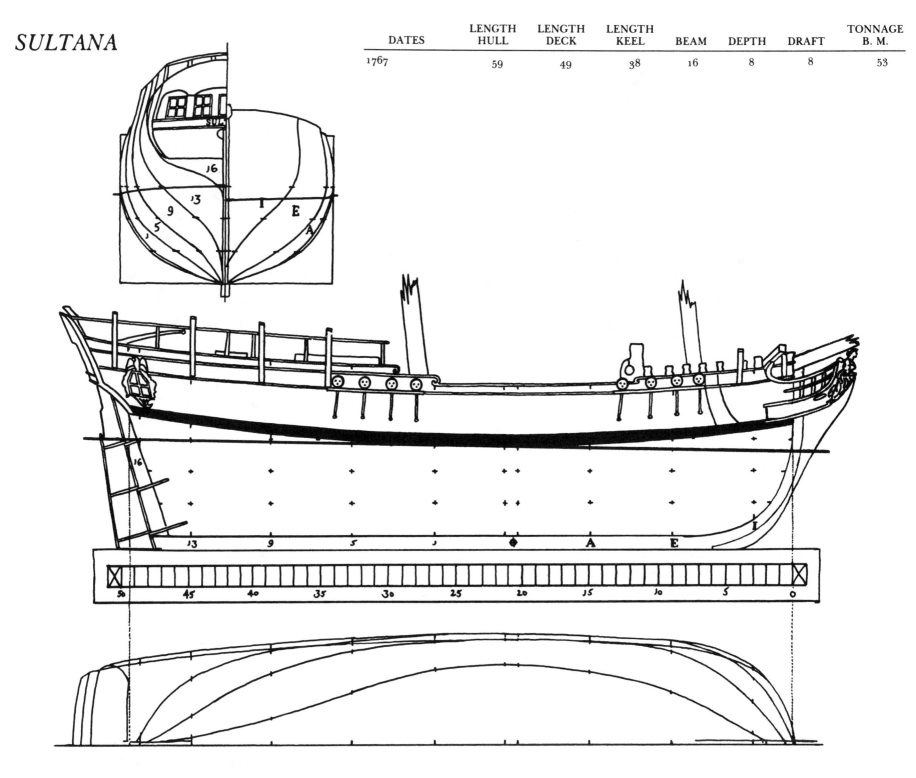

SURPRISE, 10

A 10-GUN lugger was bought on 1 May 1777 at Dunkirk by William Hodge, the Continental agent. She was named *Surprise* and Gustavus Conyngham was put in command of her with a motley crew of Americans and Frenchmen. A few days later she returned to France, having taken two prizes. Unfortunately, one of the prizes was no ordinary merchant ship, but the Royal Mail packet *Prince of Orange;* mail packets were considered sacrosanct, so the British protested more than usual. Therefore, all three vessels were seized by the French government; the two prizes were returned to the British with effusive apologies and *Surprise* was sold to the highest bidder. As for Conyngham, the French threw him in prison to keep up appearances, but they quietly let him out again after only a short time.

No lines or dimensions of *Surprise* have survived. However, there is a contemporary Dutch engraving of her taking the *Prince of Orange,* in which she looks practically as small as a longboat next to the large packet. Luggers varied little from vessel to vessel, so we have taken the profile and section of a typical lugger of the same size and period as *Surprise* and cross-referenced it with the Dutch engraving. The typical lugger hull will be seen to have been identical to the typical cutter hull of the period.

SURPRISE, 10

DATES	LENGTH HULL	LENGTH DECK	LENGTH KEEL	BEAM	DEPTH	DRAFT	TONNAGE B. M.
fl. 1777	ESTIMATED 66	56	48	21	10	11	90

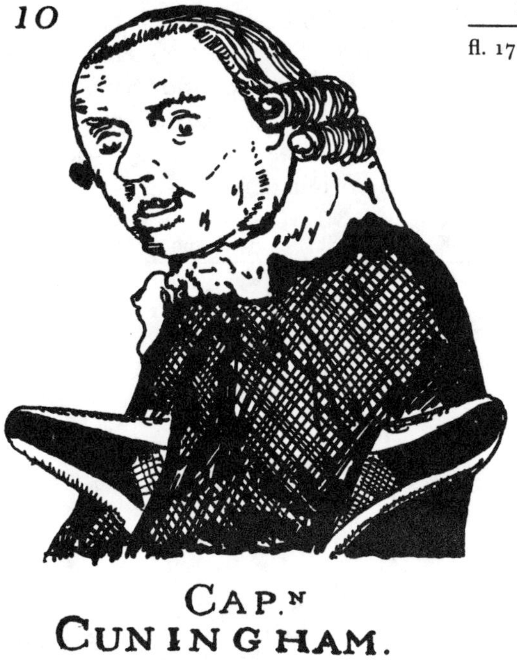

Captain Gustavus Conyngham.

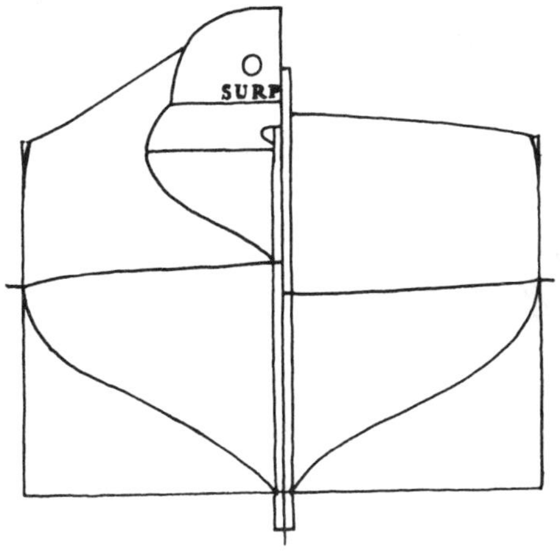

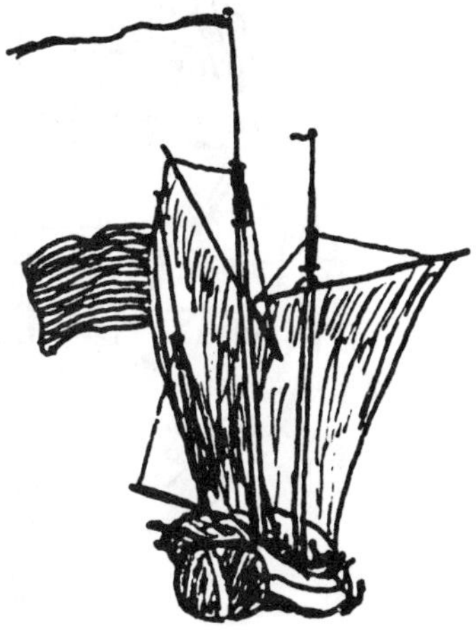

Lugger *Surprise*
From an anonymous Dutch engraving, ca. 1777

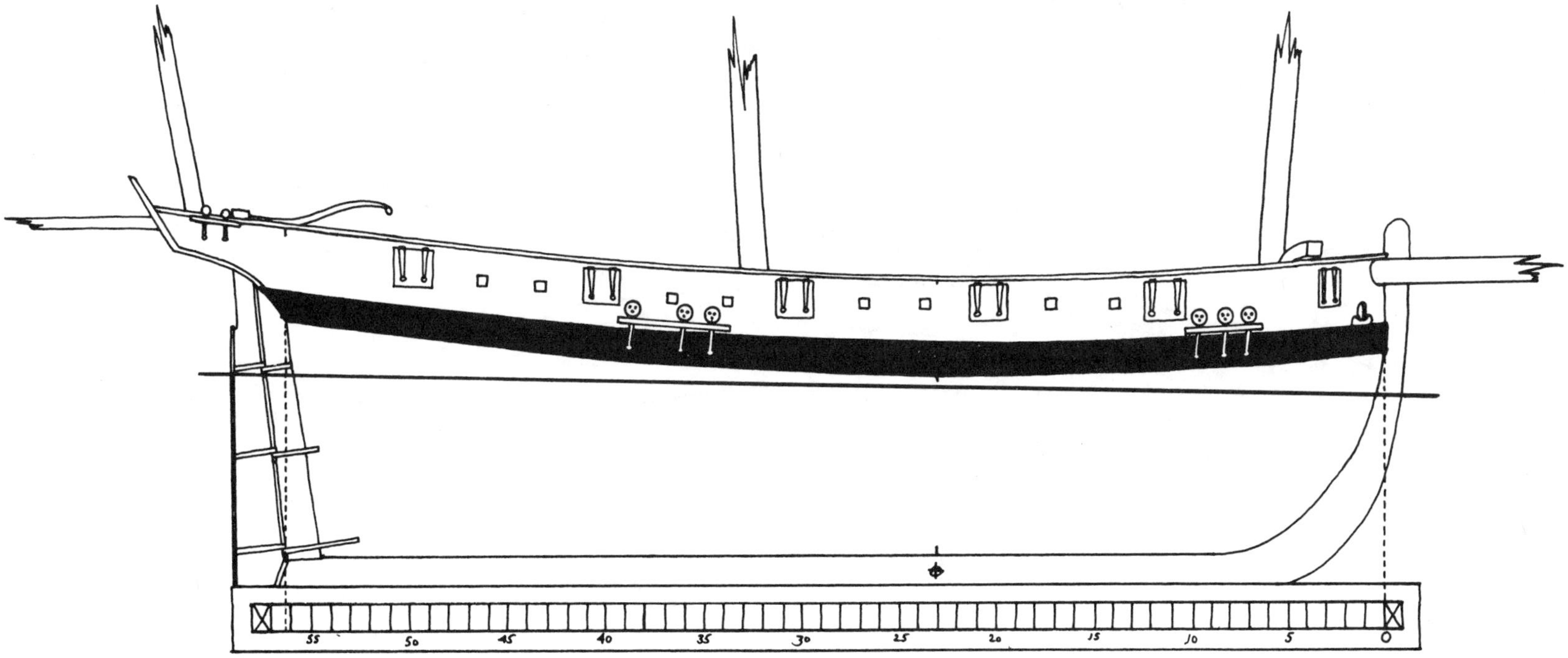

SWIFT, 10

THE 10-gun brig Swift was built in America (probably the Chesapeake area) in 1778. Judging from her ornate finish and her sharp lines, which were designed for high speed and low carrying capacity, she was probably intended to be a mail packet between the United States and France; she had a wreath on the stern with three fleurs-de-lys in it, the French national arms. She was captured by the Royal Navy in 1779, although the records do not specify the circumstances; in fact the records are extremely confusing, for there were at least two other vessels in the Royal Navy at that time with the name *Swift,* one of 8 guns that was purchased in 1773 and sold in 1784, and another of 16 guns that was also captured from the Americans in 1779 and then captured by the French in 1782. Our *Swift* remained in the navy until her sale at the end of 1783 or the beginning of 1784.

She mounted 10 three-pounders and had a crew of forty men. When her lines were drawn at Deptford in 1783, the Admiralty surveyor noted that she was oversparred, and he recommended that her sail area be drastically reduced, her crew brought down to thirty men and her guns reduced to six, while at the same time her ballast should be greatly increased. It is doubtful that these modifications were ever carried out. She must have been lightly built, with large frame spacing and thin planks so that her hull weight did not cause her to sink too deep into the water, thus losing the advantage of her sharp lines. Her deadrise was very steep, and continued above the waterline into flared topsides. Her plans are on file with the National Maritime Museum at Greenwich.

This design has proved popular with modern people. One copy called *Swift of Ipswich* was built in Massachusetts for William Robinson in the 1930s, was briefly owned by actor James Cagney and is now chartered in California.

Dennis Holland of Costa Mesa, California took twelve years and all his savings to build an enlarged copy called *Pilgrim of Newport*, launched in 1982 for charter, but he felt free to alter the design and choose a modern color-scheme. A third copy, called *Spirit of Chemainus*, is being built in British Columbia at the time of writing. None of these ships has retained the original *Swift*'s rig.

SWIFT, 10

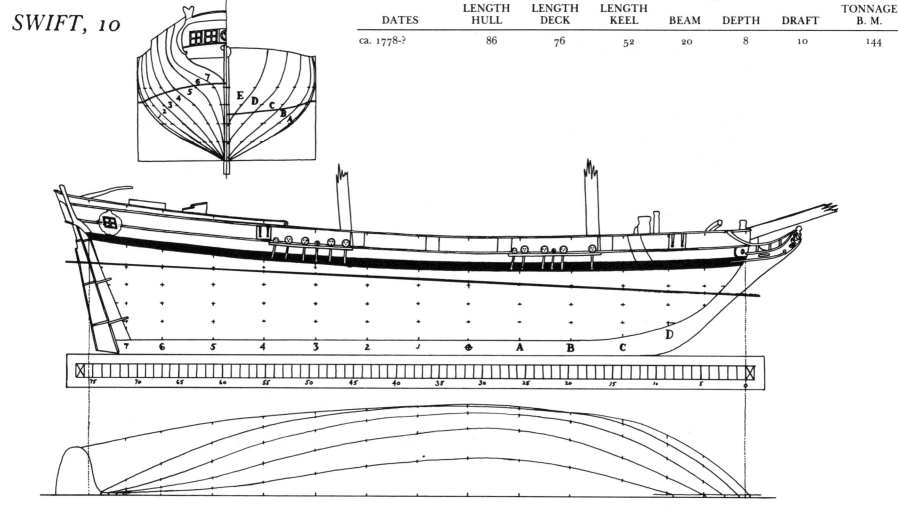

DATES	LENGTH HULL	LENGTH DECK	LENGTH KEEL	BEAM	DEPTH	DRAFT	TONNAGE B. M.
ca. 1778-?	86	76	52	20	8	10	144

SWIFT

ONE of the delightful little pilot schooners that appeared immediately after the Revolution was *Swift*, built at Norfolk, Virginia, about 1788. She was bought in 1794 by the British consul for sending dispatches back and forth to England, but he found he did not need her for that purpose so, when a Royal Navy captain named Oakes arrived in America after the ship on which he had been a passenger home from India had been captured by a French squadron, the consul turned the schooner over to him and she carried Oakes (and other passengers and crew from the ship Oakes had been riding on) to Cork, Ireland, arriving there 30 June 1794.

The admiral of the Cork station decided to use her, first for the "impress service" and later, after some repairs, for surveying. She was then turned over to the commanding officer of the Portsmouth Dockyard for his personal use. Her lines were taken off there and are now on file at the National Maritime Museum at Greenwich. On 23 March 1803, she was formally taken into the Royal Navy and ordered fitted out and her bottom coppered. After that date, we can find no specific record of her, although the Royal Navy was obviously pleased by her performance, for they ordered twelve schooners built to her design, only to a larger scale, in Bermuda. However, the Bermudans had other ideas and refused to follow the designs that the Admiralty had sent to them.

DATES	LENGTH HULL	LENGTH DECK	LENGTH KEEL	BEAM	DEPTH	DRAFT	TONNAGE B. M.
ca. 1788-18??	52	48	34	16	6	6	46

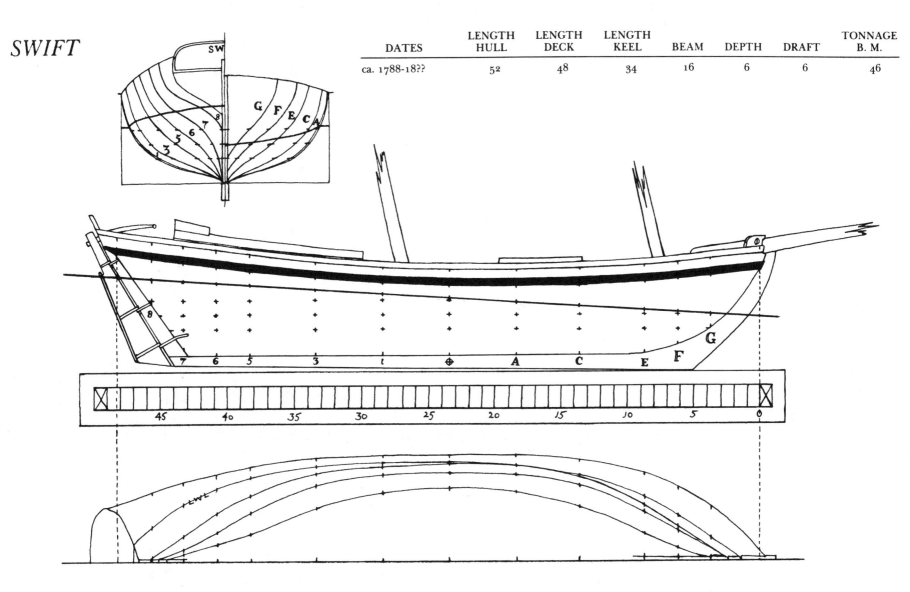

THORN & CORMORANT, 16

IN August 1779, the frigates *Deane* and *Boston* captured the British corvette *Thorn*, which they described as mounting 18 guns although her rate was supposed to have but sixteen 6-pounders. She had been launched the previous February at the village of Mistleythorn, England. She was sold in Boston as a privateer to be commanded by Daniel Waters. He used her to capture some formidable British and Loyalist opponents in 1779 and 1780. On 20 August 1782 the Royal Navy recaptured *Thorn* and took her back into service; however, Colledge says that the recapture had been from the French, which may mean that she had been sold to French owners in the mean time. Colledge also describes *Thorn* as being armed with fourteen 32-pounder carronades. It would have been quite a phenomenon if she had been so armed during her American service, for carronades had only just been invented in 1779, but British authority D. J. Lyon says that she was not fitted with carronades until after the war, and even then he says that they were only of 12-pounder size. She became a training ship for the Marine Society in 1799 and was sold for breaking up in 1816.

Thorn was only one of a numerous class of identical vessels built over two decades. Another member of the same class was *Atalanta*, built in the Sheerness Dockyard in 1775, and captured by *Alliance* on 28 May 1781. She was quickly recaptured, as was *Trepassey*, her consort, and in 1801 she was renamed *Helena*, shortly before being sold out of the service in 1802.

Cormorant was a member of the same class. She was built in 1776 at Barnard's Shipyard at Ipswich. She was captured by De Grasse's French fleet off Charleston, South Carolina on 24 August 1781 and brought with the fleet to the Chesapeake Bay for the British surrender at Yorktown in October. The French sold her to some Americans for use as a privateer, and they sold her to the Virginia State Navy in 1782 for the purpose of clearing Chesapeake Bay of Loyalist privateers. Virginia sent her to Baltimore for repairs, where they were incensed to find that Maryland insisted on levying taxes against her. The Virginia State Navy had built five frigates pierced for 20 guns (four of them ship-rigged galleys) but had never been able to find the money to arm them and man them, and so was helpless as British forces captured or destroyed all of them in a series of raids in 1781. Virginia was no more able to pay for manning *Cormorant*, and so this ship did nothing notable for the rest of the war, and was sold in 1783.

DATES	LENGTH HULL	LENGTH DECK	LENGTH KEEL	BEAM	DEPTH	DRAFT	TONNAGE B. M.
1779-1816	111	97	79	27	13	13	306

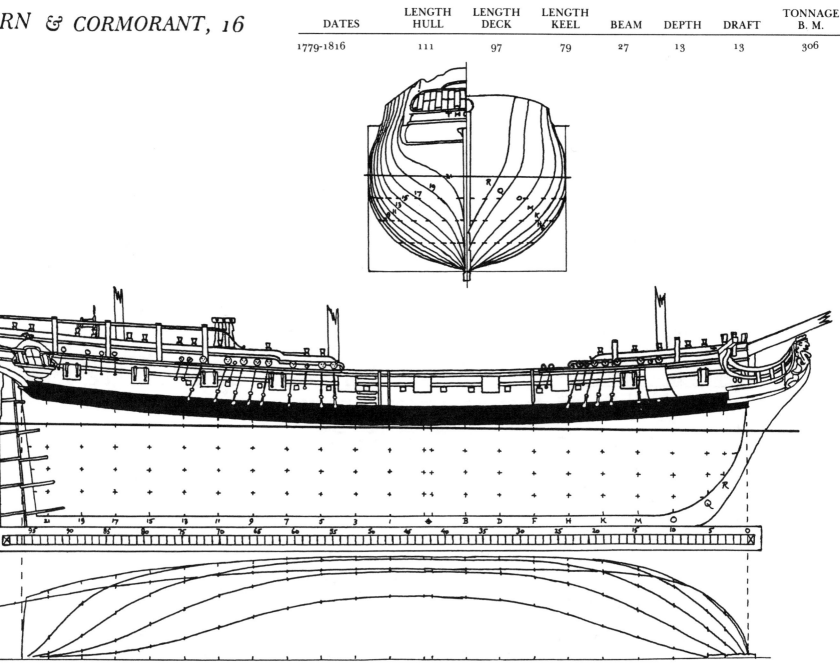

THORNTON, 20

ASHLEY BOWEN, the wide-ranging sailor of Marble-head, Massachusetts, wrote a journal of his travels in which he included color sketches of many of the ships on which he had sailed. He served as a midshipman in the Royal Navy during the siege of Quebec, having accompanied a number of New England troops to Quebec in 1759. When the city fell the provincial troops were dismissed, and somewhere between 160 and 210 of them were crammed on a transport ship called the *Thornton. Thornton* sailed from Quebec on 8 October 1759, arriving at Boston on 9 November. She had as special passengers Colonel the Honourable William Howe and his aides and servants; Howe was to return to Boston at the beginning of the Revolution as a general in an occupying army.

Bowen drew a sketch of *Thornton*, stating that she was a transport of about 500 tons from New York under captain Exshaw. Beyond that we know little about her.

Where and when was she built? The best guess is that she was a frigate built for the Royal Navy in about 1756 and converted into a transport shortly after; with the exception of the raised poop, *Thornton* was almost identical in size and shape to frigates, such as *Rose*, that were built at the beginning of the Seven Years' War, and the poop was the sort of thing that could always be quickly added to make a transport more comfortable. She was probably built in New York on speculation and was not purchased by the navy for some reason or other. She had gunports for 11 guns per side, which is rather more than a ship of her size would have had if she had been built only for the purpose of being a transport at this early date. The plans shown here are based on those of an unknown Sixth-Rate at the Science Museum, London, with appropriate alterations.

THORNTON, 20

DATES	LENGTH HULL	LENGTH DECK	LENGTH KEEL	BEAM	DEPTH	DRAFT	TONNAGE B. M.
fl. 1759	ESTIMATED 125	107	85	29	14	13	425

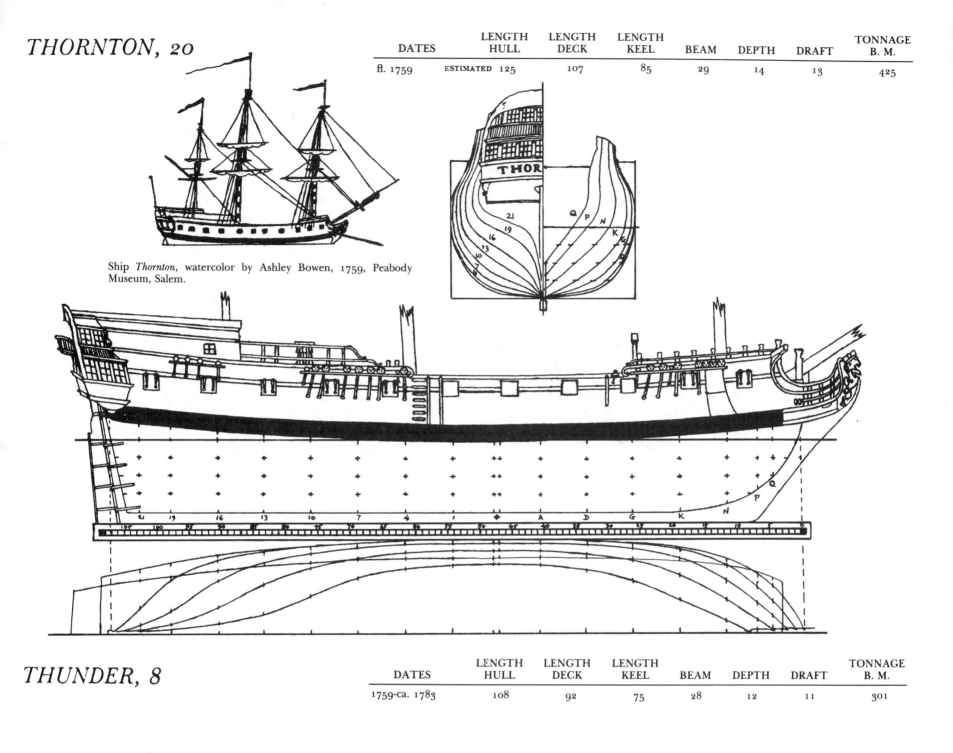

Ship *Thornton*, watercolor by Ashley Bowen, 1759, Peabody Museum, Salem.

THUNDER, 8

DATES	LENGTH HULL	LENGTH DECK	LENGTH KEEL	BEAM	DEPTH	DRAFT	TONNAGE B. M.
1759-ca. 1783	108	92	75	28	12	11	301

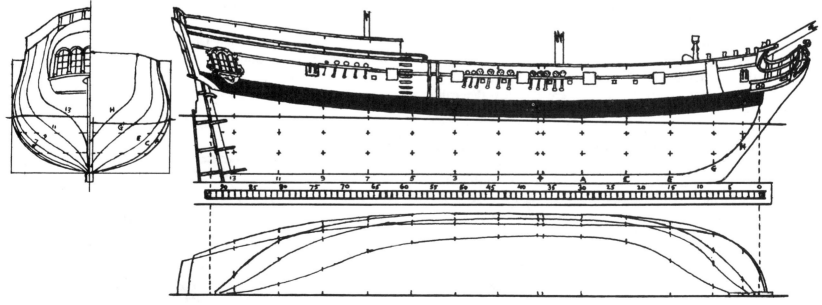

THUNDER, 8

A SHLEY Bowen, the seaman-artist of Marblehead, Massachusetts, included in his journals with no comment a sketch of what is clearly a British bomb-ketch captured by the Americans. At the head of her mainmast is her commissioning pendant over the Stars & Stripes, and at the head of her mizzen mast is a plain striped American flag over the Cross of Saint George. A second Cross of Saint George is flying from a staff on the bowsprit. No further information about this ship is available, but certain things can be deduced. She was captured some time between 1778 and 1792. The Royal Navy did not lose such a ship in that period, and therefore the ship in question had been a former Royal Naval vessel sold for use as a privateer. The transport *Mellish,* captured by the sloop *Providence,* was said to be such a vessel that had been rerigged as a ship. One possible candidate for this mystery ketch is *Thunder. Thunder,* 8 guns, was built in 1759 and sold in 1774, by which time she would have needed major repairs. Bowen's drawing, although crude, is clearly a ketch of the same design as *Thunder,* but with alterations in the height of her bulwarks to make her more seaworthy, and these alterations could easily have been done while her great repair was being accomplished. *Thunder*'s plans as originally built are kept at the National Maritime Museum at Greenwich under the name of her sistership *Basilisk* that was built the same year.

Bomb-ketch *Thunder* (?), ink sketch by Ashley Bowen, Essex Institute, Salem.

THUNDERER, 18

W HEN the British learned in the summer of 1776 that Benedict Arnold was feverishly building an American fleet on Lake Champlain to interfere with British plans to invade New York from Canada, they began to build a fleet themselves at the other end of the lake at St. John's. Some of these craft were straightforward ship-rigged or schooner-rigged lake vessels, together with a number of ships' longboats each with a cannon in the bow. However, there was one strange craft called a radeau (radeau is the French word for "raft"). This vessel, named *Thunderer,* was ketch-rigged, but her hull was like a scow. Her bottom was nearly flat, and both her bow and stern came to a flat end about half as wide as the whole vessel. To give her longitudinal strength and rigidity the topsides were slightly curved, and she had a certain amount of sheer. She also had a small raised quarterdeck aft, with a cabin below for her officers. Her sides were pierced for a total of 18 guns, and guns could also be mounted on the bow and stern if necessary; however, in spite of her capacity, she only carried 6 twenty-four-pounders and 6 twelve-pounders, together with 2 howitzers, but even this made her about the most powerful vessel on the lake. Other radeaux had appeared on the lakes during the Seven Years' War so she was really nothing new, although she is startling to our eyes.

Her construction was supervised by Lieutenant Schank of the Royal Navy, who was the inventor of the centerboard; he is said to have asked permission to in-stall one on *Thunderer,* but permission was denied and the wretched thing sailed very poorly as a result. In fact, she missed the fighting entirely at the battle of Valcour Island because she was unable to sail well enough upwind to get there before dark. Although there are no oarports indicated on the plan, one assumes that she was propelled by oars when the wind was not fair. Her great firepower was responsible for the destruction of a good part of Arnold's fleet not long after Valcour Island when Arnold personally set fire to many of the ships to avoid certain capture. Presumably she was broken up at the end of hostilities in 1783.

Thunderer appears in a number of contemporary pictures of the fleets on Lake Champlain, and her lines are on file at the National Maritime Museum at Greenwich.

DATES	LENGTH HULL	LENGTH DECK	LENGTH KEEL	BEAM	DEPTH	DRAFT	TONNAGE B. M.
1776-ca. 1783	105	92	72	34	7	6	423

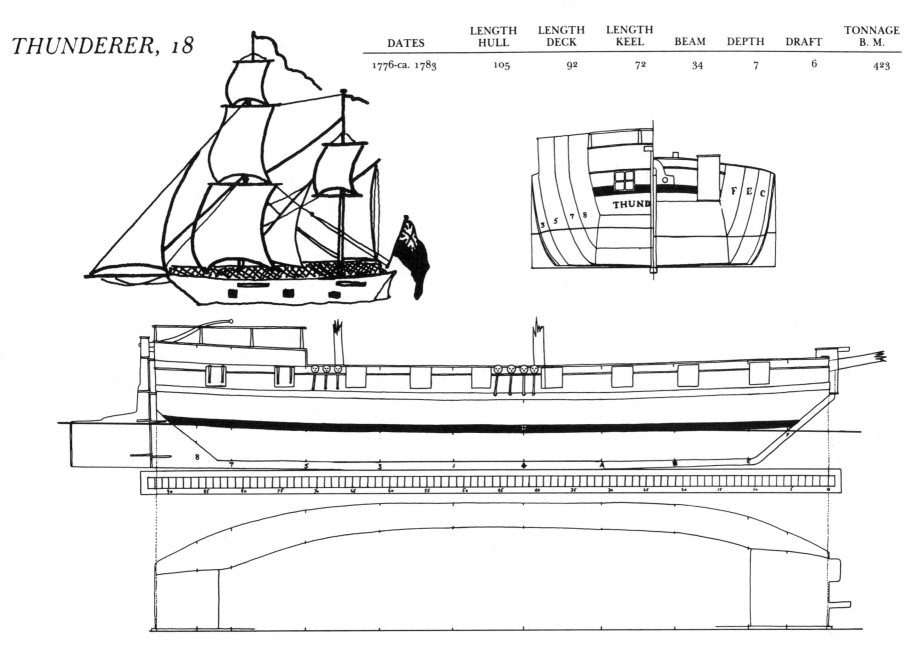

LA TRUITE, 26

WHEN French Admiral D'Estaing's siege of Savannah, Georgia failed in 1779, he left behind two of his minor ships that were of little further use to him, and transferred them to the South Carolina Navy. These were the flute (transport) *La Bricole* and gabarre (small transport) *La Truite*. Both these ships had been used to transport supplies to D'Estaing's forces and had been emptied before the siege of Savannah. Because they had shallower draft than his warships, D'Estaing had outfitted them with cannons and sent them into shallow water near Savannah in a vain effort to bombard the city into surrender. Such narrow and shallow vessels were not suited to carrying heavy batteries at sea, and yet with gunports cut into their hulls in unaccustomed places they were no longer suitable to serve him as transports. Thus, they came into the hands of South Carolina, which assigned them to guard the harbor of Charleston. *La Truite* had been armed only on the port side at Savannah, and the first thing that the South Carolina authorities did was to cut matching gunports in her starboard side. She was placed under the command of James Pyne, who was in turn told to accept orders from Continental Navy Commodore Abraham Whipple. However, when the British invasion force attacked Charleston in 1780 the American naval forces stood no chance. *La Truite* was sunk along with *La Bricole* and *Queen of France* in a futile attempt to block the harbor entrance and their guns were taken ashore, while the other American ships had to be surrendered intact as part of the terms of capitulation. Admiral Arbuthnot described *La Truite* as having formerly mounted twenty-six 12-pounders.

Jean Boudriot has located the plans of *La Truite*. She was built at Le Havre in 1776 to plans by Ginoux as an 8-gun transport measuring 350 French tons. As such, she would have been almost identical to *La Boussole* and *L'Astrolabe*, the two exploration ships that La Pérouse sailed around the Pacific in the 1780s before he was shipwrecked and eaten by cannibals. One crude picture of *La Truite* appears on a French map of Savannah.

In an interesting foreshadowing of ships in the War of 1812, the South Carolina Navy considered for a time making *La Truite* capable of carrying her armament in the open sea by cutting off her quarterdeck and forecastle, so that her gundeck would have also become her flush, bulwarked weather-deck like such corvettes as *Wasp* in later years. However, they ran out of time and money, so such an experiment was never executed.

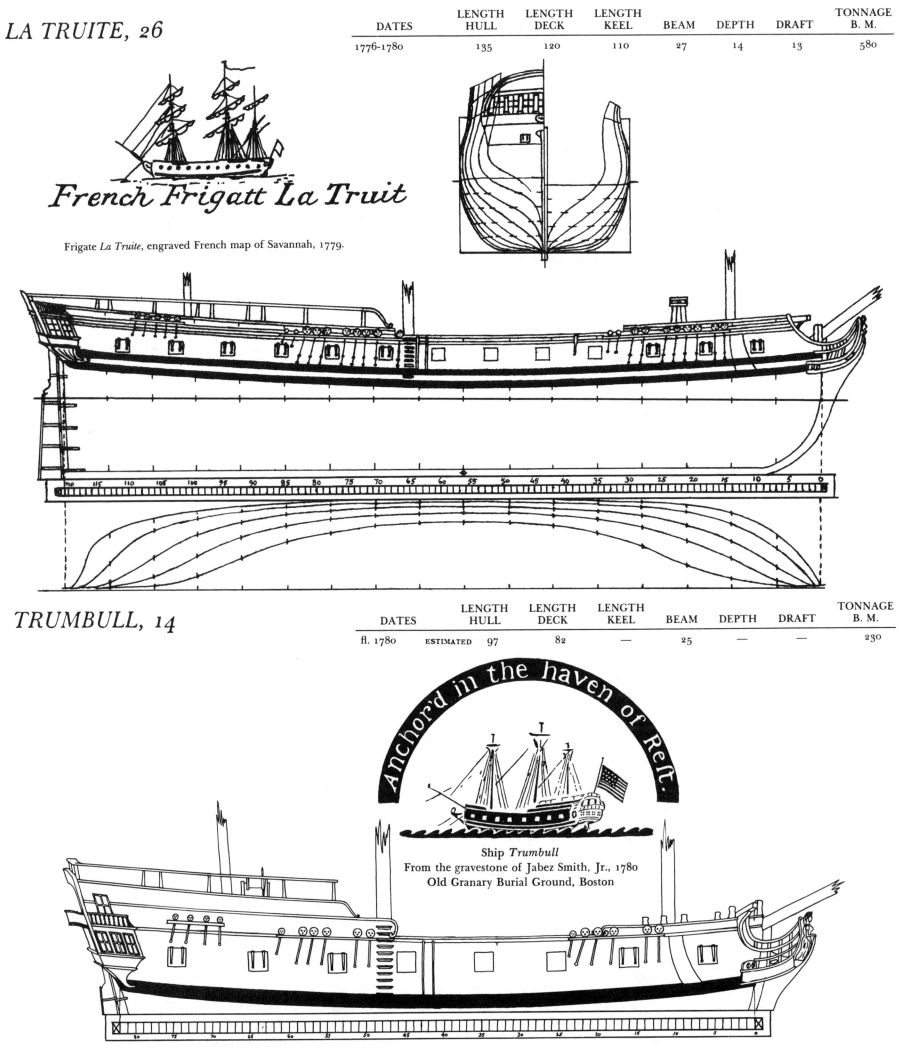

LA TRUITE, 26

DATES	LENGTH HULL	LENGTH DECK	LENGTH KEEL	BEAM	DEPTH	DRAFT	TONNAGE B. M.
1776-1780	135	120	110	27	14	13	580

Frigate *La Truite*, engraved French map of Savannah, 1779.

French Frigatt La Truit

TRUMBULL, 14

DATES	LENGTH HULL	LENGTH DECK	LENGTH KEEL	BEAM	DEPTH	DRAFT	TONNAGE B. M.
fl. 1780 ESTIMATED	97	82	—	25	—	—	230

Anchor'd in the haven of Reſt.

Ship *Trumbull*
From the gravestone of Jabez Smith, Jr., 1780
Old Granary Burial Ground, Boston

TRUMBULL, 14

AT the Old Granary Burying Ground in Boston is the gravestone of Lieutenant Jabez Smith, Jr., lieutenant of marines on the Continental frigate *Trumbull*, who died in June 1780. He had served in 1777 on the Connecticut State Navy ship *Oliver Cromwell* and later on the brig *Resistance*. He was captured when the frigate *Raleigh* was taken by the British, and was exchanged in 1779 so that he could serve on the frigate *Trumbull* as soon as she was ready for sea in 1780. The gravestone has a very fine carving in the semicircle at the top showing a 14-gun ship, probably a letter-of-marque. The problem is that one would normally think that this picture represents the frigate *Trumbull* or at least one of the other ships on which Smith had sailed, and this is absolutely impossible. Our conclusion is that the artist was told that Smith had been serving on a ship

called *Trumbull,* and that he had then gone down to the harbor to look for such a ship. There were a great many ships by that name, for Governor Jonathan Trumbull of Connecticut was a popular man, and we believe that the artist used an armed merchant ship of that name for his model.

The ship in the engraving is flying the stars and stripes, which must be about the first representation of that flag on stone. An unusual feature for a ship of her size was the two-decked stern with a balcony between the two rows of stern windows. Of course, there is always the possibility that the picture represents the frigate *Trumbull* and the artist omitted four gunports. If that is the case, then it means that the frigate, unlike her sisterships, had a doubledecked stern in the manner of some French frigates.

TURTLE

WHILE David Bushnell was a rather overaged student at Yale College he took time off from his studies to invent a successful underwater mine. After Lexington and Concord, while his classmates were joining the army around Boston, Bushnell went home to Saybrook, Connecticut, to build a submarine of his own invention, the *Turtle,* which would deliver the mine unseen to an enemy ship. The submarine was built in two eliptical halves made of oak staves like a barrel and well caulked with pitch. It had an entry hatch at the top that projected from a small conning tower, in which were set eight small glass windows and two schnorkels. At the bottom was a lead keel made in two pieces for ballast and neutral buoyancy; the fixed part of the keel weighed 700 pounds, and the other part, which could be jettisoned, weighed 200 pounds and could also be used as an anchor if needed. A foot-operated valve allowed water into the craft so it could submerge, and a pump could force it out again. A compass and a depth gauge were both illuminated by "foxfire" phosphorescence. The rudder was operated with a long tiller, and propulsion was effected by two hand-cranked screws, one for vertical motion and the other for horizontal motion. The mine was attached to an auger which was supposed to be able to take a bite on the bottom of a ship's hull, and the detonation system in the mine worked by clockwork and a flintlock. The vessel had only enough air for half an hour of operation submerged.

Bushnell's brother Ezra became quite proficient at operating *Turtle,* and although their original purpose of attacking a British ship in Boston had been thwarted by the British evacuation of Boston in March 1776, they were delighted to get the chance to try it out in New York when the British occupied that city in the summer of 1776. However, Ezra Bushnell became ill and David had not enough strength to operate *Turtle.* George Washington sought a replacement from his army and chose Sergeant Ezra Lee. Lee made an attack on the British 64-gun flagship *Eagle* after midnight on 7 September 1776, but the auger failed to take a bite on the bottom

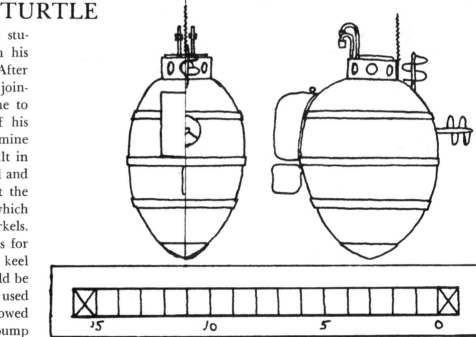

of the ship, for the little submarine had no way of exerting a force on the other end. Lee abandoned the attempt as dawn neared and propelled *Turtle* several miles against the current on the surface. Exhausted, he watched with glee as the British took fright at the mine blowing up harmlessly in the middle of the harbor. He made two more attempts within a few days, but with no more success.

On 9 October, the British made an attack up the Hudson, and in the fight the sloop carrying *Turtle* on her deck was sunk. *Turtle* was apparently recovered a few days later by the industrious Bushnell, but she was never used again. She is believed to have been destroyed after Washington's defeat at White Plains on 28 October 1776 to avoid capture.

Bushnell may have been the first to use a submarine for military purposes, but he was by no means the first to use a submarine. The Dutchman Cornelius Van Drebbel carried England's King James I in his submarine fifteen feet under the Thames River in 1624. An English inventor named Symons had also used a relatively sophisticated submersible in 1747, and in 1774 another Englishman, James Day, built two submarines, one successful to a depth of 30 feet and the other not; the latter killed him. It is not known whether Bushnell was aware of the work of his predecessors.

VIRGINIA

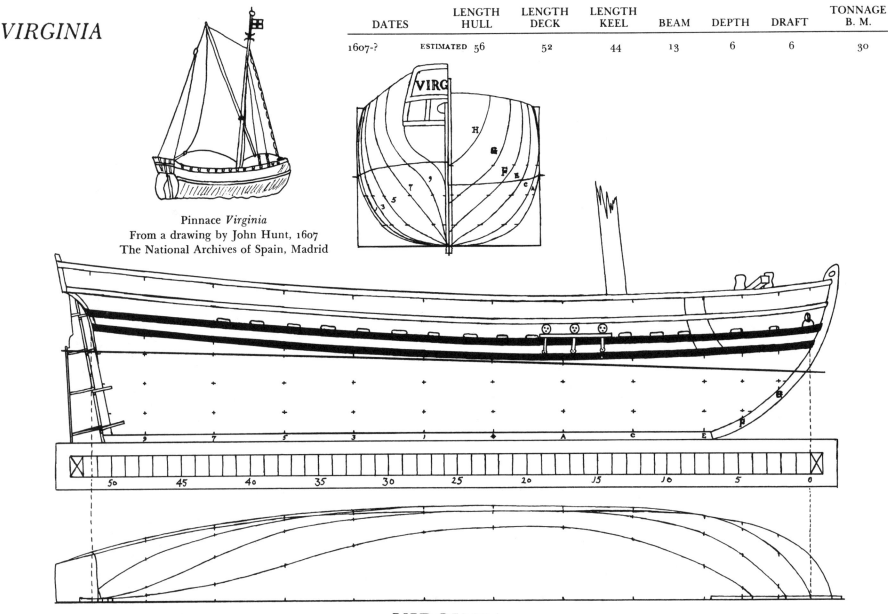

DATES		LENGTH HULL	LENGTH DECK	LENGTH KEEL	BEAM	DEPTH	DRAFT	TONNAGE B. M.
1607-?	ESTIMATED	56	52	44	13	6	6	30

Pinnace *Virginia*
From a drawing by John Hunt, 1607
The National Archives of Spain, Madrid

VIRGINIA

As far as we know, the first sailing vessel built by Englishmen in the Americas was the 30-ton pinnace *Virginia*. She was constructed under the direction of Sir George Popham by a shipwright named Digby at St. George's Fort, Sagadahoc, Maine, at the mouth of the Kennebec River in 1607. The same year as another British expedition had settled Jamestown, Virginia, Popham's group of adventurers founded their fort in Maine for the purpose of fishing and trading for furs with the Indians. The settlers found that they did not care for the severe winter weather they had to face in Maine, so they built *Virginia* in order to escape, or so we are told. Since the settlement was visited by other ships from time to time, we suspect that the real reason for building her was to explore the coast.

She returned the settlers safely to England and then made several more transatlantic crossings in her life. The date and manner of her end is not recorded. A Spanish visitor to the fort drew a picture of the fort with *Virginia* moored alongside; that is the only knowledge we have of her appearance. She was a tubby boat, rigged as a sloop with a huge lateen yard or sprit on which was set the mainsail, if the picture is to be believed (some experts think the picture represents some other boat, because pinnaces often had two masts in those days). A model based on the picture and on research by William A. Baker was built by Carl Langbehn and is on display at the Bath Marine Museum at Bath, Maine.

French settlers in Florida built a transatlantic-type vessel on the Saint John's River as early as 1562-3, but no record survives to show how it looked. Dutch explorer Adriaen Block watched his ship *Tyger* burn in New York in 1613, so he built a yacht called *Onrust* (Restless) to escape and to continue exploring the northeast American coast. Her dimensions were: 44½ feet length on deck, 33 feet length of keel, beam 11½ feet.

VIRGINIA, CONGRESS, EFFINGHAM, TRUMBULL & VIRGINIA II, 28

DATES	LENGTH HULL	LENGTH DECK	LENGTH KEEL	BEAM	DEPTH	DRAFT	TONNAGE B.M.
1776-1782	151	126	106	34	11	18	682
1776-1777							
1776-1778							
1776-1781							
1779-1779							

Frigate *Virginia*
From an oil painting by Dominic Serres, 1780
National Maritime Museum, Greenwich, England

Captain James Nicholson.

Captain James Barron

IN December 1775 Congress passed the second half of the Rhode Island Navy Bill, which called for the construction of thirteen frigates as soon as possible. Five of these frigates were to be of 28 guns, and of these only the *Providence,* built in Rhode Island, appears to have been constructed to plans other than the official drafts supplied by Congress. The four others were *Congress,* built either by Lancaster Burling or by Lawrence & Tudor at Poughkeepsie, New York; *Effingham,* built by Grice & Company at Philadelphia; *Trumbull,* built by John Cotton at Chatham, Connecticut; and *Virginia,* built by George Wells of Baltimore, Maryland.

Construction of *Congress* and her 24-gun consort *Montgomery,* built in the same place, was slowed to allow men and material to be devoted to Benedict Arnold's fleet on Lake Champlain. Since the British had occupied New York City from midsummer 1776 onward and a powerful army was advancing along Lake Champlain toward the Hudson under General Burgoyne, it was decided to burn both ships about ten miles downriver from where they were built (they may still lie on the bottom of the river, waiting for intrepid marine archaeologists to discover them). They were burned in an unfinished condition. *Congress*'s captain was Thomas Grinnell of New York.

Effingham, named after the Elizabethan sea dog, fared little better. She had been launched at Philadelphia not long before the British occupied that city, and she was sunk upriver from there to avoid capture about 20 November 1777. She was raised shortly thereafter to serve as winter barracks for some of Washington's men, but when the British made a raid up the river in May 1778 she and her 32-gun consort *Washington* were burned to avoid capture. Her captain was John Barry.

It was announced on 24 January 1777 that *Virginia* was ready for sea, but Captain James Nicholson claimed he was short of supplies, officers, and men, so he remained at anchor. In June he ventured down the Chesapeake as far as the York River, but was quickly chased back by a British patrol. After much prodding from Congress, Nicholson finally got underway again with a fresh breeze at his back and an experienced pilot sailing ahead to guide him in the clear night. The British patrols failed to see him, but suddenly *Virginia* grounded on a sandbar; when she passed into deeper water on the other side, it was found that the rudder had come off, so Nicholson rowed ashore, neglecting to take or destroy his secret papers or to give orders to burn the ship. Command of the ship devolved on eighteen-year-old Lieutenant Joshua Barney, but he could do no more than surrender the ship on April Fools Day 1778 when the British spotted her the next morning, for the crew had broken into the rum supply and were drunk to a man.

Virginia was taken into the Royal Navy under her original name, but was rated as a 32-gun ship. On 3 August 1779, she left New York in Commodore Sir George Collier's squadron that was headed for the Penobscot Bay in Maine; their arrival there caused the destruction of an enormous American fleet, including the frigate *Warren,* the corvettes *Hampden* and *General Putnam,* and the sloop *Providence.* An oil painting of this incident by Dominic Serres shows a stern view of *Virginia* and can be seen at the National Maritime Museum at Greenwich. In 1780, she took part in the British capture of Charleston, South Carolina. British records state that she was then sailed to England where she was drawn in drydock (her lines are on file at the National Maritime Museum at Greenwich), and was then ordered broken up as unsound in December 1782 (although Chapelle says she was not sold until 1786).

Trumbull, named after Connecticut's popular Governor Jonathan Trumbull, was put under command of Captain Dudley Saltonstall. She turned out to draw too much water to get over the sandbar at the mouth of the Connecticut River, so she was trapped. Benedict Arnold, home briefly on leave, suggested that she be buoyed up with lighters, but he was ignored. A British raiding party nearly got close enough to burn her in April 1777. In September 1778 her crew were taken off to man the frigate *Raleigh,* and in 1779 Saltonstall was replaced by Elisha Hinman, who had just been absolved of all blame in the loss of the *Alfred.* In two months he got out of the river, tying on empty water casks to float her higher, and took her to New London for a crew. He was suddenly relieved, for no stated reason, by James Nicholson, who had earlier lost *Virginia.* He got her to sea in May 1780 and had a furious battle with the 36-gun Liverpool privateer *Watt* (ex-East Indiaman). *Trumbull* lost her main- and mizzenmasts, and *Watt* limped away in desperate condition. On 8 August 1781 she left Philadelphia as escort for twenty-eight merchant ships, but the next day a storm carried away her main and fore topmasts. While she was making repairs she was attacked by the 32-gun frigate *Iris* (formerly *Hancock*) and the 20-gun corvette *General Monk* (formerly *General Washington*) and quickly captured. She was in such bad condition that *Iris* had to tow her back to New York and there she was sold to be broken up. There is a possibility that *Trumbull* differed from her sisterships in having a double-decked stern like East Indiamen and some French frigates (see the discussion in the text about the ship *Trumbull*). Incidentally, the *Trumbull* that was taken into the Royal Navy as *Tobago* was a completely different ship.

Another 28-gun frigate, perhaps constructed to the same design, was built for the Continental Congress at Gosport, Virginia. She was to have been named *Virginia* and was assigned to Captain James Barron, but Commodore Sir George Collier's squadron arrived and burned her along with many other ships just as she was ready for launching in 1779. Ironically, the previous *Virginia* was a member of Collier's squadron.

WARREN (ex-AMERICA), 32

DATES	LENGTH HULL	LENGTH DECK	LENGTH KEEL	BEAM	DEPTH	DRAFT	TONNAGE B. M.
1776-1779	152	132	111	34	11	17	690

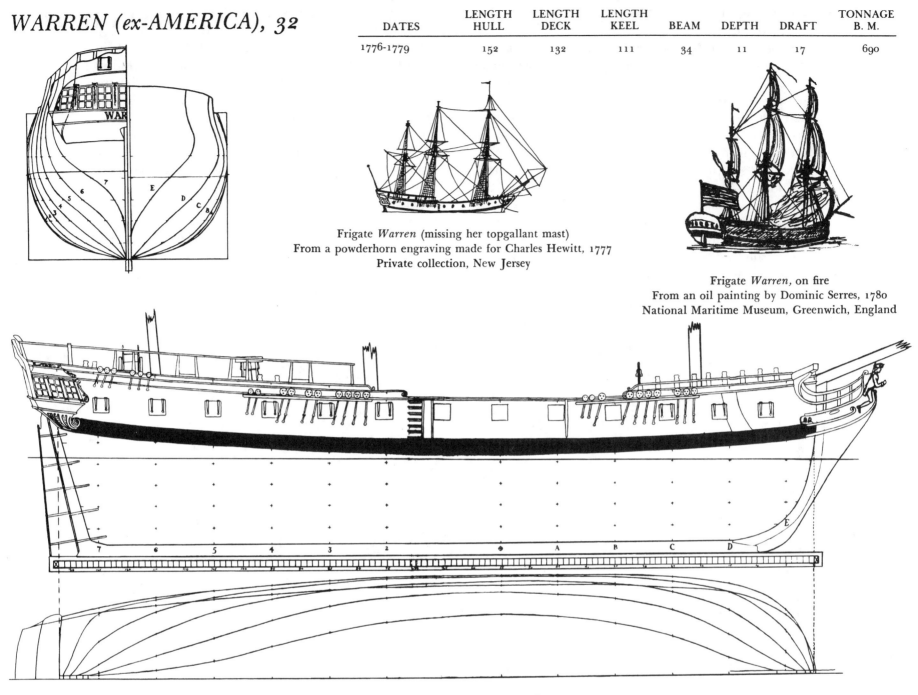

Frigate *Warren* (missing her topgallant mast)
From a powderhorn engraving made for Charles Hewitt, 1777
Private collection, New Jersey

Frigate *Warren,* on fire
From an oil painting by Dominic Serres, 1780
National Maritime Museum, Greenwich, England

WARREN (ex-AMERICA), 32

THE most powerful of all the original thirteen frigates authorized by Congress in December 1775 was the 32-gun *Warren,* for she was armed with eighteen-pounders rather than the twelve-pounders used by the others. She was the first of all the American frigates launched, on 15 May 1776 at Providence, Rhode Island, and was originally named *America,* according to the Newport *Mercury.* She was soon renamed, however, after Dr. Joseph Warren, the Massachusetts patriot who had died at Bunker Hill in 1775 and whose body had been dug up and reinterred in Boston only a short time before the launching. Some historians have thought that she might have been named for the town of Warren, Rhode Island (the Indian village where founder Roger Williams had first lived) or Commodore Peter Warren* (who had coordinated the successful New England attack on Louisbourg, Nova Scotia, in 1745). Her builders were Talman & Bowers, who were also building the 28-gun *Providence* and would later build the 20-gun *General Washington.* It is our belief that they were also the builders of the 16-gun privateer *Oliver Cromwell,* whose lines are on file at the National Maritime Museum at Greenwich, and we have based our reconstruction of *Warren* on these plans.

Command of the *Warren* was given to Captain John B. Hopkins, son of Commodore Esek Hopkins. After she was rigged, she was hove down for some work on her bottom and the rotten rope that had been supplied at great personal profit by John Brown (a prominent member of the state committee that was overseeing construction of the ships) snapped, thus breaking many of her spars. An engraving of her on a powderhorn in February 1777 shows her still without her main topgallant mast.

* A New Yorker in Royal Navy service, who was extremely popular in America.

It was not until early March 1778 that Hopkins was able to get her to sea through the tight blockade imposed by British ships at Newport, and even then she was damaged in both hull and rigging by British shots. The weather being very cold and the crew only having thin clothing with them, Hopkins cruised to Bermuda, taking two prizes before returning to Boston on 23 March. Once there the crew deserted, and Hopkins spent the rest of the year looking for a crew. A year later, she still only had 70 men out of over 200 that she should have had. Finally, in late March 1779 Hopkins got her to sea with an adequate crew in company with *Queen of France*, and on 7 April they took eight out of ten ships in a British convoy off the Delaware, including the escort. Contrary to orders, they took all their ships back to Boston, where the crew deserted immediately and Hopkins was suspended for some irregularities in the distribution of prize money. Command of *Warren* was

then given to Dudley Saltonstall, who for years had failed to get his frigate *Trumbull* out of the Connecticut River.

Saltonstall did hardly any better for *Warren*. He used her as his flagship for the huge American fleet that sailed to the Penobscot Bay in Maine. They arrived at the Penobscot in 27 July 1779, but coordination between the sea and land forces was so pathetic that they failed to dislodge the tiny British force at Castine. In the meantime, a small British fleet of seven ships, only one of them a two-decker, arrived on 13 August and the Americans fled up to the head of the bay, where they burned their ships. In this way, the whole fleet was lost, including *Warren, Hampden, General Putnam*, and the sloop *Providence*, while together they might have made a stand or escaped to sea. *Warren* appears in the background of an oil painting of the incident by Dominic Serres that can be seen at the National Maritime Museum at Greenwich.

WASHINGTON, CONGRESS, GATES & TRUM-BULL, LADY WASHINGTON, INDE-PENDENCE/DEPENDENCE, PUT-NAM/CORNWALLIS & SPITFIRE, 12

DATES	LENGTH HULL	LENGTH DECK	LENGTH KEEL	BEAM	DEPTH	DRAFT	TONNAGE B. M.
1776-ca. 1783 1776-1777 1777-1777 1776-1777	80	72	61	20	6	7	123

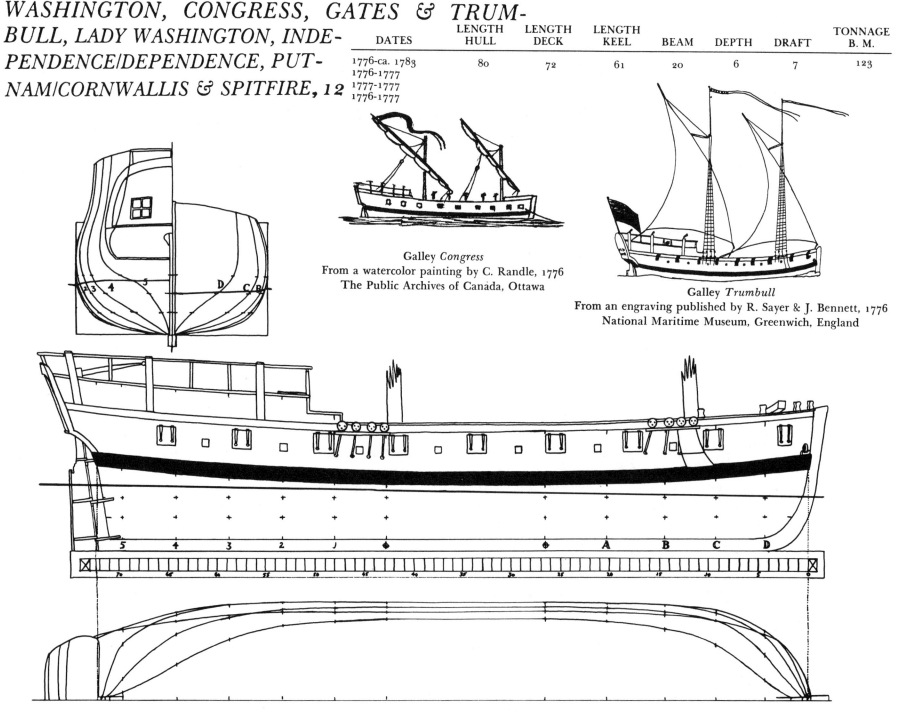

Galley *Congress*
From a watercolor painting by C. Randle, 1776
The Public Archives of Canada, Ottawa

Galley *Trumbull*
From an engraving published by R. Sayer & J. Bennett, 1776
National Maritime Museum, Greenwich, England

Galley *Washington*
From an engraving published by R. Sayer & J. Bennett, 1776
National Maritime Museum, Greenwich, England

150 Schooner-rigged galley *Lady Washington* on the Hudson River, from a powderhorn engraving, 1777, in a private collection, Kingston, New York. Despite her different rig, the hull of this vessel is thought to have been almost identical to the Lake Champlain galleys; all the principal galleys on Lake Champlain, the Hudson River and the Delaware River were designed by the same Philadelphian except for those that were converted from existing hulls.

WASHINGTON, CONGRESS, GATES & TRUMBULL, LADY WASHINGTON, INDE-PENDENCE/DEPENDENCE, PUTNAM/CORNWALLIS & SPITFIRE, 12

WHEN Benedict Arnold built his little fleet on Lake Champlain in the summer of 1776 the most important elements of it were the four galleys *Washington, Gates, Trumbull,* and *Congress. Washington* was commanded by General David Waterbury; her crew numbered 110 men, and she mounted two eighteen-pounders, four twelve-pounders, two nine-pounders, and four four-pounders, plus a few swivels. After the battle of Valcour Island she and *Congress,* with the cutter *Lee,* formed the rearguard as the Americans retreated quietly toward Crown Point. Unfortunately, the British caught up with them and captured both *Washington* and *Lee.* They released Waterbury and his men on parole after only a few days, and the men praised the British for their good treatment. *Washington,* though heavily damaged, was repaired and taken into the British forces on the lake. Chapelle reports that she was rerigged as a brig, but an engraving of the British fleet in 1777 shows her rigged as she originally was: with large lateen sails on two masts.

When the schooner *Royal Savage* was put out of action at the battle of Valcour Island, Benedict Arnold made *Congress* his flagship. She had one eighteen-pounder, one twelve-pounder, two nine-pounders, six six-pounders, and some swivels. After the battle, *Congress* formed part of the rearguard for the retreating Americans, and she was so badly damaged by the advancing British that Arnold ran her ashore at Buttonmould Bay, about ten miles north of Crown Point on the Vermont shore. Arnold personally set fire to her. Some timbers that were said to be her remains were discovered around 1900 and placed on display.

Trumbull was the only American vessel on the lake to be commanded by a genuine sailor: Seth Warner from Connecticut. He led the way out of the American position after the battle of Valcour Island, and skillfully piloted the fleet past the British ships in the foggy night without alerting the British. *Trumbull* and most of the rest of the fleet reached Crown Point in safety, and the British turned back to St. John's because it was already so late in the year. The next year the British fleet swept south along the lake with more ships than before, so *Trumbull* was destroyed to avoid capture in the summer of 1777. Pieces of the wreck were recovered in 1954 and displayed for a time at Fort Ticonderoga.

The fourth galley, named after General Horatio Gates, was not actually finished in time for the battle of Valcour Island, and when she was finished the season was over. In the summer of 1777, when the British fleet advanced along the lake, *Gates* had to be blown up to avoid capture. Thus ended her brief career without her having accomplished anything.

A plan of *Washington* was drawn after her capture, and that can be seen at the National Maritime Museum at Greenwich. There are various contemporary portraits of the galleys at the National Maritime Museum, at the Royal Collection at Windsor Castle, in the Public Archives of Canada, and at Fort Ticonderoga.

Galleys were built for American forces during the Revolution in many places. Most of them, like the Lake Champlain galleys, had two masts with lateen sails, known as a xebec rig. Some were even xebec-rigged on three masts. Four galleys were built on the Hudson River in 1776 to hull plans thought to have been identical to the Lake Champlain galleys, but they were rigged as topsail schooners. Of them, *Lady Washington* was never captured, but the other three were taken by the British, two of them before they were completed. *Independence* in British service became *Dependence*, and remained in the Royal Navy until 1786. *Putnam* was renamed *Cornwallis*, but she was sold out of the service in 1780. The fourth galley was not completed until 1778, when she was named *Spitfire*; she was captured on 19 April 1779 by the French ship *La Surveillante* in Rhode Island. Galleys were used in Pennsylvania, North Carolina, South Carolina and Georgia. Virginia built four ship-rigged galleys each pierced for twenty guns, about 100 feet in hull length, but could not afford to arm or man them properly, and thus lost them all to British raids in 1781.

AFRICA (ex-SAN JOSÉ), 70

The Spanish Admiral Gaztañeta proposed the construction of a series of more modern ships early in the eighteenth century at Havana, Cuba. For the 60-gun size, see our entry under the ship *Principe de Asturias*. The *Africa* was built to Gaztañeta's 70-gun design at Havana in 1732. After that date, French engineers produced new designs for these classes. The remarks made about the designs of the 60-gun ships apply equally to the 70-gun class, so they are not repeated here. The Royal Navy reported that the *Africa* was scuttled by its Spanish crew at Cartagena, Colombia in March 1741 in order to avoid capture by the large British invasion force, but by this time the Spanish had down-rated her to a 60-gun ship.

AFRICA (ex-SAN JOSÉ), 70

DATES	LENGTH HULL	LENGTH DECK	LENGTH KEEL	BEAM	DEPTH	DRAFT	TONNAGE B. M.
1732–1741	184	152	131	43	20	22	1180

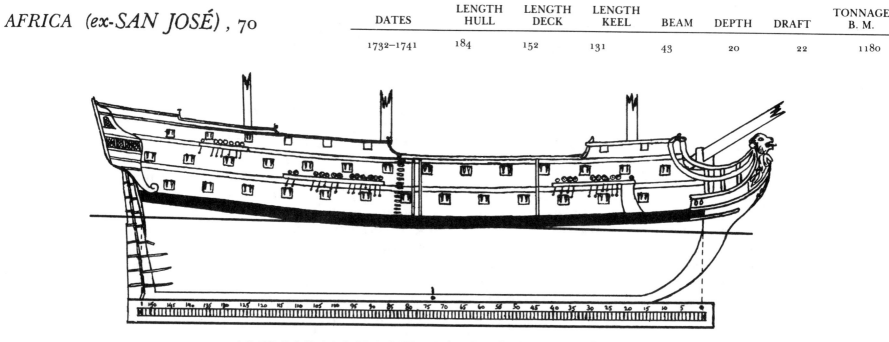

AMERICAN TARTAR/HINCHENBROKE, 28

Information about this ship arrived too late to be included in the proper place in this book. According to her dimensions as recorded by the British, she measured within inches the same as the Continental frigate *Boston* and the Massachusetts State frigate *Protector* (see pages 63–4), although her tonnage was calculated at 557 while *Boston* came to 514 and *Protector* to 586; because of non-standard measurement practices in that era the tonnage differences are regarded as meaningless.

American Tartar was built in Massachusetts as a privateer in 1777, presumably using the same plans as the frigate *Boston*. She sailed for a few days in company with the frigates *Hancock* and *Boston* and a number of other privateers under contract to the State, but all the private vessels took advantage of a storm to break their contract; if *American Tartar* had remained in company with the frigates, there is a good chance that *Fox* would not have been recaptured and *Hancock* would not have been taken. In the summer, *American Tartar* sailed to Europe in search of rich prizes, and on the way she fell in with the Liverpool privateer *Pole* (later captured by *Confederacy*). *Pole* was fitted for a trading voyage with only 16 of her 24 six-pounders mounted and only 40 men aboard, while *Ameri-can Tartar* had a crew of over 200 with 20 nine-pounders and up to 12 smaller carriage guns. Under the circumstances, *Pole* was fortunate to escape.

A few days after the battle with *Pole*, *American Tartar* was captured off Norway by the 64-gun British ship *Bienfaisant* on 28 August, 1777. *American Tartar*'s captain was John Grimes of Rhode Island. She was renamed *Hinchenbroke* and taken into the Royal Navy as a 28-gun frigate; Sir Edward Montagu, Viscount Hinchenbroke and First Earl of Sandwich, had been appointed as head of the British Navy during the Commonwealth and had been active in restoring Charles II to the throne.

Hinchenbroke became attached to the West Indies Squadron, and in June 1779 Horatio Nelson was promoted to be her captain, a few months short of his 21st birthday. He was ordered to escort an expedition of soldiers who were to cross Nicaragua and bother America's Spanish allies on the Pacific coast. Nelson exceeded his orders by accompanying the soldiers on their boat expedition up the San Juan River to the siege of Fort San Juan, where nearly the entire expedition was killed by yellow fever and malaria. Nelson, very ill, was withdrawn and replaced in March 1780 by his older friend Cuthbert Collingwood in command of *Hin-

chenbroke; Collingwood had previously followed Nelson in command of the brig *Badger* (see pages 82–3). Collingwood was soon promoted to command of a larger ship, so he was not aboard when *Hinchenbroke* foundered in a hurricane off Jamaica in 1782, commanded by George Stoney.

If the British ever recorded *Hinchenbroke's* lines, they have since been lost. Even the records are confusing, and Colledge gives incorrect listings for this frigate. I am grateful to John Sayen, Jr. for his suggestions.

Nelson, in 1784, sketched by Collingwood. (right) Cuthbert Collingwood drawn by Nelson.

CASTILLA, 64

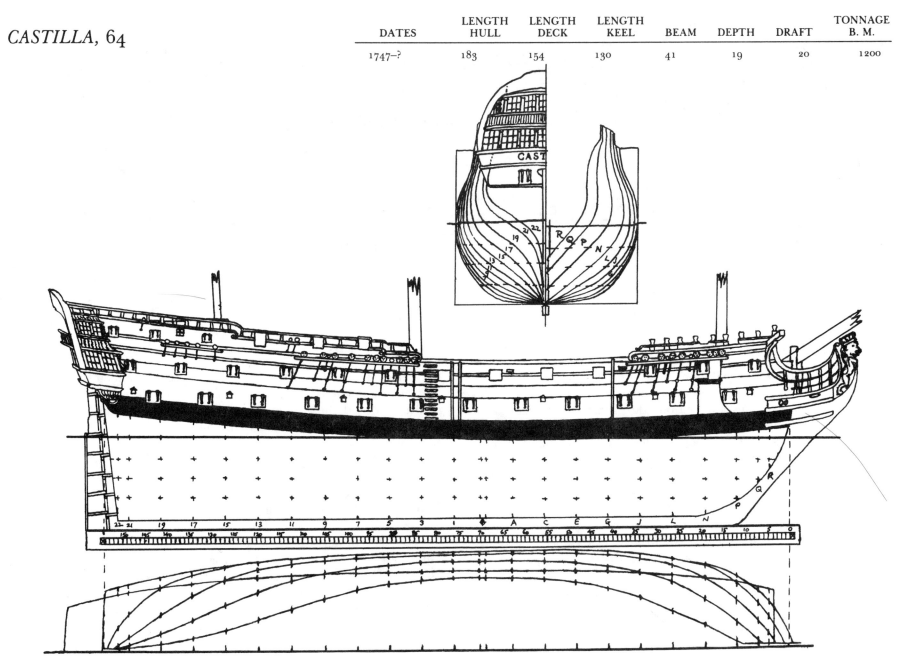

DATES	LENGTH HULL	LENGTH DECK	LENGTH KEEL	BEAM	DEPTH	DRAFT	TONNAGE B. M.
1747–?	183	154	130	41	19	20	1200

The Spanish Navy built about a third of its ships during the eighteenth century at Havana, Cuba, because of the ideal local shipbuilding timber, Cuban mahogany (now unfortunately extinct). Some of these ships were built by Spanish shipwrights, some by hired French shipwrights, and many by hired English shipwrights. One may well wonder about the details of the situation of such English masterbuilders when Spain and Britain found themselves at war with each other, as they frequently did throughout the century.

Such was the case with the 64-gun ship *Castilla*, built at Havana in 1747. Except for the addition of an extra knee on the cutwater and a handful of ventilation ports on the lower gundeck, she was absolutely identical to the latest designs for this class of warship being produced in England, which suggests that the Spanish resorted to espio-

nage during the so-called War of Jenkins' Ear. One up-to-date feature is the placement of the channels, which had previously been placed a deck lower. *Centurion*, a British ship of almost the same design but at a slightly smaller scale, was ironically completing her trip around the world at the time that *Castilla* was launched; *Centurion* had caused the Spanish no end of problems with attacks on their ports and shipping on the west coast of South America, and had then captured the fabulously wealthy Manila treasure galleon off the Philippines. No details on the career of *Castilla* have come to light, but her plans—including the English shipwright's use of English measurements—are preserved in the *Album of Jorge Juan*, 1750, at the Museo Naval in Madrid, although her actual name does not appear in the book.

FLORA (ex-SANTA ROSALIA), 24

DATES	LENGTH HULL	LENGTH DECK	LENGTH KEEL	BEAM	DEPTH	DRAFT	TONNAGE B.M.
1747–?	134	113	93	32	12	14	511

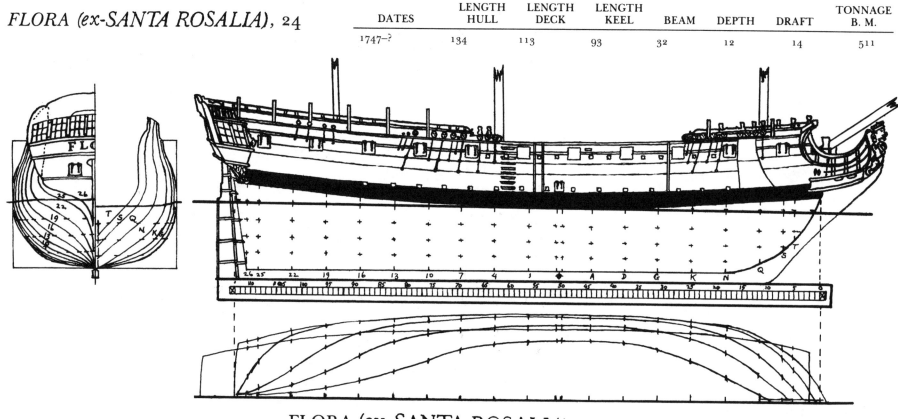

FLORA (ex-SANTA ROSALIA), 24

In the 1960s, the British aircraft industry produced four excellent new civilian airliner designs which however did not generally sell well outside Britain. Within months of the first flights of the British aircraft, Soviet airliners of identical size and shape made an appearance, and whenever the British engineers made minor alterations to the designs the same identical modifications soon appeared on their Soviet counterparts; most notably imitated were the Vickers VC-10 and the Concorde.

While Anglo-Soviet relations in the 1960s were somewhat frosty, the two countries were technically at peace. The same cannot be said for Britain and Spain in the 1740s, and yet the Spanish Navy managed to produce copies of the latest British ship designs before they could

have had an opportunity to capture or even see at sea their British counterparts. In 1747, the shipyards in Havana, Cuba produced the 64-gun ship *Castilla* and the 24-gun ship *Flora*, which were identical to the latest British designs, but with the addition of a few improvement suggested by the Spanish. For example, while some British 24-gun ships had a few oar-ports either interspersed between the gunports or arranged along the lower deck, *Flora* combined the two. She had ten ports a side on the upper deck and fifteen on the lower deck, thus making her a bireme of sorts. A ship of her size could be rowed to advantage over short distances with fifty oars. No information about *Flora's* subsequent career has come to light. Her plans survive in the *Album of Jorge Juan* of 1750 at the Museo Naval in Madrid, although without her name actually on them.

NUESTRA SEÑORA DE GUADALUPE, NUESTRA SEÑORA DE LA MERCEDES & SANTA MATILDE/HAMADRYAD, 34

DATES	LENGTH HULL	LENGTH DECK	LENGTH KEEL	BEAM	DEPTH	DRAFT	TONNAGE B. M.
1786–1799	149	123	104	39	16	14	670
1786–1804	or	or	or	or	or	or	or
1788–1815	164	135	114	43	18	15	966

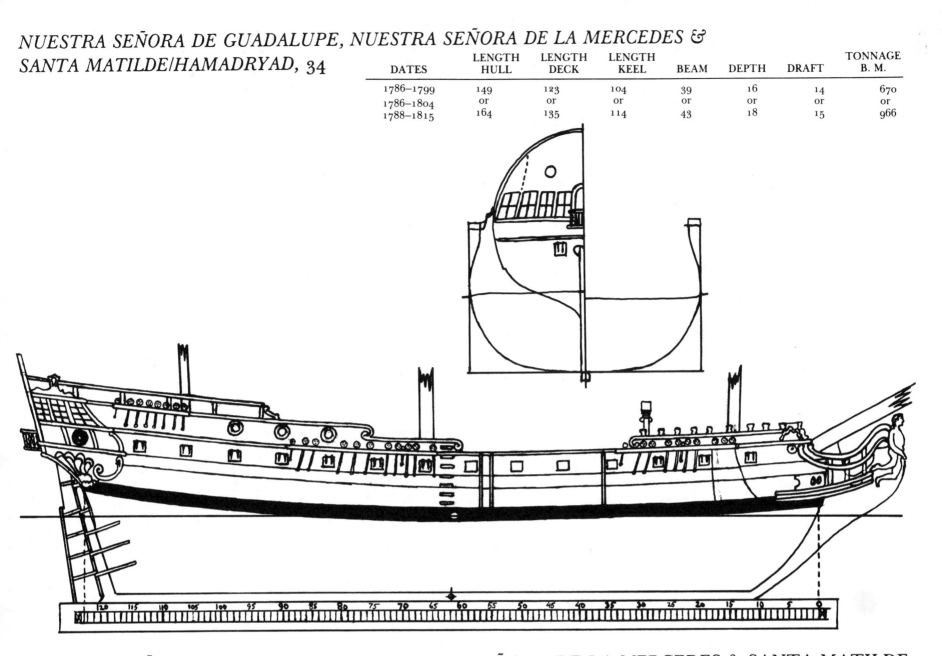

NUESTRA SEÑORA DE GUADALUPE, NUESTRA SEÑORA DE LA MERCEDES & SANTA MATILDE /HAMADRYAD, 34

At the beginning of the eighteenth century, Spanish ship design was hopelessly out of date in comparison to ships of other European nations. Admiral Gaztañeta attempted reforms about 1720, but they were too little and too late. Accordingly, French engineers were hired for a few years and then British shipwrights to design and construct the Spanish Navy's finest ships, both in Spain and in Cuba. Doubtless the local Spanish shipwrights, who continued to build some ships for the Spanish Navy (while the Englishmen built the most important ships), resented the influence of the foreigners.

The Archivo General de Indias in Seville has plans of a few ships built at Havana, including a splendid one decorated in watercolors for a 1785 frigate of 34 guns. The design is pure Spanish and owes nothing to any French or English influence, and it is tempting to say that it is inferior as a result. The most notable features of the design are the ship's excessive beam and shallow draft, harkening back to the pre-Gaztañeta period. The ship also had the out-of-date square stern, which causes drag in the water and makes the ship more vulnerable to raking fire. The ship carried fourteen small guns—probably nine-pounders—on

each side of the main deck and three more guns on the quarterdeck, whose round ports were unusual in that they were exactly above the corresponding ports on the deck below. A small poop cabin had enormous quarter windows but no stern windows, while the cabin under the quarterdeck had no quarter windows but eight windows in the stern with a small balcony in the middle. The stem had a pronounced rake which was carried into an unusually large cutwater.

Three ships appear to have been built at Havana to this design, as well as many others built at various ports in Spain. The three were *Nuestra Señora de Guadalupe* and *Nuestra Señora de la Mercedes* (Our Lady of Mercy), both built in 1786 while British shipwrights were constructing 112-gun battleships in the next building-ways, and *Santa Matilde*, built in 1788. Little is presently known about their careers, but it is known that *Guadalupe* was chased onto the rocks in the Mediterranean by *Centaur*, 74 and *Cormorant*, 20 on 16 March 1799. *Mercedes* along with three other frigates was carrying treasure from South America to Spain as secret aid for Napoleon (Spain was theoretically neutral at the time) when they were intercepted by a squadron of British frigates who knew about the secret treasure. Three of the Spanish frigates were captured, but *Mercedes* was blown up in the action, which took place on 5 October 1804 a few hundred miles west of Spain. *Matilde* was captured by the British ships *Donegal*, 80 and *Medusa*, 38 off Cadiz on 25 November 1804, and she was taken into the Royal Navy as *Hamadryad*. She was sold at the end of the war in August 1815. Her tonnage was listed as 966, which is considerably larger than the dimensions on the Spanish drawing would indicate; if the tonnage figure is correct, it probably means that the Spanish feet (a variable measure) on the drawing equal about 1.1 English feet rather than par, in which case the dimensions given here should be multiplied by 1.1.

BATEAU

A FLAT-BOTTOMED, flat-sided, double-ended craft that was used in rivers and lakes in New England and Canada was called a bateau, after the French word for boat. With the sides flaring outward, the bateau was a stable platform for the carriage of cargo on inland waters. Bateaux came in a variety of sizes, but the plans for only one have been discovered (they were so simple that they probably needed no plans for most builders to turn them out).

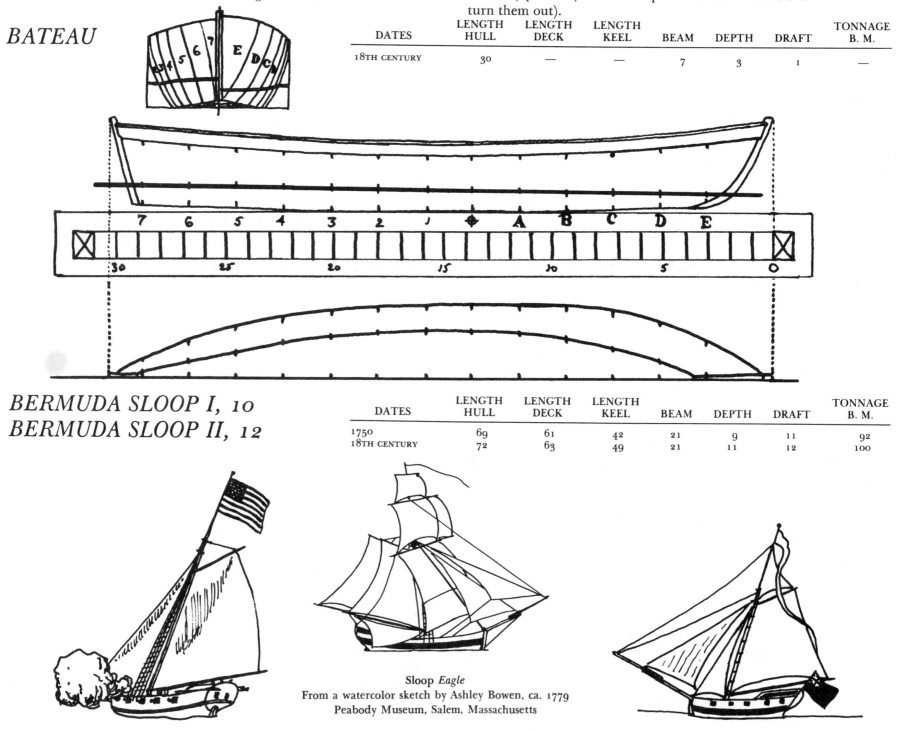

BATEAU

DATES	LENGTH HULL	LENGTH DECK	LENGTH KEEL	BEAM	DEPTH	DRAFT	TONNAGE B. M.
18TH CENTURY	30	—	—	7	3	1	—

BERMUDA SLOOP I, 10
BERMUDA SLOOP II, 12

DATES	LENGTH HULL	LENGTH DECK	LENGTH KEEL	BEAM	DEPTH	DRAFT	TONNAGE B. M.
1750	69	61	42	21	9	11	92
18TH CENTURY	72	63	49	21	11	12	100

American sloop at Boston, 1778, detail of grisaille by Pierre Ozanne, Library of Congress.

Sloop *Eagle*
From a watercolor sketch by Ashley Bowen, ca. 1779
Peabody Museum, Salem, Massachusetts

New England sloop with gaff-topsail, embroidery ca. 1740, Museum of Fine Arts, Boston.

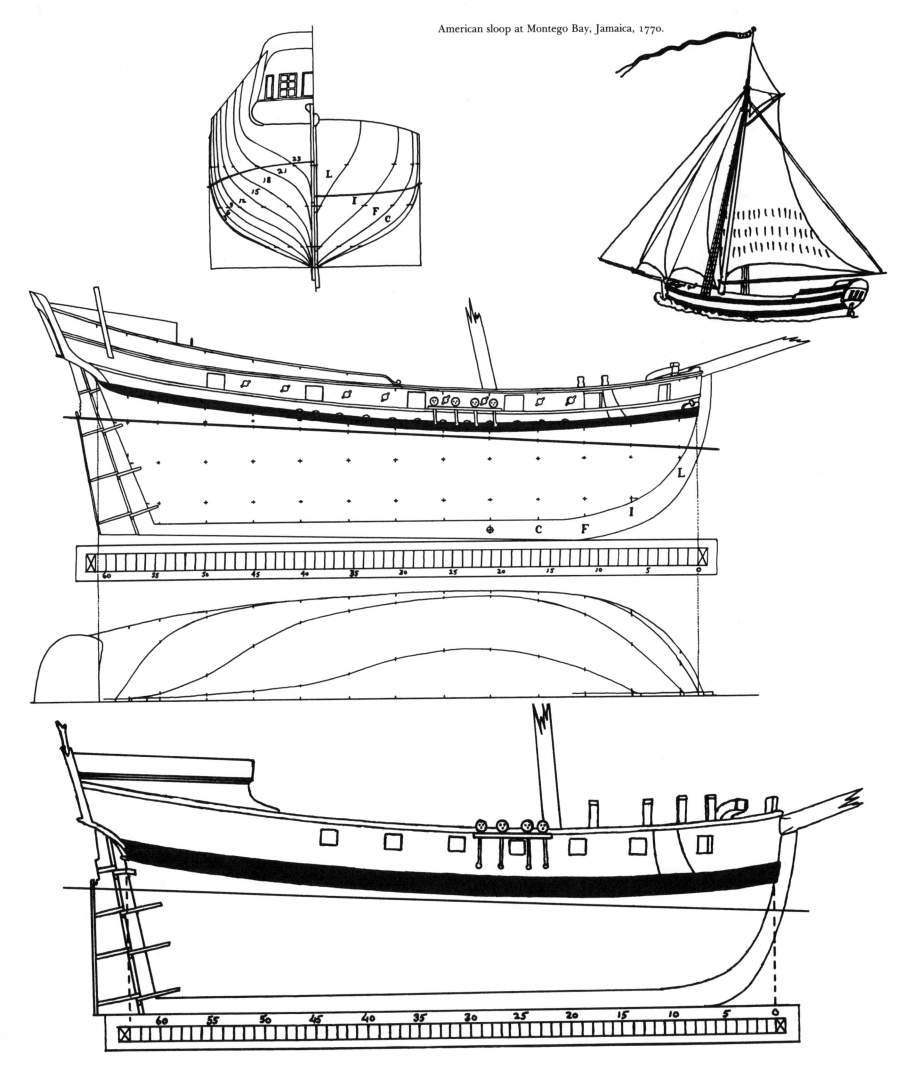

American sloop at Montego Bay, Jamaica, 1770.

213

American sloop, sketch by P. or N. Ozanne, Musée de la Marine, Paris.

American sloop at anchor off Cap François, Haiti, ca. 1765, engraving by P. and N. Ozanne, Musée de la Marine, Paris.

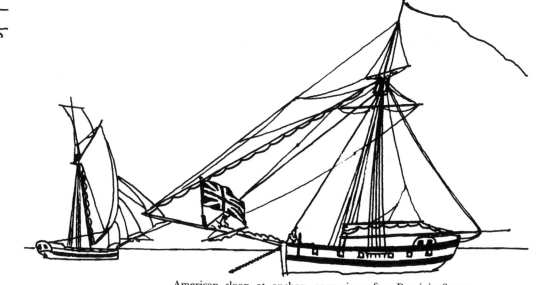

American sloop at anchor, engraving after Dominic Serres, National Maritime Museum, Greenwich.

BERMUDA SLOOP I, 10
BERMUDA SLOOP II, 12

INCLUDED in his book *Architectura Navalis Mercatoria*, published in the 1760s, Chapman showed the plans for a 10-gun "Bermuda" sloop. This kind of vessel, although called "Bermuda," was actually produced with few variations in Bermuda, Jamaica, and the Chesapeake Bay. The earliest picture of this type so far found is dated 1707, and we know that they continued to be produced after the American Revolution. They were particularly handy for sailing to, from, and around the West Indies. They made good smugglers, too, for with their sloop or schooner rigs they could escape quickly to windward while frigates and brigs were stymied from being now so close-winded. These vessels were characterized by their sharp lines, their deadrise, and the little cabin perched high on their sterns.

A crude model exists of a similar Bermuda-type sloop in the Marinmuseum, Karlskrona, Sweden. She has seven gunports a side and a decorated canvas extension to the bulwarks held up by the stanchions of the swivel-guns.

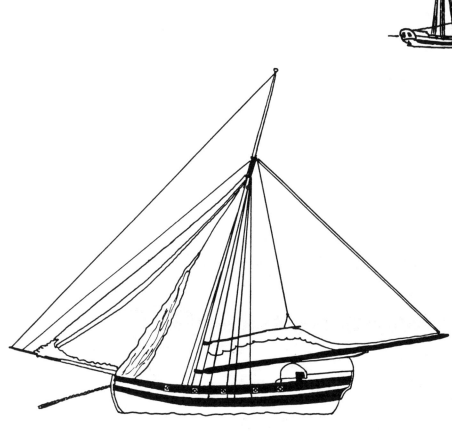

American sloop at anchor, Saint Croix, ca. 1760, engraving, National Park Service, Saint Croix.

	DATES	LENGTH HULL	LENGTH DECK	LENGTH KEEL	BEAM	DEPTH	DRAFT	TONNAGE B. M.
	1786-?	101	84	70	27	7	8	200

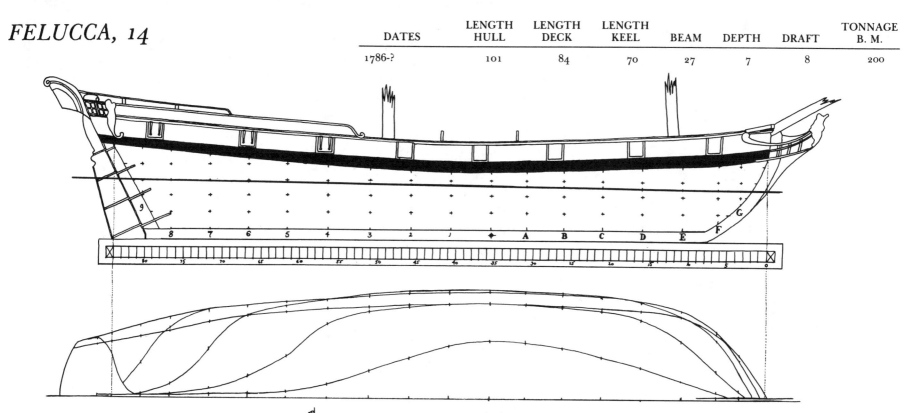

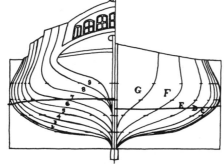

FELUCCA, 14

ONE of the smaller vessels built by the Spanish at Havana was a felucca whose plans survive, included in Admiral Paris's great work *Souvenirs de la Marine*. A felucca was a Mediterranean type of vessel, often rigged with large lateen sails, and roughly equivalent in size to a brig. This particular felucca (and there may have been dozens of them built at Havana over the years) mounted about 14 guns, although it was pierced for 16. Admiral Paris or his typesetter made serious errors with the scale, so we have had to invent our own scale, based mainly on the size and spacing of the gunports. Because of the difficulty in consulting Spanish and Cuban records we know no more about this ship than her plan and date of building, which was 1786. Research in this field would be a welcome addition to the field of eighteenth-century shipbuilding. The hull shape of this felucca was not so far different from the sketches of Simon Metcalf for vessels to be built on Lake Champlain, but of course the resemblance is only a matter of coincidence.

FRANKLIN'S YACHT

BENJAMIN Franklin turned his fertile brain to many fields and it would have been extraordinary if he had not spent some time on projects of a maritime nature. In fact, in the 1780s he designed an ideal wind-powered pleasure-craft for lounging and fishing on the Delaware River. His surviving drawings show that the hull was that of a typical rowing-boat of his day, but the sail was a rigid structure that could pivot around on a short mast. The more unusual feature of this rig was that the sail could also pivot on the horizontal axis, so that it served as an awning or shelter when not needed as a sail, and presumably when pivoted part-way it would have the same effect as if the sail were reefed. No record has been found of such a boat ever having been built or used.

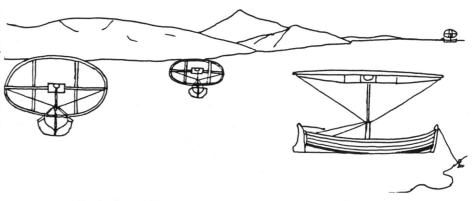

Benjamin Franklin's sketch of some of his proposed yachts.

DATES	LENGTH HULL	LENGTH DECK	LENGTH KEEL	BEAM	DEPTH	DRAFT	TONNAGE B. M.
ca. 1785	20	17	15	6	—	2	—

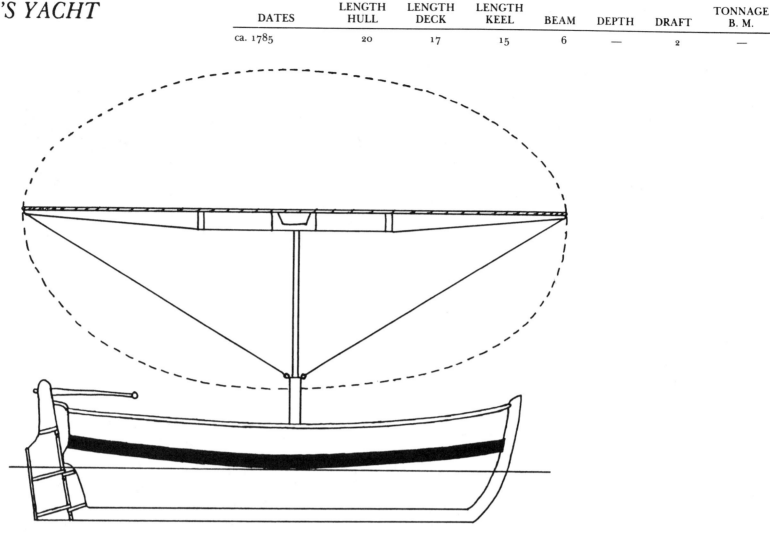

HAVANA GALLEY, 2

The shipyards at Havana, Cuba built some of the most impressive battleships for the Spanish Navy in the eighteenth century, but they also built a number of lesser craft. One of the latter was a row-galley built for the Spanish Coast Guard in 1695. She had two masts, each setting one large lateen sail; in fact, if the scale of the drawing can be accurately interpreted, the main yard was almost 100 feet in length. A long platform projected out from her stern, and a long, low, pointed beak was attached to the bow, both for attaching the forestay and for ramming the windward sides of enemy ships. The galley had rowing-stations for sixteen oars per side, each probably manned by two or three prisoners or slaves. Locations are shown for six large swivel-guns and two heavy bowchaser cannons above her low bow. Her freeboard was so low that she would no doubt have been confined to harbor service only. The Spanish used numerous such vessels in the Mediterranean, but without great effect.

HAVANA GALLEY, 2

DATES	LENGTH HULL	LENGTH DECK	LENGTH KEEL	BEAM	DEPTH	DRAFT	TONNAGE B. M.
1695-?	133	103	97	—	5	8	150

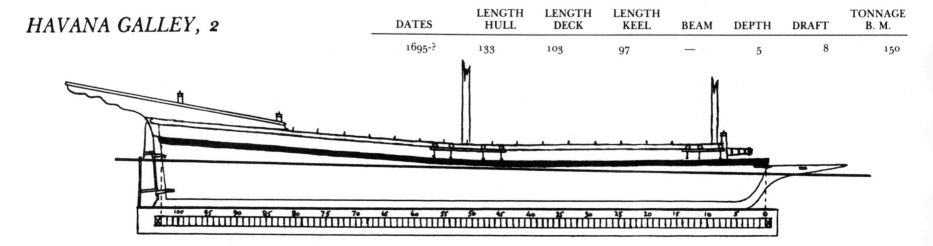

	DATES	LENGTH HULL	LENGTH DECK	LENGTH KEEL	BEAM	DEPTH	DRAFT	TONNAGE B. M.
	1776-ca. 1783	65	57	44	20	9	8	90

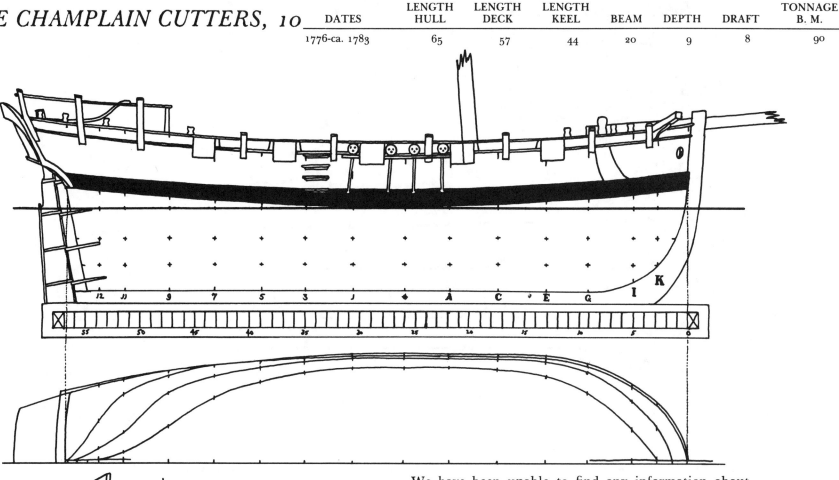

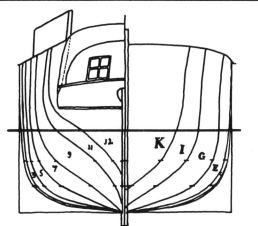

2 LAKE CHAMPLAIN CUTTERS, 10

I N the collection of Admiralty drafts at the National Maritime Museum at Greenwich is the plan for two 10-gun sloops to be built on Lake Champlain in 1776.

We have been unable to find any information about whether they were actually built. They were certainly not employed at the battle of Valcour Island, but they may have been incorporated into the British fleet in 1777 and thus completed about the same time as the corvette *Royal George*. Their profile was far more like a British sloop or cutter than an American, and they had a small cabin aft that was covered by a quarterdeck raised only half a deck-height above the main deck. Although they had the usual flattish bottom found on most lake vessels, they were deeper than the normal lake boats, so they may have sailed quite well. In addition to the carriage guns, they mounted about 20 swivels.

The general concept of this design appears to have been used for the construction of a modern copy of the Great Lakes sloop *Welcome*, built in 1975. No plans or dimensions survive for the original *Welcome*, but this rather smaller sloop could not have been very different from the Lake Champlain sloops.

LAKE CHAMPLAIN GUNBOATS, 1

W HEN Arnold built his 56-foot, 3-gun gondolas on Lake Champlain in the summer of 1776, the British were also building smaller gun-boats at St. John's at the northern end of the lake. Some were built on the Richelieu River in 1775 and others on the lake in 1776. They had one nine-pounder gun in the bow on a raised platform, and had wide, rounded bottoms. These gun-boats were used at the battle of Valcour Island, but there is no report as to how many were disabled or sunk by American fire.

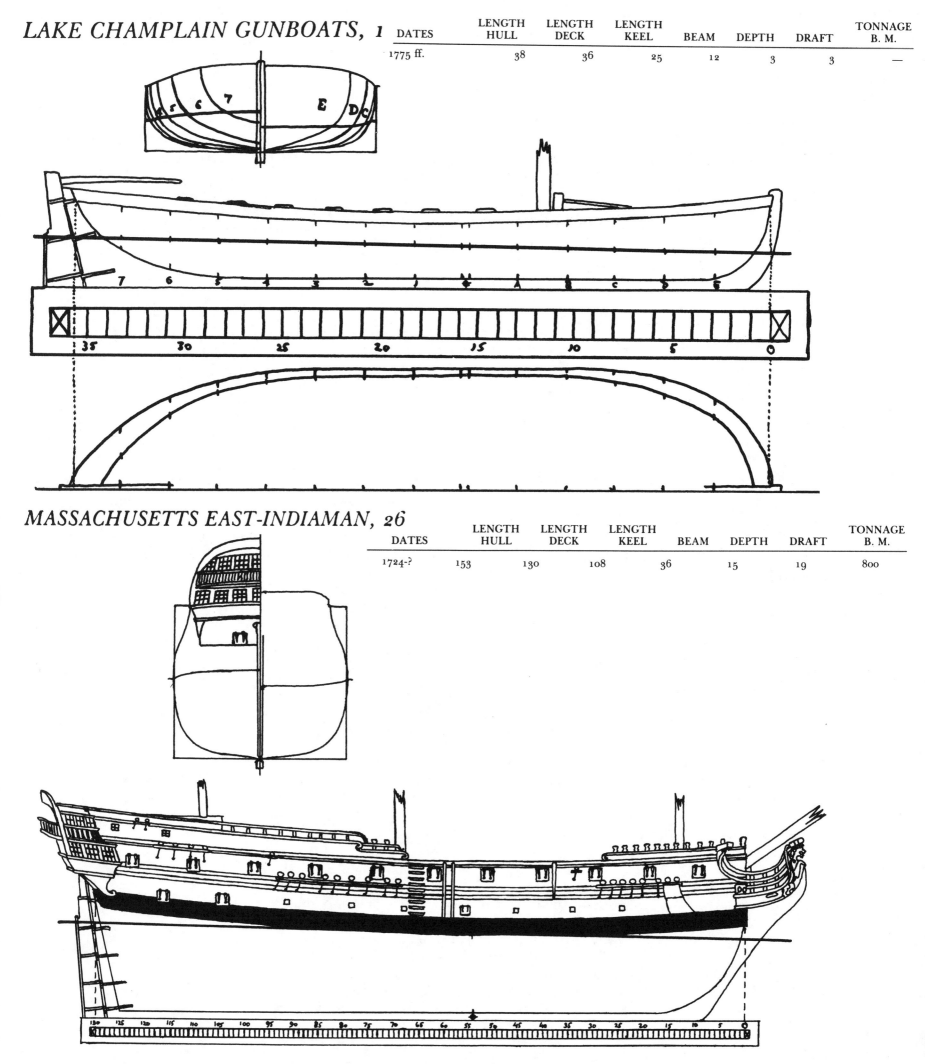

LAKE CHAMPLAIN GUNBOATS, 1

DATES	LENGTH HULL	LENGTH DECK	LENGTH KEEL	BEAM	DEPTH	DRAFT	TONNAGE B. M.
1775 ff.	38	36	25	12	3	3	—

MASSACHUSETTS EAST-INDIAMAN, 26

DATES	LENGTH HULL	LENGTH DECK	LENGTH KEEL	BEAM	DEPTH	DRAFT	TONNAGE B. M.
1724-?	153	130	108	36	15	19	800

Cabin of an East Indiaman, ca. 1810, cartoon engraved after George Cruikshank.

MASSACHUSETTS EAST-INDIAMAN, 26

Joseph Goldenberg, in his *Shipbuilding in Colonial America*, reports that Massachusetts builders launched a 130-foot merchant ship of twenty guns in 1724, with "1,000 tons displacement (*sic*)." The ship was undoubtedly an East Indiaman, and she was sold in England or Europe, but her name and fate are unknown, although it is possible to guess at her identity.

A ship of her length would have measured about 800 tons (not 1000), but no ships of that tonnage appear on the East India Company list in that period. The reason is that British law required all ships of 500 tons or more to carry a chaplain, so even though most East Indiamen measured about 800 tons they were officially listed at under 500 tons! The East India Company acquired two ships of nominally 480 tons in 1724, *Grantham II*, that made four voyages to the Orient and served until 1735, and *Marlborough II*, that also made four voyages and served until 1741. Perhaps the Massachusetts ship was one of these two. The plans shown here represent a typical East Indiaman of 1724. One feature of ships of this period is the low placement of the channels, which made them particularly vulnerable to both bad weather and damage by contact with piers or other vessels.

MASSACHUSETTS PRIVATEER FRIGATE, 36

Joseph Goldenberg's *Shipbuilding in Colonial America* notes that Boston shipbuilder Benjamin Hallowell constructed a large privateer frigate of 36 guns and 680 tons in 1758, but her name, her owners, her fate and her exact appearance remain unknown. After the British capture of Quebec in 1759 hardly any French ships could be captured within thousands of miles of Boston, so few New England privateers paid for themselves. Unless this mystery ship cruised in the Caribbean she was undoubtedly a disappointment to her owners, for the larger the privateer the more prizes she had to capture in order to meet expenses. She was large; a contemporary 36-gun frigate in the Royal Navy, *Pallas*, measured only slightly larger at 718 tons, and the 32-gun Revolutionary War frigate *Raleigh* at 697 tons was almost exactly her size. Since no plans or dimensions survive of this important ship, speculative plans have been drawn, based on an up-dating of the plans of the earlier frigate *Boston* which had been designed and built by Hallowell.

	DATES	LENGTH HULL	LENGTH DECK	LENGTH KEEL	BEAM	DEPTH	DRAFT	TONNAGE B. M.
	1758-?	155	130	109	36	17	17	680

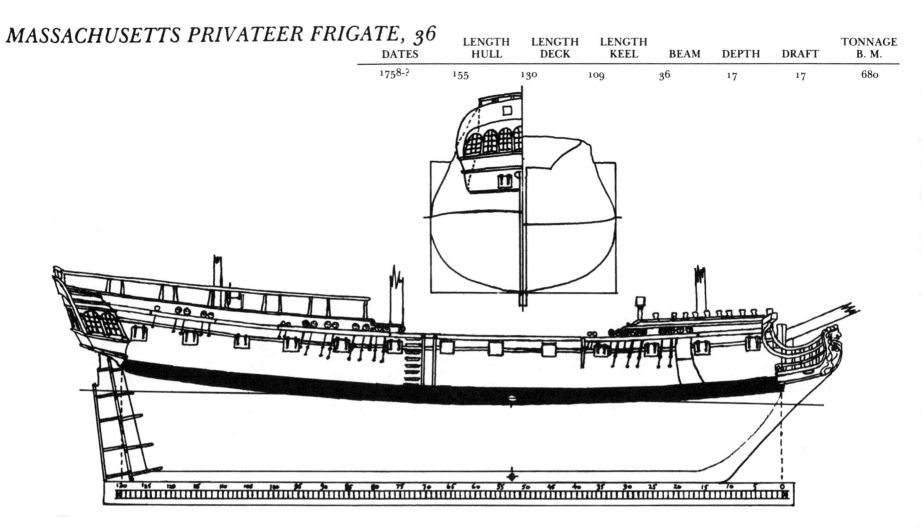

METCALF'S CORVETTE, 18; RADEAU, 6; SCHOONER, 14; SLOOP, 6.

O NE artistic and enthusiastic American in the Lake Champlain area, named Simon Metcalf, took the trouble to make rough plan drawings of four vessels he hoped he could get Arnold or someone else to build for use on the lake. They were a radeau, a sloop, a schooner, and a corvette. None was ever built, but we have included the drawings anyway. The radeau (French word for "raft") had three masts, six guns, and six oars, and was steered with two long rudders. Otherwise, it had a very simple rectangular shape with a bevel in the bow and stern from the bottom to the waterline. With one of Schank's drop-keels it might have sailed on a reach, but otherwise it would only have been able to run before the wind; in that case, why the three masts?

Metcalf's corvette mounted about 18 guns (pierced for 20), and was quite a respectable design, except for its remarkable sheer: the bow and stern stick up almost like the ends of a banana. The bow, as with the sloop and schooner, was fitted with a fiddlehead.

The sloop, which also mounted six guns, had a raked stem with a fiddlehead, but otherwise the profile was not too far from normal. It was in its sections that this sloop was unusual. It was pinched in rather sharply to the stern, which, among other things, would have left virtually no room in the tiny cabin in the stern.

Metcalf's schooner mounted 14 carriage guns and was rather larger than most schooners of the day. She had the same raked stem and fiddlehead as the sloop, but her stern was not pinched in. She had more deadrise than the sloop.

No discussion of American ships of this period would be entirely complete without these odd vessels designed by Metcalf, but on the other hand Metcalf's work should not be taken any more seriously by us than it was by the American strategists to whom he presumably submitted these designs as proposals.

	DATES		LENGTH HULL	LENGTH DECK	LENGTH KEEL	BEAM	DEPTH	DRAFT	TONNAGE B. M.
METCALF'S CORVETTE, 18	1777	ESTIMATED	105	88	77	29	7	8	200
METCALF'S RADEAU, 6	1777		40	40	33	18	2	3	30
METCALF'S SCHOONER, 14	1777		95	75	55	22	7	7	120
METCALF'S SLOOP, 6	1777		55	45	36	18	5	6	45

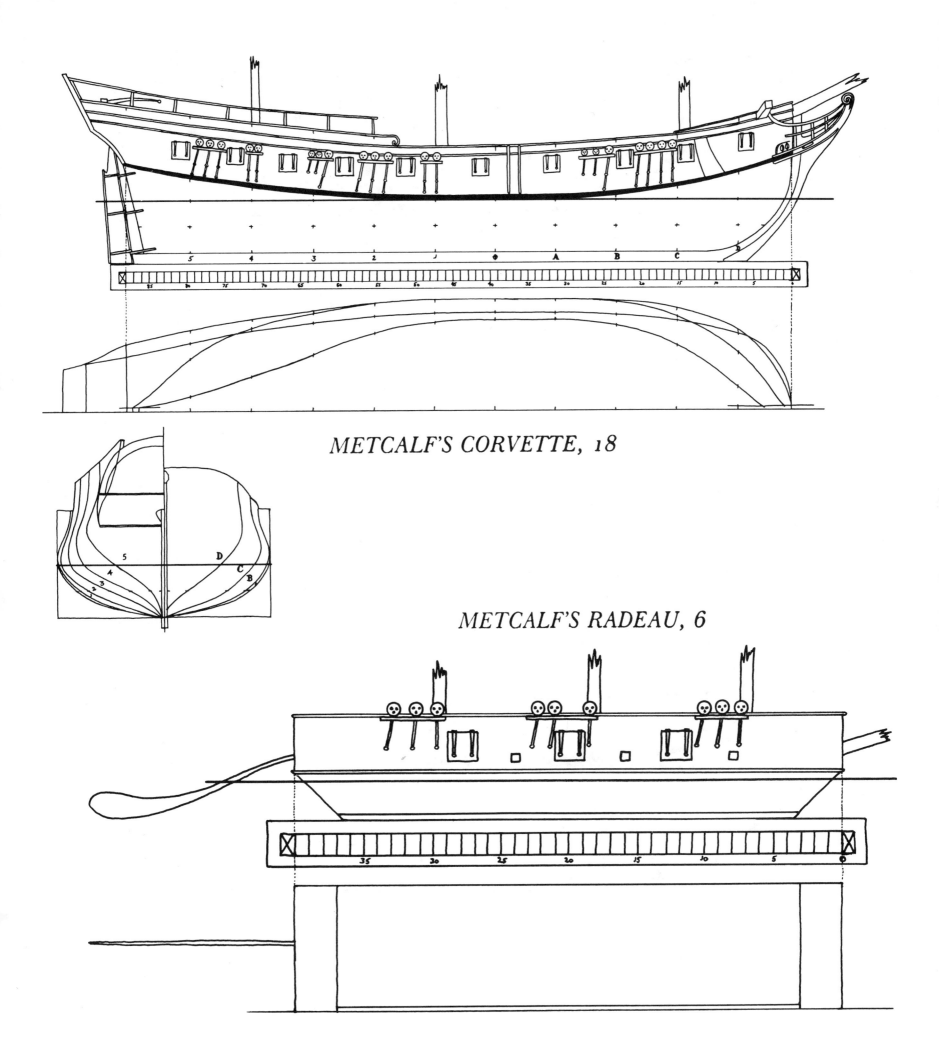

METCALF'S CORVETTE, 18

METCALF'S RADEAU, 6

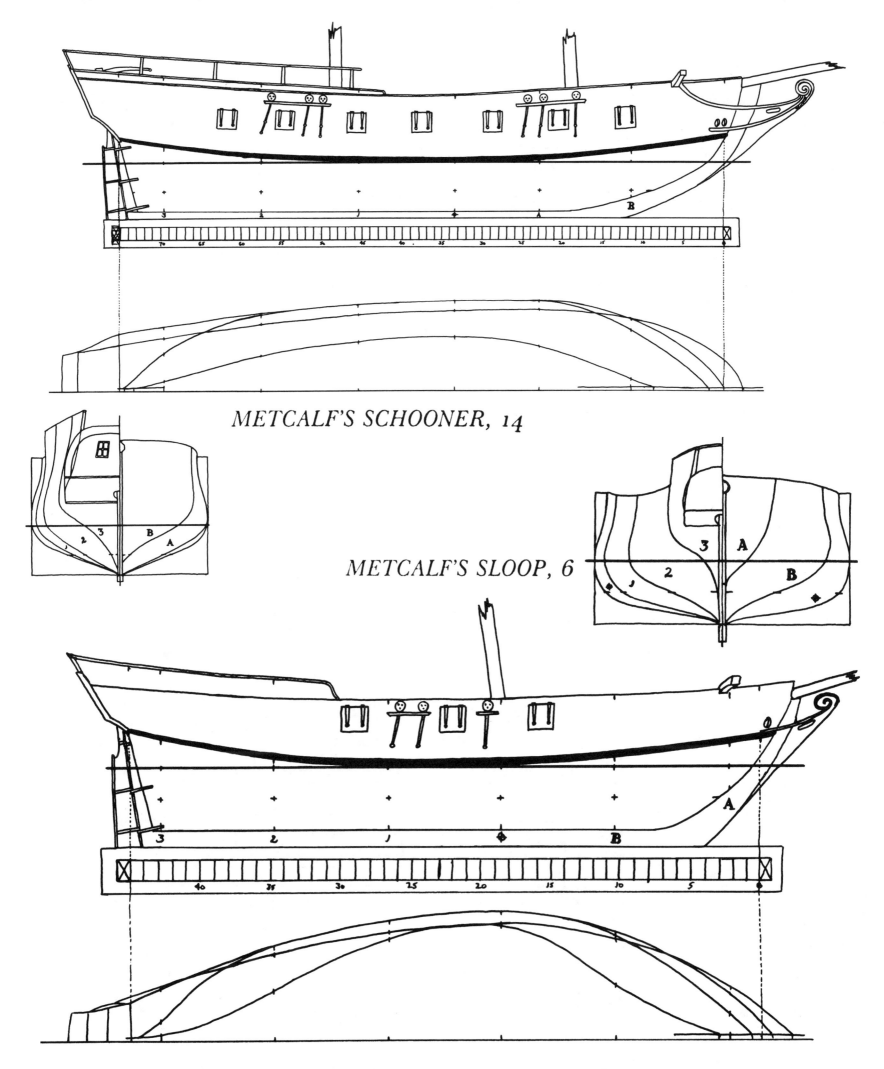

METCALF'S SCHOONER, 14

METCALF'S SLOOP, 6

DATES		LENGTH HULL	LENGTH DECK	LENGTH KEEL	BEAM	DEPTH	DRAFT	TONNAGE B. M.
fl. 1790	ESTIMATED	51	46	41	17	6	4	45

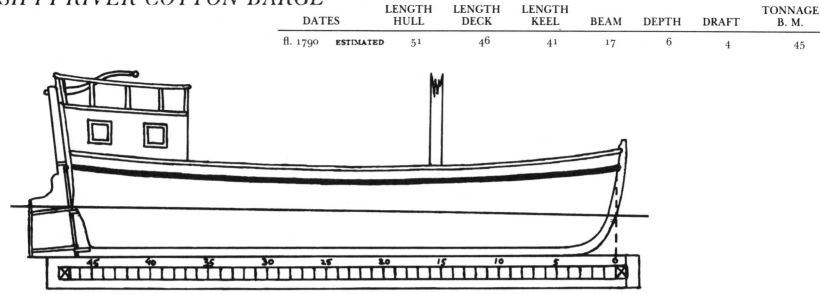

MISSISSIPPI RIVER COTTON BARGE

A FRENCHMAN with the historical name of Christophe Colomb painted an attractive painting of his father-in-law's neo-Palladian plantation house White Hall on the Mississippi about 1790. The artist has shown himself in the foreground executing a sketch from his seat on the river-bank next to his little yacht with its elaborate canopy in the stern. In the middle of the river a cotton barge is proceeding under a single square sail and the oar-power of six slaves. The barge has a raised cabin in the stern, on top of which sits the helmsman. Cotton bales are piled up between the cabin and the mainmast, and the slaves row from atop the forecastle. This is a type of vessel that must have been common not only on the Mississippi but on many American rivers, but it is seldom represented in pictures or descriptive text.

Mississippi River cotton barge in front of White Hall Plantation, Louisiana, painting by Christophe Colomb ca. 1790, private collection.

NEWBURYPORT SHIP I, 8

Aᴛ the Peabody Museum at Salem, Massachusetts, is a contemporary model of an 8-gun merchant ship of about 1760. The model is rather crude, and one suspects that it is not entirely accurate, especially with regard to deadrise and sheer. However, we have drawn it as we saw it, and we are sure that it represents a ship that once existed. Of particular interest is the figurehead, which is a two-headed horse; the reason for its having two heads is quite simply that a horse sculpture always looks better if the head is slightly inclined toward the viewer, and if the ship has two sides then there have to be two heads, one to incline each way.

The scale of the model is not given, so we had to calculate our own scale, based primarily on the size and spacing of gunports. These measurements make this an extremely short ship, a hull that would be more likely to have appeared as a schooner or even a sloop than a ship, but the ship rig was apparently necessary to drive the large beam and draft of the vessel through the water.

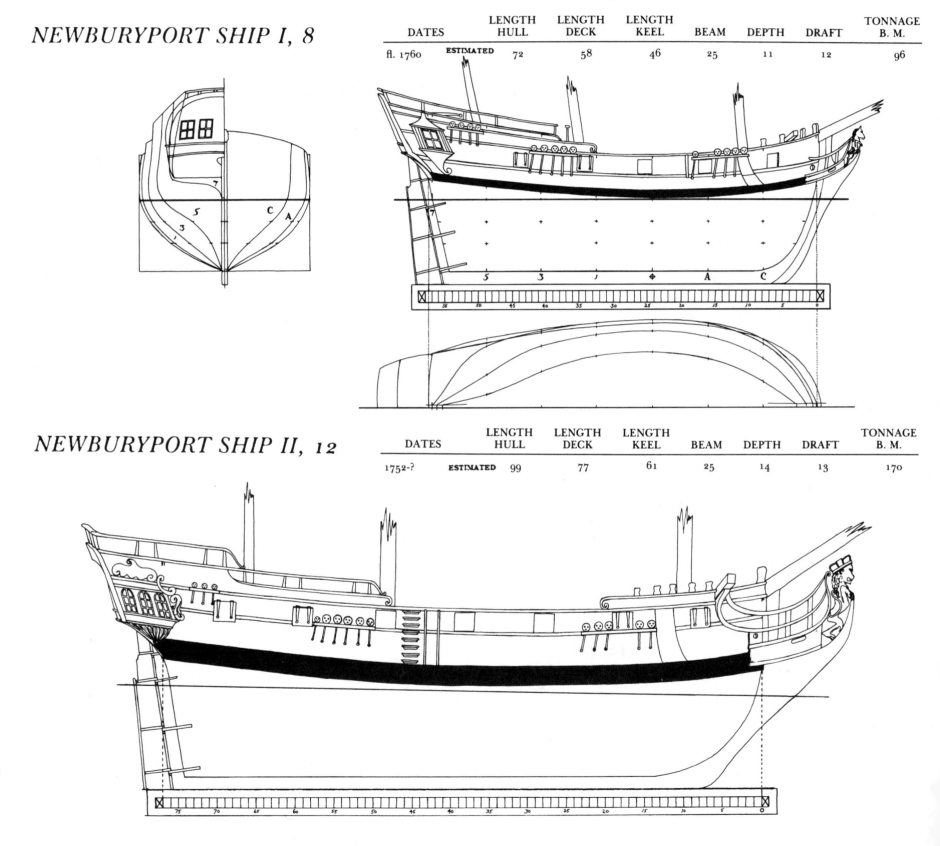

NEWBURYPORT SHIP I, 8

DATES		LENGTH HULL	LENGTH DECK	LENGTH KEEL	BEAM	DEPTH	DRAFT	TONNAGE B. M.
fl. 1760	ESTIMATED	72	58	46	25	11	12	96

NEWBURYPORT SHIP II, 12

DATES		LENGTH HULL	LENGTH DECK	LENGTH KEEL	BEAM	DEPTH	DRAFT	TONNAGE B. M.
1752-?	ESTIMATED	99	77	61	25	14	13	170

At the Peabody Museum at Salem is an extraordinary punchbowl, dated 1752 and titled "A Ship at Lanch [sic] Jonathan Greenleaf." It was sent by an Edinburgh, Scotland, merchant to Jonathan Greenleaf, a well-known shipwright of Newburyport, Massachusetts. It depicts a three-masted ship about to be launched, and she is pierced by fourteen gunports.

Jonathan Greenleaf (almost a quarter-century later, the Newburyport firm of Greenleaf & Cross was to build the frigates *Boston* and *Hancock* for the Continental Navy) was probably typical of American shipwrights in that they frequently built a ship with no special customer in mind, in the hopes of selling it in Britain. Occasionally, a grateful British shipowner would order another ship from the same yard, and I assume that this punchbowl represents such a second transaction. A Scottish merchant from Edinburgh presumably ordered a second ship from Greenleaf, and arranged for a sketch of the launching of that ship to be worked onto a punchbowl which he then sent to Greenleaf. Of course, it is entirely possible that the punchbowl sketch represents no more than a British artist's impression of the launching of a ship, and of no particular ship at that. However, the ship in the picture looks quite similar to other New England-built vessels of the period, so we can not be far amiss in including it in this book.

The ship has the usual lion figurehead, quarter galleries, and an unusual rail for the quarterdeck; this rail steps up partway along the quarterdeck as if it were to accommodate a poop, but it is by no means high enough for a poop. Either the Great Cabin was given a foot of extra headroom or the helmsman was given more protection against the weather.

A Newburyport ship, from a British porcelain punchbowl, 1752, Peabody Museum, Salem.

NEWFOUNDLAND PINK

DATES	LENGTH HULL	LENGTH DECK	LENGTH KEEL	BEAM	DEPTH	DRAFT	TONNAGE B. M.
fl. ca. 1750	49	40	—	13	—	—	35

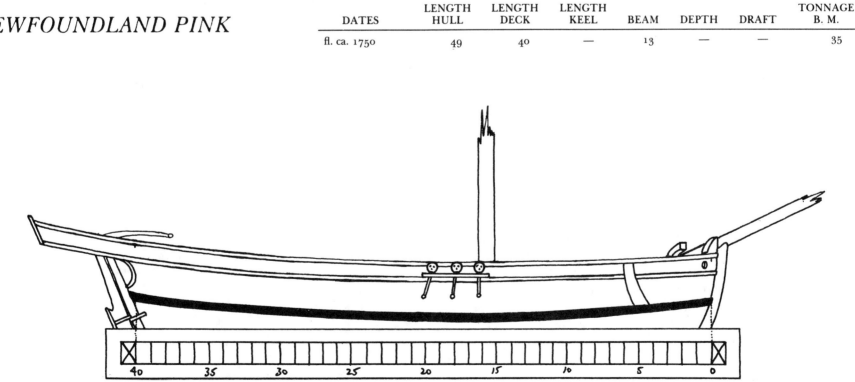

Bilander, ship and pink at a Newfoundland fishing station, anonymous 18th-century oil painting, private collection.

NEWFOUNDLAND PINK

THERE is a semiprimitive oil painting of three vessels anchored in a bay on the Newfoundland coast with a fourth vessel mostly out of the picture. Experts believe the scene to represent New England vessels from the cod fisheries about 1760; hundreds of cod were shown stretched out in the foreground to dry in the sun. The largest of these three vessels was ship-rigged. She could have passed as a typical merchant ship with no windows on the quarter, but a full head, and raised forecastle and quarterdeck.

The second vessel was rigged as a bilander (almost the same as a brig or a snow), and she had a full head,

a raised quarterdeck, and windows on the quarter.

The third vessel was a pink with a sloop or cutter rig. A pink had an unusual stern that projected abaft the rudder to a narrow, high transom. Pinks were very popular among fishermen (see the section on the ship *Diligence*) because of their sea-keeping qualities. Like a modern canoe-stern, the pink stern harmlessly dispersed the dangerous forces in following waves, forces that occasionally inflicted serious damage on vessels with broad sterns. The pink in the painting may have done most of the actual fishing while the ship and the bilander may have been present merely to transport the dried fish back to Boston or some other major port.

NIEUW AMSTERDAM YACHT; NEW YORK YACHT

NEW YORK, once known as Nieuw Amsterdam, was the largest and most important city in the Dutch possessions in seventeenth-century America. It would be fairly natural, then, for Dutch concepts of ship design to wield considerable influence in New York, even after the British had taken over the city from the Dutch. The most obviously Dutch feature that can be noticed in local vessels in pictures of seventeenth-century New York is the concept of the *Staten Jacht;* this was a sloop with a large and high cabin in the stern. We have chosen one of many from old views of the city, a yacht from a picture dated 1661. Judging from the picture, which is unfortunately rather primitive, the yacht was quite small, although she could have been slightly bigger than we have drawn her. It would have been possible to make comfortable overnight passages on this yacht, but the next one we have chosen, from a 1679 picture, was smaller, with no large cabin, so she would have been used strictly as a day-sailer. She was also rigged as a sloop:

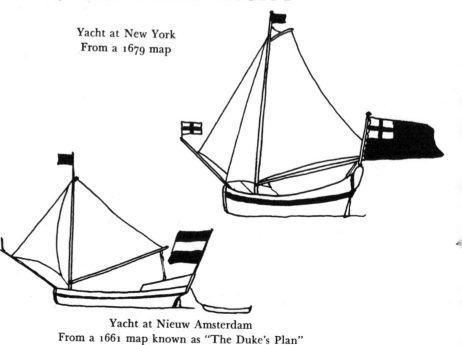

Yacht at New York
From a 1679 map

Yacht at Nieuw Amsterdam
From a 1661 map known as "The Duke's Plan"

226

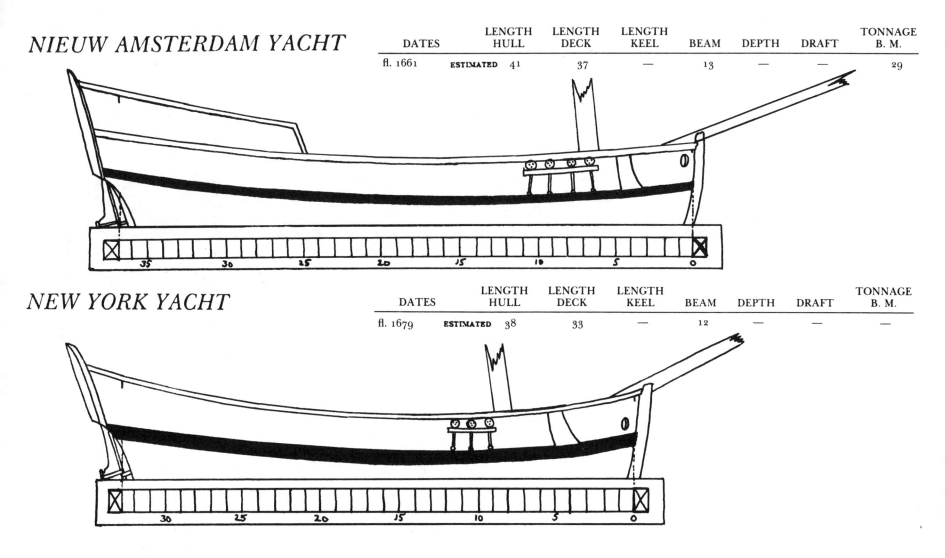

NIEUW AMSTERDAM YACHT

DATES		LENGTH HULL	LENGTH DECK	LENGTH KEEL	BEAM	DEPTH	DRAFT	TONNAGE B. M.
fl. 1661	ESTIMATED	41	37	—	13	—	—	29

NEW YORK YACHT

DATES		LENGTH HULL	LENGTH DECK	LENGTH KEEL	BEAM	DEPTH	DRAFT	TONNAGE B. M.
fl. 1679	ESTIMATED	38	33	—	12	—	—	—

RHODE ISLAND SHIP, 16

IT was a fairly common practice to paint an impressive ship in the background of the portrait of a prosperous eighteenth-century American merchant, and many such ship pictures survive. Because of lack of space on the canvas the majority of them are shown with stern-on-views, which tells us little about the ships, and those with broadside views are too distant and vague in most cases to enable us to reconstruct them.

However, there is one early portrait in the Newport Historical Society of Benjamin Ellery, Senior, executed about 1720, showing a fine privateer ship in the background. Most Rhode Island vessels in the Colonial period were sloops of up to 100 tons or so, but there were occasional ships as well, and this one was armed with 14 guns and also could be rowed with five oars per side. She had the characteristic stern and quarter galleries found on British ships of about the year 1700. Another painting, a view of Newport Harbor in 1740, shows an almost identical ship, and it may in fact be the same ship.

Rhode Island ship, detail of anonymous oil portrait of Benjamin Ellery, Sr., ca. 1720, Newport Historical Society, Newport, RI.

RHODE ISLAND SHIP, 16

DATES	LENGTH HULL	LENGTH DECK	LENGTH KEEL	BEAM	DEPTH	DRAFT	TONNAGE B. M.
fl. ca. 1720 ESTIMATED 91	76	63	24	11	10	180

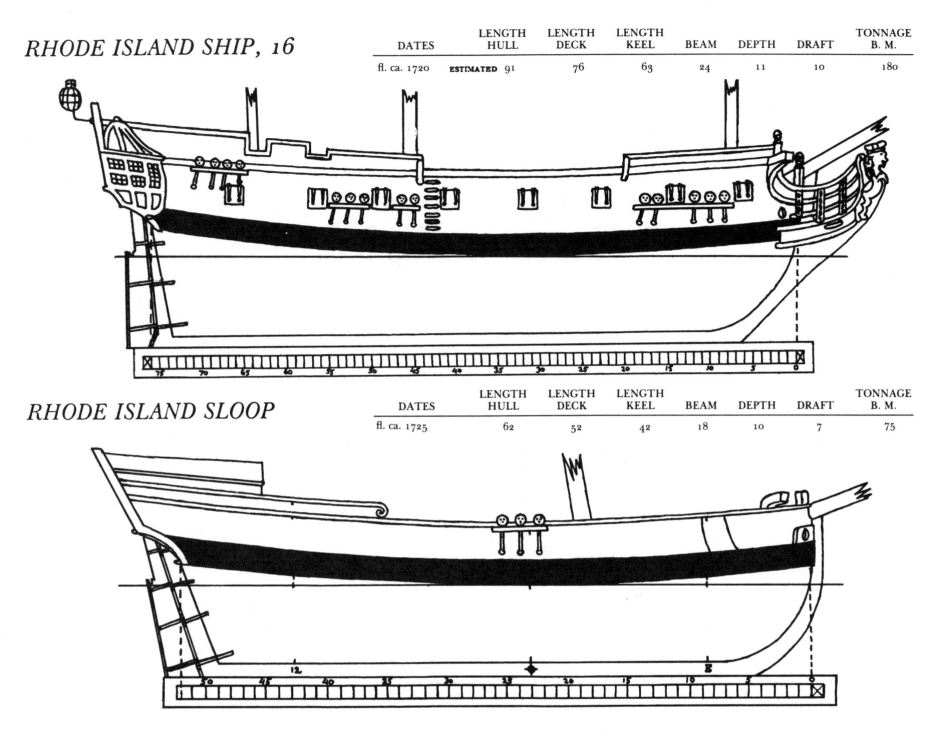

RHODE ISLAND SLOOP

DATES	LENGTH HULL	LENGTH DECK	LENGTH KEEL	BEAM	DEPTH	DRAFT	TONNAGE B. M.
fl. ca. 1725	62	52	42	18	10	7	75

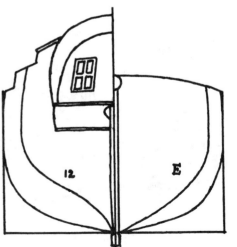

RHODE ISLAND SLOOP

IN 1977, house-restorer Robert Baker discovered a plank on the attic floor of a house in Warren, Rhode Island built in the 1740s. The plank was clearly scribed on its underside with the design of an early sloop, even though the wood had slightly distorted the design over the years. The late William A. Baker (no relation) wrote about the find in the *American Neptune* and published the design. The design is reproduced here, but with the part above the wale reconstructed; evidently, the builder did not need to draw for himself what he intended to build above the level of the wale. The drawing, which is typical of many colonial sloops built from New Hampshire to Jamaica, is probably the earliest surviving builder's draft of an American vessel. Baker thought it was drawn about 1725.

228

Two Rhode Island sloops, *Racehorse* of Providence and *Robin* of Newport, watercolors by Ashley Bowen ca. 1750, Peabody Museum, Salem.

RONSON SHIP (MORTIMER?)

Late in 1981, the ground was being excavated for a new skyscraper at 175 Water Street, New York City when a ship was discovered. The developer, an Englishman named Ronson, quickly called in a team of archaeologists led by Warren Riess and his wife Sheli from Maine, and gave them 30 days to excavate whatever they needed. At great expense to himself, Ronson extended the deadline for a further 30 days. The diggers had time to measure almost the entire ship and to save the bow section; to save the whole ship would have cost over $5 million additional and taken several more months. They discovered that the ship had been built in the Chesapeake Bay area because of the types of oak and pine used in it, and that it had been sunk as part of a landfill operation to extend the shores of Manhattan about 1740-1756. Various items datable to the 1740s were found in her, including a pile of rejected shoes that had fallen through into her hold from a cobbler's shop built on her deck; miraculously, foundation walls built over her deck without any shoring had never collapsed! The researchers also discovered from the types of teredo worms in the wood that the ship had sailed in the Caribbean, down the east coast of South America and possibly to Europe. Her hold was arranged in such a way that she would have been suited to carry hogsheads of tobacco, but not slaves.

The ship appeared to have been built about 1730. Researchers guessed that the shipwright had been trained in England and that he had not been in America long enough to acquire any bad habits. A number of interesting features were found: the principal hatch had no ladder, but what is called a monkey-pole instead; the panelling in the great cabin was tongue-in-groove; and the framing in the bow was surprisingly not like the cant frames found on many warships of the period, but instead bevelled transverse frames marched all the way up the stem in the manner of twentieth-century wooden fishing-dragger construction in New England and Maritime Canada.

When no New York museum stepped forward to guarantee the money necessary to conserve the pieces of the bow, the project was handed over to the Mariners Museum, Newport News, Virginia, where the pieces are presently being soaked in preservative solutions. The preserved section is to be re-assembled for permanent display in a few years, and it will stand 16 feet high, 18 feet wide and 20 feet long, one of the most valuable artifacts on view anywhere from the eigtheenth century. The plan shown here, adapted by the author, is courtesy of Warren and Sheli Riess and the Mariners Museum, from whom more detailed plans may be purchased.

It should be noted that since the lower part of the island of Manhattan has been greatly expanded by means of landfill almost from its earliest years of settlement, the Ronson Ship is not the only buried treasure in the area. Using tired old ships as bulkheads in order to fill in the space between the ships and the former shoreline is an old practice used around the world. The remains of ships from the Gold Rush days are occasionally being found in parts of San Francisco. While it is greatly to Mr. Ronson's credit that he took the trouble to have his ship properly investigated, it is a minor tragedy that all the other hulls unearthed in Manhattan have been quickly and quietly destroyed. At the construction site of the World Trade Center, several ships, including some from the seventeenth century, were discovered and mercilessly demolished as quickly as possible for fear that the interests of archaeologists might cause delays and thus add to the cost of the building. At least in this case, the interests of archaeologists can be clearly seen to be in tune with rest of the world, and the developers of the World Trade Center should hang their heads in shame.

	DATES	LENGTH HULL	LENGTH DECK	LENGTH KEEL	BEAM	DEPTH	DRAFT	TONNAGE B. M.
	ca. 1730-ca. 1745	93	77	65	27	11	12	200

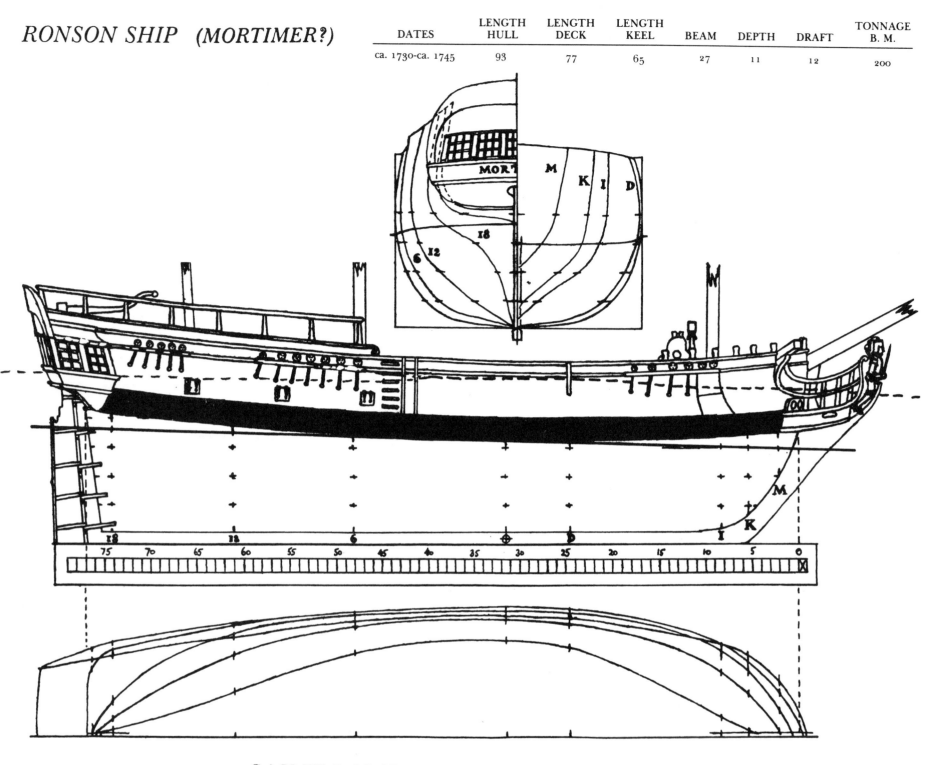

SAINT LAWRENCE RIVER GALLEYS, 1

BY 1759, due to the brilliant campaigning of James Wolfe and Jeffery Amherst, the British had captured both Louisbourg and Quebec from the French, and Montreal was the only large French settlement remaining in the northeast. Amherst carefully planned a joint attack on Montreal, with one force coming upriver from Quebec and another coming downriver from Lake Ontario. In 1760, with advice from Thomas Davies, an artist who was serving as an officer of Royal Artillery, Amherst built at least four sloop-rigged row galleys, with which he hoped he could sweep away any resistance on the St. Lawrence between Lake Ontario and Montreal. This proved to be prudent, for the French were waiting for him at Fort La Galette (now Ogdensburg, New York) with the 18-gun brig *L'Outaouaise*. Although

each galley had no more than one twelve-pounder and some swivels, their superior maneuverability enabled them to capture the brig, and Montreal surrendered shortly after without firing a shot. Davies commanded one of the galleys.

Davies painted a charming picture of the engagement with *L'Outaouaise,* now at the National Gallery of Canada in Ottawa, but the picture shows little in the way of detail on the galleys. However, Davies also painted a sketch-portrait of one of the galleys with all sails set (now in the Public Archives of Canada), which, although it contains some obvious inaccuracies, is fairly useful in reconstructing the general appearance of Amherst's galleys. They had ports for as many as eleven oars a side, but the painting of the battle shows that only

SAINT LAWRENCE RIVER GALLEYS, 1

DATES		LENGTH HULL	LENGTH DECK	LENGTH KEEL	BEAM	DEPTH	DRAFT	TONNAGE B. M.
1760-?	ESTIMATED	61	50	45	14	4	4	30

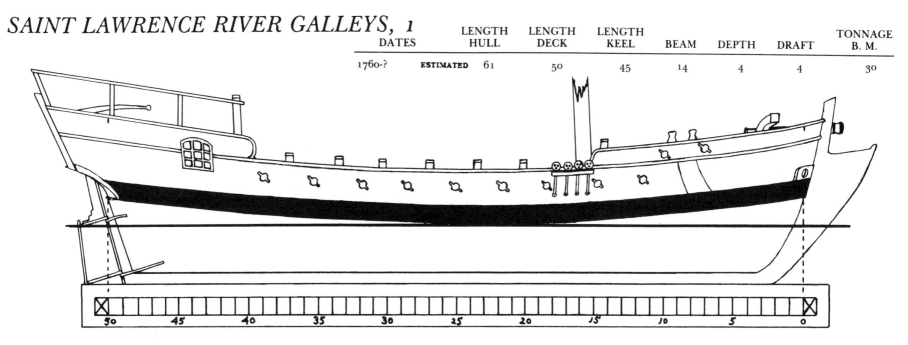

about six or seven of those were normally in use. The galleys had a small, raised quarterdeck aft, under which was a cabin with a large window on each side. On the raised forecastle was mounted the large cannon, which fired through a port cut slightly to the left of the stem.

There were stocks for eight swivels on each side along the waist. The rig was simple: a gaff mainsail could be extended with a triangular studdingsail, and there was only one jib, set on the forestay which led to the stem; no bowsprit was indicated, although one could have been fitted.

SALEM SHIP, 12

DATES		LENGTH HULL	LENGTH DECK	LENGTH KEEL	BEAM	DEPTH	DRAFT	TONNAGE B. M.
fl. ca. 1750	ESTIMATED	86	71	54	23	10	11	130

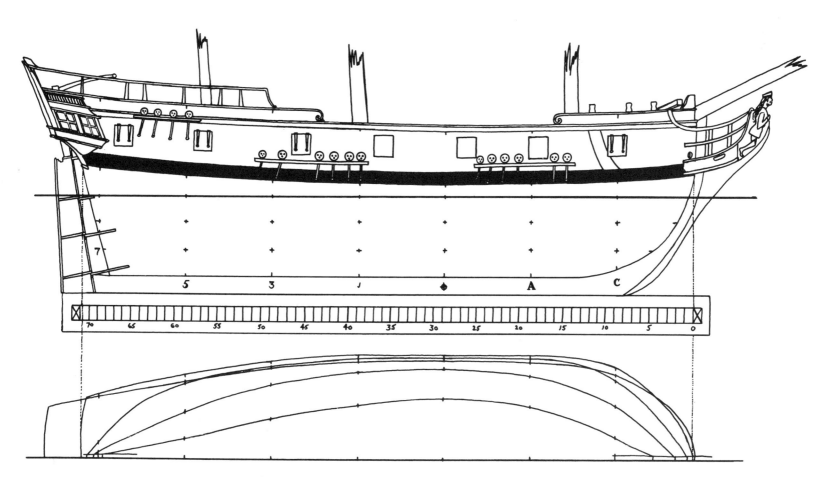

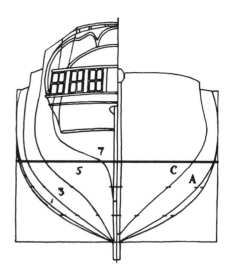

SALEM SHIP, 12

AT the Peabody Museum at Salem, Massachusetts, is a contemporary model of a 12-gun merchant ship of about 1750. The model may not be terribly accurate in some respects, particularly the deadrise of the midship section, which seems excessive. This ship had a raised quarterdeck and forecastle, and quarter galleries. She could well have served as a useful letter-of-marque during the Seven Years' War. The model had no scale marked on it, so we have calculated our own scale, based primarily on the size and spacing of the gunports. If our calculations are correct, this ship was small to be ship-rigged, although not as small as the Newburyport ship.

SALEM SLOOP

DATES	LENGTH HULL	LENGTH DECK	LENGTH KEEL	BEAM	DEPTH	DRAFT	TONNAGE B. M.
fl. ca. 1770	ESTIMATED 63	55	44	22	13	12	80

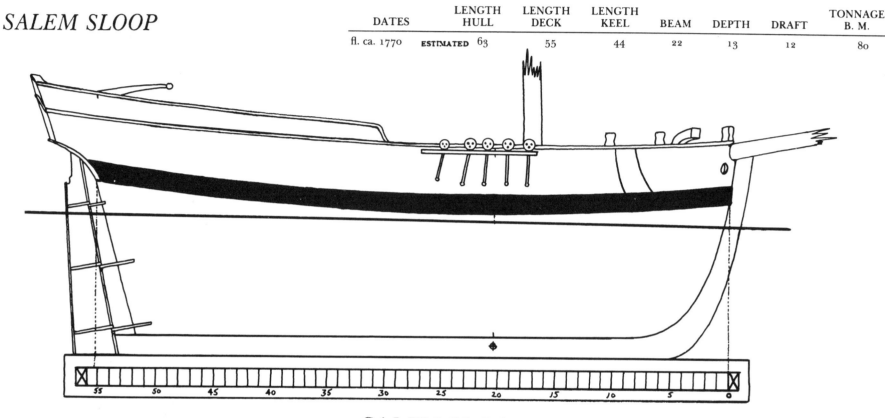

SALEM SLOOP

ONE of the models of early American ships at the Peabody Museum at Salem, Massachusetts, is an eighteenth-century unarmed sloop. The model was apparently used as a child's toy and could be sailed, but it is now minus its rig, its rudder, and any details of interest. Because this sloop at least reflects the general appearance of New England sloops of the mid-eighteenth century, and may even represent a specific vessel that was perhaps owned by the child's father, we have decided to include a profile of it in this book. We were not able to spend enough time with the model to take off its complete lines, and the inexact nature of the model made it seem not worth our while returning to investigate it further, especially since it was not on regular display and not readily accessible. There was no scale attached to the model, so we have reconstructed it as best we could.

SOUTH CAROLINA SCHOONER

THE so-called Ronson Ship, uncovered at the construction site of a New York skyscraper in 1981-2, represents an ocean-going American ship of about 1730. In 1976, archaeologists from the University of South Carolina raised the remains of a river craft of about the same date at Brown's Ferry on the Black River, South Carolina. The double-ended, two-masted vessel had a cargo of 25 tons of bricks when she sank. Perhaps her most unusual feature is her keel, which widens amidships until it is one third the width of the entire vessel. She was schooner-rigged, for her mainmast amidships was much larger in diameter than her foremast, but what kind of sails were fitted—whether gaff sails, gunter sails, sprit sails or triangular Bermudian sails—can not be determined. Also, because the top of the stem was missing it remains unknown whether she had a bowsprit. She could presumably have also been propelled by oars.

J. Richard Steffy wrote the report on the recovery and drew a reconstruction of her lines, which have been adapted for this book (much of the topsides were missing).

The vessel itself has been preserved and is to be on display at Georgetown, South Carolina. David M. Brewer has supplied valuable information.

SOUTH CAROLINA SCHOONER

DATES	LENGTH HULL	LENGTH DECK	LENGTH KEEL	BEAM	DEPTH	DRAFT	TONNAGE B. M.
fl. ca. 1740	55	50	43	14	4	3	30

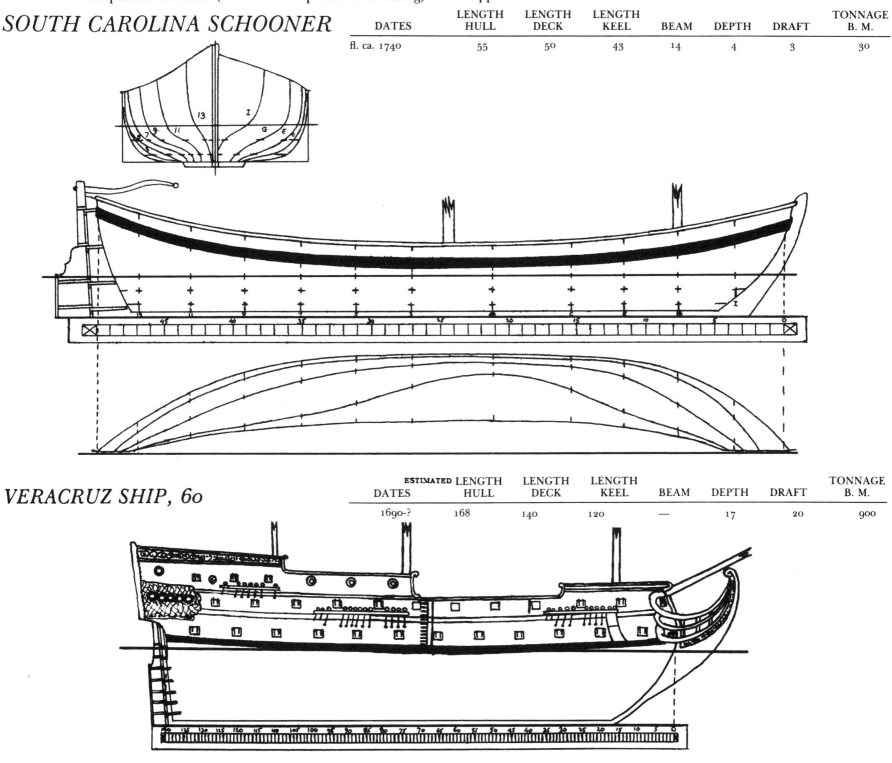

VERACRUZ SHIP, 60

ESTIMATED DATES	LENGTH HULL	LENGTH DECK	LENGTH KEEL	BEAM	DEPTH	DRAFT	TONNAGE B. M.
1690-?	168	140	120	—	17	20	900

VERACRUZ SHIP, 60

This book contains a number of formidable warships built for the Spanish Navy at Havana, Cuba. In fact, a third of the Spanish Navy's ships in the eighteenth century were built at Havana, due to the abundance of Cuban mahogany, the finest shipbuilding timber then available anywhere in the world; this species of tree is unfortunately extinct today, because no replanting program was ever undertaken. Forests of less suitable but adequate timber were also available to the Spanish throughout Central America, and one important shipyard was established at Veracruz, Mexico to make use of that timber.

Dr. Douglas Inglis of Seville, Spain, has kindly supplied a copy of a profile drawing of a 60-gun ship built at Veracruz in 1690. Her name and subsequent history is unknown, but it is possible that the drawing represents a ship called *Nuestra Señora de Guadalupe*, flagship of the Spanish Caribbean squadron (known as the Armada de Barlovento).

Her lower-deck guns are uncomfortably close to the waterline, and her excessive beam combined with her square-tuck stern would have made her very slow and unweatherly. Her narrow, high poop recalls designs of 50 and 100 years earlier. The upper part of her stem slopes aft in order to provide a plane of planking best suited for placement of bow-chaser cannons.

VIRGINIA SCHOONER I, 12

IN David Steel's book *Elements and Practice of Naval Architecture* (published 1805) are the offsets and specifications for "a fast-sailing schooner" obviously of American build, and Chapelle thinks she was a privateer built possibly before the end of the American Revolution. Chapelle redrew her from the table of offsets, and we have made our drawing based on his. She was lightly built, with open rails instead of bulwarks, and truly looked forward to the era of the Baltimore clipper schooners. She had moderate deadrise, sharp lines, raked stem and sternpost, and a square-tuck stern. She may have been owned by the French and captured from them by the British in the early 1790s, for Steel usually obtained his plans from the Admiralty and the Admiralty was not then enlightened enough to look for such a schooner to purchase, even if they did not mind capturing one. There is no Admiralty record, however, among the incomplete lists of captures made by ships of the Royal Navy, of the capture of a schooner that matches these dimensions. She would have been very fast, as long as she was not overloaded, which would have been all too easy to do. She was rather long for a schooner rig in this period, most being under 70 feet in deck length. She could carry 12 light carriage guns.

VIRGINIA SCHOONER I, 12

DATES	LENGTH HULL	LENGTH DECK	LENGTH KEEL	BEAM	DEPTH	DRAFT	TONNAGE B. M.
ca. 1785	85	77	50	20	8	9	140

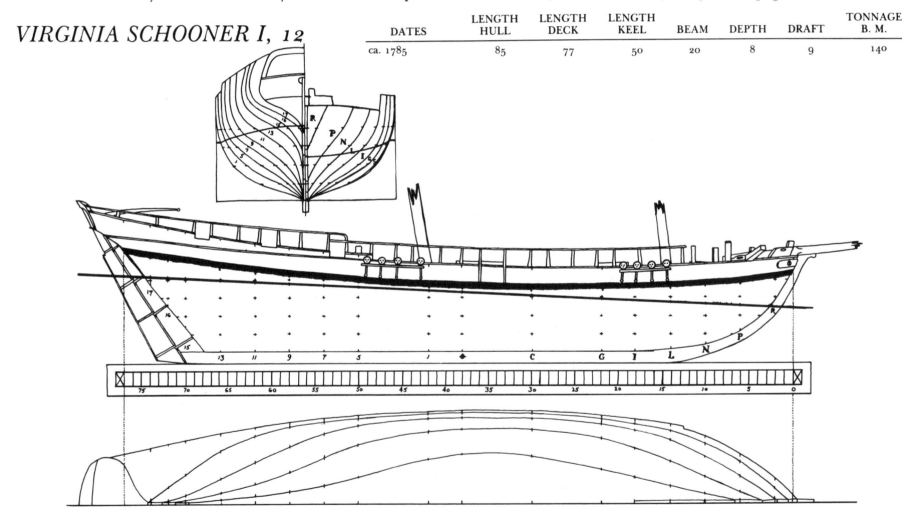

VIRGINIA SCHOONER II, 12

DAVID STEEL, an Admiralty agent and publisher in the 1790s and early 1800s, wrote a number of books about design and construction of ships. In one of these, *Elements and Practice of Naval Architecture* (1805), he included the draft for an American privateer schooner of 12 light carriage guns and 10 swivels. This was a fast-looking design which Steel claimed had come from Virginia, but the word Virginia was always used rather loosely, so we may safely assume this schooner was from the Chesapeake Bay region in the period 1781–1789. The schooner was apparently owned for a while by the French and was captured by the British around 1793, although no record can be found of a captured vessel of her dimensions. She had very sharp lines

and considerable deadrise, low freeboard, and quite a
bit of sheer. Her stern was a square tuck, and her stem
was sharply raked.

VIRGINIA SCHOONER II, 12

DATES	LENGTH HULL	LENGTH DECK	LENGTH KEEL	BEAM	DEPTH	DRAFT	TONNAGE B. M.
ca. 1785	87	78	61	22	9	12	158

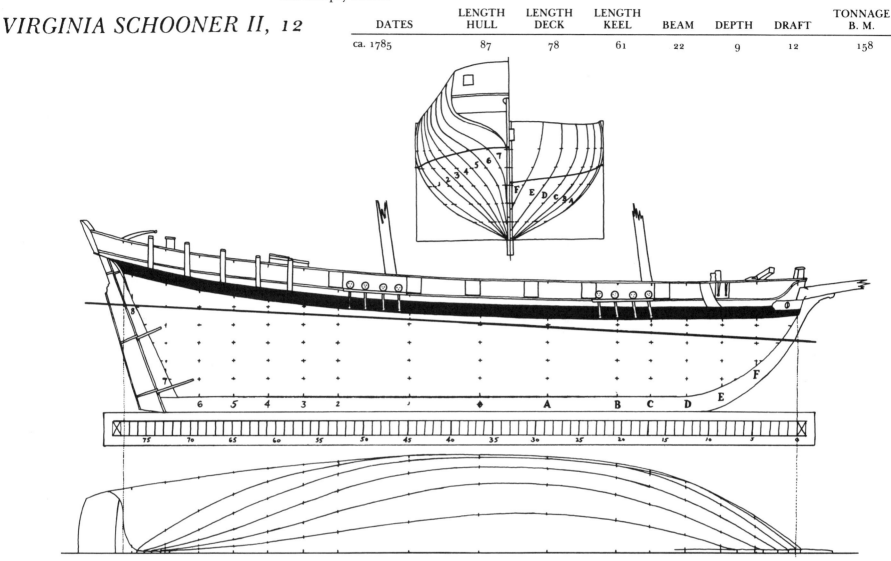

VIRGINIA SLOOP, 6

THE late Howard Chapelle of the Smithsonian Institution was often searching through European
archives in search of records of American ships. One
design that he and his researchers found that was not
included in any of his books was that of a 6-gun fast
sloop built in Virginia or the Chesapeake area in 1768.
He apparently obtained the lines from a Dutch copy of
a French drawing, and a model of her was subsequently
made for the Smithsonian. Presumably she had been
purchased by the French shortly after she was built.

She appears to be a transitional design, somewhere
between the sloop *Mediator* and the Bermuda sloop of
Chapman, on the one hand, and the two Virginia schooners found in Steel's book, on the other hand. She had
the standard aft cabin with rounded roof found on the
earlier designs, and she had the lower freeboard, steep
deadrise, and sharp lines of the later designs. She had
four gunports and four posts for swivel guns on each
side. She also had oarports of a special design that enabled the blade to be retracted only at a certain
angle; this caused less wear on the oars than the more
normal square oarports. She was steered with a wheel,

as were most small vessels with a high aft cabin. Numerous contemporary pictures show similar sloops in
the Chesapeake, Bermuda, Jamaica, and all over the
West Indies, so this sloop was far from unusual.

Two Virginia sloops on the York River, anonymous watercolor,
1755.

DATES	LENGTH HULL	LENGTH DECK	LENGTH KEEL	BEAM	DEPTH	DRAFT	TONNAGE B. M.
1768-?	54	49	41	16	6	8	42

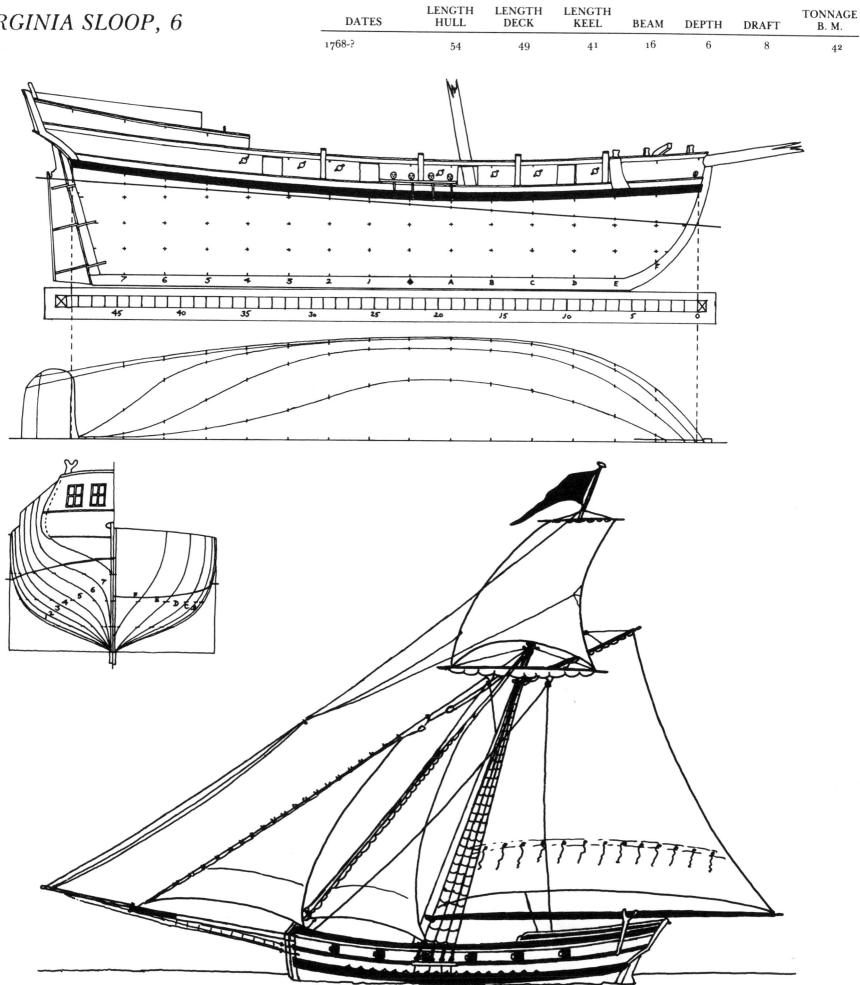

Armed Virginia sloop, 1779, sketch by Karzhavine, Soviet National Archives, Moscow.

WHALE BOAT

Nineteenth-century whaling is identified with Nantucket, New Bedford and other New England ports as much as nineteenth-century cowboys are identified with Texas and other parts of the Old West. While the New England whalers of that period may have been the most prolific practitioners of that art, pelagic whaling in American waters had been conducted by European ships perhaps before Columbus came to the West Indies (Captain John Lloyd of Bristol, England is now known to have reached Newfoundland and returned in 1483, nine-years before Columbus' first voyage to America, and Lloyd is believed to have done no more than follow fishermen and whalers who already frequented those waters). The whaling industry developed a special type of rowing-boat for assisting the mother-ship and for shore-based whaling. These whaleboats were double-ended and lightly-built so they could be easily hoisted aboard or ashore. Whaleboats were also used as coastal privateers to waylay unarmed merchantships during the Revolution, particularly in Long Island Sound.

Paul Dudley wrote in 1725,

I would take notice of the Boats our Whale-men use in going from the Shoar after the Whale. They are made of Cedar Clapboards, and so very light that two Men can conveniently carry them, yet they are twenty Feet long, and carry Six Men. . . .

Later in the century, whaleboats were described as anywhere from 24 to 32 feet long, and even one as big as 42 feet. Chapman shows plans for a 24-foot whaleboat and Steel shows one of 33 feet, but there is no indication that these were American. Henry Hall's *Report on the Ship-Building Industry of the United States*, 1882, shows the profile of a 1789 whaleboat that, unlike its nineteenth-century descendant, had a skeg and rudder; a 1760 engraving of military operations on Lake George shows boats of the same shape. Such boats could rig one or two masts when convenient for sailing, but oars were their primary motive power. The 1789 drawing has been adapted here.

WHALE BOAT

DATES	LENGTH HULL	LENGTH DECK	LENGTH KEEL	BEAM	DEPTH	DRAFT	TONNAGE B. M.
fl. 1789	ESTIMATED 26	24	15	6	—	2	—

APPENDIX
The Founding of the Continental Navy

MUCH ink has been spilled over the years about how, where and by whom the Continental Navy was founded. Since readers of this book may be interested in getting to the bottom of the controversy, this brief account is being included in the Appendix.

Some say that the Navy was founded on Lake Champlain on 18 May 1775, when Ethan Allen and Benedict Arnold pressed into service the yacht *Katharine*, the British armed sloop *George* and the armed schooner *Royal Savage*. However, Arnold and Allen were acting only on behalf of the Province of Massachusetts that had commissioned them (in spite of the quotation attributed to Allen at the capture of Fort Ticonderoga: "In the name of the great Jehovah and the Continental Congress."). The only conclusion is that Massachusetts thereby was the first of the Colonies to acquire a navy during the Revolution.

Another claim has been advanced on behalf of the event at Machias, Maine on 12 June 1775, when an *ad hoc* group of locals chased and captured the small British survey schooner *Margaretta*. This may have been the first actual battle on the sea, but the American forces involved had no Congressional authorization and regarded themselves as Massachusetts militia and volunteers.

Others say that the commissioning of the armed fishing schooner *Hannah* by George Washington on 2 September 1775 was the start of the Continental Navy, either at Marblehead or Beverly, Massachusetts. Because Washington was behind this little naval force it was legally a Continental entity, but Washington's commission was solely an army affair. Thus, to be precise, Washington's schooners were a naval force under the jurisdiction of the Continental Army and were not the Continental Navy, in much the same way as today's U. S. Army or Navy helicopters are not part of the Air Force.

The Continental Navy could be founded only by an act of the Continental Congress, and Congress acted on 13 October 1775. The story of how this came to happen is exciting but not widely known, and its seeds were sown over a century earlier.

Shortly after Charles II was restored to his father's throne in 1660, he was confronted by petitioners from Connecticut and Rhode Island who were asking him to grant their respective Colonies new charters that would give them both freedom of religion and political freedom to elect all their own public officials including the governor. Charles granted both petitions, but until 1776 these were the only self-governing colonies in the world.

Connecticut did nothing unusual with its special freedom, but the people in Rhode Island ("Rogue's Island," as many of its neighbors called it) soon found a way to take advantage of their situation. Under the charter, the king's customs inspectors were to be appointed by the governor, not by officials in London. If the governor wanted to be re-elected, he would appoint customs men who would always look the other way when smugglers arrived.

The greatest opportunity to profit from smuggling was offered by the French islands in the West Indies, whose principal crop was sugar-cane. When sugar is refined, quantities of molasses remain as a by-product, and in those days molasses was good for little but distilling into rum. However, the French government forbade the manufacture of rum for fear that the French brandy industry would suffer. The créole planters therefore were delighted to be able to sell their molasses cheaply to Rhode Island merchants.

British law said that British colonies were permitted to import molasses and rum (and most other West Indian goods) only from British islands like Jamaica, and the monopolistic Jamaican planters confidently held their prices high.

Rhode Island merchants bought all the molasses that Saint Domingue (now Haiti) could produce, imported it past the "blind" Rhode Island customs officers and distilled it into poor-quality rum. The rum was used primarily in the export trade. It was sent duty-free to all the other British colonies in North America to be used as a food-preservative (meat, fish, fruit, vegetables and even baked goods could be stored indefinitely in a barrel of rum), and it was also used in Africa as a medium of exchange to buy slaves; the slaves were taken to Haiti to be exchanged for more molasses, and thus the notorious Triangle Trade was conducted. Rhode Island's trade with Saint-Domingue also gave her the opportunity to import quantities of the excellent island mahogany that is now extinct. While Havana shipyards were building hundreds of long-lasting warships out of this wood, Newport Quaker cabinet-makers of the Townsend and Goddard families fashioned some of America's finest furniture from it.

For the most part, British officials ignored Rhode Island's smuggling while Newport grew into one of America's richest cities as a result. After all, Rhode Island appeared as no more than a fly-speck on a map of the vast British dominions, and the man in charge of the Royal Navy for many years was Sir Charles Wager, who had been brought up in Newport and therefore presumably counselled restraint. The problem arose when Britain and France found themselves embroiled in the Seven Years' War (1756-1763). Rhode Island's dilemma was whether to continue trading with French colonies and be condemned as traitors or to take part in the war against the French as vigorously as possible in the hope that the war would end before Rhode Island was financially ruined.

In the event, Rhode Island did both at once. British officials were full of praise for the unusually large number of French ships captured by Rhode Island privateers, but they were appalled when they found out the reason behind the captures.

In the eighteenth century, prisoners of war could be repatriated at any time on a special ship designated by a governor as a Cartel. Cartels were by international agreement exempt from capture. To make it an economic proposition, cartel ships were permitted to pick up a cargo at an enemy port while delivering or picking up prisoners, and this was not considered to be equivalent to the traitorous act of trading with the enemy. Of course, it was normally expected that about 200 prisoners would be shipped on a single cartel ship, but Governor Stephen Hopkins of Rhode Island could find nothing in the law that prevented him from issuing permits to 200 cartels each to carry one prisoner! In fact, more than a few Rhode Island ships sailed to Haiti on the off-chance that when they arrived there they would find one or more English or American prisoners who would like a ride to Rhode Island, and in the hope that the governor of Cap François would designate them as cartels.

By this extraordinary method, Hopkins was able to preserve the Rhode Island economy that depended so heavily on smuggling, but as soon as the war was over the British government took its revenge. The maritime trade laws were severely tightened, and enforcement was taken out of the hands of the Rhode Island customs officers by the simple expedient of having ships of the Royal Navy intercept all merchant ships before they could arrive in Newport Harbor.

Once again, economic ruin was staring Rhode Island in the face, and once again Governor Stephen Hopkins took extraordinary measures to come to the rescue. The warship that was intercepting smugglers off Newport was the schooner *Saint John*, and in an incident more fully described in the text about *Gaspee* and *Saint John*, Hopkins in effect ordered the first shots of the Revolution to be fired against the schooner on 9 July 1764.

In spite of the *Saint John* incident, the Royal Navy continued to try to stop the smugglers. In 1765, angry Newporters seized and burned the British schooner *Maidstone Tender*, and in 1769 they did the same to the sloop *Liberty*. The British reaction was remarkably restrained until a Providence mob burned the Royal Navy's schooner *Gaspee* in 1772. When their vindictive enquiry into the *Gaspee* affair failed to obtain the desired result, the British decided to send a much bigger ship to Newport to intercept the smugglers, the 24-gun frigate *Rose*, which arrived shortly before Christmas 1774. They hoped she would be large enough to avoid the fate of her predecessors. *Rose*, under Commodore Sir James Wallace, and occasional consorts did their job so well that by the summer of 1775 four-fifths of the population of Newport had been forced to depart due to unemployment, so heavily dependent upon smuggling was her economy.

In August, the Rhode Island General Assembly voted to ask Congress to establish a national navy to get rid of *Rose*, so Hopkins introduced the bill the moment Congress reconvened from its recess. After minor rewriting in committee, the bill passed on 13 October 1775. Congress then asked Stephen Hopkins to pick the right man to be commander-in-chief of the Continental Navy, and his first choice was Lieutenant Jahleel Brenton of Newport, the highest-ranking American officer then serving in the Royal Navy; the *Dictionary of National Biography* reports that Brenton declined, possibly because he valued his existing job-security; Brenton later became an admiral. Hopkins then turned to his own brother Esek Hopkins, a widely-respected seafarer who unfortunately had little experience in military matters.

For a variety of reasons, including the fact that nearly all his papers were destroyed in the great flood of the 1815

Governor Stephen Hopkins, founder of the Continental Navy and the Continental Congress, after Trumbull; sketch in the Charles Allen Munn Collection, Fordham University Library, Bronx, NY.

hurricane, Stephen Hopkins has generally not been given credit for founding the Continental Navy, nor, for that matter, for all the other work he did towards independence. For example, he was the founder of the Stamp Act Congress in 1765, of the Committees of Correspondence in 1773 as a continent-wide reaction to the illegal actions of the British commission investigating the *Gaspee* incident, and of the Continental Congress itself in 1774 in reaction to the British closure of the port of Boston after the Boston Tea Party. In fact, Hopkins has been so little studied that it was only as recently as 1971 that a documented portrait of him by Trumbull has been found (by Professor Irma Jaffe of Fordham University), proving that the man in the Quaker hat at the back of the room in Trumbull's famous picture of the Signing of the Declaration of Independence was not Hopkins at all, but John Dickinson; Hopkins, as befitted a man of his accomplishments, was seated in the front row. It should also be noted that in addition to his other achievements, Stephen Hopkins was the founder of the United States Post Office, and yet no postage stamp has ever been issued to honor his memory—perhaps readers can petition to have this oversight redressed.

Selected Bibliography

Books

Albion, Robert Greenhalgh. *Forests and Sea Power: The Timber Problem of the Royal Navy, 1652–1862.* Cambridge, Mass.: Harvard University Press, 1926.

Allen, Gardner W. *A Naval History of the American Revolution.* 2 vols. Williamstown, Mass.: Corner House, 1970.

————. *Massachusetts Privateers of the Revolution. Massachusetts Historical Society Collections,* vol. 77. Boston: Massachusetts Historical Society, 1927.

Archibald, E. H. H. *The Wooden Fighting Ship in the Royal Navy, 897–1860.* London: Blandford, 1968.

Baker, William A. *The Boston Marine Society in the American War for Independence.* Boston: The Boston Marine Society, 1976.

————. *Colonial Vessels.* Barre, Mass.: Barre, 1962.

————. *Sloops & Shallops.* Barre, Mass.: Barre, 1966.

Bird, Harrison. *Navies in the Mountains.* New York: Oxford University Press, 1962.

Boudriot, Jean. *Le Boullongne, Vaisseau de la Compagnie des Indes, 1758.* Paris: A.N.C.R.E., ca.1984.

————. *Le Cerf, 1779-1780.* Paris: A.N.C.R.E., 1982.

————. *Le Vaisseau de 74 Canons.* 4 vols. Grenoble: Éditions des Quatre Seigneurs, 1973-1977.

————. *La Vénus, 1782.* Paris: A.N.C.R.E., ca.1980.

Brewington, M. V. *Shipcarvers of North America.* Barre, Mass.: Barre, 1962; reprint ed., New York: Dover Paperbacks, 1976.

————, and Brewington, Dorothy. *Marine Painting & Drawings in the Peabody Museum.* Salem, Mass.: Peabody Museum, 1968.

Brown, Vaughan W. *Shipping in the Port of Annapolis, 1748–1775.* Annapolis, Md.: Naval Institute Press, 1965.

Bryant, Samuel W. *The Sea and the States.* New York: Thomas Y. Crowell, 1947; paperback ed., 1967.

Chapelle, Howard I. *American Small Sailing Craft.* New York: W. W. Norton & Co., 1951.

————. *The Baltimore Clipper.* 1930. Reprint. New York: Bonanza, 1976.

————. *History of American Sailing Ships.* New York: W. W. Norton & Co., 1935.

————. *History of the American Sailing Navy.* New York: W. W. Norton & Co., 1949.

————. *The Search for Speed Under Sail, 1700–1855.* New York: W. W. Norton & Co., 1967.

Chapman, Henrik Af. *Architectura navalis mercatoria.* 1968. Reprint. New York: Praeger, 1972.

Clark, William Bell. *Ben Franklin's Privateers.* New York: Greenwood, 1969.

————. *Captain Dauntless.* Shreveport, La.: Louisiana State University Press, 1949.

————, and Morgan, William James, et al., eds. *Naval Documents of the American Revolution,* 8 vols. to date. Washington, DC: U.S. Government Printing Office, 1964ff.

Coggins, Jack. *Ships and Seamen of the American Revolution.* Harrisburg, Pa.: Stackpole, 1969.

Colledge, J. J. *Ships of the Royal Navy: An Historical Index.* Vol. 1. Newton Abbott, Devon, England: David & Charles, 1969.

Dickerson, Oliver. *The Navigation Acts and the American Revolution.* 1951. Reprint. Philadelphia: University of Pennsylvania Press, 1974.

Dodds, James, and Moore, James. *Building the Wooden Fighting Ship.* London: Hutchinson, 1984.

Dodge, Ernest S. *Beyond the Capes.* Boston: Little, Brown, 1971.

Dupuy, Trevor N. *The Military History of Revolutionary War Naval Battles.* New York: Franklin Watts, 1970.

Eastman, Ralph M. *Some Famous Privateers of New England.* Boston: State Street Trust Co., 1928.

Eller, Ernest M., ed. *Chesapeake Bay in the American Revolution.* Centreville, MD: Tidewater Publishers, 1981.

Evans, Cerinda W. *Some Notes on Shipbuilding and Shipping in Colonial Virginia.* Newport News, Va.: Mariners Museum, 1957.

Falconer, William. *An Universal Dictionary of the Marine.* London, 1769; reprint ed., Newton Abbott, Devon, England: David & Charles, 1970.

Fowler, William M., Jr. *Rebels Under Sail.* New York: Scribners, 1976.

Fox, Frank. *Great Ships.* London: Conway Maritime Press, 1980.

Gardner, John. *Sail. Warships of the Royal Navy,* vol. 1. London: Evelyn, 1968.

Goldenberg, Joseph A. *Shipbuilding in Colonial America.* Charlottesville, Va.: University of Virginia Press, 1975.

Graham, Gerald S. *The Royal Navy in the War of American Independence.* London: Her Majesty's Stationery Office, 1976.

Grimwood, V. R. *American Ship Models and How to Build Them.* New York: W. W. Norton & Co., 1942.

Harland, John. *Seamanship in the Age of Sail.* London: Conway Maritime Press, 1984.

Henry, John Frazier. *Early Maritime Artists of the Pacific Northwest Coast.* Seattle: University of Washington Press, 1984.

Howard, Frank. *Sailing Ships of War, 1400-1860.* London: Conway Maritime Press, 1979.

Hutchinson, William. *A Treatise on Naval Architecture.* London: 1794; reprint ed., London: Conway Maritime Press, 1969.

Jackson, John W. *The Pennsylvania Navy, 1775–1781.* New Brunswick, N.J.: Rutgers–The State University Press, 1974.

Jackson, Melvin H., and Miller, Helen Hill. *Tobacco and the "Brilliant."* Washington, D.C.: Smithsonian Institution, 1976.

Kaminkow, Marion, and Kaminkow, Jack, eds. *Mariners of the American Revolution.* Baltimore: Magna Carta, 1967.

Laing, Alexander. *American Sail.* New York: E. P. Dutton, 1961.

————. *Seafaring America.* New York: American Heritage, 1974.

Lavery, Brian, *74 Gun Ship Bellona.* London: Conway Maritime Press, 1985.

————. *The Ship of the Line,* 2 vol. London: Conway Maritime Press, 1983.

Lees, James. *The Masting and Rigging of English Ships of War, 1625-1860.* London: Conway Maritime Press, 1979.

Longridge, C. Nepean. *The Anatomy of Nelson's Ships.* London: Percival Marshall, 1955.

MacGregor, David R. *Fast Sailing Ships, 1775–1875*. Lymington, Hampshire, England: Nautical Publishing Co., Ltd., 1973.

————. *Merchant Sailing Ships*. London: Argus Books, 1980.

Mahan, Alfred Thayer. *The Influence of Seapower upon History, 1660–1783*. 1890. Reprint. New York: Hill & Wang, 1957.

————. *The Major Operations of the Navies in the War of American Independence*. Boston: Little, Brown, 1969.

Manning, T. D., and Walker, D. F. *British Warship Names*. London: Putnam, 1959.

Marcus, G. J. *Heart of Oak: A Survey of British Sea Power in the Georgian Era*. London: Oxford University Press, 1975.

McCusker, John J. *Alfred, the First Continental Flagship*. Washington, D.C.: Smithsonian Institution, 1973.

McKee, Christopher. *Edward Preble*. Annapolis, Md.: Naval Institute Press, 1972.

Middlebrook, Louis F. *History of Maritime Connecticut During the American Revolution*. 2 vols. Salem, Mass.: 1925.

Miller, Nathan. *Sea of Glory: The Continental Navy Fights for Independence, 1775–1783*. New York: David McKay, 1974.

Miller, Russell, *The East Indiamen*. Alexandria, VA: Time-Life Books, 1980.

Morgan, William James. *Captains to the Northward*. Barre, Mass.: Barre, 1959.

Morison, Samuel Eliot. *John Paul Jones, A Sailor's Biography*. Boston: Little, Brown, 1959.

Nance, R. Morton. *Sailing Ship Models*. London: Holton & Truscott Smith, 1924.

Preston, Antony; Lyon, David; and Batchelor, John H. *Navies of the American Revolution*. Englewood Cliffs, N.J.: Prentice-Hall, 1975.

Rider, Hope S. *Valour Fore and Aft*. Annapolis, Md.: Naval Institute Press, 1976.

Henry Huddleston Rogers Collection of Ship Models. Annapolis, Md.: Naval Institute Press, 1972.

Ronnberg, Erik A. R., Jr. *Fair American 1780*. Bogota, NJ: Model Shipways Co., 1978.

Rosa, Narcisse. *La construction des navires à Quebec et les environs*. Quebec.

Roscoe, Theodore, and Freeman, Fred. *Pictorial History of the U.S. Navy*. New York: Scribners, 1956.

Sarducci, Guido. *A Red Hat for the Binnacle, or, The Cardinal Points of the Compass Explain'd*. Vatican City: L'Osservatore Romano, 1986.

Sheffield, William P. *Rhode Island Privateers and Privateersmen*. Newport, R.I.: 1883.

Smith, Myron J. *Navies in the American Revolution: A Bibliography*. Metuchen, N.J.: Scarecrow Press, 1973.

Smith, P. C. F. *Captain Samuel Tucker (1747–1833) Continental Navy*. Salem, Mass.: Essex Institute, 1976.

————. *Empress of China*. Philadelphia: Philadelphia Maritime Museum, 1984.

————. *Fired by Manly Zeal*. Salem, Mass.: Peabody Museum, 1977.

————, ed. *The Frigate Essex Papers*. Salem, Mass.: Peabody Museum, 1974.

————, ed. *The Journals of Ashley Bowen (1728–1813) of Marblehead*. 2 vols. Salem, Mass.: Peabody Museum, 1973.

Stout, Neil R. *The Royal Navy in America, 1760–1775*. Annapolis, Md.: Naval Institute Press, 1973.

Sutton, Jean. *Lords of the East*. London: Conway Maritime Press, 1981.

Syrett, David. *Shipping and the American War 1775–83*. London: Athlone Press, 1970.

Van Powell, W. Nowland. *The American Navies of the Revolutionary War*. New York: G. P. Putnam's Sons, 1974.

————. *War at Sea for Liberty*. Memphis, Tenn.: Memphis Council, Navy League of the U.S., 1975.

Wilbur, C. Keith. *Picture Book of the Revolution's Privateers*. Harrisburg, Pa.: Stackpole, 1973.

Wilcox, Leslie. *The War of Independence: A Bicentennial Exhibition of Marine Paintings*. Bethesda, Md.: Wm. Blair, Ltd., 1976.

Periodicals

The American Neptune (Quarterly). Peabody Museum, Salem, Mass.

Model Ship Builder (Bimonthly). Cedarburg, Wisconsin.

Model Ships & Boats (Bimonthly), edited by Frank W. Miller. Model Ships & Boats, Inc., New York, New York.

The Model Shipwright (Quarterly). Conway Maritime Press, London.

Nautical Research Journal (Quarterly), edited by Merritt A. Edson, Jr. Nautical Research Guild, Washington, D.C.

Scale Ship Modeler (Bimonthly). Challenge Publications, Canoga Park, California.

Warship (Quarterly). Conway Maritime Press, London.

GENERAL INDEX

ELIZABETHAN COUNTRY DANCES

by JOHN FITZHUGH MILLAR

Dancing was the principal recreation for Elizabethans of all social classes—the equivalent of our football, basketball, baseball, tennis and golf all rolled into one—and Country Dancing is just as much fun today. For the most part, Country Dancing is easy to learn, and this book shows how.

This book contains a brief history of Country Dancing, instructions in the basic figures, and music and directions for 86 dances with about 100 tunes—including sixteen 400-year-old Square Dances and eighteen Contras—with song-words to accompany the tunes, plus a bibliography and discography. The dances are graded from easy to difficult. The tunes, although anonymous, are some of the finest from the Golden Age of English music—the age of Byrd, Gibbons, Morley, Dowland and Weelkes—making the book invaluable for its music alone.

The dances in this book are ideally suited for adding color to historic re-enactments and anniversaries, increasing the authenticity of Shakespeare performances, bringing museums to life, teaching in schools and just plain fun.

9x12   114pp., ill., mus., bibl., index   LC. 85-51583

0-934943-00-1 *paperback* $12.95 (sewn for long life)
0-934943-03-6 *hardcover* $19.95 (intended for libraries)

A COMPLETE LIFE OF CHRIST

compiled by JOHN FITZHUGH MILLAR

Here, at long last, is the book that Christians have been waiting for. It combines a complete amalgamation of the Four Gospels, following the latest scholarship, in modern English, with the other facts that are known about the life and teachings of Christ. These include writings of Roman and Jewish historians in the early Christian era; fragmentary "lost" gospels, most of which had disappeared before the Bible was assembled in 382 AD and have been found only recently by archaeologists; and a brief account of the findings of the distinguished historians and scientists who have lately examined the famous Shroud of Turin. This book does not, however, include any of the numerous false books written about Christ, such as the Book of the Infancy or the Acts of Pilate.

While it is not intended to replace the regular reading of the Bible, many readers will find this easy-to-read book makes the historical Christ more readily accessible than has hitherto been possible.

The quotations from sources other than the New Testament are set in italic type so as to leave no doubt in the reader's mind as to the extent of Biblical authority in the text.

Combining, as it does, the Biblical, historical, archaeological and scientific record, this book is "must" reading for anyone who wants to see clearly the historical person of Christ and his teachings.

6x9   178pp., ill., maps, app.   LC. 85-51584

0-934943-01-x *paperback* $8.95 (sewn for long life)
0-934943-04-4 *hardcover* $15.95 (intended for libraries)

CLASSICAL ARCHITECTURE IN RENAISSANCE EUROPE 1419-1585   by JOHN FITZHUGH MILLAR

This book contains text and elevation drawings (and a few ground-plans) of nearly 400 classical buildings in Europe from 1419 to 1585. It shows the spread of classical architecture outwards from Florence and Rome to an area stretching from Portugal to Moscow, from Wales to Romania, from Scotland to Yugoslavia, from Denmark to Malta, and from Poland to Spain.

The book examines works by over 160 architects, including the more familiar Brunelleschi, Alberti, Bramante, the San Gallos, Leonardo da Vinci, Michelangelo, Raffaello, Giulio Romano, Serlio, Palladio, Vignola, Herrera, and De l'Orme, as well as many undeservingly obscure figures; for example, the previously unknown Flemish architect Hendrik van Paesschen (or van de Passe) emerges as an astonishing 'Palladio of the North.'

In the Appendix are biographical sketches of all the architects and an extensive illustrated Glossary of architectural terms.

This book appeals to expert and layman alike, and will be particularly helpful to students in art and architectural history courses, as well as to tourists planning visits to parts of Europe.

12 x 12   250pp., ill., maps, app., glos., bibl., index

LC 86-50560

0-934943-06-0 paperback $19.95 (sewn for long life)

0-934943-07-9 hardcover $34.95 (intended for libraries)

Thirteen Colonies Press

710 SOUTH HENRY STREET, WILLIAMSBURG, VIRGINIA 23185